ESSENTIALS OF CLINICAL RESEARCH

A COMPREHENSIVE GUIDE TO DRUG DEVELOPMENT AND CLINICAL TRIALS

PROF.S.SHOBHARANI & PROF.A.MURALIDHAR RAO

Made with ♥ on the Notion Press Platform
www.notionpress.com

Contents

Preface

"Essentials of Clinical Research- A Comprehensive Guide to Drug Development and Clinical Trials" designed to illuminate the path through the complex landscape of clinical research. This book aims to serve as a cornerstone resource for students and professionals in the fields of Pharmacy (Pharm.D), Master of Pharmacy (M.Pharm), Bachelor of Pharmacy (B.Pharm), and those engaged in pharmaceutical research.

The impetus for this book arises from a need for an integrative understanding of the myriad processes involved in the development of new drugs—from concept through to market. We recognize that while the journey of drug development is exhilarating, it is also riddled with challenges and intricacies that require a thorough grounding in clinical research principles.

Each chapter of this book is carefully crafted to guide you through different phases of clinical research, including the design, implementation, regulation, and ethical considerations of clinical trials. Our approach is to provide not only the theoretical foundations but also practical insights and examples that draw on recent advancements and case studies from the field.

"Essentials of Clinical Research" is structured to facilitate ease of understanding, starting with basic concepts and moving towards more complex ideas. This progression is intended to cater to a wide range of readers, from those new to the field to seasoned practitioners who may be looking for a refresher or an update on new methodologies and regulations.

Moreover, this book also addresses the regulatory landscape that governs clinical research, providing updates on the latest guidelines and how they impact the planning and approval of new therapeutic agents. We delve into the ethical considerations that are fundamental to conducting clinical research, ensuring that readers are well-versed in the responsibilities that come with the development of medical innovations.

As you embark on your journey through this book, it is our hope that "Essentials of Clinical Research" will not only educate but also inspire you.

Dr.S.Shobharani
Professor and Head ,CPS, UCESTH,
JNTUH, Kukatpally,Hyderabad
Dr. A. Muralidhar Rao Akkaladevi
professor and Principal,St. Mary's College of Pharmacy,Secunderabad

Essentials Of Clinical Research

A Comprehensive Guide to Drug Development and Clinical Trials

BY

Dr .S.Shobharani
Professor and Head ,CPS, UCESTH,
JNTUH, Kukatpally, Hyderabad
&
Dr.Muralidhar Rao Akkaladevi
Professor and Principal St.Mary's College of Pharmacy,
Secunderabad

Published By
Notion Press Media Pvt Ltd, #7, Red Cross Road,
Egmore, Chennai, Tamil Nadu 600008
Email ID: publish@notionpress.com
Notion Press, Inc.
800, West EI Camino Real #180,
California USA 94040

CHAPTER ONE

INTRODUCTION TO DRUG DEVELOPMENT

1.1 Overview of the Drug Development Process

1.1.1 Definition and Importance of Drug Development

Drug development is a vital process that involves the discovery, formulation, testing, and regulatory approval of medications intended for human use. The core objective of drug development is to identify new compounds that can effectively treat, cure, or prevent diseases with minimal side effects. This complex process begins with the identification of potential therapeutic targets and extends through pre-clinical studies, clinical trials, and ultimately, regulatory approval.

The significance of drug development cannot be overstated. It stands at the heart of medical advances, directly impacting health outcomes and quality of life across the globe. Through drug development, diseases that were once deemed untreatable are now manageable or even curable. This process also continuously adapts to emerging challenges, such as evolving pathogens or new health crises, thereby safeguarding public health.

Moreover, drug development drives economic growth and innovation in the pharmaceutical industry. It fosters an environment of research and development that is crucial for the advancement of science and technology in health care. This dynamic field requires the integration of various scientific disciplines, including biology, chemistry, pharmacology, and medicine, making it a pinnacle of interdisciplinary research.

Additionally, the drug development process is governed by stringent regulatory standards to ensure that new drugs are safe and effective. This regulatory oversight is crucial as it maintains the trust of healthcare providers and patients in pharmaceutical products, and ensures that only those therapies that meet rigorous safety and efficacy criteria reach the market.

1.1.2 Key Stages in Drug Development

1.1.2.1 Discovery and Preclinical Testing

The initial stage in the drug development process is marked by discovery and preclinical testing, which are critical for setting the foundation of a potentially successful new drug.

Discovery: This phase starts with the identification of a disease target—a molecule or pathway in the body that can be modified by a drug to produce a desired therapeutic effect. Researchers use a variety of methods to identify and validate potential targets, including genetic analysis, biochemical assays, and computational models. Once a target is confirmed, the search for a lead compound that can interact with the target begins. This involves screening thousands, sometimes millions, of compounds using high-throughput screening technologies. The most promising compounds—those that demonstrate the desired interaction with the target without harmful effects—are selected for further development.

Preclinical Testing: Before a new drug can be tested in humans, it must undergo extensive preclinical testing to determine its safety and efficacy. This phase involves laboratory experiments and animal studies to assess how the drug affects living organisms. Researchers study the pharmacokinetics (how the drug is absorbed, distributed, metabolized, and excreted in the body) and pharmacodynamics (how the drug affects the body) of the compounds. Toxicology tests are conducted to identify any potential adverse effects. The data gathered from these tests help in understanding the safety profile of the compound and its mechanism of action.

These initial steps are crucial as they provide the necessary evidence to justify moving forward with human trials. The success rate during this phase is relatively low; only a small percentage of compounds that enter preclinical testing will progress to clinical trials. Despite this, the discovery and preclinical stages are essential for ensuring that only the most promising and safest compounds are considered for further development, thereby safeguarding human subjects in subsequent phases. This careful and thorough investigation helps to maintain the integrity and efficacy of the drug development process.

1.1.2.2 Clinical Trials

Following successful preclinical testing, a drug candidate moves into the clinical trials phase, which is pivotal in evaluating its safety and effectiveness in humans. Clinical trials are conducted in a series of sequential steps, known as phases, each designed to answer specific research questions.

Phase I Trials: These initial trials are designed to assess the safety of a drug. The primary goal is to determine the drug's safe dosage range and identify side effects. Phase I trials typically involve a small number of healthy volunteers (20 to 100), though in the case of cancer drugs, patients may be used. Researchers monitor participants closely for any adverse reactions as they gradually increase the dose.

Phase II Trials: If a drug is found to be safe in Phase I, it progresses to Phase II, which tests the drug's efficacy and further evaluates its safety. This phase involves up to several hundred patients who have the condition that the drug is meant to treat. Phase II trials provide researchers with additional data on optimal dosing and are often the first indication of the drug's effectiveness in a larger, more diverse population.

Phase III Trials: These are larger trials involving several hundred to thousands of participants and are designed to confirm the drug's effectiveness, monitor side effects, compare it to commonly used treatments, and collect information that will allow the drug to be used safely. Phase III trials are typically multicenter trials conducted in different geographical locations, which help ensure the results are applicable across various populations. Successful completion of Phase III is usually the basis for regulatory approval.

Phase IV Trials: Also known as post-marketing surveillance, these trials are conducted after a drug has been approved for use. Phase IV trials monitor the long-term effectiveness and impact of the drug in a much larger patient population and over an extended period. These studies may also explore additional potential uses of the drug outside of the original indications.

Clinical trials are a critical component of the drug development process, as they provide comprehensive data about a drug's performance and safety before it becomes widely available to the public. They are rigorously designed, reviewed, and monitored to uphold the highest standards of scientific and ethical integrity. Regulatory bodies, such as the FDA in the United States, require detailed clinical trial data before approving a drug for the market, ensuring that only those medications that are proven to be safe and effective are made available to patients.

1.1.2.3 Approval and Post-Marketing Surveillance

The final stages of the drug development process encompass regulatory approval and post-marketing surveillance, which are essential for ensuring the continued safety and effectiveness of new medications on the market.

Regulatory Approval: After a drug has successfully completed Phase III clinical trials, the next step is to seek regulatory approval from relevant health authorities, such as the U.S. Food and Drug Administration (FDA), the European Medicines Agency (EMA), or other national bodies depending on the geographical location. The approval process involves a thorough review of all data collected from the drug's discovery, preclinical testing, and clinical trials. The manufacturer must submit a comprehensive dossier that includes detailed information on the drug's pharmacology, toxicology, manufacturing process, and clinical trial results, commonly known as a New Drug Application (NDA) in the USA. The regulatory authority evaluates the data to determine whether the drug's benefits outweigh its risks and if it should be approved for use in the general population.

Post-Marketing Surveillance (Phase IV Trials): Even after a drug is approved, its journey is not complete. Post-marketing surveillance, also referred to as Phase IV trials, is conducted to monitor the effects of the drug in the general population over a longer period and in a much larger group than is possible during clinical trials. This stage is crucial for detecting rare or long-term adverse effects that may not have been apparent in previous trials. Companies are required to report any adverse reactions identified during this phase to regulatory authorities. Additionally, Phase IV trials can be used to assess the drug's effectiveness and safety in different subgroups (such as children or the elderly), or for different dosages and combinations with other drugs.

Impact of Regulatory Actions: Regulatory bodies have the authority to issue updates on drug labels, require additional studies, or in some cases, withdraw a drug from the market if post-marketing data suggest significant safety issues. This ongoing oversight helps ensure that the benefits of a drug continue to outweigh its risks as more is learned about its long-term usage.

1.1.3 Timeline and Costs Involved

The process of developing a new drug is both time-consuming and costly, reflecting the complexity and rigorous standards required to bring a safe and effective product to market.

Timeline: On average, it takes approximately 10 to 15 years for a drug to move from the initial discovery phase to reaching the market. The timeline can be broken down into several key stages:

- **Discovery and Preclinical Testing**: Typically takes 1 to 6 years. Researchers identify potential drug targets, perform initial tests in the lab, and conduct animal studies to determine if the drug is safe enough to test in humans.
- **Clinical Trials**: Can last from 6 to 7 years, divided across Phase I, II, and III trials. Each phase progressively involves more participants and longer durations to thoroughly assess the drug's safety and effectiveness.
- **Regulatory Review**: Following the completion of clinical trials, the regulatory approval process itself can take 1 to 2 years, depending on the complexity of the data and the therapeutic impact of the drug.

Costs: The financial investment required to develop a new drug is substantial, with estimates often exceeding $1 billion. This figure includes:

- **Research and Development (R&D)**: The cost of conducting laboratory research, preclinical tests, and clinical trials. These expenses are high due to the need for specialized equipment, high-quality materials, and compensation for a large number of highly skilled personnel.
- **Regulatory Costs**: Fees associated with submitting an application for drug approval and the costs of maintaining compliance with regulatory standards throughout the process.
- **Failed Trials and Projects**: A significant portion of the costs comes from projects that do not succeed. Only a small percentage of drug candidates that enter preclinical testing will make it to market, meaning the investment in failed trials must be recouped through the successful drugs.

Economic Implications: The high costs and long timelines are significant barriers for pharmaceutical companies, especially smaller or mid-size firms. This economic burden also impacts the pricing of new drugs, as companies seek to recover their substantial investment and fund ongoing research activities.

Despite these challenges, the drug development process is crucial for advancing medical science and improving public health. Pharmaceutical companies, governments, and other stakeholders continue to seek ways to reduce both the time and costs associated with drug development, such as through regulatory incentives or innovations in technology that streamline research and trials.

1.2 Key Concepts in Drug Discovery

1.2.1 Target Identification and Validation

Target identification and validation are foundational steps in the drug discovery process, focusing on determining the best molecular targets for a new drug. These targets are typically proteins, such as enzymes, ion channels, or receptors that are implicated in a disease process and can be modulated by a therapeutic agent.

Target Identification: The first step, target identification, involves finding a biological entity that plays a key role in disease pathology. This can be achieved through various methods including genomics, where researchers look for genes associated with diseases; proteomics, which involves studying the proteins involved in disease; and metabolomics, focusing on metabolic changes. Advanced techniques like high-throughput screening (HTS) are also used to evaluate a large number of potential targets quickly. Computational biology plays a crucial role as well, using algorithms and databases to predict and prioritize potential targets based on biological and chemical data.

Target Validation: Once potential targets are identified, they must be validated to confirm their role in the disease and their potential as a drug target. This involves demonstrating that manipulating the target through genetic, pharmacological, or other means alters the disease process in a predictable way. Techniques such as RNA interference (RNAi) and CRISPR-Cas9 are commonly used for gene silencing or editing to study the effects of increasing or decreasing a target's activity. Additionally, animal models and cell lines are used to study the biological consequences of targeting a specific molecule in complex living systems.

Validating a target is crucial because it confirms the biological relevance of the target to the disease and its potential to impact the disease positively when modulated by a drug. This step reduces the risk of failure in later stages of drug development by ensuring the chosen target can feasibly lead to a successful therapeutic intervention.

1.2.2 High Throughput Screening (HTS)

High Throughput Screening (HTS) is a pivotal technique in drug discovery that allows researchers to quickly evaluate thousands to millions of compounds to identify potential drugs that act on a chosen biological target. This method utilizes automation, miniaturized assays, and large libraries of chemicals to efficiently test the effects of compounds on biological or biochemical processes.

Process of HTS: The process begins with the preparation of the target, which could be a protein, DNA segment, or whole cells, placed into wells of a microtiter plate—a flat plate with multiple "wells" used as small test tubes. Each well receives a different compound from the library. Advanced robotic systems add the compounds and necessary reagents to the wells, and then measure the reactions between the compounds and the target. The reactions are typically measured using various detection methods such as fluorescence, luminescence, or absorbance, which indicate how each compound affects the target.

Data Analysis and Hit Identification: After screening, the data collected is analyzed to identify "hits," or compounds that have a desirable effect on the target, such as inhibiting an enzyme or activating a receptor. These hits undergo further validation and testing to confirm their activity and assess their potential as drug candidates.

Advantages of HTS: One of the major advantages of HTS is its ability to rapidly identify active compounds among a vast array of possibilities, which significantly accelerates the early stages of drug discovery. It also allows for the exploration of compound interactions that may not have been considered in more traditional, hypothesis-driven research, broadening the potential for novel therapeutic discoveries.

Challenges: Despite its efficiency, HTS does face challenges such as high costs associated with setting up and maintaining the required technology and the potential for high rates of false positives or negatives, which require careful subsequent validation. Additionally, the complexity of biological systems means that hits from HTS still require extensive further testing to determine their suitability as drug candidates.

1.2.3 Lead Optimization

Lead optimization is a crucial phase in drug discovery where chemical compounds, identified as potential drug candidates during the earlier stages such as High Throughput Screening (HTS), are modified to improve their efficacy, selectivity, and safety. The goal of this stage is to refine these "lead" compounds to produce a drug candidate that is suitable for clinical trials.

Process of Lead Optimization: This process involves a series of modifications to the chemical structure of the lead compounds. Chemists make systematic changes to various parts of the molecule, assessing how these changes affect the compound's interaction with the target, its activity in biological models, and its overall drug-like properties. Common parameters optimized during this stage include the compound's potency, stability, solubility, and absorption characteristics. Toxicological properties are also a critical focus, as the drug must not only be effective but also safe for human use.

Techniques and Technologies Used: Lead optimization utilizes various advanced techniques, including:

- **Structure-activity relationships (SAR)**: This involves analyzing how changes in the molecular structure of a compound affect its activity against the target.
- **Computer-aided drug design (CADD)**: Computational tools predict how structural changes will impact the compound's properties and interactions with biological targets.
- **Pharmacokinetics and pharmacodynamics studies**: These studies assess the absorption, distribution, metabolism, excretion (ADME), and toxicological data of the compounds.
- **In vitro and in vivo testing**: Laboratory and animal studies are used to evaluate the biological efficacy and safety of the modified compounds.

Challenges: Lead optimization faces several challenges. Balancing the improvement of one property without detrimentally affecting others is a complex task. For instance, increasing the solubility of a compound might reduce its potency. Moreover, predicting how changes will perform in humans based on preclinical models can be uncertain.

Outcome of Lead Optimization: The outcome of successful lead optimization is a "drug candidate" that demonstrates optimal interaction with the target, possesses suitable pharmacokinetic properties, and shows a reasonable expectation of safety in humans. This candidate moves forward into preclinical and clinical development phases.

1.3 Preclinical Testing

1.3.1 In Vitro Tests

In vitro tests are a crucial component of the preclinical testing phase in drug development. These tests are conducted using cells, tissues, or biological molecules outside their normal biological context—typically in a controlled environment like a test tube or petri dish. In vitro testing provides early insight into a compound's efficacy and safety before proceeding to in vivo tests involving whole organisms.

Purpose and Types of In Vitro Tests: The primary purpose of in vitro tests is to assess the biological activity and toxicity of new compounds on a cellular level. These tests can include:

- **Cytotoxicity assays**, which evaluate whether a compound is toxic to cells.
- **Enzyme inhibition assays**, to determine how a compound affects the activity of specific enzymes involved in disease processes.
- **Binding assays**, which assess the ability of a compound to bind to targeted receptors or other molecules.
- **Gene expression studies**, where the impact of a compound on the expression levels of certain genes is analyzed, helping to predict its effects on various biological pathways.

Advantages of In Vitro Testing: These tests are valued for their speed and cost-effectiveness compared to in vivo studies. They allow researchers to quickly screen large numbers of compounds and identify those with the most promising profiles for further development. Moreover, in vitro tests can be highly controlled, enabling researchers to manipulate conditions to study specific interactions without the complexity of a living organism.

Challenges and Limitations: While in vitro tests are an essential first step in drug screening, they have limitations. The main challenge is the extrapolation of results to humans. Cells or biological systems used in these tests may not fully replicate the conditions found in a living organism, leading to discrepancies between in vitro and in vivo outcomes. Furthermore, some biological processes, such as metabolism or multi-organ interactions, cannot be effectively mimicked in vitro.

Role in Drug Development: Despite these challenges, in vitro tests play an indispensable role in the initial stages of drug development. They are instrumental in identifying and optimizing potential drug candidates before more extensive and expensive in vivo testing begins. By effectively eliminating compounds with poor activity or significant toxicity early in the process, in vitro tests enhance the overall efficiency and safety of drug development.

1.3.2 Animal Models

Animal models are an integral part of preclinical testing, providing a crucial bridge between in vitro studies and human clinical trials. These models involve using non-human animals to study the effects of drug candidates on whole biological systems, offering insights that cannot be obtained from cell-based tests alone.

Purpose and Types of Animal Models: The primary aim of using animal models is to evaluate the pharmacokinetics (PK), pharmacodynamics (PD), toxicity, and efficacy of a drug candidate within a living organism. Common types of animal models include:

- **Rodent models**, typically mice and rats, which are used because of their genetic and physiological similarities to humans, short life cycles, and ease of handling.
- **Non-rodent models** such as rabbits, dogs, or monkeys, are used when specific aspects of human physiology or disease need to be replicated more closely than rodent models can provide.

Selection of Animal Models: The choice of an animal model depends on the specific disease being studied and the biological pathways involved. Models are selected based on their ability to mimic human disease states or drug metabolism. Genetic engineering techniques, such as transgenic or knockout models, are often employed to enhance the relevance of the models to human conditions.

Advantages of Animal Models: These models provide valuable data on how a drug behaves in a complex biological system, including its absorption, distribution, metabolism, and excretion (ADME). They also allow researchers to observe potential side effects and adjust dosing regimens. Furthermore, animal models can show how a drug affects not just a specific cellular target but whole body systems, which is critical for understanding potential therapeutic and adverse effects.

Ethical Considerations: The use of animal models in research is subject to stringent ethical regulations. Researchers must follow the principles of the 3Rs—Replacement, Reduction, and Refinement:

- **Replacement** refers to methods that permit a reduction in the number of animals used or employ alternative techniques such as in vitro models.
- **Reduction** involves strategies to obtain comparable levels of information from fewer animals or more information from the same number of animals.
- **Refinement** means modifying procedures to minimize stress and suffering to the animals involved.

Challenges and Limitations: While animal models are invaluable, they are not without limitations. Differences in drug metabolism between animals and humans can lead to inaccurate predictions about drug behavior in human subjects. Moreover, ethical concerns and regulatory restrictions can limit the scope of studies that can be conducted using animal models.

Role in Drug Development: Despite these challenges, animal models remain a critical component of drug development. They provide essential data that can predict how a drug is likely to perform in humans, which is vital for designing human clinical trials. The insights gained from animal models about a drug's safety and efficacy are fundamental to ensuring that only the most promising drug candidates move forward to clinical evaluation.

1.3.3 Assessing Safety and Efficacy

Assessing the safety and efficacy of drug candidates is a critical component of preclinical testing. This phase ensures that potential pharmaceuticals are both effective in treating the intended condition and safe for future use in humans. These assessments are meticulously designed to meet rigorous regulatory standards and provide a solid foundation for advancing to clinical trials.

Safety Assessment: The primary goal of safety assessment is to identify any potential toxic effects the drug may have and determine the appropriate dose range that minimizes these risks. This involves a series of studies:

- **Toxicology Studies**: These are conducted in both in vitro systems and in vivo using animal models to evaluate the toxic responses caused by the drug, which might include organ-specific toxicity, genotoxicity (damage to genetic information within a cell), and carcinogenicity (potential to cause cancer).
- **ADME Studies (Absorption, Distribution, Metabolism, and Excretion)**: Understanding the pharmacokinetics of a drug is crucial.

These studies help determine how much of the drug reaches the target site, how it is distributed within the body, metabolized, and how it is ultimately excreted. This information is vital for setting dosing regimens and predicting potential interactions with other drugs.

Efficacy Assessment: Efficacy testing confirms that the drug effectively addresses the targeted disease or condition within the tested models.

- **Disease Models**: Using disease-specific animal models, researchers can observe how the drug affects the disease's progression and outcome. These models should closely mimic the human condition they are intended to treat.
- **Biomarker Measurements**: Biomarkers are measurable indicators of the severity or presence of some disease state. By measuring these, scientists can quantitatively assess how the drug impacts the disease during the preclinical trials.

Challenges in Assessment: One of the main challenges in assessing safety and efficacy is the extrapolation of data from animal models to humans. Differences in physiology and metabolism can lead to differing drug responses, which makes it difficult to predict human outcomes based solely on animal data.

Regulatory Considerations: Data from safety and efficacy assessments form a crucial part of the documentation required for Investigational New Drug (IND) applications, which must be approved by regulatory bodies such as the FDA or EMA before human clinical trials can begin. This data must demonstrate that the drug candidate has a reasonable safety margin and shows potential clinical benefits.

Role in Drug Development: Safety and efficacy assessments are pivotal in drug development. They provide the necessary evidence that supports the progression of drug candidates from preclinical stages to human testing. Ensuring a drug is both safe and effective before it enters clinical trials is paramount to the success of the development process, helping to minimize risks to human subjects and improve the chances of regulatory approval.

1.4 Clinical Trials: Design and Implementation

1.4.1 Types of Clinical Trials

Clinical trials are research studies performed in people that are aimed at evaluating a medical, surgical, or behavioral intervention. They are the primary way that researchers find out if a new treatment, like a new drug, diet, or medical device, is safe and effective in people. Clinical trials follow a typical series from early, small-scale, Phase 1 studies to late-stage, large scale, Phase 3 trials.

Phase 1 Trials: These are the first stage of testing in human subjects. Normally, a small group of 20-100 healthy volunteers will be selected. This phase is designed to assess the safety of a drug or device. This includes determining the effects of the drug or device on humans including how it is absorbed, metabolized, and excreted. This phase also investigates side effects that occur as dosage levels are increased. Approximately 70% of experimental drugs pass this initial phase of testing.

Phase 2 Trials: Once the initial safety of the study drug has been confirmed in Phase 1 trials, Phase 2 trials are performed on larger groups (100-300) and are designed to assess how well the drug works, as well as to continue Phase 1 safety assessments in a larger group of volunteers and patients. This phase aims to obtain preliminary data on whether the drug works in people who have a certain disease or condition. These trials are sometimes divided into Phase 2a and Phase 2b trials, where Phase 2a is specifically designed to assess dosing requirements (how much drug should be given), while Phase 2b is designed to study efficacy (how well the drug works at the prescribed dose(s)).

Phase 3 Trials: These studies involve randomized and blind testing in several hundred to several thousand patients. This large-scale testing provides the pharmaceutical company and the FDA with a more thorough understanding of the effectiveness of the drug or device, the benefits and the range of possible adverse reactions. Most Phase 3 studies are randomized and double-blind trials. The successful completion of Phase 3 testing will usually result in the pharmaceutical company applying to the FDA for New Drug Application (NDA) approval to market the drug.

Phase 4 Trials: After a drug or device has been approved by the FDA and made available to the public, Phase 4 trials can be conducted to compare a drug with other drugs already in the market, monitor the drug's long-term effectiveness and impact on a patient's quality of life, and determine the cost-effectiveness of a particular drug therapy relative to other traditional and new therapies.

Each of these phases is crucial for different reasons and helps scientists answer different questions. In addition to these, there are specific types of clinical trials that focus on other aspects:

- **Preventive trials** look for better ways to prevent disease in people who have never had the disease or to prevent a disease from returning. These approaches may include medicines, vitamins, vaccines, minerals, or lifestyle changes.
- **Screening trials** test the best way to detect certain diseases or health conditions.
- **Diagnostic trials** are conducted to find better tests or procedures for diagnosing a particular disease or condition.
- **Quality of Life trials (supportive care trials)** explore ways to improve comfort and the quality of life for individuals with a chronic illness.

Each type of trial is designed to answer specific research questions and is integral to the process of drug development and approval.

1.4.1.1 Phase I: Safety and Dosage

Phase I clinical trials are the first stage in testing a new drug or therapy in humans and are primarily focused on evaluating safety and dosage. These trials are critical for determining how a new drug should be given (orally, intravenously, etc.), how often, and at what dosage levels, while also observing for any adverse effects.

Objectives of Phase I Trials:

- **Safety Assessment:** The primary goal is to determine if the drug is safe for human use. This involves monitoring participants for any adverse effects or toxicities associated with the drug.
- **Dosage Determination:** These trials help to establish the appropriate dose of the drug that can be given safely to humans without causing serious side effects. This is done by testing different doses on different groups of participants.
- **Pharmacokinetics (PK):** Understanding how the drug is absorbed, distributed, metabolized, and excreted in the human body. PK studies help to reveal the drug's bioavailability and the rate at which the body processes it.
- **Pharmacodynamics (PD):** Assessing the effects of the drug on the body, including how it interacts with the target and any biological changes that occur as a result.

Design and Conduct:

- Phase I trials typically involve a small group of 20 to 100 volunteers, who are often healthy participants, although some trials might include patients, especially if the drug is expected to be too toxic for healthy individuals.
- The trials usually employ a dose-escalation study design. A small group of participants is given a very low dose of the drug, and if there are no adverse side effects, the next group receives a slightly higher dose. This process continues until a predetermined maximum tolerated dose (MTD) is identified or significant side effects become apparent.
- Safety monitoring is intense and continuous throughout the trial, with participants often required to stay in a clinical setting so their health can be monitored closely.

Ethical Considerations:

- Participants are fully informed of the potential risks and are closely monitored throughout the study. Ethical oversight is provided by regulatory bodies and ethics committees to ensure that the risks are as low as possible.

Outcomes:

- The results from Phase I trials can determine whether a drug proceeds to Phase II trials, where its efficacy and further safety testing are conducted in a larger group of patients.
- These outcomes are crucial for deciding dose ranges and for understanding the initial pharmacological impacts of the drug, which are essential for designing later-phase trials.

Phase I trials are foundational in the clinical development process, setting the stage for all subsequent testing of the drug. They provide the first clear indication of a drug's safety profile and help establish the parameters for its further clinical investigation.

1.4.1.2 Phase II: Efficacy and Side Effects

Phase II clinical trials are a critical step in the development of a new drug, following the initial safety assessments conducted in Phase I trials. These trials are primarily focused on evaluating the efficacy of the drug and continue to monitor its safety in a larger group of patients, often those who have the condition that the drug is intended to treat.

Objectives of Phase II Trials:

- **Efficacy Assessment**: The primary aim of Phase II trials is to determine whether the drug has a biological or clinical effect on the condition it targets. This involves evaluating the drug's therapeutic effect and determining whether it improves the outcomes for patients compared to a baseline or compared to existing treatments.
- **Side Effects Evaluation**: While the initial safety profile is established in Phase I trials, Phase II trials provide additional information on side effects as the drug is administered over a longer period and to patients who may have underlying health issues due to their condition.
- **Dose Refinement**: These trials may also refine the dosage of the drug, determining the optimal dose that maximizes efficacy while minimizing side effects. This often involves dose-ranging studies.

Design and Conduct:

- Phase II trials usually involve several hundred participants who are randomly assigned to receive either the new drug or a placebo (and sometimes, an existing standard treatment). This stage can be divided into Phase IIa (pilot studies to assess clinical efficacy and recommended dose) and Phase IIb (rigorous testing of the efficacy at the recommended dose).
- These trials are often double-blind, meaning neither the researchers nor the participants know who is receiving the drug and who is receiving the placebo, to prevent bias in the results.
- The primary endpoints vary depending on the condition being treated but typically include measurements that indicate the drug's effectiveness in treating the condition or managing symptoms.

Statistical Analysis:

- The data collected from Phase II trials are subject to rigorous statistical analysis to ascertain the significance of the observed effects. This analysis helps determine whether the results are due to the drug or merely due to chance.

Ethical Considerations:

- As with all clinical trials, ethical oversight is crucial. Participants need to provide informed consent, understanding the potential risks and benefits of participating. Ethical committees and regulatory bodies must approve the trial design.

Outcomes:

- The outcomes of Phase II trials can significantly impact the development path of a drug. If the drug demonstrates clear efficacy and an acceptable safety profile, it will proceed to Phase III trials, which involve a larger group of participants and aim to confirm these findings in a broader population.
- Conversely, if the drug does not show sufficient efficacy or if significant safety issues are identified, the development may be halted or redirected.

Phase II trials are vital for determining the therapeutic potential of new drugs. They provide essential evidence that informs decisions about further development and potential adjustments to the drug's formulation or dosing regimen. These trials balance the need to rigorously test the drug's effectiveness against the need to accelerate promising treatments to patients.

1.4.1.3 Phase III: Comparison and Confirmation

Phase III clinical trials are among the most pivotal stages in the drug development process. These trials are designed to confirm the efficacy of a new drug, monitor its side effects, and compare it to standard or equivalent treatments. Phase III trials are typically the last step before a drug is considered for approval by regulatory bodies.

Objectives of Phase III Trials:

- **Efficacy Confirmation:** The primary goal is to confirm that the drug works in the intended patient population and that its benefits outweigh any risks. This is achieved by conducting large-scale studies that provide statistically robust data.
- **Monitoring of Side Effects:** Continued surveillance of adverse effects is crucial to ensuring the drug's safety profile is acceptable, especially given the larger and more diverse patient population.

- **Comparative Analysis**: These trials often involve comparisons with standard treatments currently available on the market. This helps to establish whether the new drug is an improvement over existing therapies in terms of effectiveness, safety, and patient outcomes.

Design and Conduct:

- Phase III trials typically involve a large number of participants, ranging from several hundred to thousands, recruited from multiple sites worldwide. This diversity ensures that the findings are generalizable across various populations and medical settings.
- The trials are usually randomized and double-blind, maintaining rigorous standards to prevent bias. Many trials also use placebo controls and/or active controls (a standard treatment) to provide a clear basis for comparison.
- The endpoint of these trials is often a primary clinical outcome, such as survival rate, disease remission rate, or significant improvement in quality of life, depending on the condition being treated.

Statistical Considerations:

- Due to the large scale of these trials, sophisticated statistical methods are used to analyze the data. This includes multiple interim analyses to monitor the progress of the trial and to ensure that it can be stopped early if the drug proves to be either very effective or too dangerous.
- The significance levels set for Phase III trials are stringent, as the results can determine whether a drug will be approved for public use.

Regulatory Review and Approval:

- The results from Phase III trials form the basis of a New Drug Application (NDA) submitted to regulatory authorities like the FDA or EMA. These bodies review the trial outcomes to ensure the drug is safe and effective for its intended use.
- Approval may lead to the drug being available for prescription. However, regulatory bodies may require additional post-marketing surveillance studies, known as Phase IV, to monitor the drug's performance in the general population.

Ethical and Operational Considerations:

- Phase III trials must adhere to strict ethical standards, with oversight from multiple institutional review boards (IRBs) or ethics committees, especially since these studies impact a larger segment of the population.
- The logistics of conducting such extensive trials require significant resources and coordination, emphasizing the importance of thorough planning and management.

Outcomes:

- Successful Phase III trials can lead to a drug's approval and widespread use in medical practice. However, any concerns regarding efficacy or safety identified during these trials can necessitate additional research or lead to the rejection of the drug by regulatory authorities.

Phase III trials are critical for finalizing the clinical understanding of a drug. They not only confirm its efficacy and safety but also place it within the current medical landscape by comparing it to existing therapies. This phase is essential for ensuring that new treatments provide real benefits and meet the stringent requirements set by health authorities.

1.4.2 Patient Recruitment and Ethics

Patient recruitment and the ethical considerations involved are crucial aspects of the design and implementation of clinical trials. Ensuring that the right participants are enrolled and that their rights are protected is fundamental to the success and integrity of any clinical research study.

Patient Recruitment:

- **Target Population Identification:** Identifying the appropriate participants who meet the specific inclusion and exclusion criteria of the study is the first step. This involves a clear understanding of the patient demographics, disease state, and any other relevant characteristics that may affect the study's outcome.
- **Recruitment Strategies:** Effective recruitment strategies are essential to enroll participants in a timely manner. These can include partnerships with hospitals and clinics, use of patient registries, advertising in various media, and community outreach. Digital tools and social media are increasingly used to reach potential participants.

- **Informed Consent Process**: Every participant must go through an informed consent process, where they are fully educated about the study's aims, risks, benefits, and their rights as participants, including the right to withdraw from the study at any time without any consequences to their medical care.

Ethical Considerations:

- **Respect for Persons**: This principle requires that participants are treated as autonomous agents and that those with diminished autonomy are afforded protection. Participants must enter the study voluntarily and with adequate information.
- **Beneficence**: Researchers must take measures to ensure the study maximizes possible benefits and minimizes possible harms. The health and well-being of the participants should always be a priority.
- **Justice**: The selection of research subjects needs to be scrutinized to ensure that it is fair and equitable, avoiding any form of discrimination or exploitation. It is also important to ensure that the benefits of the research are distributed fairly among all groups in society.

Ethical Oversight:

- **Institutional Review Boards (IRBs) or Ethics Committees**: These bodies review the research protocols to ensure that they are ethical and that the risks to participants are minimized. They also monitor ongoing studies to ensure compliance.
- **Data Monitoring Committees (DMCs)**: For larger trials, especially those involving significant risks, an independent committee of experts monitors participant safety and study integrity throughout the trial.

Challenges in Patient Recruitment and Ethics:

- **Recruitment Efficiency**: One of the major challenges in clinical trials is recruiting enough participants within the projected timelines. Delays in recruitment can lead to increased costs and extended study durations.
- **Ethical Dilemmas**: Researchers may face ethical dilemmas, especially in placebo-controlled trials where participants may receive no therapeutic benefit. Balancing scientific objectives with the best interest of the

participants can be complex.

Outcomes:

- Effective patient recruitment and strict ethical adherence are not only crucial for the validity of the clinical trial but also for maintaining public trust in clinical research. Ensuring ethical conduct and protecting the rights and welfare of participants lead to more reliable and impactful research outcomes.

1.4.3 Data Management and Statistical Analysis

Data management and statistical analysis are integral components of clinical trials, ensuring the integrity, reliability, and statistical power of the study's findings. Effective management of data and rigorous statistical analysis are crucial for drawing valid conclusions from the research.

Data Management:

- **Data Collection:** Clinical trial data collection involves gathering complete and accurate data from each participant, which includes medical history, treatment data, outcomes, and side effects. This data must be collected in a consistent and standardized format across all study sites to ensure comparability.
- **Data Storage and Security:** Data must be securely stored to protect patient confidentiality and comply with regulatory requirements such as the Health Insurance Portability and Accountability Act (HIPAA) in the U.S. or the General Data Protection Regulation (GDPR) in the EU. This often involves the use of secure electronic data capture (EDC) systems that provide encrypted data transmission and storage.
- **Data Quality Assurance:** Regular audits and checks are conducted to ensure the accuracy and completeness of the data. Data quality management processes are put in place to identify, resolve, and prevent discrepancies or errors.

Statistical Analysis:

- **Design of Analysis:** Before the trial begins, a statistical analysis plan (SAP) is developed. This plan details how the collected data will be analyzed to answer the research questions posed by the trial. It includes definitions of analysis populations, primary and secondary endpoints, and statistical methods to be used.

- **Interim Analysis**: For longer trials, interim analyses may be conducted to assess the data at certain points during the trial. These analyses can help determine if the trial should continue as planned, be modified, or be stopped early due to efficacy or safety concerns.
- **Final Analysis**: After data collection is complete, the final analysis is conducted as per the SAP. This analysis typically involves a variety of statistical tests to compare the treatment effects between the drug and control groups, adjust for multiple comparisons, and handle missing data.

Challenges in Data Management and Statistical Analysis:

- **Handling Missing Data**: Missing data can bias the results and affect the power of the study. Strategies to handle missing data include using last observation carried forward (LOCF), multiple imputation, or model-based approaches like mixed-effects models.
- **Multisite Coordination**: Trials involving multiple sites require harmonization of data collection and entry procedures to ensure data consistency and reliability across all locations.
- **Adaptive Trial Designs**: These designs allow modifications to the trial procedures based on interim results. While they can make trials more flexible and efficient, they also require sophisticated statistical techniques and careful planning to maintain the integrity of the study.

Ethical Considerations:

- **Transparency and Reproducibility**: The data management and analysis processes must be transparent to allow for reproducibility of the results, which is a cornerstone of scientific research.
- **Reporting Bias**: There is a duty to report all results, including negative or inconclusive results, to prevent publication bias and provide a complete picture of the research.

Effective data management and statistical analysis are essential to the success of clinical trials. They provide the foundation for scientifically valid conclusions, ensuring that the results are robust, reproducible, and capable of supporting decision-making regarding the drug's efficacy and safety.

1.5 Regulatory Approval and Compliance

1.5.1 Drug Approval Process in Different Regions (FDA, EMA, etc.)

The drug approval process is a critical phase in the lifecycle of a pharmaceutical product. This process varies significantly across different regions due to varying regulatory requirements and procedures. The U.S. Food and Drug Administration (FDA) and the European Medicines Agency (EMA) are among the most influential regulatory bodies, with their procedures often serving as benchmarks worldwide.

FDA Approval Process (U.S.):

- **Investigational New Drug (IND) Application**: Before clinical trials can begin in the U.S., a drug sponsor must submit an IND application to the FDA. This application includes results from preclinical studies, the drug's chemical structure, manufacturing information, and the proposed clinical trial protocol.
- **Clinical Trials (Phase I-III)**: Upon IND approval, clinical trials can commence. These trials are designed to test the drug's safety, efficacy, and optimal dosage.
- **New Drug Application (NDA)**: After successful clinical trials, the sponsor submits an NDA, which provides comprehensive details about the drug's pharmacology, manufacturing specifications, formulation details, and labeling.
- **FDA Review**: The FDA reviews the NDA to ensure that the drug is safe and effective for its intended use and that the benefits outweigh the risks.
- **Post-Marketing Surveillance (Phase IV)**: After approval, the drug enters the market with continued monitoring to track long-term effects and ensure continued safety and effectiveness.

EMA Approval Process (EU):

- **Marketing Authorization Application (MAA)**: Similar to the NDA, the MAA is submitted to the EMA detailing the results from all clinical trial phases and comprehensive drug information.
- **Centralized Procedure**: This is the most common route for drug approval in the EU, where the EMA conducts a scientific assessment of the MAA and provides a recommendation for marketing authorization

valid throughout the EU.

- **Committee for Medicinal Products for Human Use (CHMP)**: This committee reviews the MAA and gives a recommendation on whether the drug should be approved.
- **Decision by the European Commission**: Based on the CHMP's recommendation, the European Commission makes a final decision on approval for the drug to be marketed across the EU.
- **Post-Authorization Safety Studies (PASS)**: Similar to the U.S., the EMA requires ongoing post-marketing studies to monitor the drug's performance and safety in the general population.

Differences in Regulatory Processes:

- **Review Times**: The time taken from submission to approval can vary significantly between the FDA and EMA, influenced by the drug's complexity, the urgency of the medical need, and the completeness of the application.
- **Adaptive Pathways**: Both agencies have provisions for accelerated or adaptive pathways for drugs that address unmet medical needs, particularly for severe conditions or where there is no existing satisfactory treatment.
- **Public and Professional Involvement**: The EMA often involves broader public and patient consultation processes compared to the FDA, reflecting European policies on public health and safety.

Common Challenges:

- **Regulatory Harmonization**: Despite efforts by international bodies like the International Council for Harmonisation of Technical Requirements for Pharmaceuticals for Human Use (ICH), significant differences still exist in regulatory requirements and processes between regions.
- **Data Requirements**: Differences in the required clinical data and the interpretation of safety and efficacy can lead to variations in drug approval decisions between regulators.

Understanding these processes is essential for pharmaceutical companies planning to market new drugs globally. Each region's specific requirements must be carefully considered to navigate the regulatory landscape successfully.

1.5.2 Requirements for Drug Labeling and Packaging

Drug labeling and packaging are critical components of pharmaceutical regulation, ensuring that medications are used safely and effectively. Regulatory agencies like the FDA (U.S.) and EMA (Europe) have specific requirements for labeling and packaging to prevent misuse and provide essential information to healthcare providers and patients.

Key Components of Drug Labeling:

- **Brand and Generic Name**: Both the brand name and the generic name of the drug must be prominently displayed on the label.
- **Dosage Form and Strength**: The form (e.g., tablet, capsule, injection) and strength of the drug must be clearly stated.
- **Indications and Usage**: This section describes the approved uses of the drug, specifying the conditions it is meant to treat.
- **Dosage and Administration**: Instructions on how to use the drug, including dosages, frequencies, routes of administration, and any special handling instructions.
- **Contraindications**: Situations in which the drug should not be used due to risks of potential harm.
- **Warnings and Precautions**: Information about any serious adverse reactions and safety hazards associated with the drug.
- **Adverse Reactions**: Details of potential side effects, typically derived from clinical trial data.
- **Drug Interactions**: Information on how the drug interacts with other medications, foods, or medical conditions.
- **Pharmacokinetics and Pharmacodynamics**: Information on how the drug is absorbed, distributed, metabolized, and excreted, as well as its mechanism of action.
- **Storage and Handling**: Instructions for proper storage conditions to maintain drug efficacy and safety.

Packaging Requirements:

- **Child-Resistant Packaging**: Many medications are required to be packaged in child-resistant containers to prevent accidental ingestion by children.

- **Tamper-Evident Packaging**: Packaging must clearly show whether it has been opened or altered to ensure consumer safety.
- **Accessibility Features**: Packaging designs may need to include features for the elderly or individuals with disabilities, such as easy-open caps or braille for visually impaired users.
- **Material Safety**: Materials used in packaging must not interact with the drug, affecting its stability or efficacy.

Regulatory Differences and Considerations:

- **FDA Guidelines (U.S.)**: The FDA requires drug labels to include a "Drug Facts" panel similar to "Nutrition Facts" on food products, which is standardized to help consumers compare and understand drug information easily.
- **EMA Guidelines (Europe)**: The EMA requires that labeling and package leaflets be provided in all official languages of the country where the drug is marketed, accommodating the diverse linguistic landscape of the EU.
- **Environmental Considerations**: Increasingly, regulators are considering the environmental impact of drug packaging, pushing for materials that are sustainable or easily recyclable.

Compliance and Updates:

- **Regular Updates**: Drug labels and packaging must be regularly updated as new information becomes available about the drug's safety, efficacy, or other relevant data.
- **Compliance Checks**: Regulatory agencies conduct periodic reviews and audits to ensure compliance with labeling and packaging guidelines.

Proper drug labeling and packaging not only comply with regulatory requirements but also serve as the final check to ensure patient safety and effective medication use. This involves a collaborative effort among regulatory bodies, pharmaceutical companies, and healthcare professionals to maintain high standards throughout the product's lifecycle.

CHAPTER TWO

APPROACHES TO DRUG DISCOVERY

2.1 Pharmacological Approaches

2.1.1 Traditional Pharmacological Screening

Traditional pharmacological screening is a foundational method in drug discovery, involving the systematic testing of chemical compounds for their biological activity. The process typically begins with the identification of a biological target or disease mechanism of interest, such as an enzyme, receptor, or cellular pathway implicated in a particular disease. Researchers then screen large libraries of chemical compounds, often natural or synthetic small molecules, to identify those that modulate the target's activity or function. This screening can be conducted using various assays, such as binding assays, enzymatic assays, or cellular assays, depending on the nature of the target and the desired mode of action of the drug candidate.

One key advantage of traditional pharmacological screening is its ability to identify compounds with diverse chemical structures that may exhibit the desired pharmacological activity. This diversity can increase the likelihood of finding a lead compound with suitable drug-like properties for further development. Additionally, traditional screening approaches can be tailored to specific target classes or therapeutic areas, allowing researchers to focus their efforts on areas of high medical need or scientific interest.

Despite its strengths, traditional pharmacological screening also has limitations. One challenge is the potential for false positives or false negatives in the screening assays, which can lead to the identification of compounds that are not truly active or the failure to identify promising leads. To mitigate this risk, researchers often conduct secondary and tertiary screens to validate hits and prioritize compounds for further study. Additionally, traditional screening approaches may overlook compounds with novel mechanisms of action or complex modes of interaction with biological targets, limiting the discovery of truly innovative drugs.

In recent years, traditional pharmacological screening has been complemented by advanced screening technologies, such as high-throughput screening (HTS) and virtual screening, which allow for the rapid screening of large compound libraries and the in silico prediction of compound activity, respectively. These technologies have significantly accelerated the drug discovery process and enabled the identification of novel drug candidates more efficiently. However, traditional pharmacological screening remains a valuable tool in drug discovery, particularly in the early stages of target identification and validation, where its flexibility and versatility are essential for exploring diverse chemical space and identifying promising lead compounds.

2.1.2 Target-Based Drug Discovery

Target-based drug discovery is a strategic approach that focuses on identifying and modulating specific biological targets implicated in disease pathogenesis. These targets can include proteins, enzymes, receptors, nucleic acids, or other molecules involved in key disease processes such as signaling pathways, gene expression, or protein-protein interactions. The primary goal of target-based drug discovery is to develop small molecule or biologic therapeutics that selectively modulate the activity or function of the target, thereby restoring normal physiological function or inhibiting pathological processes.

One of the key advantages of target-based drug discovery is its rational and systematic approach to drug development. By elucidating the molecular mechanisms underlying disease pathogenesis and identifying specific targets involved, researchers can design and optimize drug candidates with greater precision and efficacy. This approach enables the development of drugs with improved selectivity, potency, and safety profiles, reducing the risk of off-target effects and adverse reactions.

Target-based drug discovery typically involves several key steps, including target identification, validation, and characterization, followed by the design and optimization of drug candidates that modulate the target's activity. Target identification may involve a variety of approaches, including genomic and proteomic analyses, functional genomics, and bioinformatics, to identify genes, proteins, or pathways associated with disease susceptibility or progression. Once a target has been identified, its relevance to disease pathogenesis must be validated through genetic, biochemical, or pharmacological studies, confirming its potential as a therapeutic target.

After target validation, researchers design and screen chemical libraries or biologic compounds to identify lead molecules that selectively modulate the target's activity. This process often involves high-throughput screening (HTS) of large compound libraries using biochemical or cell-based assays tailored to the target of interest. Hits identified from screening are then subjected to further optimization through medicinal chemistry or protein engineering approaches to enhance their potency, selectivity, and pharmacokinetic properties. Lead optimization involves iterative cycles of compound design, synthesis, and testing to identify drug candidates with suitable drug-like properties for preclinical and clinical development.

While target-based drug discovery offers numerous advantages, it also presents several challenges. One limitation is the potential for target validation failures, where drugs designed to modulate a specific target fail to demonstrate efficacy in clinical trials due to unforeseen complexities in disease biology or drug-target interactions. Additionally, target-based approaches may overlook targets with poorly characterized roles in disease pathogenesis or targets involved in complex biological networks that are difficult to modulate selectively.

2.1.3 Phenotypic Screening

Phenotypic screening is a powerful approach in drug discovery that focuses on evaluating the effects of chemical compounds on whole cells, tissues, or organisms, rather than targeting specific molecular pathways or biological targets. Unlike target-based drug discovery, which relies on a priori knowledge of disease mechanisms and molecular targets, phenotypic screening allows researchers to identify novel drug candidates based on their ability to produce a desired phenotypic change or biological response in a relevant biological system.

One of the key advantages of phenotypic screening is its ability to identify drug candidates with unexpected or unanticipated effects on disease-relevant phenotypes. By screening large compound libraries in cellular or animal models of disease, researchers can discover compounds that produce desirable changes in disease-associated phenotypes, such as cell proliferation, apoptosis, differentiation, or metabolic activity, without prior knowledge of the underlying molecular mechanisms. This unbiased approach enables the identification of novel drug targets and pathways that may not have been previously implicated in disease pathogenesis.

Phenotypic screening typically involves several key steps, including the selection of an appropriate biological model or assay system that recapitulates key aspects of the disease phenotype, the screening of chemical libraries or compound collections to identify hits that produce the desired phenotypic response, and the validation and optimization of hit compounds for further development. Assay systems used in phenotypic screening may range from simple cellular assays in vitro to complex animal models in vivo, depending on the disease target and the desired level of physiological relevance.

One challenge of phenotypic screening is the identification of the molecular targets and mechanisms of action of hit compounds. Unlike target-based drug discovery, where the molecular target is known a priori, phenotypic screening often yields hits with unknown or poorly characterized targets, making it challenging to elucidate the underlying mechanisms of action. To overcome this challenge, researchers often employ a variety of approaches, including target deconvolution studies, chemical proteomics, and functional genomics, to identify the molecular targets and pathways modulated by hit compounds.

2.1.4 Rational Drug Design

Rational drug design is an innovative approach in drug discovery that leverages our understanding of the molecular mechanisms underlying disease pathogenesis to design and optimize drug candidates with high specificity and efficacy. Unlike traditional screening methods, which rely on empirical testing of large compound libraries, rational drug design starts with the identification of a specific molecular target implicated in the disease process, such as a protein, enzyme, or receptor, and aims to develop drugs that selectively modulate the activity or function of that target.

One of the key advantages of rational drug design is its ability to accelerate the drug discovery process by focusing efforts on targets with well-defined roles in disease biology. By elucidating the three-dimensional structure of the target protein through techniques such as X-ray crystallography, nuclear magnetic resonance (NMR) spectroscopy, or homology modeling, researchers can identify binding pockets and potential drug-binding sites on the target surface. This structural information serves as the basis for computer-aided drug design (CADD) approaches, which use computational algorithms and molecular modeling techniques to predict and optimize the binding affinity, selectivity, and pharmacokinetic properties of drug candidates.

Rational drug design typically involves several key steps, including target identification and validation, structure-based virtual screening, lead optimization, and preclinical characterization. Target identification may involve genomic, proteomic, or biochemical studies to identify proteins or pathways with key roles in disease pathogenesis. Once a target has been validated, researchers use computational methods to screen large chemical libraries or design new compounds that are predicted to bind to the target with high affinity and selectivity. These lead compounds are then synthesized and tested in vitro and in vivo to assess their pharmacological activity, safety, and efficacy.

One challenge of rational drug design is the accurate prediction of drug-target interactions and the optimization of drug candidates with desired properties. Despite advances in computational modeling and structural biology, predicting the binding affinity and selectivity of drug candidates remains a complex and challenging task, often requiring iterative cycles of design, synthesis, and testing to identify lead compounds with suitable drug-like properties. Additionally, rational drug design may overlook potential off-target effects or unintended consequences of modulating a specific target, highlighting the importance of comprehensive preclinical characterization and safety assessment.

2.1.5 Case Study: Discovery of Imatinib in Chronic Myeloid Leukemia

The discovery of imatinib, a breakthrough drug in the treatment of chronic myeloid leukemia (CML), exemplifies the successful application of rational drug design principles in targeting specific molecular pathways implicated in cancer pathogenesis. CML is characterized by the presence of the Philadelphia chromosome, resulting from a reciprocal translocation between chromosomes 9 and 22, which generates the BCR-ABL fusion protein with constitutive tyrosine kinase activity.

The pivotal step in the development of imatinib was the elucidation of the crystal structure of the BCR-ABL kinase domain by scientists led by Nicholas Lydon and Brian Druker. This structural insight revealed the ATP-binding pocket of the kinase domain as a potential target for small molecule inhibitors. Based on this structural information, researchers at Novartis Pharmaceuticals designed imatinib as a specific inhibitor of the BCR-ABL kinase, with the aim of disrupting the aberrant signaling pathway driving CML proliferation and survival.

Imatinib was initially tested in preclinical studies using cellular and animal models of CML, where it demonstrated potent inhibition of BCR-ABL kinase activity and induction of apoptosis in leukemic cells. Encouraged by these promising results, imatinib entered clinical trials, where it was evaluated for safety, efficacy, and tolerability in patients with CML. The results of these trials were groundbreaking, demonstrating unprecedented rates of hematologic and cytogenetic responses, and leading to accelerated approval by regulatory authorities for the treatment of CML.

Subsequent clinical trials further established the efficacy of imatinib as a frontline therapy for newly diagnosed CML patients and as a salvage therapy for patients resistant or intolerant to prior treatments. Imatinib revolutionized the management of CML, transforming it from a fatal disease to a chronic, manageable condition for many patients. Moreover, the success of imatinib sparked interest in targeted therapies and rational drug design approaches across the pharmaceutical industry, leading to the development of numerous other kinase inhibitors for the treatment of various cancers and other diseases.

2.2 Toxicological Aspects

2.2.1 ADMET (Absorption, Distribution, Metabolism, Excretion, Toxicity) Profiling

ADMET profiling is a crucial aspect of drug discovery and development, focusing on evaluating the pharmacokinetic and toxicological properties of drug candidates to assess their safety, efficacy, and suitability for further development. The acronym ADMET stands for Absorption, Distribution, Metabolism, Excretion, and Toxicity, representing key processes that influence the pharmacokinetics and pharmacodynamics of drugs in vivo.

Absorption: Absorption refers to the process by which a drug enters the bloodstream from its site of administration. It involves the passage of the drug across biological barriers, such as the gastrointestinal tract (oral administration), respiratory tract (inhalation), or skin (topical administration). ADMET studies evaluate factors affecting drug absorption, such as solubility, permeability, and the presence of efflux transporters, to predict the bioavailability of a drug and its potential for oral absorption.

Distribution: Distribution involves the transport of a drug from the bloodstream to various tissues and organs throughout the body. It is influenced by factors such as plasma protein binding, tissue permeability, and the presence of active transport mechanisms. ADMET profiling assesses the distribution of a drug in different tissues and organs, as well as its potential for accumulation in specific tissues or compartments, which can impact both therapeutic efficacy and toxicity.

Metabolism: Metabolism refers to the enzymatic conversion of a drug into metabolites, which may be pharmacologically active or inactive. The liver is the primary site of drug metabolism, where enzymes such as cytochrome P450 (CYP) enzymes catalyze the biotransformation of drugs into metabolites that are more hydrophilic and easier to excrete. ADMET studies evaluate the metabolic stability of drug candidates, their potential for drug-drug interactions, and the formation of toxic metabolites that may contribute to adverse effects or toxicity.

Excretion: Excretion involves the removal of drugs and their metabolites from the body, primarily through the kidneys (urine) and liver (bile). Renal excretion is particularly important for hydrophilic compounds, while hepatic excretion via bile is more relevant for lipophilic compounds. ADMET profiling assesses the routes and kinetics of drug excretion, as well as factors influencing renal clearance, such as glomerular filtration, tubular secretion, and reabsorption.

Toxicity: Toxicity evaluation is a critical component of ADMET profiling, focusing on identifying and characterizing potential adverse effects of drug candidates on various organ systems and physiological processes. Toxicological studies assess acute and chronic toxicity, genotoxicity, carcinogenicity, reproductive toxicity, and other safety endpoints to ensure the safety of drug candidates for human use. ADMET profiling aims to identify and mitigate potential toxicities early in the drug development process, guiding the selection of safe and efficacious drug candidates for further development.

2.2.2 Predictive Toxicology Methods

Predictive toxicology methods are essential tools in drug discovery and development, aimed at identifying and evaluating potential toxicities of drug candidates early in the development process. These methods utilize in vitro, in silico, and in vivo approaches to predict the toxicological effects of drugs on various organ systems and physiological processes, enabling researchers to prioritize safe and efficacious drug candidates for further development.

In vitro Methods: In vitro methods involve the use of cultured cells, tissues, or organs to assess the toxicological effects of drugs. Cell-based assays, such as cytotoxicity assays, cell proliferation assays, and cell viability assays, are commonly used to evaluate the effects of drugs on cell viability, proliferation, apoptosis, and cellular function. Organotypic models, such as liver spheroids, kidney organoids, and lung epithelial cultures, can mimic the structure and function of specific organs and tissues, enabling more physiologically relevant toxicity testing. In vitro methods are valuable for screening large numbers of compounds in a high-throughput manner and for investigating mechanisms of toxicity at the cellular and molecular levels.

In silico Methods: In silico methods involve computational modeling and simulation techniques to predict the toxicological properties of drugs based on their chemical structure, physicochemical properties, and biological activity. Quantitative structure-activity relationship (QSAR) models, pharmacophore modeling, molecular docking, and machine learning algorithms are commonly used to predict drug toxicity, metabolism, and pharmacokinetic properties. In silico methods can screen large chemical libraries, prioritize compounds for experimental testing, and identify structural features associated with toxicological liabilities, guiding the design and optimization of safer drug candidates.

In vivo Methods: In vivo methods involve the use of animal models to evaluate the toxicological effects of drugs in living organisms. Animal studies assess acute and chronic toxicity, organ toxicity, reproductive toxicity, carcinogenicity, and other safety endpoints to assess the overall safety profile of drug candidates. Rodents (e.g., mice, rats) are commonly used for toxicology studies due to their small size, ease of handling, and short reproductive cycles. Non-human primates and other species may be used for certain toxicology studies to better predict human responses to drugs. In vivo studies provide valuable information on systemic toxicity, organ-specific effects, and potential adverse reactions that may occur in humans.

2.2.3 In vitro and In vivo Toxicity Testing

In vitro and in vivo toxicity testing are integral components of the drug development process, aiming to evaluate the safety profile of drug candidates by assessing their potential adverse effects on biological systems. These testing methods employ different approaches to predict and characterize toxicological responses, providing valuable information to guide decision-making and mitigate risks associated with drug development.

In vitro Toxicity Testing:

In vitro toxicity testing involves the use of cultured cells, tissues, or organs to assess the toxicological effects of drug candidates at the cellular and molecular levels. Cell-based assays are widely used to evaluate various aspects of toxicity, including cytotoxicity, genotoxicity, and organ-specific toxicity. Common in vitro assays include:

1. **Cytotoxicity Assays**: These assays measure the viability and proliferation of cells following exposure to drug candidates. Techniques such as the MTT assay, the LDH release assay, and the ATP assay are commonly used to assess cell viability and cytotoxic effects.
2. **Genotoxicity Assays**: Genotoxicity assays assess the potential of drug candidates to induce DNA damage or mutations in cells. The Ames test, the micronucleus assay, and the comet assay are commonly used to evaluate genotoxic effects.
3. **Organotypic Models**: Organotypic models involve the use of three-dimensional cell cultures or tissue slices that mimic the structure and function of specific organs or tissues. These models, such as liver spheroids, kidney organoids, and lung epithelial cultures, provide more physiologically relevant platforms for toxicity testing.

In vitro toxicity testing offers several advantages, including high throughput, cost-effectiveness, and the ability to assess mechanistic aspects of toxicity at the cellular level. However, in vitro models may not fully capture the complexity of in vivo systems and may have limited predictive value for certain toxicological endpoints.

In vivo Toxicity Testing:

In vivo toxicity testing involves the evaluation of the toxicological effects of drug candidates in living organisms, typically using animal models. These studies assess acute and chronic toxicity, organ toxicity, reproductive toxicity, carcinogenicity, and other safety endpoints to determine the overall safety profile of drug candidates. Common animal models used for toxicity testing include rodents (e.g., mice, rats), non-human primates, and other species.

In vivo toxicity testing provides valuable information on systemic toxicity, organ-specific effects, and potential adverse reactions that may occur in humans. These studies assess the pharmacokinetics and pharmacodynamics of drug candidates in vivo, including absorption, distribution, metabolism, and excretion (ADME), to identify potential safety concerns and optimize dosing regimens.

However, in vivo toxicity testing also has limitations, including ethical considerations, species-specific differences in drug metabolism and toxicity, and the high cost and time associated with conducting animal studies. In addition, extrapolating results from animal models to humans may be challenging due to interspecies variability and differences in physiology, metabolism, and drug response.

2.2.4 Case Study: Thalidomide Disaster and the Importance of Toxicological Assessment

The thalidomide disaster stands as a tragic reminder of the critical importance of rigorous toxicological assessment in drug development. Thalidomide, initially introduced in the late 1950s as a sedative and antiemetic, became infamous for its devastating teratogenic effects when prescribed to pregnant women, resulting in thousands of babies born with severe birth defects.

Thalidomide was marketed without sufficient preclinical toxicological evaluation, and its teratogenic effects were not adequately assessed prior to widespread clinical use. In the absence of robust toxicological data, the drug was prescribed to pregnant women to alleviate morning sickness, leading to a public health catastrophe of unprecedented scale.

The thalidomide disaster highlighted several key lessons regarding the importance of toxicological assessment in drug development:

1. **Preclinical Evaluation**: Thalidomide's teratogenic effects could have been predicted and prevented through comprehensive preclinical toxicological studies. However, inadequate testing and oversight allowed the drug to reach the market without sufficient evidence of its safety profile.
2. **Species-Specific Differences**: Thalidomide's teratogenic effects were not evident in animal studies conducted prior to its clinical use. This discrepancy underscored the importance of considering species-specific differences in drug metabolism, toxicity, and teratogenicity when extrapolating preclinical data to humans.
3. **Risk Communication and Regulation**: The thalidomide disaster prompted regulatory agencies worldwide to reevaluate their approval processes and regulations for drug safety. It led to the establishment of more rigorous guidelines for preclinical testing, risk assessment, and post-marketing surveillance to ensure the safety of drugs for human use.

4. **Ethical Considerations**: The thalidomide tragedy raised ethical questions about the responsibility of pharmaceutical companies, regulatory agencies, and healthcare providers in ensuring the safety of drugs. It highlighted the need for transparency, accountability, and ethical oversight throughout the drug development process.

In response to the thalidomide disaster, regulatory agencies implemented stricter requirements for preclinical toxicological assessment, including the evaluation of reproductive and developmental toxicity, genotoxicity, carcinogenicity, and other safety endpoints. These measures have significantly improved the safety and efficacy of drugs, reducing the risk of adverse effects and protecting public health.

2.3 Initial Drug Characterization

2.3.1 Physicochemical Properties Evaluation

Physicochemical properties evaluation is a crucial step in the initial characterization of drug candidates, providing valuable insights into their chemical structure, stability, solubility, permeability, and other key properties that influence their pharmacokinetics and pharmacodynamics. By assessing these properties early in the drug discovery process, researchers can identify promising lead compounds and prioritize candidates for further development.

Molecular Structure: The evaluation of molecular structure involves determining the chemical composition, stereochemistry, and conformational flexibility of drug candidates. Techniques such as nuclear magnetic resonance (NMR) spectroscopy, X-ray crystallography, and mass spectrometry are used to elucidate the three-dimensional structure of molecules, providing insights into their physical and chemical properties.

Solubility: Solubility is a critical determinant of oral bioavailability, affecting the rate and extent of drug absorption in the gastrointestinal tract. Poorly soluble compounds may exhibit erratic or incomplete absorption, leading to variable pharmacokinetics and reduced efficacy. Various methods, such as shake-flask method, equilibrium solubility measurement, and high-throughput screening assays, are employed to assess the solubility of drug candidates under different pH conditions and formulation strategies.

Permeability: Permeability refers to the ability of a drug to cross biological membranes, such as the intestinal epithelium, blood-brain barrier, or cellular membranes. High permeability is essential for oral absorption and tissue distribution, while low permeability may limit drug delivery to target tissues. Permeability assessments are typically performed using in vitro cell-based assays, such as the Caco-2 cell permeability assay or the parallel artificial membrane permeability assay (PAMPA), to predict the absorption potential of drug candidates.

Stability: Stability evaluation assesses the chemical and physical stability of drug candidates under various environmental conditions, including temperature, pH, humidity, and light exposure. Stability studies aim to identify degradation pathways, degradation kinetics, and potential degradation products that may affect drug potency, safety, and shelf life. Accelerated stability testing, forced degradation studies, and stability-indicating assay methods are commonly used to evaluate the stability of drug candidates.

Particle Size and Morphology: Particle size and morphology influence the dissolution rate, bioavailability, and formulation stability of drug candidates. Techniques such as microscopy, laser diffraction, and dynamic light scattering are used to characterize the particle size distribution, shape, surface area, and surface charge of drug particles, providing insights into their physical properties and behavior in different dosage forms.

Hygroscopicity and Moisture Uptake: Hygroscopicity assessment evaluates the tendency of drug substances to absorb moisture from the environment, leading to changes in physical properties, stability, and formulation performance. Techniques such as gravimetric moisture sorption analysis and dynamic vapor sorption are used to measure moisture uptake kinetics and assess the hygroscopic behavior of drug candidates.

2.3.2 Pharmacokinetic Profiling

Pharmacokinetic profiling is a fundamental aspect of initial drug characterization, focusing on the study of a drug's absorption, distribution, metabolism, and excretion (ADME) in biological systems. This comprehensive assessment provides critical insights into the pharmacokinetic behavior of drug candidates, guiding decisions regarding formulation optimization, dosing regimens, and further development.

Absorption: Absorption refers to the process by which a drug enters the systemic circulation following administration. Pharmacokinetic studies evaluate the route, rate, and extent of drug absorption, as well as factors influencing absorption kinetics such as solubility, permeability, and formulation characteristics. Common methods for assessing absorption include in vitro permeability assays, in situ intestinal perfusion studies, and in vivo pharmacokinetic studies in animal models or humans.

Distribution: Distribution involves the transport of a drug from the bloodstream to various tissues and organs throughout the body. Pharmacokinetic studies assess the volume of distribution (Vd) of a drug, reflecting its distribution in different tissues relative to plasma concentrations. Techniques such as tissue distribution studies, imaging techniques (e.g., positron emission tomography), and pharmacokinetic modeling are used to characterize the distribution kinetics of drugs in vivo.

Metabolism: Metabolism refers to the biotransformation of a drug into metabolites, primarily in the liver and other metabolic organs. Pharmacokinetic studies evaluate the metabolic stability of drug candidates, their susceptibility to metabolism by cytochrome P450 enzymes and other metabolic pathways, and the formation of metabolites with pharmacological activity or toxicity. In vitro microsomal metabolism assays, in vivo clearance studies, and metabolite profiling analyses are commonly used to assess drug metabolism.

Excretion: Excretion involves the elimination of drugs and their metabolites from the body, primarily through renal excretion and hepatic metabolism. Pharmacokinetic studies evaluate the renal and hepatic clearance of drug candidates, as well as factors influencing their elimination kinetics such as renal function, protein binding, and metabolism. Techniques such as urinary excretion studies, bile duct cannulation, and pharmacokinetic modeling are used to assess drug excretion pathways and kinetics.

Pharmacokinetic Parameters: Pharmacokinetic profiling generates a variety of quantitative parameters to characterize the pharmacokinetic behavior of drug candidates, including area under the concentration-time curve (AUC), maximum plasma concentration (Cmax), time to reach Cmax (Tmax), elimination half-life ($t_{1/2}$), clearance (CL), and bioavailability (F). These parameters provide valuable information on drug absorption, distribution, metabolism, and excretion, as well as overall exposure and duration of action.

Pharmacokinetic Modeling and Simulation: Pharmacokinetic modeling and simulation are valuable tools for predicting and optimizing the pharmacokinetic behavior of drug candidates. Physiologically-based pharmacokinetic (PBPK) models, compartmental models, and population pharmacokinetic modeling are used to simulate drug concentration-time profiles, assess dosing regimens, and predict drug-drug interactions and variability in patient populations.

2.3.3 Pharmacodynamic Assessment

Pharmacodynamic assessment is an essential component of initial drug characterization, focusing on understanding the biological effects of drug candidates on target tissues, cells, and physiological systems. By elucidating the pharmacological mechanisms of action and dose-response relationships, pharmacodynamic studies provide critical insights into the efficacy, potency, and safety of drug candidates, guiding decisions regarding further development and optimization.

Target Engagement: Pharmacodynamic assessment begins with the evaluation of target engagement, assessing the ability of drug candidates to bind to and modulate their molecular targets. Techniques such as receptor binding assays, enzyme activity assays, and functional assays are used to measure target occupancy, activation, or inhibition in vitro and in vivo.

Biological Effects: Pharmacodynamic studies evaluate the biological effects of drug candidates on cellular and physiological processes relevant to disease pathogenesis. These effects may include changes in cell signaling pathways, gene expression profiles, protein synthesis, and cellular function. In vitro cell-based assays, tissue culture studies, and animal models are used to assess the pharmacological activity and mechanism of action of drug candidates.

Dose-Response Relationships: Pharmacodynamic assessment involves establishing dose-response relationships to determine the potency and efficacy of drug candidates. Dose-response studies assess the effects of varying drug concentrations on biological endpoints, such as receptor binding, enzyme activity, or physiological responses. Graphical analysis, mathematical modeling, and statistical analysis are used to quantify dose-response relationships and derive pharmacodynamic parameters, such as EC50 (half-maximal effective concentration) and Emax (maximum effect).

Pharmacological Biomarkers: Pharmacodynamic assessment may involve the identification and validation of pharmacological biomarkers, molecular or cellular markers that reflect drug activity or disease progression. Pharmacological biomarkers serve as surrogate endpoints for drug efficacy and safety, providing valuable tools for monitoring drug response, predicting clinical outcomes, and stratifying patient populations. Biomarker assays, imaging techniques, and omics technologies are used to identify and validate pharmacological biomarkers in preclinical and clinical studies.

Safety Pharmacology: Pharmacodynamic assessment also includes the evaluation of potential adverse effects and safety pharmacology endpoints associated with drug candidates. Safety pharmacology studies assess the effects of drugs on vital organ systems, such as the cardiovascular, respiratory, central nervous, and gastrointestinal systems, to identify potential safety concerns and inform risk mitigation strategies. Functional assays, physiological monitoring, and behavioral assessments are used to evaluate safety pharmacology endpoints in animal models and early-phase clinical trials.

2.3.4 Safety Assessment

Safety assessment is a pivotal aspect of initial drug characterization, aiming to identify and evaluate potential adverse effects and safety concerns associated with drug candidates. By conducting comprehensive safety assessments, researchers can mitigate risks, optimize drug candidates, and ensure the safety and well-being of patients during clinical development and subsequent use.

Toxicity Studies: Safety assessment begins with the evaluation of toxicological properties of drug candidates through a series of in vitro and in vivo studies. These studies assess acute and chronic toxicities, genotoxicity, carcinogenicity, reproductive toxicity, organ toxicity, and other safety endpoints. Various regulatory guidelines outline the requirements for conducting toxicology studies to assess the safety of drug candidates prior to clinical trials.

ADME Studies: Safety assessment also involves pharmacokinetic studies to evaluate the absorption, distribution, metabolism, and excretion (ADME) properties of drug candidates. Understanding the pharmacokinetic behavior of drugs is critical for predicting and minimizing potential safety risks, such as drug accumulation, metabolite formation, and drug-drug interactions. ADME studies provide valuable insights into the systemic exposure, tissue distribution, and elimination kinetics of drug candidates.

Safety Pharmacology: Safety assessment includes safety pharmacology studies to assess the effects of drug candidates on vital organ systems, such as the cardiovascular, respiratory, central nervous, and gastrointestinal systems. These studies evaluate potential adverse effects on organ function, hemodynamics, electrocardiography, respiratory parameters, and other physiological endpoints. Safety pharmacology studies aim to identify potential safety concerns early in the drug development process and inform risk mitigation strategies.

Clinical Safety Studies: Safety assessment extends to clinical trials, where drug candidates are evaluated for safety, tolerability, and adverse effects in human subjects. Phase I clinical trials focus on assessing safety, pharmacokinetics, and tolerability in healthy volunteers, while later-phase trials involve larger patient populations to evaluate efficacy and safety in specific disease indications. Adverse event monitoring, safety assessments, and laboratory tests are conducted throughout clinical trials to detect and manage potential safety concerns.

Risk Assessment and Mitigation: Safety assessment involves risk assessment and mitigation strategies to identify and manage potential safety risks associated with drug candidates. Risk assessment involves evaluating the probability and severity of adverse effects based on preclinical and clinical data, while risk mitigation strategies aim to minimize or prevent adverse effects through dose optimization, patient selection criteria, monitoring protocols, and labeling recommendations.

2.3.5 Case Study: Initial Characterization of Aspirin as an Analgesic and Anti-inflammatory Drug

The initial characterization of aspirin stands as a seminal example of the importance of systematic drug evaluation in identifying therapeutic properties and safety profiles. Aspirin, or acetylsalicylic acid, is a nonsteroidal anti-inflammatory drug (NSAID) widely used for its analgesic, antipyretic, and anti-inflammatory effects.

Discovery and Development: Aspirin's therapeutic properties can be traced back to ancient times when the bark of the willow tree was used medicinally to alleviate pain and fever. However, it was not until the late 19th century that scientists elucidated the active compound responsible for these effects. In 1897, Felix Hoffmann, a chemist at Bayer, synthesized acetylsalicylic acid, leading to the development of aspirin as a pharmaceutical product.

Initial Pharmacological Characterization: Early studies on aspirin focused on characterizing its pharmacological effects and mechanisms of action. Aspirin was found to inhibit the enzyme cyclooxygenase (COX), thereby blocking the synthesis of prostaglandins, which are mediators of pain, inflammation, and fever. This mechanism of action underlies aspirin's analgesic, anti-inflammatory, and antipyretic properties.

Clinical Efficacy: Clinical trials conducted in the early 20th century demonstrated the efficacy of aspirin in relieving pain, reducing fever, and alleviating inflammation in various conditions, including rheumatic diseases and infectious illnesses. Aspirin's effectiveness in providing symptomatic relief and improving quality of life in patients with inflammatory conditions contributed to its widespread acceptance and adoption as a therapeutic agent.

Safety Profile: Despite its therapeutic benefits, aspirin was also found to be associated with certain safety concerns, particularly gastrointestinal irritation and bleeding. Early clinical observations and post-marketing surveillance studies identified gastrointestinal adverse effects as common side effects of aspirin use, leading to efforts to develop safer formulations and dosing regimens to minimize these risks.

Optimization and Formulation: Over the years, aspirin has undergone optimization and formulation improvements to enhance its pharmacokinetic properties, safety profile, and patient adherence. Enteric-coated formulations were developed to reduce gastrointestinal irritation, while low-dose regimens were introduced for cardiovascular prophylaxis. These advancements have expanded the therapeutic utility of aspirin and improved its safety and tolerability in diverse patient populations.

Ongoing Research: Despite its long history of clinical use, ongoing research continues to uncover new insights into aspirin's pharmacological effects and therapeutic applications. Recent studies have explored aspirin's potential role in cancer prevention, cardiovascular disease management, and neurodegenerative disorders, highlighting its diverse pharmacological effects and potential clinical benefits beyond its traditional indications.

2.4 Drug Optimization and Lead Identification

2.4.1 Structure-Activity Relationship (SAR) Studies

Structure-Activity Relationship (SAR) studies are a cornerstone of drug optimization and lead identification, providing crucial insights into how chemical structure influences the pharmacological activity of compounds. By systematically modifying the structure of lead compounds and evaluating their biological activity, SAR studies aim to optimize potency, selectivity, and pharmacokinetic properties, guiding the rational design of drug candidates with improved therapeutic profiles.

Lead Compound Selection: SAR studies typically begin with the identification of lead compounds, molecules with initial pharmacological activity against a target of interest. Lead compounds may be discovered through high-throughput screening, virtual screening, natural product isolation, or rational design approaches. Once identified, lead compounds serve as starting points for SAR studies to elucidate structure-activity relationships and optimize their pharmacological properties.

Chemical Modification: SAR studies involve the systematic modification of lead compounds to explore the impact of structural changes on biological activity. Chemical modifications may include altering functional groups, substituents, stereochemistry, or scaffold architecture to optimize pharmacodynamic and pharmacokinetic properties. These modifications are guided by hypotheses based on known structure-activity relationships, molecular modeling, bioinformatics analysis, and empirical observations.

Biological Evaluation: Modified compounds generated through SAR studies are evaluated for their biological activity using in vitro and in vivo assays relevant to the target of interest. Pharmacological assays assess the potency, selectivity, efficacy, and mechanism of action of modified compounds, providing quantitative data on their pharmacodynamic properties. Structure-activity relationships are established by correlating structural features with changes in biological activity across a series of analogs.

Optimization Criteria: SAR studies aim to optimize lead compounds based on predefined criteria, such as potency, selectivity, metabolic stability, solubility, permeability, and safety profile. Optimization strategies may prioritize enhancing potency against the target while minimizing off-target effects, improving drug-like properties to optimize pharmacokinetics and bioavailability, or mitigating safety concerns associated with lead compounds.

Iterative Process: SAR studies are iterative processes involving cycles of chemical modification, biological evaluation, and structure-activity analysis. By systematically exploring the structure-activity landscape of lead compounds, researchers iteratively refine chemical structures to optimize pharmacological properties and identify promising drug candidates for further development.

Application Across Therapeutic Areas: SAR studies are applied across a wide range of therapeutic areas, including oncology, infectious diseases, central nervous system disorders, cardiovascular diseases, and metabolic disorders. SAR-guided drug discovery has led to the development of numerous clinically important drugs, including small molecules, biologics, and targeted therapies, with improved efficacy, safety, and therapeutic outcomes.

2.4.2 Hit-to-Lead Optimization

Hit-to-Lead Optimization is a critical phase in drug discovery where promising initial hits from high-throughput screening or other lead identification methods are refined and optimized to develop lead compounds with improved potency, selectivity, and pharmacokinetic properties. This process involves a series of iterative steps aimed at transforming hit compounds into lead candidates suitable for further preclinical and clinical development.

Hit Identification: Hit-to-Lead Optimization begins with the identification of promising hits from screening libraries, natural product extracts, or virtual screening approaches. Hits are compounds that exhibit initial activity against a biological target of interest, typically identified through biochemical, cell-based, or computational assays. Hits serve as starting points for further optimization to improve their drug-like properties and efficacy.

Structure-Activity Relationship (SAR) Studies: Hit compounds undergo SAR studies to explore the relationship between chemical structure and biological activity. By systematically modifying the chemical structure of hit compounds and evaluating their activity, SAR studies identify key structural features responsible for potency, selectivity, and other pharmacological properties. Rational design strategies, molecular modeling, and computational chemistry techniques are used to guide chemical modifications and optimize lead compounds.

Medicinal Chemistry Optimization: Medicinal chemistry optimization involves synthesizing and evaluating analogs of hit compounds to improve their potency, selectivity, and pharmacokinetic properties. Medicinal chemists iteratively modify the chemical structure of hit compounds based on SAR insights and computational predictions, aiming to enhance drug-target interactions, optimize physicochemical properties, and minimize off-target effects. Optimization strategies may include structural modifications, stereochemical adjustments, scaffold hopping, and functional group alterations.

ADME/T Properties Optimization: Optimization of Absorption, Distribution, Metabolism, Excretion, and Toxicity (ADME/T) properties is crucial for developing lead compounds with favorable pharmacokinetic profiles and safety profiles. Lead candidates undergo ADME/T studies to assess their absorption, distribution, metabolism, excretion, and toxicity characteristics. Optimization strategies aim to enhance oral bioavailability, increase metabolic stability, reduce clearance, minimize toxicity, and improve overall drug-like properties.

Functional Assays and In vivo Studies: Lead candidates are evaluated using functional assays and in vivo studies to assess their biological activity, efficacy, and safety in relevant disease models. Functional assays measure the ability of lead compounds to modulate target activity, signaling pathways, or physiological functions, providing insights into their mechanism of action and therapeutic potential. In vivo studies assess the pharmacodynamic effects, pharmacokinetics, and toxicity of lead candidates in animal models, helping to prioritize promising candidates for further development.

Lead Identification and Candidate Selection: Hit-to-Lead Optimization culminates in the identification and selection of lead candidates with the most promising pharmacological properties for further preclinical and clinical development. Lead candidates undergo rigorous evaluation to assess their potency, selectivity, efficacy, safety, and drug-like properties, helping to prioritize candidates with the highest likelihood of success for advancement into preclinical studies and clinical trials.

2.4.3 High-Throughput Screening (HTS) Methods

High-Throughput Screening (HTS) methods are pivotal in drug discovery, allowing for the rapid and efficient screening of large compound libraries to identify hits with potential therapeutic activity against specific biological targets. HTS enables the exploration of chemical space and the identification of lead compounds for further optimization and development. Several methods and technologies are employed in HTS to streamline the screening process and enhance efficiency.

Assay Development: HTS begins with the development of robust biochemical, cellular, or functional assays that reflect the biological activity of the target of interest. Assay development involves optimizing assay conditions, including assay format, detection method, substrate concentration, and assay robustness, to ensure reliable and reproducible results. Assays are designed to accommodate high-throughput screening requirements, such as miniaturization, automation, and compatibility with multiwell plates.

Compound Libraries: HTS utilizes diverse compound libraries containing thousands to millions of small molecules, natural products, peptides, or other chemical entities for screening. Compound libraries may include commercial libraries, in-house libraries, natural product extracts, fragment libraries, or virtual libraries generated computationally. Libraries are curated to encompass chemical diversity, structural complexity, and drug-like properties to maximize the chances of identifying hits with desired pharmacological activity.

Automation and Robotics: HTS platforms are equipped with robotic systems and automation technologies to streamline the screening process and increase throughput. Automated liquid handling systems, robotic workstations, plate handlers, and integrated software solutions enable the rapid dispensing, manipulation, and analysis of compounds and assay components in a high-throughput manner. Automation minimizes manual intervention, reduces experimental variability, and enhances the efficiency of screening campaigns.

Detection Technologies: HTS employs a variety of detection technologies to measure assay readouts and quantify biological responses. Detection methods include fluorescence, luminescence, absorbance, fluorescence polarization, time-resolved fluorescence, and label-free techniques. These detection technologies offer sensitivity, specificity, and dynamic range suitable for detecting changes in enzymatic activity, receptor-ligand binding, cellular signaling, or other biological endpoints with high throughput and accuracy.

Data Analysis and Management: HTS generates large volumes of data that require sophisticated informatics tools and data analysis workflows for processing, analysis, and interpretation. Data analysis pipelines incorporate statistical methods, data mining algorithms, and visualization techniques to identify hits, assess screening quality, and prioritize compounds for further validation. HTS data management systems facilitate data storage, retrieval, annotation, and sharing, ensuring the integrity and reproducibility of screening results.

Hit Confirmation and Validation: Hits identified through HTS undergo confirmation and validation assays to verify their activity, potency, and specificity. Secondary assays, counter screens, dose-response studies, and orthogonal assays are employed to validate hits, eliminate false positives, and characterize their pharmacological properties. Hit validation ensures the reliability and reproducibility of screening results, guiding decisions regarding hit-to-lead optimization and lead candidate selection.

2.4.4 Computational Approaches in Lead Identification

Computational approaches play a crucial role in lead identification, complementing experimental methods to accelerate the drug discovery process, rationalize compound design, and prioritize candidates for further evaluation. By leveraging computational tools, algorithms, and modeling techniques, researchers can explore chemical space, predict molecular interactions, and optimize lead compounds with enhanced potency, selectivity, and pharmacokinetic properties.

Virtual Screening: Virtual screening is a computational approach used to identify potential lead compounds from large chemical libraries or databases by predicting their binding affinity to a target of interest. Structure-based virtual screening involves docking small molecules into the binding site of the target protein and scoring their binding poses to prioritize compounds with favorable interactions. Ligand-based virtual screening utilizes molecular similarity or pharmacophore-based methods to identify compounds structurally similar to known ligands or active compounds.

Structure-Based Drug Design (SBDD): SBDD relies on computational modeling techniques, such as molecular docking, molecular dynamics simulations, and free energy calculations, to predict the binding mode and affinity of lead compounds to the target protein. By analyzing the three-dimensional structure of the target protein and its interactions with ligands, SBDD enables the rational design of novel compounds with optimized binding affinity, selectivity, and pharmacokinetic properties.

Ligand-Based Drug Design (LBDD): LBDD involves the analysis of structure-activity relationships (SAR) and quantitative structure-activity relationship (QSAR) modeling to predict the biological activity of lead compounds based on their chemical structure and physicochemical properties. LBDD methods include pharmacophore modeling, quantitative structure-activity relationship (QSAR) modeling, and machine learning algorithms to correlate molecular descriptors with biological activity and guide compound optimization.

Fragment-Based Drug Design (FBDD): FBDD is a computational approach that involves screening small, low molecular weight fragments against a target protein to identify fragment hits with weak but favorable binding interactions. Fragment hits are then elaborated into larger lead compounds through structure-based or ligand-based optimization strategies. FBDD enables the exploration of chemical space, identification of novel scaffolds, and optimization of fragment hits into lead compounds with improved potency and selectivity.

Machine Learning and Artificial Intelligence: Machine learning (ML) and artificial intelligence (AI) algorithms are increasingly used in lead identification to analyze large datasets, predict compound properties, and guide compound optimization. ML models can predict compound activity, toxicity, and ADME properties based on chemical structure, biological assays, and experimental data, facilitating lead selection and optimization. AI-driven approaches, such as generative models and reinforcement learning, can generate novel chemical structures with desired properties and optimize lead compounds in silico.

Integration of Experimental and Computational Approaches: Integration of experimental and computational approaches enables a synergistic and iterative drug discovery process, where computational predictions guide experimental design, and experimental data inform computational modeling. By combining computational screening, modeling, and optimization with experimental validation, researchers can efficiently identify and optimize lead compounds with enhanced pharmacological properties and therapeutic potential.

2.4.5 Case Study: Optimization of Statins for Cholesterol Lowering

Statins are a class of drugs widely used for lowering cholesterol levels and reducing the risk of cardiovascular diseases. The optimization of statins serves as a notable case study in drug discovery, illustrating the iterative process of lead optimization to enhance therapeutic efficacy, safety, and patient outcomes.

Discovery of Statins: The discovery of statins can be traced back to the 1970s when researchers identified lovastatin, the first statin isolated from the fungus Aspergillus terreus. Lovastatin was found to inhibit 3-hydroxy-3-methylglutaryl-coenzyme A (HMG-CoA) reductase, a key enzyme involved in cholesterol biosynthesis. Subsequent efforts led to the development of other statins, including simvastatin, atorvastatin, and rosuvastatin, with improved potency, selectivity, and pharmacokinetic properties.

Structure-Activity Relationship (SAR) Studies: SAR studies played a pivotal role in optimizing statins for cholesterol lowering. By systematically modifying the chemical structure of lovastatin and other early statins, researchers elucidated key structural features essential for inhibiting HMG-CoA reductase and lowering cholesterol levels. Structural modifications, such as altering the lactone ring, substituting side chains, and introducing lipophilic groups, were explored to enhance potency, metabolic stability, and pharmacokinetic properties.

Medicinal Chemistry Optimization: Medicinal chemistry optimization of statins focused on improving potency, selectivity, and pharmacokinetic properties to enhance their clinical efficacy and safety. Chemical modifications aimed to increase the lipophilicity, bioavailability, and metabolic stability of statins, optimizing their absorption, distribution, metabolism, and excretion (ADME) properties. Rational design strategies, combinatorial chemistry, and structure-based drug design were employed to generate statin analogs with improved pharmacological profiles.

Clinical Efficacy and Safety: Clinical trials demonstrated the efficacy of statins in lowering cholesterol levels and reducing the risk of cardiovascular events, such as heart attacks and strokes. Statins were shown to lower low-density lipoprotein cholesterol (LDL-C) levels by inhibiting HMG-CoA reductase, the rate-limiting enzyme in cholesterol synthesis. Additionally, statins exhibited pleiotropic effects, including anti-inflammatory, antioxidant, and endothelial function-improving properties, contributing to their cardiovascular benefits.

Safety Profile and Tolerability: Optimization of statins also involved improving their safety profile and tolerability to enhance patient adherence and reduce the risk of adverse effects. While statins are generally well-tolerated, they may be associated with side effects such as myopathy, liver toxicity, and gastrointestinal disturbances. Optimization efforts focused on minimizing off-target effects, drug-drug interactions, and dose-related toxicity through dose optimization, formulation improvements, and patient monitoring strategies.

Diverse Formulations and Dosage Regimens: Optimization of statins led to the development of diverse formulations and dosage regimens to accommodate individual patient needs and preferences. Statins are available in various formulations, including immediate-release tablets, extended-release formulations, and combination therapies with other lipid-lowering agents. Different dosage strengths and administration schedules allow for personalized treatment approaches tailored to patient lipid profiles, comorbidities, and cardiovascular risk factors.

2.5 Preclinical Development

2.5.1 Safety Pharmacology Studies

Safety pharmacology studies are a critical component of preclinical development, aiming to evaluate the potential effects of drug candidates on vital organ systems and physiological functions. These studies assess the safety profile of drug candidates, identify potential adverse effects, and inform risk mitigation strategies before advancing to clinical trials. Safety pharmacology studies encompass a range of in vitro and in vivo assessments to comprehensively evaluate the pharmacological effects of drug candidates on vital organ systems.

Cardiovascular System: Safety pharmacology studies evaluate the effects of drug candidates on the cardiovascular system, including the heart rate, rhythm, blood pressure, and cardiac electrophysiology. In vitro assays, such as isolated tissue preparations and cardiac ion channel assays, assess the direct effects of drugs on cardiac function and electrophysiology. In vivo studies using telemetry or invasive hemodynamic monitoring assess cardiovascular parameters in conscious animals to evaluate the potential for adverse cardiovascular effects, such as arrhythmias, QT prolongation, or hemodynamic instability.

Central Nervous System: Safety pharmacology studies assess the effects of drug candidates on the central nervous system (CNS), including sedation, locomotor activity, motor coordination, and cognitive function. Behavioral assays, such as open field tests, rotarod assays, and passive avoidance tests, evaluate the CNS effects of drugs in animal models. Electrophysiological recordings and imaging techniques may also be used to assess neuronal activity and CNS function in response to drug treatment.

Respiratory System: Safety pharmacology studies evaluate the effects of drug candidates on the respiratory system, including respiratory rate, tidal volume, and pulmonary function. In vivo studies using plethysmography or whole-body plethysmography assess respiratory parameters in conscious animals exposed to drug treatment. Respiratory reflexes, such as cough reflex and respiratory drive, may also be evaluated to assess potential respiratory depressant effects of drugs.

Renal and Hepatic Function: Safety pharmacology studies assess the effects of drug candidates on renal and hepatic function, including renal excretion, hepatic metabolism, and biochemical markers of organ toxicity. In vivo studies measure urine output, renal blood flow, serum creatinine, and blood urea nitrogen levels to assess renal function. Hepatic function tests evaluate liver enzymes, such as alanine transaminase (ALT) and aspartate transaminase (AST), to assess hepatic injury or dysfunction.

Gastrointestinal Function: Safety pharmacology studies evaluate the effects of drug candidates on gastrointestinal function, including gastric motility, intestinal transit time, and gastrointestinal secretions. In vivo studies using gastrointestinal transit assays or charcoal meal tests assess the effects of drugs on gastrointestinal motility and transit. Gastrointestinal endoscopy or histopathological examination may also be performed to assess mucosal integrity and identify potential gastrointestinal lesions or ulcers.

Other Organ Systems: Safety pharmacology studies may also assess the effects of drug candidates on other organ systems, such as the immune system, endocrine system, and reproductive system. Immunotoxicity assays evaluate the effects of drugs on immune cell function and cytokine production. Endocrine function tests assess hormonal levels and reproductive parameters in animal models exposed to drug treatment.

2.5.2 Pharmacokinetic/Pharmacodynamic (PK/PD) Modeling

Pharmacokinetic/pharmacodynamic (PK/PD) modeling is a key component of preclinical development, aiming to quantitatively characterize the relationship between drug exposure (pharmacokinetics) and pharmacological effects (pharmacodynamics). PK/PD modeling integrates data from in vivo pharmacokinetic studies with pharmacodynamic endpoints to elucidate the drug's efficacy, potency, and safety profile, providing valuable insights into dose-response relationships and guiding dose selection for clinical trials.

Pharmacokinetic Studies: PK/PD modeling begins with the characterization of drug pharmacokinetics, including absorption, distribution, metabolism, and excretion (ADME) properties. Pharmacokinetic studies measure drug concentrations in plasma or other biological matrices over time following drug administration. Non-compartmental analysis (NCA) and compartmental modeling techniques, such as one-, two-, or multi-compartmental models, are used to describe the pharmacokinetic behavior of drugs and estimate pharmacokinetic parameters, such as clearance, volume of distribution, and half-life.

Pharmacodynamic Studies: PK/PD modeling involves the assessment of pharmacodynamic endpoints, which reflect the drug's effects on biological systems or disease processes. Pharmacodynamic studies measure biomarkers, physiological responses, or clinical endpoints in animal models or in vitro systems exposed to drug treatment. Pharmacodynamic endpoints may include changes in enzyme activity, receptor occupancy, signaling pathway activation, or disease biomarkers relevant to the drug's mechanism of action and therapeutic indication.

PK/PD Modeling Approaches: PK/PD modeling integrates pharmacokinetic and pharmacodynamic data using mathematical models to quantify the relationship between drug exposure and pharmacological effects. PK/PD models may be empirical or mechanistic in nature, depending on the underlying biological mechanisms and available data. Empirical models, such as Emax models or sigmoidal Emax models, describe the concentration-effect relationship based on observed data without consideration of underlying biological processes. Mechanistic models, such as indirect response models or turnover models, incorporate physiological or biochemical mechanisms to describe the dynamic interactions between drug concentrations and pharmacological effects.

Dose-Response Analysis: PK/PD modeling enables dose-response analysis to characterize the relationship between drug dose, drug exposure, and pharmacodynamic effects. Dose-response curves are generated to quantify the drug's potency (EC50 or ED50), efficacy (maximum effect), and slope of the response curve. PK/PD modeling facilitates the prediction of pharmacodynamic responses at different dose levels, guiding dose selection for clinical trials to achieve optimal therapeutic outcomes while minimizing the risk of adverse effects.

Model Validation and Simulation: PK/PD models are validated using independent datasets or experimental studies to assess their predictive performance and robustness. Model validation ensures that the PK/PD model accurately describes the observed data and can be extrapolated to predict pharmacodynamic responses under different conditions or scenarios. Once validated, PK/PD models can be used for simulation and prediction to optimize dosing regimens, evaluate alternative dosing strategies, or predict the effects of drug-drug interactions or patient covariates on drug response.

2.5.3 In vivo Efficacy Testing

In vivo efficacy testing is a crucial component of preclinical development, providing essential insights into the therapeutic potential and effectiveness of drug candidates in relevant disease models. These studies evaluate the ability of drug candidates to modulate disease-related endpoints, such as tumor growth inhibition, symptom relief, or disease progression, in animal models or experimental systems. In vivo efficacy testing plays a pivotal role in identifying lead candidates, validating drug targets, and informing decision-making for further development.

Selection of Disease Models: In vivo efficacy testing involves selecting appropriate disease models that recapitulate the pathophysiology, etiology, and clinical features of the target disease or condition. Disease models may include genetically engineered animal models, xenograft models, patient-derived xenografts (PDX), syngeneic models, or chemically-induced models of disease. The choice of disease model depends on factors such as disease relevance, biological complexity, and translational validity to human disease.

Study Design and Endpoint Selection: In vivo efficacy studies are designed to evaluate the effects of drug candidates on relevant disease endpoints using standardized protocols and experimental procedures. Study design considerations include sample size calculation, randomization, blinding, and allocation concealment to minimize bias and ensure robust and reproducible results. Endpoint selection may include measurements of tumor volume, disease severity scores, survival rates, biomarker expression levels, or functional assessments relevant to the disease phenotype.

Dose-Response Assessment: In vivo efficacy testing involves assessing dose-response relationships to determine the optimal dose or dose range for achieving therapeutic effects while minimizing toxicity. Drug candidates are administered at different dose levels, often using dose escalation or dose titration protocols, to evaluate their effects on disease endpoints across a range of concentrations. Dose-response curves are generated to quantify the relationship between drug dose and efficacy outcomes, guiding dose selection for further studies.

Evaluation of Therapeutic Efficacy: In vivo efficacy testing evaluates the therapeutic efficacy of drug candidates based on predefined efficacy endpoints and criteria. Therapeutic efficacy may be assessed by measuring changes in disease progression, tumor growth kinetics, symptom severity, or survival rates in treated animals compared to control groups. Efficacy outcomes are quantified using objective measurements, such as imaging techniques, histopathological analysis, or molecular assays, to provide quantitative data on treatment effects.

Comparison with Standard Therapies: In vivo efficacy studies often include comparison with standard-of-care therapies or reference compounds to benchmark the effectiveness of drug candidates against existing treatments. Comparative efficacy studies assess whether drug candidates provide superior, equivalent, or inferior therapeutic outcomes compared to standard therapies in terms of efficacy, safety, tolerability, and other relevant parameters. Comparative data inform decision-making regarding the clinical potential and competitive positioning of drug candidates in the treatment landscape.

Interpretation and Translation to Clinical Relevance: In vivo efficacy testing provides valuable insights into the potential clinical relevance and translatability of drug candidates to human disease. Interpretation of efficacy data involves considering factors such as species differences, disease heterogeneity, pharmacokinetic-pharmacodynamic relationships, and predictive validity of animal models. Preclinical efficacy data are used to support rationale for clinical development, inform dose selection, design clinical trials, and predict potential therapeutic outcomes in humans.

2.5.4 Regulatory Requirements in Preclinical Development

Regulatory agencies impose stringent requirements on preclinical development to ensure the safety, efficacy, and quality of investigational drugs before they can advance to clinical trials. Compliance with regulatory guidelines is essential for obtaining approval to initiate clinical studies and ultimately market approval. Key regulatory requirements in preclinical development include:

Good Laboratory Practice (GLP): Preclinical studies must be conducted in accordance with GLP regulations, which establish standards for the conduct, documentation, and reporting of nonclinical laboratory studies. GLP compliance ensures the integrity, reliability, and traceability of preclinical data, supporting regulatory submissions and decision-making. GLP requirements cover aspects such as study design, personnel qualifications, standard operating procedures (SOPs), data management, quality assurance, and facility inspections.

Study Protocols and Reports: Preclinical studies require comprehensive study protocols outlining the objectives, experimental procedures, endpoints, and data analysis plans. Study protocols must be approved by Institutional Animal Care and Use Committees (IACUC) or equivalent ethics committees to ensure animal welfare and compliance with regulatory standards. Preclinical study reports document study conduct, results, interpretations, and conclusions in a format suitable for regulatory submission, providing detailed documentation of study methods, findings, and conclusions.

Pharmacology and Toxicology Studies: Regulatory agencies require a comprehensive pharmacology and toxicology assessment to evaluate the safety, efficacy, and pharmacokinetic properties of investigational drugs in preclinical species. Pharmacology studies assess the pharmacological effects, mechanisms of action, and therapeutic potential of drugs using relevant animal models and endpoints. Toxicology studies assess the potential adverse effects, target organ toxicity, and dose-response relationships of drugs through acute, subchronic, and chronic toxicity testing in multiple species.

Safety Pharmacology: Safety pharmacology studies evaluate the effects of investigational drugs on vital organ systems and physiological functions, including cardiovascular, respiratory, central nervous, and renal systems. These studies assess potential adverse effects, such as cardiac arrhythmias, respiratory depression, CNS toxicity, and renal impairment, using standardized assays and endpoints. Safety pharmacology assessments inform risk assessment, dose selection, and safety monitoring strategies for clinical trials.

Genotoxicity and Carcinogenicity Testing: Preclinical development includes genotoxicity and carcinogenicity testing to evaluate the potential mutagenic and carcinogenic effects of investigational drugs. Genotoxicity assays assess the ability of drugs to induce mutations or DNA damage using in vitro and in vivo tests, such as Ames tests, chromosome aberration assays, and micronucleus assays. Carcinogenicity studies assess the long-term effects of drugs on tumor incidence and progression in animal models over extended durations.

Regulatory Submissions and Interactions: Regulatory submissions for preclinical development include Investigational New Drug (IND) applications or equivalent regulatory filings, which provide detailed information on the preclinical data, study protocols, manufacturing processes, and clinical development plans for investigational drugs. Regulatory interactions involve discussions with regulatory agencies to obtain feedback, address questions, and resolve issues related to preclinical data, study design, or regulatory requirements, facilitating the advancement of drug development programs.

2.5.5 Case Study: Preclinical Development of Monoclonal Antibodies for Cancer Therapy

Monoclonal antibodies (mAbs) have revolutionized cancer therapy by targeting specific molecular pathways involved in tumor growth, proliferation, and survival. The preclinical development of mAbs for cancer therapy involves a series of rigorous assessments to evaluate their safety, efficacy, and pharmacological properties before advancing to clinical trials. This case study outlines the preclinical development of a hypothetical mAb for cancer therapy:

Target Selection and Validation: The preclinical development of mAbs begins with the identification and validation of an appropriate molecular target implicated in cancer pathogenesis. Target selection may involve genomic, proteomic, or bioinformatics analyses to identify overexpressed or dysregulated proteins in cancer cells. The selected target should have a clear mechanistic rationale, clinical relevance, and potential for therapeutic intervention.

Antibody Generation and Characterization: Once the target is validated, mAbs are generated using hybridoma technology, phage display libraries, or other antibody engineering platforms. Antibodies are screened for specificity, affinity, and binding characteristics to ensure selective targeting of the intended antigen. In vitro assays, such as enzyme-linked immunosorbent assays (ELISA) and flow cytometry, assess antibody-antigen interactions and select lead candidates with optimal binding properties.

In vitro Efficacy Studies: Lead mAb candidates undergo in vitro efficacy studies to evaluate their ability to inhibit tumor cell growth, induce apoptosis, or modulate signaling pathways relevant to cancer progression. Cell-based assays, such as proliferation assays, apoptosis assays, and signaling pathway analysis, assess the anti-tumor effects of mAbs in relevant cancer cell lines or primary tumor cells. In vitro studies provide preliminary evidence of mAb efficacy and guide the selection of candidates for in vivo efficacy testing.

In vivo Efficacy Testing: Selected mAb candidates undergo in vivo efficacy testing using xenograft or syngeneic mouse models of cancer. Tumor-bearing mice are treated with mAbs, and tumor growth, regression, or metastasis is monitored over time using imaging techniques or caliper measurements. Pharmacodynamic biomarkers, such as proliferation markers, apoptosis markers, or angiogenesis markers, are assessed in tumor tissues to evaluate the effects of mAbs on tumor biology and microenvironment.

Pharmacokinetic and Toxicology Studies: Preclinical development includes pharmacokinetic and toxicology studies to evaluate the pharmacokinetic properties, safety, and tolerability of mAb candidates in animal models. Pharmacokinetic studies measure mAb concentrations in plasma or tissues following administration to assess absorption, distribution, metabolism, and excretion (ADME) properties. Toxicology studies assess potential adverse effects, target organ toxicity, and immunogenicity through acute, subchronic, and chronic toxicity testing.

Regulatory Submissions and IND Filing: Preclinical data, including efficacy, pharmacokinetic, and toxicology studies, are compiled into a regulatory submission package for Investigational New Drug (IND) application filing with regulatory agencies. The IND application provides comprehensive information on the preclinical data, study protocols, manufacturing processes, and clinical development plans for mAb candidates. Regulatory interactions involve discussions with regulatory agencies to obtain feedback, address questions, and resolve issues related to preclinical data, facilitating IND approval and clinical trial initiation.

2.6 Clinical Development

2.6.1 Phases of Clinical Trials

Clinical development encompasses a series of phases designed to evaluate the safety, efficacy, and pharmacological properties of investigational drugs in human subjects. Each phase of clinical trials serves distinct objectives and contributes to the accumulation of evidence supporting the approval and marketing of new therapeutics. The phases of clinical trials include:

Phase 0: Phase 0 trials, also known as exploratory investigational new drug (eIND) studies, involve microdosing of small amounts of the investigational drug in a small number of subjects (typically fewer than 15) to obtain initial pharmacokinetic and pharmacodynamic data. Phase 0 trials are exploratory in nature and provide preliminary insights into drug behavior in humans, guiding dose selection and study design for subsequent phases.

Phase I: Phase I trials are the first-in-human studies designed to assess the safety, tolerability, pharmacokinetics, and pharmacodynamics of the investigational drug. Phase I trials typically involve a small number of healthy volunteers or patients and aim to determine the maximum tolerated dose (MTD), dose-limiting toxicities (DLTs), and preliminary evidence of efficacy. Phase I trials may include dose escalation or dose expansion cohorts to evaluate different dose levels and dosing regimens.

Phase II: Phase II trials are conducted in a larger cohort of patients with the target disease or condition to assess the preliminary efficacy, dose-response relationship, and safety profile of the investigational drug. Phase II trials aim to provide initial evidence of therapeutic activity, identify patient subpopulations likely to benefit from the drug, and refine dose selection for further evaluation in larger phase III trials. Phase II trials may include randomized controlled trials (RCTs) or single-arm studies, depending on the study objectives and design.

Phase III: Phase III trials are pivotal studies conducted in a large patient population to confirm the safety and efficacy of the investigational drug, demonstrate its superiority or non-inferiority compared to standard-of-care treatments, and support regulatory approval and marketing authorization. Phase III trials are typically randomized, controlled, multicenter studies with predefined primary and secondary endpoints. Phase III trials aim to provide conclusive evidence of clinical benefit and establish the risk-benefit profile of the drug for regulatory review.

Phase IV: Phase IV trials, also known as post-marketing surveillance or pharmacovigilance studies, are conducted after regulatory approval to monitor the long-term safety, effectiveness, and real-world use of the drug in a broader patient population. Phase IV trials assess outcomes such as rare adverse events, drug interactions, patient adherence, and health economic outcomes in real-world clinical practice settings. Phase IV trials provide ongoing evidence to support post-market regulatory commitments, label updates, and clinical guideline revisions.

Each phase of clinical trials builds upon the evidence generated in earlier phases and contributes to the overall understanding of the investigational drug's safety, efficacy, and therapeutic potential. The progression from phase to phase is contingent upon the accumulation of favorable data and regulatory approval at each stage. Through systematic evaluation in clinical trials, investigational drugs are rigorously tested to ensure their safety and effectiveness, ultimately leading to their approval and availability for patient care.

2.6.2 Designing Clinical Trials

Designing clinical trials is a meticulous process that involves careful planning, consideration of ethical principles, and adherence to regulatory requirements to generate reliable and clinically meaningful data. Several key elements must be addressed when designing clinical trials:

Research Question and Objectives: The first step in designing a clinical trial is clearly defining the research question and objectives. This includes specifying the primary and secondary endpoints that will be used to evaluate the efficacy and safety of the investigational drug. The research question should be relevant, feasible, and address an unmet medical need.

Study Population: Determining the appropriate study population is crucial for ensuring the relevance and generalizability of trial results.

Inclusion and exclusion criteria should be defined to identify eligible participants based on factors such as age, gender, disease stage, comorbidities, and prior treatments. Sample size calculations should be performed to ensure adequate statistical power to detect meaningful treatment effects.

Study Design: The study design defines the overall framework and methodology of the clinical trial. Common study designs include randomized controlled trials (RCTs), non-randomized trials, crossover trials, factorial trials, and adaptive trials. The choice of study design depends on factors such as the research question, ethical considerations, feasibility, and practical constraints. Randomization and blinding are essential components of study design to minimize bias and ensure the reliability of trial results.

Treatment Allocation: The method of treatment allocation determines how participants are assigned to different study groups or treatment arms. Randomization, stratification, and allocation concealment are used to ensure that treatment assignment is unbiased and not influenced by factors such as patient characteristics or investigator preferences. Randomization minimizes selection bias and allows for the comparison of treatment groups with similar baseline characteristics.

Control Group: Clinical trials often include a control group that receives standard-of-care treatment or placebo to provide a basis for comparison with the investigational treatment. The choice of control group depends on ethical considerations, the availability of effective treatments, and the objectives of the trial. Control groups may include placebo, active comparator, or standard-of-care treatments, depending on the study design and research question.

Treatment Regimens: Clinical trials evaluate different treatment regimens, including dosing schedules, drug combinations, and treatment durations, to optimize therapeutic outcomes. Treatment regimens should be based on preclinical data, pharmacokinetic-pharmacodynamic relationships, and clinical experience to ensure safety and efficacy. Dose escalation, dose finding, and dose optimization may be incorporated into trial designs to identify the optimal dose for further evaluation.

Data Collection and Analysis: Data collection procedures and analysis plans should be predefined to ensure consistency, accuracy, and reliability of trial results. Case report forms (CRFs) are used to collect standardized data on participant demographics, medical history, treatment administration, and study endpoints. Statistical analysis plans (SAPs) outline the statistical methods and procedures for data analysis, including hypothesis testing, subgroup analyses, and sensitivity analyses.

Ethical Considerations: Clinical trial design must adhere to ethical principles and guidelines to protect the rights, safety, and well-being of trial participants. Clinical trials should be conducted in accordance with the Declaration of Helsinki, Good Clinical Practice (GCP) guidelines, and local regulatory requirements. Institutional review board (IRB) or ethics committee approval is required before initiating any clinical trial, and informed consent must be obtained from all participants.

2.6.3 Patient Recruitment and Informed Consent

Patient recruitment and informed consent are critical aspects of clinical trial conduct that ensure the ethical and voluntary participation of individuals in research studies. Effective patient recruitment strategies and comprehensive informed consent processes are essential for protecting participants‘ rights, safety, and welfare while facilitating the advancement of medical knowledge. Key considerations for patient recruitment and informed consent include:

Patient Recruitment Strategies:

1. **Identification of Eligible Participants**: Eligible participants are identified based on predefined inclusion and exclusion criteria, which are specified in the study protocol. Recruitment efforts may involve collaboration with healthcare providers, patient advocacy groups, community organizations, and clinical trial recruitment services to identify potential participants.
2. **Recruitment Channels**: Various recruitment channels are utilized to reach potential participants, including physician referrals, electronic medical records (EMRs), clinical trial databases, social media platforms, patient registries, community outreach events, and advertising campaigns. Recruitment materials should be clear, accurate, and non-coercive, providing information about the study purpose, eligibility criteria, potential risks and benefits, and contact details for further inquiry.
3. **Patient Education and Engagement**: Patient education and engagement are essential for fostering informed decision-making and promoting active participation in clinical trials. Educational materials, such as brochures, websites, videos, and interactive tools, provide

comprehensive information about the study protocol, procedures, treatment options, and potential outcomes. Patient engagement activities, such as informational sessions, support groups, and peer mentoring programs, facilitate dialogue, address concerns, and empower participants to make informed choices.

4. **Cultural Sensitivity and Diversity**: Recruitment efforts should be culturally sensitive and inclusive to ensure diversity and representation of different demographic groups in clinical trials. Cultural and linguistic barriers should be addressed through translated materials, interpreter services, and culturally tailored recruitment strategies to enhance access and participation among underrepresented populations.
5. **Patient Advocacy and Support**: Patient advocacy groups play a crucial role in promoting awareness, facilitating recruitment, and providing support to individuals considering participation in clinical trials. Collaboration with patient advocacy organizations, disease foundations, and community stakeholders can enhance recruitment efforts, build trust, and address patient concerns throughout the trial process.

Informed Consent Process:

1. **Content and Format**: Informed consent documents (ICDs) provide detailed information about the study purpose, procedures, risks, benefits, confidentiality, compensation, and voluntary nature of participation. ICDs should be written in plain language, tailored to the target audience, and structured to facilitate comprehension. The informed consent process should include opportunities for participants to ask questions, seek clarification, and discuss concerns with study staff or investigators.
2. **Voluntary Participation**: Informed consent is a voluntary process that requires participants to freely choose whether to participate in a clinical trial without coercion or undue influence. Participants should be informed of their right to withdraw from the study at any time without repercussion and provided with sufficient time to consider their decision before signing the consent form.
3. **Capacity and Understanding**: Informed consent is obtained from individuals who have the capacity to understand the information presented and make autonomous decisions about participation. Investigators should assess participants' comprehension of the study

details, risks, and procedures to ensure informed decision-making. Special considerations are made for vulnerable populations, such as minors, individuals with cognitive impairments, and non-English-speaking participants, to safeguard their rights and interests.

4. **Documentation and Signature**: Participants or their legally authorized representatives are required to sign the informed consent form to indicate their voluntary agreement to participate in the clinical trial. The consent process should be documented in the participant's medical record, and a copy of the signed consent form should be provided to the participant for their records.
5. **Ongoing Communication and Consent**: The informed consent process is an ongoing dialogue between participants and study staff throughout the trial duration. Participants should be kept informed of any changes to the study protocol, procedures, or risks that may affect their decision to continue participation. Consent may need to be reconfirmed or updated periodically to ensure continued voluntary participation and informed decision-making.

2.6.4 Safety Monitoring in Clinical Trials

Safety monitoring is a fundamental component of clinical trial conduct aimed at assessing and managing the safety profile of investigational drugs throughout the trial duration. The systematic collection, evaluation, and reporting of safety data enable early detection of adverse events (AEs), adverse drug reactions (ADRs), and unexpected safety concerns, thereby ensuring the protection of participants‘ welfare and informing risk-benefit assessments. Key aspects of safety monitoring in clinical trials include:

Pre-Trial Safety Assessment:

1. **Investigational New Drug (IND) Application**: Before initiating clinical trials, sponsors are required to submit an IND application to regulatory authorities, providing comprehensive information about the investigational drug's safety, pharmacology, pharmacokinetics, and proposed clinical development plan. Regulatory review of the IND application ensures that adequate preclinical safety data support the initiation of human studies.
2. **Ethical Review and Protocol Approval**: Clinical trial protocols undergo ethical review and approval by Institutional Review Boards (IRBs) or Ethics Committees to assess the study's scientific merit, ethical conduct,

and participant safety. IRB review includes evaluation of the proposed safety monitoring plan, informed consent process, risk mitigation strategies, and provisions for participant safety and welfare.

Safety Monitoring during Clinical Trials:

1. **Adverse Event Reporting:** Investigators are responsible for monitoring and documenting AEs reported by trial participants during the course of the study. AEs are classified based on severity, relationship to the investigational drug, and expectedness. Serious AEs (SAEs), including death, life-threatening events, hospitalizations, and persistent or significant disabilities, are subject to expedited reporting requirements to regulatory authorities, ethics committees, and study sponsors.
2. **Safety Assessments and Monitoring Visits:** Scheduled safety assessments and monitoring visits are conducted to evaluate participants' clinical status, vital signs, laboratory parameters, and other safety-related endpoints specified in the study protocol. Safety assessments may include physical examinations, laboratory tests, electrocardiograms (ECGs), imaging studies, and functional assessments, depending on the trial design and investigational drug's safety profile.
3. **Data Safety Monitoring Board (DSMB):** Independent DSMBs may be established to provide oversight and review of safety data throughout the trial duration. DSMBs comprise clinicians, biostatisticians, and other experts who evaluate safety endpoints, interim analyses, and cumulative safety data to ensure participant safety, data integrity, and study conduct. DSMB recommendations may include protocol modifications, continuation, or termination of the trial based on safety considerations.
4. **Safety Data Collection and Analysis:** Safety data are systematically collected, monitored, and analyzed throughout the trial duration using electronic data capture systems or case report forms (CRFs). Data management procedures ensure timely identification, coding, and classification of AEs and SAEs according to standardized terminology (e.g., Medical Dictionary for Regulatory Activities - MedDRA). Statistical analysis of safety data includes descriptive summaries, frequency distributions, and comparative analyses between treatment groups to detect potential safety signals or trends.

Safety Reporting and Communication:

1. **Safety Reporting to Regulatory Authorities:** Investigators, sponsors, and regulatory authorities have obligations to report AEs, SAEs, and other safety-related information in a timely manner according to regulatory requirements. Expedited safety reporting timelines and criteria are specified in regulatory guidelines, ensuring prompt assessment and appropriate regulatory action to protect participant safety.
2. **Safety Communication to Investigators and Participants:** Investigators are responsible for communicating safety-related information to trial participants, including potential risks, AEs, and precautions associated with the investigational drug. Participants receive written informed consent documents outlining the nature and likelihood of potential AEs, procedures for reporting AEs, and contact information for study staff or sponsor representatives.
3. **Safety Updates and Risk Mitigation Strategies:** Ongoing safety monitoring enables the identification of emerging safety concerns or changes in the risk-benefit profile of the investigational drug. Safety updates, protocol amendments, and risk mitigation strategies are implemented based on safety data reviews, regulatory feedback, and DSMB recommendations to optimize participant safety and trial conduct.

2.6.5 Case Study: Clinical Development of Remdesivir for COVID-19 Treatment

The emergence of the novel coronavirus SARS-CoV-2 and the subsequent COVID-19 pandemic prompted urgent efforts to identify effective treatments to mitigate disease severity and reduce mortality. Remdesivir, a broad-spectrum antiviral drug developed by Gilead Sciences, emerged as a promising candidate for the treatment of COVID-19 due to its demonstrated activity against other coronaviruses and RNA viruses in preclinical studies. The clinical development of remdesivir for COVID-19 treatment exemplifies a rapid and collaborative approach to drug development in response to a global public health crisis.

Preclinical Studies and Early Clinical Trials:

1. **Preclinical Evaluation**: Preclinical studies demonstrated the antiviral activity of remdesivir against SARS-CoV-2 and other coronaviruses in cell culture and animal models. These findings provided the rationale for further evaluation of remdesivir in clinical trials for the treatment of COVID-19.
2. **Phase I Clinical Trial**: A Phase I clinical trial of remdesivir in healthy volunteers evaluated the safety, pharmacokinetics, and tolerability of the drug. The study demonstrated that remdesivir was well-tolerated at various dose levels and supported its further evaluation in patients with COVID-19.
3. **Phase II Clinical Trials**: Phase II clinical trials of remdesivir in hospitalized patients with COVID-19 assessed the safety, efficacy, and optimal dosing regimen of the drug. These studies provided preliminary evidence of remdesivir's ability to reduce viral load, improve clinical outcomes, and shorten the time to recovery compared to placebo or standard of care.

Phase III Clinical Trials and Regulatory Approval:

1. **Adaptive Trial Design**: Gilead Sciences initiated multiple Phase III clinical trials of remdesivir in patients with moderate to severe COVID-19 using adaptive trial designs to expedite the evaluation of the drug's efficacy and inform regulatory decision-making. These trials included randomized, double-blind, placebo-controlled studies conducted at multiple sites worldwide.
2. **Preliminary Results**: Preliminary results from Phase III trials, such as the Adaptive COVID-19 Treatment Trial (ACTT) conducted by the National Institute of Allergy and Infectious Diseases (NIAID), demonstrated that remdesivir significantly reduced the time to recovery and showed a trend toward lower mortality rates compared to placebo in hospitalized patients with COVID-19.
3. **Emergency Use Authorization (EUA)**: Based on the preliminary efficacy and safety data from clinical trials, the U.S. Food and Drug Administration (FDA) issued an Emergency Use Authorization (EUA) for remdesivir in hospitalized patients with severe COVID-19, allowing for the emergency use of the drug in clinical practice while additional data were being collected.

4. **Full Approval and Global Access:** Subsequent to the EUA, remdesivir received full approval from regulatory authorities in various countries, including the FDA in the United States and the European Medicines Agency (EMA) in Europe, for the treatment of COVID-19. Gilead Sciences also entered into agreements with governments and international organizations to expand access to remdesivir in low- and middle-income countries.

2.7 Regulatory Approval and Post-Marketing Surveillance

2.7.1 Regulatory Submission Process

The regulatory submission process is a critical step in gaining approval for a new drug or therapeutic intervention from regulatory agencies such as the U.S. Food and Drug Administration (FDA), the European Medicines Agency (EMA), and other national regulatory authorities. This process involves compiling comprehensive data on the safety, efficacy, quality, and manufacturing of the investigational product and submitting it to regulatory authorities for review. Key components of the regulatory submission process include:

Preparation and Compilation of Regulatory Dossier:

1. **Clinical Data:** Clinical data from preclinical studies and all phases of clinical trials are compiled to demonstrate the safety and efficacy of the investigational product. This includes detailed study protocols, informed consent forms, clinical study reports, and statistical analyses of trial outcomes.
2. **Nonclinical Data:** Nonclinical data from pharmacology, toxicology, and pharmacokinetic studies provide evidence of the investigational product's mechanism of action, safety profile, and potential risks. Nonclinical studies are conducted in accordance with regulatory guidelines and Good Laboratory Practice (GLP) standards.
3. **Chemistry, Manufacturing, and Controls (CMC):** CMC data encompass information on the chemistry, manufacturing process, and quality control of the investigational product. This includes documentation of drug substance synthesis, formulation development, analytical methods, stability testing, and manufacturing facilities.

Regulatory Submissions:

1. **Investigational New Drug (IND) Application**: In the United States, the IND application is submitted to the FDA to obtain authorization to conduct clinical trials in humans. The IND application includes preclinical and clinical data, study protocols, investigator information, and manufacturing details. The FDA reviews the IND application to ensure participant safety and data integrity before clinical trials can commence.
2. **New Drug Application (NDA) or Biologics License Application (BLA)**: Upon completion of clinical trials, sponsors submit an NDA or BLA to the FDA for marketing approval of a new drug or biologic product, respectively. The NDA/BLA contains comprehensive data on the safety, efficacy, and quality of the investigational product, including results from preclinical and clinical studies, CMC information, labeling, and risk management plans.
3. **Marketing Authorization Application (MAA)**: In the European Union (EU), the MAA is submitted to the EMA or national regulatory agencies for approval to market a new drug or biologic product. The MAA includes similar data to the NDA/BLA and undergoes a centralized or decentralized review process involving multiple EU member states.

Regulatory Review and Approval:

1. **Review Process**: Regulatory agencies conduct a thorough review of the submitted data to assess the safety, efficacy, and quality of the investigational product. This review may involve multiple disciplines, including clinical pharmacology, biostatistics, pharmacovigilance, and regulatory affairs. The goal is to evaluate whether the benefits of the product outweigh its risks for the proposed indication.
2. **Advisory Committees**: In some cases, regulatory agencies convene advisory committees of external experts to provide independent evaluation and recommendations on the investigational product's safety and efficacy. Advisory committee meetings may involve public hearings and deliberations to inform regulatory decision-making.
3. **Approval Decision**: Based on the review of the regulatory submission and advisory committee recommendations, regulatory agencies make a decision to approve or reject the marketing application. Approval may be granted with specific conditions, such as post-marketing commitments or risk management measures, to ensure ongoing safety monitoring and

data collection.

Post-Approval Commitments and Surveillance:

1. **Post-Marketing Surveillance**: Following approval, sponsors are required to conduct post-marketing surveillance activities to monitor the safety and effectiveness of the product in real-world clinical practice. This includes ongoing pharmacovigilance, adverse event reporting, and periodic safety updates submitted to regulatory agencies.
2. **Risk Evaluation and Mitigation Strategies (REMS)**: Regulatory agencies may require sponsors to implement REMS programs to manage specific risks associated with the product, such as medication errors, misuse, or adverse effects. REMS programs may include elements such as medication guides, communication plans, and restricted distribution systems.
3. **Phase IV Clinical Trials**: Phase IV clinical trials are conducted after approval to further evaluate the long-term safety, effectiveness, and comparative effectiveness of the product in larger patient populations or real-world settings. Phase IV trials may also explore new indications, dosing regimens, or patient populations not studied in preapproval trials.

2.7.2 Post-Marketing Surveillance and Pharmacovigilance

Post-marketing surveillance (PMS) and pharmacovigilance play crucial roles in monitoring the safety, effectiveness, and quality of pharmaceutical products after they have been approved for marketing and are available to patients in real-world clinical practice. These processes involve systematic data collection, analysis, and evaluation of adverse events (AEs), adverse drug reactions (ADRs), medication errors, and other safety-related information to ensure ongoing assessment of the benefit-risk profile of drugs and biologic products. Key components of post-marketing surveillance and pharmacovigilance include:

Adverse Event Reporting:

1. **Spontaneous Reporting**: Healthcare professionals, patients, and pharmaceutical companies are encouraged to report AEs and suspected ADRs to regulatory authorities and drug manufacturers through spontaneous reporting systems. Spontaneous reports provide valuable information about potential safety concerns associated with

pharmaceutical products and contribute to signal detection and risk assessment.

2. **Expedited Reporting**: Certain serious AEs, such as death, life-threatening events, hospitalizations, and congenital anomalies, are subject to expedited reporting requirements, mandating timely submission of safety data to regulatory agencies. Expedited reporting ensures prompt assessment and regulatory action to mitigate risks and protect patient safety.

Pharmacovigilance Activities:

1. **Signal Detection**: Pharmacovigilance activities involve the systematic detection, assessment, and investigation of potential safety signals or new ADRs associated with pharmaceutical products. Signal detection methods include data mining of spontaneous reporting databases, literature review, epidemiological studies, and analysis of post-authorization safety studies (PASS) and risk management plans (RMP).
2. **Risk Assessment and Benefit-Risk Evaluation**: Pharmacovigilance experts conduct risk assessments to evaluate the potential risks associated with pharmaceutical products in relation to their therapeutic benefits. Benefit-risk assessments consider factors such as the severity and frequency of AEs, patient population characteristics, treatment alternatives, and therapeutic indications to inform regulatory decision-making and risk management strategies.

Risk Management Strategies:

1. **Risk Minimization Measures**: Regulatory authorities may require sponsors to implement risk minimization measures, such as Risk Evaluation and Mitigation Strategies (REMS), to mitigate specific risks associated with pharmaceutical products. REMS programs may include elements such as medication guides, communication plans, restricted distribution systems, and healthcare provider training to enhance safe prescribing, dispensing, and use of the product.
2. **Labeling Updates and Safety Communications**: Post-marketing surveillance data inform labeling updates, safety advisories, and communication strategies to healthcare professionals, patients, and the public. Regulatory authorities issue safety alerts, drug safety

communications, and public health advisories to disseminate important safety information and promote awareness of potential risks associated with pharmaceutical products.

Post-Authorization Safety Studies (PASS):

1. **Phase IV Clinical Trials**: Post-authorization safety studies (PASS) are conducted after regulatory approval to further evaluate the safety, effectiveness, and real-world use of pharmaceutical products in larger patient populations or specific subgroups. Phase IV clinical trials assess long-term outcomes, treatment patterns, comparative effectiveness, and rare or delayed ADRs not captured in preapproval studies.
2. **Registry Studies and Observational Research**: Registry studies and observational research utilize healthcare databases, electronic health records (EHRs), and patient registries to assess the safety and effectiveness of pharmaceutical products in routine clinical practice. These studies provide real-world evidence to complement data from controlled clinical trials and inform post-marketing surveillance efforts.

2.7.3 Labeling and Packaging Requirements

Labeling and packaging requirements are critical aspects of pharmaceutical product regulation aimed at ensuring safe and effective use, accurate identification, and proper handling of medications by healthcare professionals, patients, and consumers. Regulatory authorities, such as the U.S. Food and Drug Administration (FDA) and the European Medicines Agency (EMA), establish guidelines and standards for labeling and packaging to provide clear, comprehensive, and standardized information about pharmaceutical products. Key components of labeling and packaging requirements include:

Labeling Requirements:

1. **Prescription Drug Labeling**: Prescription drug labeling includes essential information for healthcare professionals, such as the drug name, strength, dosage form, route of administration, indications, contraindications, warnings, precautions, adverse reactions, drug interactions, and instructions for use. Prescription drug labeling also contains the product's National Drug Code (NDC), lot number, expiration date, and storage conditions.

2. **Over-the-Counter (OTC) Drug Labeling**: Over-the-counter drug labeling provides similar information as prescription drug labeling but is designed for consumer use. OTC drug labeling includes clear directions for use, warnings, precautions, and information on when to consult a healthcare professional. OTC drug labeling also includes the Drug Facts panel, which presents standardized information about active ingredients, purpose, uses, warnings, directions, and inactive ingredients.
3. **Package Inserts**: Package inserts, also known as prescribing information or patient information leaflets, accompany pharmaceutical products and provide detailed information about the product's properties, uses, dosing, administration, precautions, and potential side effects. Package inserts are intended to assist healthcare professionals and patients in making informed decisions about the safe and effective use of medications.

Packaging Requirements:

1. **Child-Resistant Packaging**: Certain pharmaceutical products, such as prescription drugs and OTC medications, are required to be packaged in child-resistant containers to reduce the risk of accidental ingestion by children. Child-resistant packaging features special closures or mechanisms that require adult-level dexterity or strength to open, thereby preventing access by young children.
2. **Tamper-Evident Packaging**: Tamper-evident packaging is designed to provide visual evidence of tampering or manipulation of pharmaceutical products, thereby ensuring product integrity and safety. Tamper-evident features may include seals, bands, shrink wraps, or other barriers that are visibly damaged upon opening, alerting consumers to potential tampering and prompting them to discard the product.
3. **Unit-Dose Packaging**: Unit-dose packaging involves individually packaging pharmaceutical products in single-dose or unit-of-use containers, such as blister packs, ampules, or prefilled syringes. Unit-dose packaging improves medication safety, accuracy, and convenience by reducing dosing errors, cross-contamination, and medication waste.

Labeling and Packaging Standards:

1. **Regulatory Compliance**: Labeling and packaging must comply with applicable regulatory requirements and standards set forth by regulatory authorities, such as the FDA, EMA, and national health authorities. Compliance ensures that pharmaceutical products meet quality, safety, and efficacy standards and are appropriately labeled and packaged for distribution and use.
2. **Standardized Formats**: Labeling and packaging may follow standardized formats and templates to ensure consistency, clarity, and readability of information across different products and manufacturers. Standardized formats help healthcare professionals and consumers easily identify and interpret essential information about pharmaceutical products.
3. **Multilingual Labeling**: Pharmaceutical products distributed in international markets may require multilingual labeling to accommodate diverse language preferences and regulatory requirements. Multilingual labeling provides instructions for use, warnings, and precautions in multiple languages to facilitate safe and effective use by global populations.

2.7.4 Risk Management Plans (RMPs)

Risk Management Plans (RMPs) are strategic documents developed by pharmaceutical companies in collaboration with regulatory authorities to identify, characterize, and mitigate risks associated with the use of medicinal products. RMPs are an essential component of pharmacovigilance and regulatory oversight, providing a framework for assessing, minimizing, and communicating risks throughout the product lifecycle. Key elements of RMPs include:

1. Risk Identification and Characterization:

- **Risk Assessment**: RMPs begin with a comprehensive assessment of potential risks associated with the medicinal product, including known and potential adverse reactions, off-label use, medication errors, misuse, and other safety concerns. Risk assessment considers factors such as the severity, frequency, and predictability of adverse events, patient population characteristics, and pharmacological properties of the product.
- **Risk Factors**: RMPs identify risk factors that may contribute to the occurrence or exacerbation of adverse events, such as patient-related factors (e.g., age, gender, comorbidities), drug-related factors (e.g., dose,

duration of treatment, route of administration), and environmental factors (e.g., concomitant medications, healthcare settings).

2. Risk Minimization and Mitigation Strategies:

- **Risk Minimization Measures:** RMPs outline specific risk minimization measures to reduce the likelihood or severity of identified risks associated with the medicinal product. Risk minimization measures may include educational interventions, healthcare provider training programs, patient counseling materials, medication guides, and communication strategies to raise awareness of potential risks and promote safe prescribing, dispensing, and use.
- **Risk Communication:** RMPs define communication strategies for effectively communicating risk information to healthcare professionals, patients, and other stakeholders. Risk communication strategies may include product labeling updates, safety advisories, Dear Healthcare Professional letters, public health alerts, and educational materials to enhance awareness of potential risks and facilitate informed decision-making.

3. Pharmacovigilance and Safety Monitoring:

- **Post-Marketing Surveillance:** RMPs establish pharmacovigilance activities and post-marketing surveillance systems to monitor the safety and effectiveness of the medicinal product in real-world clinical practice. Pharmacovigilance activities include the systematic collection, analysis, and evaluation of adverse events, adverse drug reactions, medication errors, and other safety-related information to detect, assess, and mitigate potential risks.
- **Periodic Safety Updates:** RMPs define procedures for preparing periodic safety update reports (PSURs) or periodic benefit-risk evaluation reports (PBRERs) summarizing the safety data collected during post-marketing surveillance. PSURs/PBRERs provide an overview of the product's safety profile, including new or emerging safety concerns, regulatory actions taken, and risk management activities implemented.

4. Risk Evaluation and Benefit-Risk Assessment:

- **Benefit-Risk Evaluation**: RMPs facilitate ongoing benefit-risk assessments to evaluate the balance between the therapeutic benefits and potential risks associated with the medicinal product. Benefit-risk assessments consider factors such as the severity of the disease, availability of alternative treatments, patient preferences, and the overall public health impact to inform regulatory decision-making and risk management strategies.
- **Risk Evaluation and Response**: RMPs outline procedures for evaluating new safety data, signal detection findings, and risk-benefit assessments to determine appropriate risk management actions and regulatory responses. Regulatory authorities may require modifications to the product labeling, implementation of additional risk minimization measures, or updates to the RMP based on evolving safety information.

2.7.5 Case Study: Withdrawal of Rofecoxib (Vioxx) Due to Cardiovascular Risks

The withdrawal of rofecoxib (brand name Vioxx) serves as a prominent case study highlighting the importance of post-marketing surveillance and pharmacovigilance in identifying and managing drug safety concerns. Rofecoxib, a selective cyclooxygenase-2 (COX-2) inhibitor, was approved by regulatory authorities for the treatment of osteoarthritis, rheumatoid arthritis, and acute pain conditions.

Background:

1. **Approval and Market Availability**: Rofecoxib was approved by the U.S. Food and Drug Administration (FDA) in 1999 and subsequently marketed globally as a safer alternative to traditional nonsteroidal anti-inflammatory drugs (NSAIDs) due to its reduced gastrointestinal side effects.
2. **Emerging Safety Concerns**: Despite initial enthusiasm for rofecoxib, concerns began to emerge regarding its cardiovascular safety profile based on clinical trial data and post-marketing surveillance reports.

Post-Marketing Surveillance Findings:

1. **VIGOR Study**: The Vioxx Gastrointestinal Outcomes Research (VIGOR) study, published in 2000, compared rofecoxib with naproxen in patients with rheumatoid arthritis. The study found an increased risk of

myocardial infarction (heart attack) and other cardiovascular events in patients receiving rofecoxib compared to naproxen.

2. **Observational Studies and Meta-Analyses**: Subsequent observational studies and meta-analyses confirmed the association between rofecoxib use and an elevated risk of cardiovascular events, including myocardial infarction and stroke. These findings raised concerns about the overall cardiovascular safety of COX-2 inhibitors.

Regulatory Action and Market Withdrawal:

1. **FDA Advisory Panel Meeting**: In September 2004, an FDA advisory panel convened to review the cardiovascular safety of COX-2 inhibitors, including rofecoxib. The panel concluded that rofecoxib posed an increased risk of cardiovascular events and recommended regulatory action.
2. **Voluntary Withdrawal by Merck**: In response to the FDA advisory panel's recommendations and growing safety concerns, Merck & Co., the manufacturer of rofecoxib, voluntarily withdrew Vioxx from the market on September 30, 2004. The decision to withdraw rofecoxib was based on an analysis of additional clinical trial data indicating an increased risk of cardiovascular events with long-term use.

Impact and Lessons Learned:

1. **Public Health Impact**: The withdrawal of rofecoxib had significant implications for public health, as it underscored the importance of post-marketing surveillance and timely regulatory action in identifying and addressing drug safety concerns. The withdrawal of rofecoxib prompted healthcare professionals and patients to reevaluate the use of COX-2 inhibitors and NSAIDs in clinical practice.
2. **Regulatory Oversight**: The rofecoxib case led to enhanced regulatory oversight and scrutiny of drug safety throughout the product lifecycle, including premarket approval, post-marketing surveillance, and risk management. Regulatory agencies implemented stricter guidelines for assessing cardiovascular risks associated with new drug approvals and requiring comprehensive safety monitoring and risk mitigation strategies.

3. **Litigation and Settlements**: The withdrawal of rofecoxib resulted in numerous lawsuits and legal settlements against Merck & Co. alleging harm caused by the drug's cardiovascular risks. Merck ultimately settled thousands of lawsuits related to rofecoxib for billions of dollars, highlighting the financial and reputational impact of drug safety controversies on pharmaceutical manufacturers.

CHAPTER THREE

REGULATORY SUBMISSIONS AND APPROVALS

3.1 Investigational New Drug (IND) Application Process

3.1.1 Overview of IND Application Process

The Investigational New Drug (IND) application process serves as a critical milestone in the development of a new pharmaceutical product, facilitating its progression from preclinical studies to human clinical trials. It represents a comprehensive submission to regulatory authorities, typically the Food and Drug Administration (FDA) in the United States, seeking authorization to initiate clinical investigation of the investigational drug in human subjects. The primary objective of the IND application is to provide sufficient data and information to demonstrate the safety and preliminary efficacy of the investigational product, while ensuring the protection of human subjects participating in clinical trials. The process is governed by regulatory guidelines and statutes aimed at safeguarding public health and promoting innovation in drug development.

The IND application encompasses a multifaceted compilation of scientific, technical, and regulatory documentation, meticulously prepared by the sponsor or applicant. Central to the application is the submission of preclinical data generated from laboratory and animal studies, which elucidate the pharmacological properties, toxicological profile, and potential risks associated with the investigational drug. These preclinical findings are pivotal in informing the design and conduct of subsequent clinical trials, guiding dosage selection, and identifying potential safety concerns. Additionally, the IND application includes detailed clinical trial protocols outlining the objectives, study design, participant eligibility criteria, treatment regimens, and endpoints of the proposed clinical investigations. These protocols are designed to ensure the ethical conduct of clinical trials and the generation of reliable data to support the safety and efficacy of the investigational product.

Furthermore, the IND application incorporates comprehensive information pertaining to the manufacturing process and quality control of the investigational drug product. This includes detailed descriptions of the drug substance and drug product, manufacturing facilities, analytical methods, and specifications for ensuring product consistency, purity, and stability. The submission also includes data on the chemistry, manufacturing, and controls (CMC) aspects of the investigational product, demonstrating compliance with current Good Manufacturing Practice (cGMP) regulations to ensure product quality and integrity throughout the clinical trial process.

Importantly, the IND application serves as a communication tool between the sponsor and regulatory authorities, facilitating ongoing dialogue and collaboration throughout the drug development process. Regulatory review of the IND application involves a thorough assessment of the scientific rationale, study design, safety data, manufacturing processes, and regulatory compliance, with the aim of evaluating the feasibility and ethicality of initiating clinical trials. Upon successful review and acceptance of the IND application, the sponsor receives authorization, typically in the form of an IND number, allowing initiation of clinical trials at approved trial sites. Throughout the clinical trial phase, sponsors are required to adhere to regulatory reporting requirements, including the submission of safety updates, protocol amendments, and annual reports, to ensure ongoing oversight and evaluation of the investigational product's safety profile.

3.1.2 Components of an IND Application

3.1.2.1 Preclinical Data Requirements

Preclinical data represent a cornerstone of the Investigational New Drug (IND) application, providing essential insights into the pharmacological properties, toxicological profile, and potential risks associated with the investigational drug. The preclinical data package is designed to comprehensively characterize the safety profile of the drug candidate and to inform the design and conduct of subsequent clinical trials. Key components of the preclinical data requirements include:

1. **Pharmacology Studies:** Pharmacology studies aim to elucidate the mechanism of action, pharmacokinetic parameters, and pharmacodynamic effects of the investigational drug in relevant animal models. These studies provide essential information regarding the drug's absorption, distribution, metabolism, and excretion (ADME), as well as its potential interactions with physiological systems and other medications.

2. **Toxicology Studies:** Toxicology studies are conducted to assess the safety profile of the investigational drug and to identify potential adverse effects or toxicities. These studies typically involve the administration of escalating doses of the drug to animal subjects, followed by comprehensive evaluation of systemic toxicity, organ-specific effects, and potential carcinogenicity. Acute, subchronic, and chronic toxicity studies are conducted to assess the dose-response relationship and to establish safe dose levels for human trials.

3. **ADME Studies:** ADME studies provide critical information regarding the drug's absorption, distribution, metabolism, and excretion properties in animal models, helping to predict its behavior in humans. These studies evaluate the bioavailability, tissue distribution, metabolic pathways, and elimination kinetics of the investigational drug, informing dosage selection and administration regimens for clinical trials.

4. **Safety Pharmacology Studies:** Safety pharmacology studies assess the potential effects of the investigational drug on vital physiological functions, such as cardiovascular, respiratory, and central nervous system function. These studies aim to identify any adverse effects or safety concerns related to the drug's pharmacological activity, guiding risk mitigation strategies and monitoring parameters for clinical trials.

5. **Genotoxicity and Carcinogenicity Studies:** Genotoxicity and carcinogenicity studies evaluate the potential of the investigational drug to induce genetic mutations or carcinogenic effects in animal models. These studies assess the drug's potential to cause DNA damage, chromosomal abnormalities, or tumor formation, providing critical information for assessing long-term safety risks and informing regulatory decisions regarding human exposure.

3.1.2.2 Clinical Protocols and Investigator Information

Clinical protocols and investigator information constitute integral components of the Investigational New Drug (IND) application, providing detailed plans for the conduct of clinical trials and identifying the individuals responsible for overseeing the research. These components serve to ensure the ethical and scientific integrity of clinical investigations, safeguarding the rights and welfare of human subjects participating in the trials.

Clinical Protocols: Clinical protocols outline the objectives, design, methodology, and statistical considerations of proposed clinical trials, providing a roadmap for conducting the research in accordance with regulatory standards and ethical principles. Key elements of clinical protocols include:

- **Study Objectives:** Clearly defined primary and secondary endpoints, hypotheses to be tested, and rationale for the study.
- **Study Design:** Description of the study design (e.g., randomized controlled trial, observational study), treatment arms, allocation ratio, blinding procedures, and duration of the study.
- **Participant Eligibility Criteria:** Inclusion and exclusion criteria specifying the characteristics of eligible participants, including age, gender, medical history, and disease severity.
- **Treatment Regimens:** Detailed descriptions of investigational drug dosing regimens, route of administration, dose escalation plans, and concomitant medications.
- **Study Procedures:** Procedures for participant screening, enrollment, randomization, treatment administration, follow-up assessments, and data collection.
- **Safety Monitoring:** Plans for monitoring participant safety, including adverse event reporting, laboratory assessments, and criteria for study discontinuation.
- **Data Analysis:** Statistical methods for data analysis, sample size calculations, and considerations for controlling bias and confounding variables.
- **Ethical Considerations:** Measures to ensure compliance with ethical principles, protection of participant confidentiality, and informed consent procedures.

Investigator Information: The IND application includes comprehensive information about the principal investigator(s) and study team members responsible for conducting the clinical trials. This information typically includes:

- **Principal Investigator:** The individual responsible for the overall conduct of the clinical trial, including protocol development, participant recruitment, data collection, and regulatory compliance.
- **Co-Investigators:** Additional investigators involved in the study, contributing to patient care, data collection, and study oversight.
- **Clinical Site Information:** Details of the clinical trial sites where the research will be conducted, including site-specific protocols, facilities, resources, and personnel qualifications.
- **Qualifications and Experience:** Documentation of the qualifications, training, and experience of investigators and study personnel, demonstrating their competence to conduct clinical research and ensure participant safety.
- **Financial Disclosures:** Declarations of any financial interests, conflicts of interest, or relationships with sponsors or entities that may influence the conduct or interpretation of the research.

3.1.2.3 Manufacturing Information

Manufacturing information is a critical component of the Investigational New Drug (IND) application, providing comprehensive details about the manufacturing process, quality control measures, and specifications for the investigational drug product. This information is essential for ensuring the consistency, quality, and integrity of the drug product throughout the clinical trial phase and is subject to rigorous regulatory review to ensure compliance with current Good Manufacturing Practice (cGMP) regulations.

Drug Substance Manufacturing: The IND application includes detailed information regarding the manufacturing process for the drug substance, including:

- **Synthetic Route:** Description of the chemical synthesis or extraction process used to produce the drug substance, including starting materials, reaction conditions, and purification steps.
- **Characterization:** Analytical methods and specifications for assessing the identity, purity, and potency of the drug substance, including tests for impurities, residual solvents, and degradation products.
- **Batch Records:** Documentation of manufacturing batch records, detailing the production steps, in-process controls, and quality checks performed at each stage of the manufacturing process.

- **Stability Studies:** Data from stability studies evaluating the physical, chemical, and microbiological stability of the drug substance under various storage conditions, demonstrating its long-term stability and shelf-life.

Drug Product Manufacturing: Information about the manufacturing process for the drug product (formulation, packaging, labeling) is also included in the IND application, covering:

- **Formulation Development:** Description of the formulation composition, excipients, and manufacturing process used to prepare the drug product, ensuring uniformity, stability, and bioavailability of the active ingredient.
- **Packaging and Labeling:** Specifications for packaging materials, container closure systems, and labeling requirements for the investigational drug product, including instructions for use, storage conditions, and cautionary statements.
- **Quality Control Testing:** Analytical methods and specifications for quality control testing of the drug product, including tests for identity, strength, purity, and uniformity, to ensure compliance with regulatory standards.
- **Batch Release Testing:** Procedures for batch release testing, including sampling, testing, and documentation requirements to verify compliance with specifications before release for clinical use.

Manufacturing Facilities and Controls: The IND application provides information about the manufacturing facilities and quality control systems used to produce the investigational drug, including:

- **Facility Description:** Details of manufacturing facilities, equipment, utilities, and controls used in drug substance and drug product manufacturing, demonstrating compliance with cGMP regulations.
- **Quality Assurance Systems:** Documentation of quality assurance systems, procedures, and personnel responsible for ensuring compliance with regulatory requirements and maintaining product quality and integrity.
- **Validation Studies:** Validation studies demonstrating the suitability and consistency of manufacturing processes, equipment, and analytical

methods, ensuring reproducibility and reliability of the drug product.

3.1.2.4 Pharmacology and Toxicology Data

Pharmacology and toxicology data are pivotal components of the Investigational New Drug (IND) application, providing essential insights into the pharmacological properties, therapeutic potential, and safety profile of the investigational drug. These data are derived from preclinical studies conducted in laboratory settings and animal models, aiming to elucidate the drug's mechanism of action, pharmacokinetic parameters, and potential adverse effects.

Pharmacology Data: Pharmacology data encompass a comprehensive assessment of the drug's pharmacodynamic and pharmacokinetic properties, including:

- **Mechanism of Action:** Detailed elucidation of the drug's mechanism of action, including its molecular targets, biochemical pathways, and physiological effects.
- **Pharmacodynamic Effects:** Characterization of the drug's pharmacological effects on target tissues, cells, or physiological systems, including dose-response relationships and duration of action.
- **Pharmacokinetics:** Evaluation of the drug's absorption, distribution, metabolism, and excretion (ADME) properties in animal models, including bioavailability, plasma concentration-time profiles, and metabolic pathways.
- **Drug Interactions:** Assessment of potential drug-drug interactions, including metabolism-based interactions (e.g., cytochrome P450 inhibition/induction) and pharmacodynamic interactions (e.g., additive or synergistic effects).

Toxicology Data: Toxicology data aim to assess the safety profile of the investigational drug and identify potential adverse effects or toxicities, including:

- **Acute Toxicity:** Evaluation of acute toxicity following single-dose administration of the drug in animal models, determining the maximum tolerated dose (MTD) and identifying target organs or systems affected.
- **Subchronic and Chronic Toxicity:** Assessment of subchronic and chronic toxicity following repeated administration of the drug over

extended periods, identifying dose-dependent adverse effects, organ toxicity, and potential carcinogenicity.

- **Reproductive and Developmental Toxicity:** Evaluation of potential effects on reproductive function and embryo-fetal development following exposure to the drug during pregnancy, including assessments of fertility, embryo-fetal viability, and teratogenicity.
- **Genotoxicity:** Assessment of the drug's potential to induce genetic mutations or chromosomal damage in in vitro and in vivo assays, including tests for gene mutations, chromosomal aberrations, and DNA damage.
- **Safety Pharmacology:** Evaluation of potential effects on vital physiological functions, including cardiovascular, respiratory, and central nervous system function, to identify any safety concerns related to pharmacological activity.

3.2 Dosage Form Considerations

3.2.1 Importance of Dosage Form in Drug Development

The choice of dosage form plays a pivotal role in drug development, influencing various aspects of efficacy, safety, patient compliance, and marketability. Dosage form selection is not merely a matter of convenience but a strategic decision that impacts the overall success of a pharmaceutical product. Several key factors underscore the importance of dosage form in drug development:

1. Pharmacokinetics and Bioavailability: Different dosage forms exhibit distinct pharmacokinetic profiles, affecting the absorption, distribution, metabolism, and excretion (ADME) of the active pharmaceutical ingredient (API). For instance, immediate-release formulations may achieve rapid onset of action but shorter duration of effect, whereas extended-release formulations offer sustained drug levels over an extended period, reducing dosing frequency and improving patient compliance. The choice of dosage form can significantly influence the bioavailability and therapeutic efficacy of the drug product.

2. Patient Acceptance and Compliance: The acceptability and ease of administration of a dosage form are critical factors in patient adherence to prescribed therapy. Dosage forms that are convenient, palatable, and easy to swallow are more likely to enhance patient compliance and treatment outcomes. Patient-centric considerations, such as taste preferences, swallowing difficulties, and dosing frequency, should be taken into account when selecting the optimal dosage form to improve patient acceptance and adherence to therapy.

3. Stability and Formulation Compatibility: The physical and chemical stability of the drug substance and formulation components are essential considerations in dosage form development. Different dosage forms may require specific formulation approaches, excipients, and manufacturing processes to ensure product stability, integrity, and shelf-life. Factors such as moisture sensitivity, light exposure, and temperature fluctuations can influence the stability of the dosage form and may necessitate formulation modifications or packaging considerations to maintain product quality.

4. Manufacturing and Quality Control: Dosage form selection can impact manufacturing complexity, production scale-up, and quality control measures. Each dosage form may require unique manufacturing processes, equipment, and controls to ensure consistent product quality, uniformity, and compliance with regulatory standards. Formulation optimization and process validation are essential steps in dosage form development to achieve reproducible manufacturing and meet cGMP requirements.

5. Market Differentiation and Branding: The choice of dosage form can also contribute to product differentiation, market positioning, and branding strategies. Innovative dosage forms, such as orally disintegrating tablets, transdermal patches, or controlled-release formulations, may offer competitive advantages in terms of patent protection, market exclusivity, and patient preference. Strategic selection of a novel dosage form can enhance product differentiation, market penetration, and commercial success in an increasingly competitive pharmaceutical landscape.

3.2.2 Factors Influencing Dosage Form Selection

3.2.2.1 Drug Properties

The selection of an appropriate dosage form is influenced by various factors, with drug properties playing a pivotal role in determining the most suitable formulation approach. Understanding the physicochemical characteristics, pharmacokinetic profile, and therapeutic requirements of the drug substance is essential for optimizing dosage form selection. Several key drug properties influence dosage form selection:

1. Solubility and Permeability: The solubility and permeability of the drug substance are critical determinants of its bioavailability and absorption characteristics. Poorly water-soluble drugs may benefit from formulation approaches that enhance solubility and dissolution rates, such as micronization, complexation, or lipid-based formulations. Similarly, drugs with low permeability may require dosage forms that improve mucosal absorption or bypass first-pass metabolism, such as transdermal patches, nasal sprays, or sublingual tablets.

2. **Stability and Degradation Profile:** The stability and degradation profile of the drug substance influence formulation stability, shelf-life, and compatibility with different dosage forms. Drugs prone to degradation, hydrolysis, or oxidation may require protective formulation strategies, such as encapsulation, pH adjustment, or inert packaging materials, to prevent chemical degradation and maintain product integrity. Formulation optimization is essential to minimize degradation pathways and ensure long-term stability under various storage conditions.

3. **Molecular Weight and Size:** The molecular weight and size of the drug molecule impact its pharmacokinetic properties, including absorption, distribution, and elimination. Large molecular weight drugs may exhibit limited oral bioavailability due to poor membrane permeability or extensive first-pass metabolism. In such cases, alternative routes of administration, such as parenteral or inhalation delivery, may be preferred to bypass gastrointestinal barriers and improve systemic exposure. Formulation considerations for large molecules also include stability, aggregation, and immunogenicity concerns.

4. **pH and Ionization Characteristics:** The pH and ionization characteristics of the drug substance influence its solubility, dissolution behavior, and absorption across biological membranes. Weakly acidic or basic drugs may exhibit pH-dependent solubility, dissolution, and permeability properties, necessitating formulation adjustments to optimize drug release and absorption. pH modifiers, buffering agents, or pH-responsive delivery systems may be employed to enhance drug solubility and stability within the physiological pH range of target tissues.

5. **Partition Coefficient (Log P):** The partition coefficient (Log P) reflects the lipophilicity of the drug molecule and its propensity to partition between aqueous and lipid phases. Drugs with high lipophilicity may preferentially accumulate in lipophilic compartments, influencing their distribution, metabolism, and elimination. Formulation strategies to enhance drug solubility and bioavailability may include lipid-based formulations, self-emulsifying drug delivery systems (SEDDS), or nanoparticulate carriers to improve drug dispersibility and absorption.

3.2.2.2 Patient Population

When selecting a dosage form, considerations related to the patient population are paramount. Different patient demographics, including age, medical conditions, and preferences, influence the suitability of various dosage forms. Tailoring the dosage form to the specific needs and characteristics of the target patient population enhances medication adherence, therapeutic outcomes, and overall patient satisfaction. Several key factors related to the patient population impact dosage form selection:

1. **Age Group:** Patient age is a critical factor in dosage form selection, as it affects swallowing ability, taste preferences, and medication acceptance. Pediatric and geriatric populations may have unique challenges related to dosage form administration. Pediatric patients often require age-appropriate formulations, such as liquids, chewable tablets, or orally disintegrating tablets, to facilitate administration and improve palatability. Conversely, geriatric patients may benefit from dosage forms that are easy to swallow, such as small tablets, liquids, or transdermal patches, to minimize the risk of choking or aspiration.

2. **Disease State:** The underlying medical condition and disease state of the patient population influence dosage form selection. Patients with gastrointestinal disorders, such as dysphagia, gastroesophageal reflux disease (GERD), or gastroparesis, may require dosage forms that bypass the gastrointestinal tract or provide controlled release to minimize gastrointestinal irritation or variability in drug absorption. Similarly, patients with chronic conditions, such as diabetes, hypertension, or Parkinson's disease, may benefit from dosage forms that offer sustained release, dose titration, or simplified dosing regimens to optimize therapeutic outcomes and improve treatment adherence.

3. **Cognitive and Physical Impairments:** Patients with cognitive or physical impairments may face challenges in medication administration, handling, or adherence. Dosage forms that offer ease of use, dosing flexibility, and simplified administration procedures are essential for enhancing medication compliance and safety in these populations. Caregiver-friendly dosage forms, such as pre-filled syringes, metered-dose inhalers, or transdermal patches, may be preferable for patients requiring assistance with medication administration or those with limited dexterity or coordination.

4. **Lifestyle and Preferences:** Patient lifestyle factors, preferences, and cultural considerations also influence dosage form selection. Patients with busy lifestyles, travel requirements, or unpredictable schedules may prefer

dosage forms that offer convenience, portability, and flexibility in dosing. For example, once-daily formulations, such as extended-release tablets or patches, may be preferred over multiple daily dosing regimens to simplify medication adherence and improve patient convenience. Additionally, cultural preferences, religious beliefs, or dietary restrictions may influence the acceptability of certain dosage forms, necessitating culturally sensitive approaches to medication delivery and administration.

3.2.2.3 Administration Route

The administration route is a critical factor influencing dosage form selection, as it determines the route of drug delivery, absorption kinetics, and systemic distribution within the body. Tailoring the dosage form to the optimal administration route ensures efficient drug delivery, therapeutic efficacy, and patient acceptance. Consideration of various administration routes is essential for selecting the most appropriate dosage form for the target patient population. Several key factors related to administration routes influence dosage form selection:

1. **Oral Administration:** Oral administration is the most common and preferred route for drug delivery due to its convenience, patient acceptance, and versatility. Dosage forms for oral administration include tablets, capsules, powders, solutions, suspensions, and chewable formulations. Factors such as patient swallowing ability, taste preferences, and dosing frequency influence the choice of oral dosage form. Immediate-release formulations offer rapid drug absorption and onset of action, while extended-release formulations provide sustained drug levels and less frequent dosing.

2. **Parenteral Administration:** Parenteral administration involves delivering drugs directly into the bloodstream or target tissues via injection or infusion. Parenteral dosage forms include solutions, suspensions, emulsions, and lyophilized powders for reconstitution. Subcutaneous, intramuscular, and intravenous routes are commonly used for parenteral drug delivery, offering rapid onset of action and high bioavailability. Parenteral dosage forms require sterile preparation, specialized administration techniques, and careful handling to minimize the risk of infection or tissue damage.

3. **Topical Administration:** Topical administration involves applying drugs directly to the skin or mucous membranes for localized or systemic effects. Topical dosage forms include creams, ointments, gels, patches, foams, and sprays. Topical administration offers targeted drug delivery to

specific anatomical sites, minimizing systemic exposure and adverse effects. Factors such as skin permeability, drug solubility, and formulation viscosity influence the choice of topical dosage form. Transdermal patches provide sustained drug release and systemic absorption over an extended period, offering convenience and improved patient compliance.

4. Inhalation Administration: Inhalation administration delivers drugs directly to the respiratory tract via inhalation devices, such as metered-dose inhalers, dry powder inhalers, nebulizers, and nasal sprays. Inhalation dosage forms include aerosols, powders, and solutions for inhalation. Inhalation administration is used for local treatment of respiratory conditions, such as asthma or chronic obstructive pulmonary disease (COPD), as well as systemic delivery of drugs with rapid onset of action. Factors such as particle size, inhalation technique, and lung deposition influence the efficacy and safety of inhalation dosage forms.

5. Rectal and Vaginal Administration: Rectal and vaginal administration delivers drugs to the rectal or vaginal mucosa for local or systemic effects. Rectal dosage forms include suppositories, enemas, and foams, while vaginal dosage forms include creams, gels, tablets, and inserts. These routes of administration offer targeted drug delivery to specific anatomical sites, avoiding first-pass metabolism and gastrointestinal irritation. Factors such as formulation compatibility, patient comfort, and ease of administration influence the choice of rectal or vaginal dosage form.

3.2.3 Dosage Form Optimization Strategies

3.2.3.1 Solid Dosage Forms

Solid dosage forms are widely used in pharmaceutical formulations due to their ease of manufacturing, stability, patient acceptance, and dose accuracy. Optimization strategies for solid dosage forms aim to enhance drug delivery, bioavailability, and patient compliance while ensuring product quality, uniformity, and regulatory compliance. Several key strategies for optimizing solid dosage forms include:

1. Formulation Optimization: Formulation optimization involves selecting excipients, modifying drug release profiles, and enhancing drug stability to improve the performance of solid dosage forms. Excipient selection plays a crucial role in optimizing drug solubility, dissolution, and bioavailability. Use of solubilizing agents, surfactants, and co-solvents can enhance drug solubility and dissolution rates, particularly for poorly water-soluble drugs. Controlled-release technologies, such as matrix systems, osmotic pumps, and multiparticulate formulations, offer tailored drug release profiles, extended duration of action, and reduced dosing frequency.

2. Particle Engineering: Particle engineering techniques, such as micronization, nanosizing, and spray drying, are used to optimize the physical properties of drug particles and improve drug dissolution and bioavailability. Reduction of drug particle size increases surface area and enhances drug dissolution rates, leading to faster onset of action and improved therapeutic outcomes. Nanoparticle formulations offer advantages in terms of enhanced drug solubility, stability, and targeted drug delivery to specific tissues or cells, overcoming limitations associated with conventional solid dosage forms.

3. Process Optimization: Process optimization involves refining manufacturing processes, equipment, and controls to ensure reproducible production of solid dosage forms with consistent quality and performance. Implementation of quality by design (QbD) principles, process analytical technology (PAT), and continuous manufacturing approaches enables real-time monitoring and control of critical process parameters, reducing variability and enhancing product quality. Adoption of advanced manufacturing technologies, such as hot melt extrusion, spray coating, and 3D printing, offers opportunities for precise control over drug release kinetics, particle morphology, and dosage form design.

4. Dosage Form Design: Dosage form design encompasses the selection of appropriate dosage forms, such as tablets, capsules, powders, or granules, based on patient needs, drug properties, and therapeutic requirements. Design considerations include dosage form size, shape, color, and surface properties to optimize patient acceptance, swallowability, and ease of administration. Modified-release formulations, such as enteric-coated tablets, film-coated tablets, and extended-release capsules, provide controlled drug release, reduced dosing frequency, and improved patient compliance.

5. Quality Assurance and Regulatory Compliance: Quality assurance and regulatory compliance are integral aspects of solid dosage form optimization to ensure product safety, efficacy, and compliance with regulatory standards. Implementation of good manufacturing practices (GMP), quality control testing, and batch release procedures ensures product quality, uniformity, and purity. Comprehensive documentation, stability testing, and regulatory submissions demonstrate compliance with regulatory requirements and facilitate product registration, approval, and commercialization.

3.2.3.2 Liquid Dosage Forms

Liquid dosage forms offer advantages in terms of dose flexibility, ease of administration, and rapid drug absorption, making them suitable for patients with swallowing difficulties, pediatric populations, and those requiring precise dosing. Optimization strategies for liquid dosage forms aim to enhance drug stability, palatability, accuracy of dosing, and patient acceptance while ensuring product quality, uniformity, and regulatory compliance. Several key strategies for optimizing liquid dosage forms include:

1. **Solubility Enhancement:** Solubility enhancement techniques are employed to improve the solubility and dissolution rates of poorly water-soluble drugs in liquid dosage forms. Use of co-solvents, surfactants, solubilizing agents, and complexation agents enhances drug solubility, ensuring uniform drug distribution and accurate dosing. Nanotechnology-based approaches, such as nanoemulsions, liposomes, and nanosuspensions, offer advantages in terms of enhanced drug solubility, stability, and bioavailability, overcoming limitations associated with conventional liquid formulations.

2. **Taste Masking:** Taste masking strategies are employed to improve the palatability and acceptability of liquid dosage forms, particularly for pediatric and geriatric populations. Masking bitter or unpleasant tastes using sweetening agents, flavoring agents, and masking agents enhances patient compliance and medication adherence. Encapsulation of drugs within taste-masked microspheres, nanoparticles, or lipid-based carriers provides sustained release and controlled drug delivery, minimizing taste perception and enhancing patient comfort.

3. **Stability Enhancement:** Stability enhancement techniques are utilized to improve the chemical and physical stability of liquid dosage forms, ensuring product integrity and shelf-life under various storage conditions. Use of antioxidants, chelating agents, buffering agents, and preservatives protects against degradation pathways, oxidation, microbial growth, and pH fluctuations. Lyophilization or freeze-drying techniques offer advantages in terms of improved stability, reconstitution convenience, and extended shelf-life for liquid formulations, particularly for biologics and injectable drugs.

4. **Dosing Accuracy and Precision:** Dosing accuracy and precision are critical considerations in liquid dosage form optimization to ensure accurate and consistent dosing, particularly for potent or narrow therapeutic index

drugs. Use of calibrated measuring devices, such as oral syringes, droppers, or dosing cups, facilitates precise measurement and administration of liquid medications. Implementation of standardized dosing instructions, dose titration schedules, and dosing aids enhances medication safety and minimizes dosing errors, particularly in pediatric or elderly patients.

5. Compatibility and Interactions: Compatibility and interactions between drug substances, excipients, and packaging materials are important considerations in liquid dosage form optimization to prevent chemical degradation, physical instability, or leaching of harmful contaminants. Compatibility testing, container closure integrity testing, and compatibility studies with administration devices ensure product quality, safety, and regulatory compliance. Use of inert, pharmaceutical-grade materials, such as glass, plastic, or silicone, minimizes interactions and ensures compatibility with liquid formulations.

3.2.3.3 Semisolid Dosage Forms

Semisolid dosage forms, including creams, ointments, gels, and pastes, offer advantages in terms of localized drug delivery, enhanced skin penetration, and prolonged drug release, making them suitable for topical and transdermal drug administration. Optimization strategies for semisolid dosage forms aim to improve drug solubility, skin permeation, formulation stability, and patient acceptability while ensuring product quality, uniformity, and regulatory compliance. Several key strategies for optimizing semisolid dosage forms include:

1. Base Selection and Formulation: Base selection is a critical consideration in semisolid dosage form optimization, as it influences drug solubility, skin penetration, and formulation stability. Various bases, such as hydrophilic bases (e.g., water-in-oil emulsions), lipophilic bases (e.g., oil-in-water emulsions), and gel bases (e.g., hydrogels), offer advantages in terms of drug release, skin hydration, and compatibility with different drug substances. Selection of appropriate emulsifiers, thickeners, and stabilizers ensures uniform distribution of drug particles, consistent rheological properties, and optimal drug release kinetics.

2. Drug Solubility and Penetration Enhancement: Drug solubility and penetration enhancement techniques are employed to improve drug absorption, skin permeation, and therapeutic efficacy in semisolid dosage forms. Use of penetration enhancers, such as surfactants, fatty acids, and chemical permeation enhancers, facilitates drug diffusion through the stratum corneum and enhances skin penetration. Nanoencapsulation, lipid nanoparticles, and microemulsions offer advantages in terms of enhanced drug solubility, stability, and targeted drug delivery, overcoming limitations associated with conventional semisolid formulations.

3. Stability Enhancement: Stability enhancement strategies are utilized to improve the chemical and physical stability of semisolid dosage forms, ensuring product integrity and shelf-life under various storage conditions. Use of antioxidants, preservatives, chelating agents, and pH modifiers protects against oxidation, microbial growth, and degradation pathways. Incorporation of stabilizing agents, such as viscosity enhancers, thickeners, and gelling agents, improves formulation stability, texture, and consistency, minimizing phase separation, syneresis, or crystallization.

4. Dosing Precision and Patient Acceptability: Dosing precision and patient acceptability are important considerations in semisolid dosage form optimization to ensure accurate and consistent drug delivery, minimize wastage, and enhance patient compliance. Use of calibrated dispensing devices, such as tubes, jars, pumps, or applicators, facilitates precise measurement and administration of semisolid medications. Optimization of formulation texture, appearance, and sensory properties enhances patient acceptance, comfort, and satisfaction, promoting adherence to prescribed therapy.

5. Compatibility and Irritation Potential: Compatibility and irritation potential of semisolid dosage forms with skin, mucous membranes, and external surfaces are important considerations in formulation optimization to prevent skin irritation, sensitization, or allergic reactions. Compatibility testing, skin irritation studies, and safety assessments ensure product safety, tolerability, and regulatory compliance. Use of hypoallergenic ingredients, fragrance-free formulations, and skin-friendly excipients minimizes the risk of adverse reactions and enhances patient safety.

3.2.4 Case Study: Formulation Challenges and Solutions in Dosage Form Development

In the development of a novel oral medication for the treatment of a chronic inflammatory condition, a pharmaceutical company, Therapeutic Innovations Ltd., encountered several formulation challenges that required innovative solutions to achieve optimal drug delivery and therapeutic efficacy.

Background: Therapeutic Innovations Ltd. aimed to develop a once-daily oral tablet formulation containing a poorly water-soluble drug with low bioavailability. The drug exhibited high permeability but suffered from dissolution rate-limited absorption, leading to suboptimal therapeutic outcomes and variable drug exposure in clinical trials.

Formulation Challenges:

1. **Poor Solubility:** The drug substance displayed poor aqueous solubility, resulting in limited dissolution and erratic absorption upon oral administration. Conventional formulation approaches, such as immediate-release tablets or capsules, failed to achieve adequate drug solubility and bioavailability, leading to suboptimal therapeutic outcomes.
2. **Dose Dumping:** Formulation attempts to enhance drug solubility using solubilizing agents or surfactants resulted in dose dumping, characterized by rapid drug release and unpredictable plasma concentration profiles. This posed safety concerns related to drug overdose, systemic toxicity, and adverse effects, necessitating dose titration and controlled drug release strategies.
3. **Gastrointestinal Irritation:** The drug substance exhibited irritant effects on the gastrointestinal mucosa, leading to gastrointestinal irritation, nausea, and vomiting in clinical trials. Formulation optimization was required to mitigate gastrointestinal side effects, improve patient tolerability, and enhance medication compliance.

Solution Strategies:

1. **Nanoformulation Approach:** Therapeutic Innovations Ltd. employed a nanoformulation approach to enhance drug solubility, dissolution rates, and oral bioavailability. Nanoparticle formulations, such as solid lipid nanoparticles (SLNs) or nanostructured lipid carriers (NLCs), were developed to encapsulate the drug substance within lipid matrices, improving drug dispersibility and dissolution behavior. Nanoencapsulation offered advantages in terms of enhanced drug solubility, stability, and absorption, overcoming limitations associated with conventional formulations.
2. **Controlled-Release Technology:** To address dose dumping and achieve controlled drug release, Therapeutic Innovations Ltd. incorporated controlled-release technology into the formulation design. Modified-release tablets or multiparticulate systems, such as matrix tablets, osmotic pumps, or coated pellets, were developed to provide sustained

drug release, prolonged drug exposure, and reduced dosing frequency. Controlled-release formulations offered advantages in terms of dose titration, safety, and improved patient compliance, minimizing the risk of adverse effects associated with rapid drug release.

3. **Gastrointestinal Protection:** To mitigate gastrointestinal irritation and enhance patient tolerability, Therapeutic Innovations Ltd. implemented gastroprotective strategies in the formulation design. Enteric coating, pH-sensitive polymers, or mucoadhesive coatings were utilized to protect the drug substance from gastric acidity, delay drug release in the stomach, and target drug delivery to the small intestine. Gastrointestinal protection offered advantages in terms of reduced irritation, improved tolerability, and enhanced absorption, optimizing therapeutic outcomes and patient satisfaction.

Outcome: Through innovative formulation strategies and collaborative efforts between formulation scientists, pharmacologists, and regulatory experts, Therapeutic Innovations Ltd. successfully developed a novel oral tablet formulation with improved drug solubility, controlled drug release, and enhanced gastrointestinal tolerability. The optimized formulation demonstrated superior pharmacokinetic profiles, therapeutic efficacy, and patient compliance in preclinical and clinical studies, paving the way for regulatory approval and commercialization as a novel treatment option for the chronic inflammatory condition.

3.3 Abbreviated New Drug Application (ANDA)

3.3.1 Introduction to ANDA Process

The Abbreviated New Drug Application (ANDA) process is a regulatory pathway in the United States for the approval of generic pharmaceutical products. Unlike the New Drug Application (NDA) process, which is applicable to innovative drugs requiring full clinical data, the ANDA pathway allows for the approval of generic drugs based on the demonstration of bioequivalence to a reference listed drug (RLD). The ANDA process streamlines the approval of generic medications by relying on the safety and efficacy data of the RLD, provided that the generic product is pharmaceutically equivalent and bioequivalent to the reference product.

Key Components of the ANDA Process:

1. **Generic Drug Equivalence:** The foundation of the ANDA process lies in demonstrating the equivalence of the generic drug product to the RLD in terms of pharmaceutical formulation, active ingredient(s), strength, dosage form, route of administration, and labeling. The generic drug must be shown to be pharmaceutically equivalent and bioequivalent to the RLD to ensure therapeutic equivalence and interchangeability.
2. **Bioequivalence Studies:** Bioequivalence studies are conducted to compare the pharmacokinetic parameters of the generic drug product and the RLD following administration to healthy volunteers or patients. These studies assess the rate and extent of drug absorption, peak plasma concentration (Cmax), time to reach peak concentration (Tmax), and area under the plasma concentration-time curve (AUC). The generic drug must demonstrate bioequivalence to the RLD within predefined statistical criteria (e.g., 80-125% confidence interval for the ratio of AUC and Cmax).
3. **Pharmaceutical Equivalence:** Pharmaceutical equivalence refers to the identical qualitative and quantitative composition of active ingredients, excipients, dosage form, strength, and route of administration between the generic drug and the RLD. In vitro studies, such as dissolution testing, are conducted to demonstrate comparable drug release profiles and dissolution characteristics between the generic product and the RLD.
4. **Labeling Requirements:** The labeling of the generic drug product must be identical or closely similar to the RLD, including indications, dosage and administration instructions, warnings, precautions, adverse reactions, and other relevant information. The generic drug label must also include bioequivalence information, indicating its therapeutic equivalence to the RLD.
5. **Patent and Exclusivity Considerations:** Generic drug applicants must address patent and exclusivity issues related to the RLD during the ANDA process. Applicants are required to certify the status of patents listed in the FDA's Orange Book and provide notice to patent holders of their intent to market the generic product. Various patent challenges, including Paragraph IV certifications and patent litigation, may occur during the ANDA review process, impacting the timing of generic product approval.
6. **Regulatory Review and Approval:** The ANDA submission undergoes regulatory review by the U.S. Food and Drug Administration (FDA) to

assess the safety, efficacy, quality, and compliance of the generic drug product with regulatory requirements. The FDA reviews the scientific data, bioequivalence studies, manufacturing processes, labeling, and other relevant information to determine whether the generic product meets the standards for approval. Upon successful review, the FDA grants approval for the generic drug product, allowing it to be marketed and distributed in the United States.

3.3.2 Components of an ANDA

3.3.2.1 Chemistry, Manufacturing, and Controls (CMC) Information

The Chemistry, Manufacturing, and Controls (CMC) section of an Abbreviated New Drug Application (ANDA) provides comprehensive information about the pharmaceutical formulation, manufacturing process, and quality control measures for the generic drug product. This section is critical for demonstrating the pharmaceutical equivalence and bioequivalence of the generic product to the reference listed drug (RLD). Key components of the CMC section include:

1. **Drug Substance Description:** This subsection provides detailed information about the active pharmaceutical ingredient (API) used in the formulation of the generic drug product. It includes the chemical structure, physicochemical properties, synthesis route, and specifications of the drug substance, such as purity, impurities, and characterization data.
2. **Drug Product Description:** This subsection describes the composition, formulation, and dosage form of the generic drug product. It includes the ingredients, excipients, strength, dosage form (e.g., tablets, capsules, injections), and packaging configuration of the drug product. The physical characteristics, appearance, and specifications of the finished dosage form are also provided.
3. **Manufacturing Process:** This subsection outlines the manufacturing process used to produce the generic drug product, including unit operations, equipment, controls, and critical process parameters. It describes the steps involved in drug substance synthesis, formulation, blending, granulation, compression, coating (if applicable), and packaging. Detailed information about in-process controls, batch records, and validation studies is included to ensure consistent product quality and compliance with current Good Manufacturing Practices (cGMP).
4. **Control of Drug Substance:** This subsection describes the quality control measures and analytical methods used to assess the identity,

strength, purity, and potency of the drug substance. It includes specifications for raw materials, intermediates, and API batches, as well as analytical test methods, reference standards, and acceptance criteria. Stability data demonstrating the stability of the drug substance under various storage conditions is also provided.

5. Control of Drug Product: This subsection details the quality control measures and analytical methods used to evaluate the identity, strength, purity, potency, and uniformity of the finished dosage form. It includes specifications for the drug product, including appearance, dissolution, content uniformity, disintegration, and impurities. Stability data demonstrating the stability of the drug product throughout its shelf-life is provided to ensure product quality and performance over time.

6. Container Closure System: This subsection describes the packaging materials and container closure system used to store and protect the generic drug product. It includes specifications for primary containers (e.g., bottles, blister packs, vials) and closure systems (e.g., caps, seals) to ensure product integrity, compatibility, and stability. Compatibility studies demonstrating the suitability of the container closure system for the drug product are included.

3.3.2.2 Bioequivalence Studies

Bioequivalence studies are a crucial component of an Abbreviated New Drug Application (ANDA) for generic pharmaceutical products. These studies compare the pharmacokinetic parameters of the generic drug product with those of the reference listed drug (RLD) to demonstrate bioequivalence, indicating similar rate and extent of drug absorption in the body. Key aspects of bioequivalence studies include:

1. Study Design: Bioequivalence studies are designed to compare the systemic exposure of the generic drug product and the RLD following administration under similar conditions. Typically, these studies are conducted in healthy human volunteers or patient populations using a randomized, crossover design. Subjects receive a single dose of the generic drug product and the RLD with a washout period between administrations to minimize carryover effects.

2. Pharmacokinetic Parameters: Bioequivalence is assessed by comparing the pharmacokinetic parameters of the generic drug product and the RLD, including peak plasma concentration (Cmax), time to reach peak concentration (Tmax), area under the plasma concentration-time curve (AUC), and terminal elimination half-life ($t_{1/2}$). These parameters provide insights into the rate and extent of drug absorption, distribution, metabolism, and excretion in the body.

3. Statistical Analysis: Statistical analysis is performed to evaluate the differences between the pharmacokinetic profiles of the generic drug product and the RLD. Bioequivalence is typically assessed using the ratio of geometric means (e.g., AUC and Cmax) and 90% confidence intervals (CI) to determine if the generic product falls within the predefined acceptance criteria (e.g., 80-125% for AUC and Cmax). Nonparametric methods may be used for Tmax if necessary.

4. Study Population: Bioequivalence studies are conducted in a representative study population that reflects the intended patient population for the generic drug product. Factors such as age, sex, race, and health status may influence drug absorption, distribution, metabolism, and excretion, so study participants should be selected accordingly. Special populations, such as pediatric, geriatric, or renally impaired patients, may require specific considerations in study design and analysis.

5. Formulation Considerations: Bioequivalence studies must be conducted using the final marketed formulation of the generic drug product, including the same dosage form, strength, and route of administration as the RLD. Formulation differences, such as excipients, coatings, or manufacturing processes, may affect drug dissolution, absorption, and bioavailability, so formulation equivalence must be demonstrated through comparative dissolution testing and in vitro studies.

6. Regulatory Requirements: Bioequivalence studies must adhere to regulatory guidelines and requirements established by regulatory authorities, such as the U.S. Food and Drug Administration (FDA) or the European Medicines Agency (EMA). Guidance documents provide recommendations on study design, conduct, analysis, and reporting of bioequivalence studies to ensure scientific rigor, reliability, and reproducibility of results.

3.3.2.3 Labeling and Packaging Information

Labeling and packaging information is an essential component of an Abbreviated New Drug Application (ANDA) submission for generic pharmaceutical products. This section provides detailed documentation of the labeling and packaging materials used for the generic drug product, ensuring compliance with regulatory requirements and facilitating safe and effective use by patients and healthcare professionals. Key elements of labeling and packaging information include:

1. Labeling Content: The labeling content includes the package insert, prescribing information, patient information leaflet, and outer and inner container labels. These documents provide essential information about the generic drug product, including its name, active ingredient(s), dosage form, strength, route of administration, indications, dosage and administration instructions, warnings, precautions, adverse reactions, contraindications, drug interactions, and storage conditions.

2. Generic Name and Brand Equivalence: The generic drug product is identified by its established nonproprietary name (generic name), which is commonly known as the International Nonproprietary Name (INN). The generic name must be prominently displayed on the labeling and packaging materials to ensure accurate identification and differentiation from brand-name products. Brand equivalence may be indicated by referencing the brand-name product's proprietary name or the reference listed drug (RLD) in the labeling.

3. Dosage Form and Strength: The dosage form and strength of the generic drug product are clearly stated on the labeling and packaging materials to facilitate accurate dosing and administration by patients and healthcare providers. Dosage form descriptors (e.g., tablets, capsules, injections, topical creams) and strength designations (e.g., mg, mL) are provided in standardized format to ensure consistency and clarity in product identification.

4. Administration Instructions: Instructions for dosage and administration of the generic drug product are included in the labeling content to guide patients and healthcare professionals in safe and effective medication use. Dosage and administration instructions specify the recommended dose, frequency of administration, method of administration (e.g., oral, topical, intravenous), and any special instructions (e.g., with food, at bedtime) to optimize therapeutic outcomes and minimize risks.

5. Warnings and Precautions: Warnings and precautions highlight important safety information and potential risks associated with the use of the generic drug product. These include warnings about adverse reactions, precautions for specific patient populations (e.g., pregnant women, pediatric patients), contraindications, drug interactions, and precautions for use (e.g., driving, operating machinery). Clear and concise warnings and precautions are provided to promote patient safety and minimize medication-related harm.

6. Packaging Materials: The packaging materials used for the generic drug product, including primary containers (e.g., bottles, blister packs, vials) and closure systems (e.g., caps, seals), are described in the labeling and packaging information. Specifications for packaging materials ensure product integrity, stability, compatibility, and protection from environmental factors (e.g., light, moisture, temperature). Information about packaging materials is provided to facilitate product identification, storage, and handling by patients and healthcare professionals.

3.3.3 Regulatory Review and Approval Process for ANDA

The regulatory review and approval process for an Abbreviated New Drug Application (ANDA) involves comprehensive evaluation by regulatory authorities, such as the U.S. Food and Drug Administration (FDA) in the United States. This process assesses the safety, efficacy, quality, and regulatory compliance of the generic drug product to ensure its approval for marketing and distribution. Key steps in the regulatory review and approval process for ANDA include:

1. ANDA Submission: The process begins with the submission of the ANDA to the regulatory authority, accompanied by comprehensive documentation and scientific data supporting the safety, efficacy, and quality of the generic drug product. The ANDA submission includes various sections, such as chemistry, manufacturing, and controls (CMC) information, bioequivalence studies, labeling and packaging information, and regulatory documentation.

2. Completeness Assessment: Upon receipt of the ANDA submission, the regulatory authority conducts an initial completeness assessment to ensure that all required documentation and information are included. The completeness assessment verifies the submission's adherence to regulatory guidelines, formatting requirements, and data integrity standards. Incomplete or deficient submissions may result in requests for additional information or clarification from the applicant.

3. Review and Evaluation: The regulatory authority conducts a thorough review and evaluation of the ANDA submission to assess the scientific validity, data integrity, and regulatory compliance of the generic drug product. This review encompasses multiple disciplines, including pharmaceutical sciences, pharmacology, toxicology, clinical research, and regulatory affairs. Each component of the ANDA submission undergoes detailed scrutiny to verify compliance with regulatory requirements and standards.

4. Chemistry, Manufacturing, and Controls (CMC) Review: The CMC section of the ANDA submission is reviewed to evaluate the pharmaceutical formulation, manufacturing process, quality control measures, and packaging materials of the generic drug product. This review assesses the adequacy of manufacturing processes, adherence to current Good Manufacturing Practices (cGMP), and consistency of product quality and performance.

5. Bioequivalence Assessment: Bioequivalence studies submitted as part of the ANDA are critically evaluated to determine the therapeutic equivalence and interchangeability of the generic drug product with the reference listed drug (RLD). The pharmacokinetic data generated from bioequivalence studies are analyzed to assess the rate and extent of drug absorption, ensuring similar systemic exposure and clinical outcomes between the generic and reference products.

6. Labeling and Packaging Review: The labeling and packaging information provided in the ANDA submission is reviewed to ensure compliance with regulatory requirements and standards. This review assesses the accuracy, completeness, and clarity of labeling content, including dosage form, strength, administration instructions, warnings, precautions, and packaging materials. The goal is to ensure safe and effective medication use by patients and healthcare professionals.

7. Regulatory Decision: Following the review and evaluation process, the regulatory authority makes a regulatory decision regarding the approval or rejection of the ANDA. If the generic drug product meets the criteria for approval, including demonstration of safety, efficacy, quality, and regulatory compliance, the regulatory authority grants approval for marketing and distribution. Approval may be subject to specific conditions, labeling requirements, or post-marketing surveillance obligations to ensure continued product safety and effectiveness.

3.3.4 Case Study: Successful ANDA Submission and Approval

In this case study, we'll explore the process and key factors leading to the successful submission and approval of an Abbreviated New Drug Application (ANDA) for a generic pharmaceutical product by a fictional company, Generic Pharma Inc.

Background: Generic Pharma Inc. aimed to develop and market a generic version of a widely prescribed cardiovascular medication, CardioX, which had recently lost its patent exclusivity. The company identified an opportunity to enter the market with a cost-effective alternative to CardioX, leveraging its expertise in pharmaceutical formulation, manufacturing, and regulatory affairs.

Key Steps and Strategies:

1. **Product Selection:** Generic Pharma Inc. conducted thorough market research and feasibility studies to identify CardioX as a suitable candidate for generic drug development. The medication's high demand, established therapeutic efficacy, and patent expiration made it an attractive target for generic entry.
2. **Formulation Development:** The company invested significant resources in formulation development to produce a generic version of CardioX with equivalent pharmaceutical properties and bioequivalence to the reference listed drug (RLD). Formulation scientists conducted extensive research and optimization studies to achieve comparable drug release, dissolution profiles, and pharmacokinetic parameters.
3. **Bioequivalence Studies:** Generic Pharma Inc. designed and executed bioequivalence studies to demonstrate the therapeutic equivalence and interchangeability of its generic CardioX product with the RLD. These studies involved rigorous pharmacokinetic assessments in healthy human volunteers to compare the systemic exposure of the generic and reference products, ensuring similar rates and extents of drug absorption.
4. **Regulatory Preparation:** The company meticulously prepared the ANDA submission, compiling comprehensive documentation, scientific data, and regulatory information to support the safety, efficacy, and quality of its generic CardioX product. Regulatory experts ensured adherence to regulatory guidelines, formatting requirements, and data integrity standards throughout the submission process.
5. **Labeling and Packaging Compliance:** Generic Pharma Inc. developed labeling and packaging materials that complied with regulatory requirements and standards for generic drug products. The labeling content, including dosage form, strength, administration instructions, warnings, precautions, and packaging materials, was carefully reviewed and verified to ensure accuracy, completeness, and clarity.
6. **Regulatory Submission:** Upon completion of the ANDA preparation, Generic Pharma Inc. submitted the application to the regulatory authority, accompanied by all required documentation and supporting data. The company facilitated ongoing communication and collaboration

with regulatory reviewers to address any questions, requests for clarification, or additional information during the review process.

Outcome: Generic Pharma Inc. successfully obtained regulatory approval for its generic CardioX product following a thorough review and evaluation process by the regulatory authority. The ANDA submission demonstrated the safety, efficacy, quality, and regulatory compliance of the generic drug product, including pharmaceutical equivalence and bioequivalence to the RLD. Regulatory approval enabled Generic Pharma Inc. to market and distribute its generic CardioX medication, providing patients with a cost-effective alternative to the brand-name product and contributing to increased accessibility and affordability of cardiovascular treatment options.

Key Success Factors:

- Strategic Product Selection
- Formulation Development Expertise
- Rigorous Bioequivalence Studies
- Regulatory Compliance and Preparation
- Labeling and Packaging Compliance
- Ongoing Communication and Collaboration with Regulatory Authorities

3.4 Regulatory Pathways Comparison: IND vs. ANDA

3.4.1 Contrasting Characteristics of IND and ANDA Processes

The Investigational New Drug (IND) application process and the Abbreviated New Drug Application (ANDA) process are two distinct regulatory pathways governing the development and approval of pharmaceutical products in the United States. While both pathways are regulated by the U.S. Food and Drug Administration (FDA), they serve different purposes and involve distinct requirements and procedures. Here, we contrast the key characteristics of the IND and ANDA processes:

1. Purpose:

- **IND Process:** The IND process is intended for the submission of applications to conduct clinical trials of investigational drugs or biologics in humans. It allows sponsors to initiate clinical testing of new drugs or biologics, including first-in-human trials, to evaluate safety, efficacy, and pharmacokinetics.

- **ANDA Process:** The ANDA process is designed for the submission of applications to obtain approval for generic versions of previously approved brand-name drugs (reference listed drugs). It allows sponsors to demonstrate bioequivalence and pharmaceutical equivalence to the reference product, without the need for extensive clinical trials.

2. Product Type:

- **IND Process:** The IND process is applicable to investigational drugs, biologics, and biosimilars that have not yet been approved for marketing by the FDA. These products are typically in early stages of development and require clinical testing to assess safety and efficacy.
- **ANDA Process:** The ANDA process is applicable to generic pharmaceutical products intended to be marketed as substitutes for existing brand-name drugs that have already been approved by the FDA. These products are required to demonstrate pharmaceutical equivalence and bioequivalence to the reference product.

3. Clinical Trials:

- **IND Process:** IND sponsors are required to conduct clinical trials to assess the safety, efficacy, and pharmacokinetics of the investigational product in human subjects. These trials progress through phases (I, II, III) to gather data supporting regulatory approval.
- **ANDA Process:** Clinical trials are generally not required as part of the ANDA submission, as generic products are intended to be therapeutically equivalent to the reference product. Instead, bioequivalence studies are conducted to demonstrate comparable systemic exposure between the generic product and the reference product.

4. Data Requirements:

- **IND Process:** IND submissions must include preclinical data, clinical trial protocols, investigator information, manufacturing details, pharmacology and toxicology data, and regulatory documentation to support the proposed clinical testing.

- **ANDA Process:** ANDA submissions must include chemistry, manufacturing, and controls (CMC) information, bioequivalence studies, labeling and packaging information, and regulatory documentation demonstrating pharmaceutical equivalence and bioequivalence to the reference product.

5. Approval Criteria:

- **IND Process:** FDA approval of an IND allows sponsors to proceed with clinical trials, provided that safety and ethical standards are met. Subsequent regulatory approval for marketing (New Drug Application, Biologics License Application) requires demonstration of safety and efficacy in clinical trials.
- **ANDA Process:** FDA approval of an ANDA is based on the demonstration of pharmaceutical equivalence and bioequivalence to the reference product. Therapeutic equivalence is assumed, allowing for substitution with the reference product without additional clinical testing.

6. Market Entry:

- **IND Process:** Market entry occurs following successful completion of clinical trials and FDA approval of a New Drug Application (NDA) or Biologics License Application (BLA). Approval allows sponsors to market the drug for its indicated use.
- **ANDA Process:** Market entry occurs following FDA approval of the ANDA submission. Once approved, generic products can be marketed as therapeutically equivalent alternatives to the reference product.

3.4.2 Key Differences in Regulatory Requirements

The regulatory requirements for the Investigational New Drug (IND) application process and the Abbreviated New Drug Application (ANDA) process vary significantly due to their distinct purposes and objectives in the drug development and approval lifecycle. Here are the key differences in regulatory requirements between the two pathways:

1. Preclinical and Clinical Data:

- **IND Process:** Preclinical data, including pharmacology and toxicology studies, are required to assess the safety and potential efficacy of the investigational drug or biologic in animal models before human testing. Clinical data from human trials are subsequently generated to evaluate safety, efficacy, and pharmacokinetics in phases (I, II, III) of clinical development.
- **ANDA Process:** Preclinical and clinical data are generally not required as part of the ANDA submission, as generic products are intended to be bioequivalent to previously approved reference products. Instead, bioequivalence studies are conducted to demonstrate comparable systemic exposure between the generic product and the reference product in healthy human volunteers.

2. Manufacturing and Controls:

- **IND Process:** Detailed information about the manufacturing process, controls, and specifications for drug substance and drug product are required in the IND application. Sponsors must demonstrate the ability to manufacture the investigational product consistently and ensure product quality and stability throughout clinical development.
- **ANDA Process:** The Chemistry, Manufacturing, and Controls (CMC) section of the ANDA submission focuses on demonstrating pharmaceutical equivalence to the reference product. Sponsors must provide comprehensive information about the manufacturing process, controls, and specifications to ensure that the generic product is pharmaceutically equivalent and meets regulatory standards.

3. Bioequivalence Studies:

- **IND Process:** Bioequivalence studies are not typically required as part of the IND application process. Instead, clinical trials focus on assessing safety, efficacy, and pharmacokinetics to support regulatory approval for marketing.
- **ANDA Process:** Bioequivalence studies are a critical component of the ANDA submission, demonstrating that the generic product is therapeutically equivalent to the reference product. Sponsors must conduct comparative bioavailability and bioequivalence studies to establish similar systemic exposure and pharmacokinetic profiles

between the generic and reference products.

4. Labeling and Packaging:

- **IND Process:** Labeling and packaging requirements focus on providing clear and concise information to clinical trial participants, investigators, and institutional review boards (IRBs) regarding the investigational product's use, safety, and handling instructions.
- **ANDA Process:** Labeling and packaging requirements for generic products are similar to those for brand-name products. Sponsors must provide comprehensive labeling content, including dosage form, strength, administration instructions, warnings, precautions, and packaging materials, consistent with the reference product's labeling.

5. Approval Criteria:

- **IND Process:** FDA approval of an IND allows sponsors to initiate clinical trials, provided that safety and ethical standards are met. Subsequent regulatory approval for marketing (New Drug Application, Biologics License Application) requires demonstration of safety and efficacy in clinical trials.
- **ANDA Process:** FDA approval of an ANDA is based on the demonstration of pharmaceutical equivalence and bioequivalence to the reference product. Therapeutic equivalence is assumed, allowing for substitution with the reference product without additional clinical testing.

3.4.3 Considerations for Choosing between IND and ANDA Routes

When deciding between the Investigational New Drug (IND) application process and the Abbreviated New Drug Application (ANDA) process, sponsors and pharmaceutical companies must carefully consider various factors to determine the most appropriate regulatory pathway for their product. Here are key considerations for choosing between the IND and ANDA routes:

1. Product Type:

- **New Drug Development (IND):** If the product is a novel drug or biologic that has not been previously approved by regulatory authorities, the

IND pathway is typically the appropriate choice. This pathway allows sponsors to conduct clinical trials to evaluate safety, efficacy, and pharmacokinetics in human subjects.

- **Generic Drug Development (ANDA):** If the product is intended to be a generic version of an existing brand-name drug that has already been approved by regulatory authorities, the ANDA pathway is the appropriate choice. This pathway allows sponsors to demonstrate pharmaceutical equivalence and bioequivalence to the reference product without the need for extensive clinical trials.

2. Development Stage:

- **Early-Stage Development (IND):** If the product is in the early stages of development, such as preclinical research or phase I/II clinical trials, the IND pathway is suitable. This pathway allows sponsors to initiate clinical testing to assess safety, efficacy, and pharmacokinetics in human subjects.
- **Late-Stage Development (ANDA):** If the product is a generic version of an existing brand-name drug and has already undergone extensive clinical testing, the ANDA pathway is appropriate. This pathway allows sponsors to demonstrate bioequivalence to the reference product and obtain regulatory approval for marketing.

3. Regulatory Requirements:

- **Data Requirements (IND):** The IND pathway requires comprehensive preclinical and clinical data to support safety, efficacy, and pharmacokinetics. Sponsors must conduct extensive studies and provide detailed information about manufacturing, controls, and labeling.
- **Bioequivalence Studies (ANDA):** The ANDA pathway requires bioequivalence studies to demonstrate that the generic product is therapeutically equivalent to the reference product. Sponsors must conduct comparative bioavailability and bioequivalence studies in healthy human volunteers.

4. Time and Cost:

- **Time (IND):** The IND pathway may require more time for product development, preclinical and clinical testing, regulatory review, and approval. Clinical trials may take several years to complete before regulatory approval for marketing is obtained.
- **Cost (ANDA):** The ANDA pathway may be more cost-effective than the IND pathway, as it generally does not require extensive clinical trials. Sponsors can leverage existing clinical data for the reference product and focus on demonstrating bioequivalence to streamline development and regulatory review.

5. Market Opportunities:

- **Market Entry (ANDA):** The ANDA pathway allows for expedited market entry of generic products following regulatory approval. Generic products can capture market share quickly and compete with brand-name products, especially when patents expire and market exclusivity ends.
- **Innovation (IND):** The IND pathway allows for the development of innovative new drugs or biologics with potential for significant therapeutic impact. Sponsors may pursue this pathway to address unmet medical needs and capitalize on market opportunities for novel treatments.

3.5 Compliance and Post-Approval Obligations

3.5.1 Good Manufacturing Practices (GMP) Compliance

Good Manufacturing Practices (GMP) are essential standards that ensure the quality, safety, and efficacy of pharmaceutical products throughout the manufacturing process. Compliance with GMP regulations is a fundamental requirement for pharmaceutical manufacturers to maintain product quality and regulatory compliance. Here are the key aspects of GMP compliance:

1. Facility Design and Maintenance:

- Pharmaceutical manufacturing facilities must be designed, constructed, and maintained in a manner that prevents contamination, cross-contamination, and mix-ups. Adequate space, ventilation, and segregation of manufacturing areas are essential to ensure product quality and integrity.

2. Equipment Qualification and Calibration:

- Manufacturing equipment used in pharmaceutical production must be qualified, calibrated, and maintained according to established procedures and standards. Equipment validation ensures that it functions reliably and consistently to produce products that meet quality specifications.

3. Personnel Training and Hygiene:

- Personnel involved in pharmaceutical manufacturing must receive appropriate training and education to perform their duties effectively and in compliance with GMP regulations. Training programs cover topics such as hygiene practices, gowning procedures, and proper handling of materials to prevent contamination.

4. Raw Material Control:

- Pharmaceutical manufacturers must establish procedures for the receipt, storage, handling, and testing of raw materials used in the production process. Raw material testing ensures that materials meet specified quality standards before use in manufacturing.

5. Process Validation:

- Manufacturing processes must be validated to demonstrate consistency, reliability, and reproducibility in producing pharmaceutical products that meet predetermined specifications. Process validation involves documenting and evaluating critical process parameters to ensure product quality and performance.

6. Quality Control Testing:

- Quality control testing is conducted throughout the manufacturing process to monitor product quality and ensure compliance with specifications. In-process testing, finished product testing, and stability testing are essential components of quality control to verify product attributes and stability over time.

7. Documentation and Recordkeeping:

- Comprehensive documentation and recordkeeping are critical aspects of GMP compliance. Pharmaceutical manufacturers must maintain accurate and complete records of manufacturing activities, testing results, deviations, investigations, and corrective actions to demonstrate compliance with regulatory requirements.

8. Quality Management Systems:

- Pharmaceutical manufacturers must establish and maintain robust quality management systems (QMS) to ensure effective oversight of GMP activities and continuous improvement of processes. QMS elements include quality policies, procedures, risk management, and performance monitoring to maintain product quality and regulatory compliance.

9. Inspections and Audits:

- Regulatory authorities conduct routine inspections and audits of pharmaceutical manufacturing facilities to assess GMP compliance and adherence to regulatory standards. Inspections may be conducted by regulatory agencies such as the FDA to verify compliance with GMP regulations and identify areas for improvement.

3.5.2 Post-Market Surveillance and Reporting Requirements

Post-market surveillance (PMS) and reporting requirements are crucial elements of pharmaceutical regulation aimed at monitoring the safety, efficacy, and quality of marketed drugs and ensuring timely reporting of adverse events and product defects. Here are the key aspects of post-market surveillance and reporting requirements:

1. Adverse Event Reporting:

- Pharmaceutical companies are required to establish systems for the collection, evaluation, and reporting of adverse events associated with their marketed products. Adverse events include any untoward medical occurrence, whether expected or unexpected, occurring during the use of the drug, regardless of its causal relationship with the product.

2. Pharmacovigilance Systems:

- Pharmacovigilance systems are established to systematically monitor and assess the safety profile of marketed drugs throughout their lifecycle. These systems involve the collection, analysis, and evaluation of safety data from various sources, including spontaneous reports, clinical studies, literature, and regulatory databases.

3. Serious Adverse Event Reporting:

- Pharmaceutical companies are required to report serious and unexpected adverse events to regulatory authorities within specified timeframes. Serious adverse events are those that result in death, life-threatening conditions, hospitalization, disability, congenital anomalies, or other significant medical events.

4. Periodic Safety Update Reports (PSURs):

- Periodic Safety Update Reports (PSURs) are comprehensive summaries of the safety profile of a marketed drug submitted to regulatory authorities at predefined intervals. PSURs provide an overview of safety data, including adverse events, product complaints, and risk-benefit assessments, to support ongoing regulatory oversight.

5. Risk Evaluation and Mitigation Strategies (REMS):

- Risk Evaluation and Mitigation Strategies (REMS) are required for certain drugs with known or potential serious risks to ensure safe use by patients. REMS may include elements such as medication guides, communication plans, healthcare provider education, and restricted distribution programs to mitigate identified risks.

6. Product Quality Monitoring:

- Pharmaceutical companies are responsible for monitoring the quality of their marketed products to ensure compliance with established specifications and standards. Product quality monitoring involves routine testing, sampling, and analysis of finished products, stability studies, and ongoing assessment of manufacturing processes.

7. Field Safety Corrective Actions (FSCAs):

- In the event of product defects, quality issues, or safety concerns, pharmaceutical companies are required to implement Field Safety Corrective Actions (FSCAs) to address the issue promptly and mitigate potential risks to patients. FSCAs may include product recalls, market withdrawals, product modifications, or labeling updates.

8. Post-Market Studies:

- Post-market studies may be required by regulatory authorities to further evaluate the safety, efficacy, or use of a marketed drug in real-world clinical practice. These studies provide additional data to inform regulatory decisions, update product labeling, or address specific safety concerns identified during post-market surveillance.

9. Regulatory Reporting Obligations:

- Pharmaceutical companies have regulatory reporting obligations to communicate safety-related information to regulatory authorities in accordance with applicable regulations and guidelines. Timely and accurate reporting of adverse events, product defects, recalls, and other safety-related issues is essential for regulatory oversight and public health protection.

3.5.3 Labeling Updates and Variations

Labeling updates and variations are important aspects of pharmaceutical regulation that allow manufacturers to ensure that product labeling reflects the most current information regarding safety, efficacy, and usage. Here are key considerations regarding labeling updates and variations:

1. Labeling Updates:

- **Safety Information:** Manufacturers are required to promptly update product labeling to include new safety information, such as adverse reactions, warnings, precautions, and contraindications, identified through post-marketing surveillance, clinical studies, or regulatory review.

- **Efficacy Updates:** Labeling may also be updated to reflect new efficacy data, indications, dosing recommendations, or administration instructions resulting from clinical trials, post-market studies, or regulatory approval for expanded indications.
- **Quality Updates:** Updates to labeling may also be made to address changes in product quality, formulation, manufacturing processes, or packaging that could impact product safety, efficacy, or usage.

2. Labeling Variations:

- **Labeling Supplements:** Manufacturers submit labeling supplements to regulatory authorities to request changes to product labeling that do not require prior approval, such as editorial changes, formatting updates, or minor corrections to text or graphics.
- **Labeling Changes:** Changes to product labeling that require prior approval, such as updates to indications, dosing, safety information, or warnings, may require submission of a prior approval supplement (PAS) or a supplemental new drug application (sNDA) for review and approval by regulatory authorities.

3. Safety Labeling Changes (SLCs):

- **Safety Communication:** Safety Labeling Changes (SLCs) are updates to product labeling required by regulatory authorities to communicate new safety information, including boxed warnings, contraindications, warnings, precautions, and adverse reactions, identified through post-marketing surveillance or regulatory review.
- **Implementation Deadline:** Manufacturers are typically given a specified timeframe to implement required SLCs following regulatory approval, ensuring timely dissemination of updated safety information to healthcare providers and patients.

4. Labeling Review Process:

- **Regulatory Review:** Proposed labeling updates or variations undergo regulatory review by authorities such as the U.S. Food and Drug Administration (FDA) or the European Medicines Agency (EMA) to assess the scientific validity, accuracy, and appropriateness of the proposed changes.

- **Approval Process:** Regulatory authorities may require submission of supporting data, analyses, or justifications to support proposed labeling updates or variations. Once approved, manufacturers are authorized to implement the changes in product labeling.

5. Communication and Implementation:

- **Healthcare Provider Communication:** Manufacturers are responsible for communicating labeling updates and variations to healthcare providers through Dear Healthcare Provider (DHCP) letters, package inserts, product websites, or educational materials to ensure awareness and understanding of changes.
- **Patient Communication:** Manufacturers may also communicate labeling changes directly to patients through patient information leaflets, medication guides, or consumer websites to promote safe and effective use of the product.

3.5.4 Pharmacovigilance and Adverse Event Monitoring

Pharmacovigilance and adverse event monitoring are critical components of pharmaceutical regulation aimed at identifying, evaluating, and mitigating risks associated with the use of marketed drugs. Here are the key aspects of pharmacovigilance and adverse event monitoring:

1. Adverse Event Reporting Systems:

- Pharmaceutical companies are required to establish robust systems for the collection, evaluation, and reporting of adverse events associated with their marketed products. These systems capture information on adverse reactions, product complaints, medication errors, and other untoward medical occurrences related to drug use.

2. Spontaneous Reporting:

- Spontaneous reporting involves the voluntary submission of adverse event reports by healthcare professionals, patients, consumers, and pharmaceutical companies to regulatory authorities or drug manufacturers. Spontaneous reports provide valuable real-world data on the safety profile of marketed drugs.

3. Expedited Reporting:

- Certain serious and unexpected adverse events require expedited reporting to regulatory authorities within specified timeframes. Expedited reporting is mandatory for events such as death, life-threatening conditions, hospitalization, congenital anomalies, or other serious medical events suspected to be associated with drug use.

4. Signal Detection:

- Signal detection involves the systematic analysis of adverse event data to identify potential safety signals or new safety concerns associated with marketed drugs. Statistical algorithms, data mining techniques, and qualitative assessments are used to detect patterns, trends, or associations indicative of safety issues.

5. Risk Assessment and Evaluation:

- Once potential safety signals are identified, regulatory authorities and pharmaceutical companies conduct thorough risk assessments and evaluations to determine the significance, causality, and clinical implications of the observed safety concerns. This process involves reviewing available data, conducting epidemiological studies, and consulting expert opinions.

6. Risk Management Strategies:

- Risk management strategies are implemented to mitigate identified risks and minimize potential harm to patients. These strategies may include updating product labeling, implementing risk minimization measures, conducting post-marketing studies, or restricting drug use through Risk Evaluation and Mitigation Strategies (REMS).

7. Periodic Safety Update Reports (PSURs):

- Periodic Safety Update Reports (PSURs) are comprehensive summaries of the safety profile of a marketed drug submitted to regulatory authorities at predefined intervals. PSURs provide an overview of safety data, including adverse events, product complaints, and risk-benefit assessments, to support ongoing regulatory oversight.

8. Collaboration and Communication:

- Effective collaboration and communication among regulatory authorities, healthcare professionals, pharmaceutical companies, and patients are essential for timely identification, evaluation, and management of drug safety concerns. Regular updates, safety communications, and educational initiatives enhance awareness and understanding of drug risks and promote patient safety.

CHAPTER FOUR

CLINICAL TRIALS: AN OVERVIEW

4.1 Introduction to Clinical Trials

4.1.1 What are Clinical Trials?

Clinical trials are research studies conducted to evaluate the safety and efficacy of new drugs, medical devices, or treatment strategies in humans. These trials are fundamental to the development of new medical interventions that can offer better outcomes for patients dealing with various diseases and conditions. The primary goal of clinical trials is to gather data on the effectiveness and safety of a new intervention, ensuring that it provides a measurable improvement over existing treatments while not posing undue risk to participants.

The process begins with the development of a hypothesis based on preliminary research, which may involve laboratory studies or experiments on animal models. Once a potential treatment shows promise, it proceeds to clinical trials, which are conducted in several phases to systematically test the intervention across different populations and various medical settings. These trials are crucial for determining the appropriate dosage, understanding side effects, and establishing how the treatment interacts with the human body.

Regulatory authorities, such as the U.S. Food and Drug Administration (FDA) or the European Medicines Agency (EMA), require a rigorous and structured approach to clinical trials to ensure that any new therapy is both effective and safe before it is approved for public use. This approval process is critical as it protects the public from potential harms of untested treatments.

In addition to testing efficacy and safety, clinical trials also explore other important aspects of medical treatments, such as quality of life outcomes, cost-effectiveness, and long-term benefits and risks. This comprehensive evaluation helps in making informed decisions about whether a treatment should be used widely.

Clinical trials are not only a key step in medical research but also a crucial element in advancing medical science and improving health care. They involve collaboration among scientists, doctors, regulatory authorities, and most importantly, the participants who volunteer to be part of these trials, contributing significantly to medical advances and the development of better treatments.

4.1.2 Importance and Objectives of Clinical Trials

Clinical trials play an indispensable role in the advancement of medical science, serving as the bridge between laboratory research and clinical practice. The primary objectives of clinical trials are multifaceted, focusing on ensuring safety, determining efficacy, and enhancing medical knowledge.

Safety: The foremost objective of clinical trials is to ensure the safety of new interventions. Before any new treatment can be recommended for widespread use, it must undergo rigorous testing to evaluate its safety profile. This includes identifying any potential side effects, understanding the severity of these effects, and determining the risk factors associated with the treatment. Safety assessments help in establishing safe dosage ranges and identifying any contraindications, where the treatment should not be used.

Efficacy: Another critical objective is to test the efficacy of new treatments. Clinical trials aim to confirm that the new intervention works as intended to treat, prevent, or diagnose a disease. This is measured through specific outcomes determined before the trial begins, such as the reduction in tumor size in cancer treatment trials or improvement in mobility in trials for orthopedic devices. Efficacy trials often compare the new treatment against a placebo or the current standard treatment to gauge its relative effectiveness.

Optimization: Clinical trials also seek to optimize the use of medical interventions. This includes figuring out the most effective administration routes, timing of administration, and whether a combination of treatments is more effective than individual treatments alone. This optimization helps in tailoring treatments to individual needs, which is a key aspect of personalized medicine.

Regulatory Approval: Gaining regulatory approval is a significant objective of clinical trials. The data collected from these trials form the basis for regulatory bodies to approve or reject new treatments for use in the public. This rigorous scrutiny ensures that only those interventions that meet stringent safety and efficacy standards reach the market.

Advancing Knowledge: Beyond immediate treatment concerns, clinical trials also contribute to the broader scientific knowledge base. They can provide insights into disease mechanisms, help in identifying biomarkers for early disease detection, and foster innovations in drug development and disease management strategies.

Patient Outcomes: Ultimately, the aim of all clinical trials is to improve patient outcomes. This not only means developing treatments that are effective but also ensuring that these treatments are accessible and improve the quality of life for patients. Clinical trials often explore how treatments can reduce symptoms, prolong life, and improve the overall quality of health care delivery.

Through these objectives, clinical trials ensure that medical advancements are safe, effective, and optimized for the best possible patient outcomes, driving forward the frontiers of healthcare and treatment methodologies.

4.1.3 Ethical Considerations

Ethical considerations are central to the design and conduct of clinical trials, ensuring the rights, safety, and well-being of participants are protected while maintaining the integrity of the scientific process. The ethical principles governing clinical trials are derived from key documents like the Declaration of Helsinki and are enforced through regulations and guidelines at both international and national levels.

Informed Consent: The cornerstone of ethical clinical trials is informed consent. Participants must be fully informed about the nature of the study, including its purpose, duration, required procedures, potential risks and benefits, and their right to withdraw from the study at any time without penalty. Consent must be given voluntarily, without any coercion, and participants should understand all aspects of the trial before agreeing to partake.

Risk Minimization: Researchers are obligated to minimize potential risks to participants. This involves conducting thorough preclinical testing and ensuring that the clinical trial is scientifically sound and likely to yield meaningful results. During the trial, continuous monitoring is essential to identify and address any adverse effects that arise.

Benefit-Risk Assessment: Ethical clinical trials require a favorable benefit-risk balance. This means that the potential benefits to the participant and society must outweigh the risks involved in the study. Decisions about whether to proceed with or modify a clinical trial are often guided by an independent ethics committee or institutional review board, which evaluates the study's benefit-risk profile.

Confidentiality: Protecting the confidentiality of trial participants is another crucial ethical concern. Personal information and medical data must be handled securely and disclosed only with the participant's consent or as required by law, ensuring privacy and respecting the confidentiality of participants.

Vulnerable Populations: Special considerations are required when involving vulnerable populations in clinical trials, such as children, pregnant women, or individuals with cognitive impairments. These groups require additional protections to ensure they are not unduly burdened or coerced into participation.

Equitable Selection: The selection of participants should be equitable, ensuring that no group is unfairly burdened with the risks of research or unjustly denied the benefits of participation. Researchers must avoid exploiting vulnerable groups and ensure that the selection criteria are based on scientific objectives rather than convenience or vulnerability.

Post-Trial Access: Ethical considerations also extend beyond the end of the trial. Participants should have access to the best proven interventions identified by the study, and plans for post-trial access should be discussed as part of the informed consent process.

4.1.4 Role of Regulatory Authorities

Regulatory authorities play a crucial role in overseeing clinical trials to ensure they are conducted according to the highest standards of safety, efficacy, and ethical practice. These bodies are responsible for protecting public health by rigorously evaluating the data from clinical trials to make informed decisions about whether new medical products should be approved for market entry.

Approval and Oversight: Before a clinical trial can begin, it must receive approval from a regulatory authority, such as the U.S. Food and Drug Administration (FDA) or the European Medicines Agency (EMA). This involves reviewing the trial protocol to ensure that the study is scientifically sound and that it includes adequate measures to protect participants. The protocol review also assesses the ethical considerations, including the process for obtaining informed consent and plans for managing and reporting adverse events.

Monitoring Compliance: Once a trial is underway, regulatory authorities monitor its progress to ensure compliance with regulatory standards and good clinical practice (GCP) guidelines. This includes regular inspections of trial sites, reviewing the qualifications of the research team, and ensuring that data is collected, recorded, and reported accurately. Monitoring also involves verifying that the rights and welfare of participants are being upheld throughout the study.

Data Review and Drug Approval: After the completion of a clinical trial, regulatory authorities review the collected data to decide whether the investigated treatment is safe and effective for its intended use. This review process is comprehensive and can involve not only the data from the trial itself but also data from other relevant studies, scientific literature, and post-market surveillance reports. If the benefits of the drug or device outweigh the risks, the regulatory authority will approve it for sale and use within their jurisdiction.

Setting Standards: Regulatory authorities are also involved in setting and updating standards for clinical trial conduct. These standards include guidelines for trial design, implementation, monitoring, data integrity, and reporting. By setting these standards, regulatory bodies ensure consistency and reliability in the trials conducted within their regions, facilitating the development of safe and effective medical treatments.

Public Communication: Transparency with the public is another important role of regulatory authorities. They provide information about ongoing and completed trials, decisions made regarding drug approvals, and any safety concerns that arise from new or existing treatments. This communication helps to maintain public trust in the medical research process and the safety of medical products on the market.

Through these activities, regulatory authorities ensure that clinical trials are conducted ethically, safely, and efficiently, safeguarding public health while enabling the advancement of medical science.

4.2 Phases of Clinical Trials

Clinical trials are typically conducted in a series of phases, each designed to answer specific research questions and ensure the progressive evaluation of a new medical intervention's safety and efficacy. Each phase is critical, building on the results of earlier phases to comprehensively assess the treatment's overall value.

4.2.1 Phase I: Safety and Dosage

- **4.2.1.1 Overview of Phase I Trials**: Phase I trials are the first stage of testing in human subjects. Primarily focused on safety, these trials assess the side effects associated with increasing doses. The main goal is to determine a drug's toxicity profile and identify the maximum tolerated dose.
- **4.2.1.2 Participant Selection**: Typically involving a small number of healthy volunteers (20-100), these studies are designed to ensure a controlled environment where the pharmacokinetics and pharmacodynamics of the drug can be closely monitored.
- **4.2.1.3 Objectives and Study Design**: The design of Phase I trials is often open-label and non-randomized. This phase includes initial trials, such as first-in-human (FIH) and dose-escalation studies, to establish a safe dosage range and identify potential side effects.

4.2.2 Phase II: Efficacy and Side Effects

- **4.2.2.1 Overview of Phase II Trials**: Once the safety of the drug is confirmed in Phase I, Phase II trials focus on evaluating the efficacy of the drug for a particular indication in patients with the disease or condition. This phase aims to determine the preliminary efficacy and further assess safety.
- **4.2.2.2 Participant Selection**: These trials involve larger groups of patients (100-300) who have the condition for which the treatment is being developed. The selection is more targeted compared to Phase I.
- **4.2.2.3 Objectives and Study Design**: Phase II trials are often randomized and controlled, and can include "proof-of-concept" studies that help to determine whether a drug works in humans as it is expected based on preclinical models.

4.2.3 Phase III: Efficacy and Monitoring Adverse Reactions

- **4.2.3.1 Overview of Phase III Trials**: This phase involves randomized and blind testing in several hundred to several thousand patients. The objective is to gather more comprehensive information on efficacy and safety, and to evaluate the overall benefit-risk relationship of the drug.

- **4.2.3.2 Participant Selection**: Phase III trials have a broad population of patients who are more representative of the general public. These participants have the condition or disease the drug is meant to treat, ensuring that the results are applicable to a wider group.
- **4.2.3.3 Objectives and Study Design**: These studies are typically multicenter trials that compare the new intervention against the standard existing treatment. This phase is crucial for the approval process, providing the definitive data on which regulatory decisions are based.

4.2.4 Phase IV: Post-Marketing Surveillance

- **4.2.4.1 Overview of Phase IV Trials**: Also known as post-marketing surveillance trials, these are conducted after a drug has been approved for use by the regulatory authorities. They monitor the drug's long-term effectiveness and continued safety in a larger, more diverse population.
- **4.2.4.2 Objectives and Study Design**: The main objectives are to detect any rare or long-term adverse effects over a much larger patient population and longer time period than is possible during Phase I to III trials. These studies are crucial for optimizing drug use in clinical practice and may lead to changes in treatment recommendations or further labeling changes.

The structured progression through these phases ensures that by the time a pharmaceutical product reaches the market, it has undergone a thorough evaluation to establish its safety and effectiveness, significantly reducing the risks and uncertainties associated with new medical treatments.

4.2.1 Phase I: Safety and Dosage

4.2.1.1 Overview of Phase I Trials: Phase I trials represent the initial step in testing a new medical intervention in humans, primarily focusing on safety assessment. This phase is crucial for determining how the human body reacts to the drug, particularly in terms of safety and pharmacokinetics, which is the study of how the drug is absorbed, distributed, metabolized, and excreted in the body. These trials are generally the first-time exposure of the compound to a small group of healthy volunteers, although some drugs, especially those used in cancer treatment, might be tested directly in patients with the disease due to their potential toxicity.

4.2.1.2 Safety and Dose Determination: The primary purpose of Phase I trials is to determine the drug's safety profile and identify the maximum tolerated dose (MTD). Researchers start with a very low dose and gradually increase it among subsequent groups of participants, monitoring the subjects closely for any adverse reactions. This dose-escalation strategy helps pinpoint the dose at which the drug demonstrates the best balance between efficacy and acceptable side effects. The findings from these trials inform dosage guidelines and provide critical safety data for later phases.

4.2.1.3 Study Design and Methods: Phase I trials are typically non-randomized, open-label studies, meaning both the researchers and participants know what is being administered. This phase does not aim to show whether the drug treats the disease but rather assesses its safety, which is why a control group is often not used. Common designs include single ascending dose (SAD) and multiple ascending dose (MAD) studies. SAD studies focus on understanding the pharmacokinetics after a single dose, while MAD studies examine the effects of multiple doses.

4.2.1.4 Participant Selection: Although most Phase I trials involve healthy volunteers, the selection criteria are stringent, with participants undergoing thorough screening to ensure they have no underlying health conditions that could skew the results or put them at greater risk. In trials involving severe diseases like cancer, participants may be patients who have the condition and have not responded to other treatments.

4.2.1.5 Ethical Considerations: Ethical oversight is critical in Phase I trials, given the potential risks involved with untested treatments. Informed consent is meticulously obtained, ensuring participants are fully aware of the potential risks and their rights, including the right to withdraw from the trial at any point. Ethics committees closely monitor these studies to ensure compliance with safety protocols.

4.2.1.6 Challenges and Limitations: One of the main challenges of Phase I trials is balancing the need for information on drug safety with the ethical implications of exposing individuals to potentially harmful substances. The limited participant number also means that less common side effects may not be detected during this phase.

Phase I trials are essential for laying the groundwork for further clinical development, providing the necessary safety data to proceed with confidence in exploring the therapeutic potential of new drugs in more targeted patient populations.

4.2.1.1 Objectives and Study Design

Objectives of Phase I Trials: The primary objective of Phase I clinical trials is to evaluate the safety profile of a new drug. This initial phase of testing in humans is designed to determine the safe dosage range and identify any side effects associated with increasing doses. Specifically, these trials aim to ascertain the maximum tolerated dose (MTD) — the highest dose of the drug that can be given with acceptable side effects. Additionally, Phase I trials seek to understand the pharmacokinetics (PK) and pharmacodynamics (PD) of the drug, which involve studying how the drug is absorbed, distributed, metabolized, and excreted in the body, as well as its mechanisms of action and effects on the body.

Study Design: Phase I trials are generally conducted using an open-label, non-randomized approach. This design allows researchers to carefully monitor and adjust the dosing regimen based on real-time observations of participants' responses to the drug. The studies often employ one of the following specific designs:

- **Single Ascending Dose (SAD) Studies**: These involve administering a single dose of the drug to a small group of participants, followed by analysis of pharmacokinetic and pharmacodynamic parameters. After ensuring safety at one dose level, a higher dose is then given to a new group of participants. This escalation continues until the MTD is reached or significant side effects prevent further increases.
- **Multiple Ascending Dose (MAD) Studies**: In these studies, multiple doses of the drug are administered to the same group of participants over a period of time. The objective is to observe the effects of the drug when it is administered repeatedly, which helps in understanding its safety and efficacy over extended use.
- **Adaptive Trial Designs**: Some Phase I trials utilize adaptive designs, where the protocol allows for modifications based on interim data from participants already enrolled in the study. This flexibility can include adjustments to dosage, sample size, or eligibility criteria, which helps optimize the trial's efficiency and safety.

Participant Selection: Phase I trials typically involve a small number of healthy volunteers, though patient populations may also be included, particularly in oncology trials. The selection is rigorous, often excluding individuals with comorbid conditions that could confound the results or increase the risk of adverse effects.

Safety Monitoring: Due to the experimental nature of the treatments being tested, safety monitoring is a critical component of Phase I trials. This includes continuous oversight by medical professionals, regular health assessments, and specific protocols to manage adverse effects, ensuring the well-being of participants throughout the study.

Ethical Considerations: Given the potential risks associated with unproven treatments, ethical considerations are paramount. Informed consent must be obtained from all participants, ensuring they understand the risks and benefits and agree to the terms of participation without coercion.

By adhering to these detailed objectives and carefully designed study protocols, Phase I trials set the foundation for the subsequent phases of clinical research, focusing on establishing a thorough understanding of the safety profile of new therapeutic agents.

4.2.1.2 Selection of Participants

The selection of participants for Phase I clinical trials is a critical process, guided by specific criteria that prioritize safety and the ability to provide clear, reliable data on the pharmacological properties of the investigational drug. This process is crucial not only for the safety of the participants but also for ensuring that the results of the trial are valid and informative.

Criteria for Selection:

- **Health Status**: Most Phase I trials recruit healthy volunteers to minimize the risk of confounding factors associated with underlying diseases. However, in certain cases, such as in oncology, participants who have the disease being targeted by the drug may be included, especially when the drug's side effects might be too severe for healthy individuals.
- **Age and Gender**: Participants are usually adults, as pediatric testing requires additional safeguards and ethical considerations. Both men and women are included unless there are specific reasons related to the drug's mechanism of action or potential risks that would limit participation to one gender.
- **No Significant Comorbidities**: Participants should not have significant other health issues that might interfere with the drug's metabolism or pharmacodynamics, or that would increase the risk of adverse effects.

- **No Concomitant Medications**: Ideally, participants should not be taking other medications that could interact with the investigational drug. If certain medications are permissible, these are strictly defined in the protocol.

Screening Process:

- **Medical Evaluation**: Potential participants undergo thorough medical evaluations, including physical examinations, laboratory tests, and sometimes more specific diagnostic tests to ensure they meet the health criteria for the study.
- **Informed Consent**: Participants must provide informed consent, which involves a comprehensive discussion about the study's purpose, procedures, potential risks, and benefits, as well as the participant's rights and responsibilities. This process ensures that participants are fully aware of what participation entails and are willing to proceed.
- **Psychological Assessment**: For some trials, particularly those that may involve significant risk or long-term commitment, a psychological assessment might be conducted to ensure that participants are mentally prepared and likely to comply with the study requirements.

Ethical Considerations:

- **Voluntary Participation**: It is essential that participation in the trial is entirely voluntary, free from coercion or undue influence. Compensation for participation is carefully regulated to ensure it is not coercive.
- **Protection of Vulnerable Populations**: Extra care is taken when considering populations that might be vulnerable, such as those with limited decision-making capacity or economic disadvantages. Special ethical considerations and protections must be in place for these groups.

Ongoing Assessment:

- **Monitoring for Eligibility**: Throughout the trial, the eligibility of participants is continuously reassessed. If a participant's health status changes, or if they start a medication that could interfere with the study drug or increase their risk, they may be withdrawn from the study to protect their safety and the integrity of the data.

The careful selection and continuous re-evaluation of participants in Phase I clinical trials are fundamental to the ethical conduct of the study and to achieving reliable results that can guide the further development of the investigational drug.

4.2.2 Phase II: Efficacy and Side Effects

4.2.2.1 Objectives and Study Design

Objectives of Phase II Trials: The main objectives of Phase II clinical trials are to evaluate the efficacy of a drug and to continue the safety assessment with a focus on side effects, conducted with a larger group of patients than in Phase I. This phase is crucial for determining if the drug works in people who have the specific disease or condition it's targeting. The outcomes help decide whether the drug should move to more extensive Phase III trials.

Study Design:

- **Types of Phase II Trials**:
  - **Single-arm Trials**: All participants receive the drug. The outcomes may be compared with historical control data where the results from similar patients who received standard treatment or no treatment are considered.
  - **Randomized Controlled Trials (RCTs)**: Participants are randomly assigned to either the treatment group or a control group, which may receive a placebo or a standard treatment. RCTs are considered the gold standard for determining a drug's efficacy.

- **Endpoints**: The primary endpoint is often the drug's effectiveness, measured by specific criteria dependent on the disease. For example, in cancer treatments, effectiveness could be measured by tumor shrinkage or survival rates. Secondary endpoints include further assessment of safety and side effects, quality of life, and other therapeutic effects.
- **Sample Size**: The number of participants typically ranges from several dozen to about 300. This size is large enough to provide preliminary conclusions about the drug's efficacy while managing study costs and time.

- **Adaptive Features**: Many Phase II trials incorporate adaptive design elements, allowing modifications to the trial procedures based on interim data. This flexibility can include changes in dosage, sample size, or eligibility criteria which helps optimize the trial's efficiency and effectiveness.

Participant Selection:

- **Inclusion Criteria**: Participants are selected based on specific characteristics, including the stage or type of disease, previous treatment history, and genetic markers, among others. These criteria are designed to ensure that the study population is homogeneously affected by the condition the drug is intended to treat.
- **Exclusion Criteria**: Potential participants with certain health conditions or those on treatments that could interfere with the study outcomes are typically excluded to maintain the integrity of the trial's results.

Safety Monitoring:

- **Monitoring for Adverse Effects**: Continuous monitoring is essential to identify any side effects or adverse reactions as more participants and higher doses are involved compared to Phase I.
- **Ethical Oversight**: An independent ethics committee or institutional review board continues to review the trial's progress to ensure that ethical standards are maintained.

Data Collection and Analysis:

- **Data Integrity**: Rigorous methods are used to collect and analyze data to ensure accuracy and reliability. This includes blinding, where appropriate, to prevent bias.
- **Statistical Analysis**: Statistical techniques are applied to interpret the data and determine whether the results are statistically significant, meaning that they are likely not due to chance.

Phase II trials are a pivotal step in the clinical trial process, as they provide the first indication of a drug's effectiveness in its intended patient population and further elaborate its safety profile. These trials are integral to determining the path forward in the drug development process, including any necessary modifications before proceeding to large-scale Phase III trials.

4.2.2 Phase II: Efficacy and Side Effects

4.2.2.1 Objectives and Study Design

Objectives of Phase II Trials: The primary objective of Phase II clinical trials is to assess the efficacy of a drug in patients who have the disease or condition that the drug is intended to treat. These trials also continue to evaluate the safety profile of the drug, focusing particularly on identifying any side effects that occur when the drug is used in a larger population over a longer period. The data obtained from Phase II trials are crucial for determining whether the drug should proceed to the more extensive and expensive Phase III trials.

Study Design:

- **Trial Types**:
  - **Single-arm Trials**: In these trials, all participants receive the drug, and their outcomes are measured over time without a comparison group. This design is often used when a control group would be unethical or unfeasible.
  - **Randomized Controlled Trials (RCTs)**: Participants are randomly assigned to either receive the drug or a control (placebo or standard treatment), which is the gold standard for assessing drug efficacy. This design helps ensure that the drug's effects are being measured accurately, free from bias.
- **Endpoints**:
  - **Primary Endpoints**: Typically focus on the effectiveness of the drug, measured by clinically relevant outcomes specific to the disease. For example, in cancer trials, this could be tumor response or progression-free survival.
  - **Secondary Endpoints**: Often include additional efficacy measures, detailed safety evaluations, and quality of life assessments.
- **Sample Size and Duration**: Phase II trials involve more participants than Phase I—commonly several hundred—and are conducted over a

period that allows adequate time to observe the drug's effects and gather sufficient data on its efficacy and safety.

- **Adaptive Design**: Some Phase II trials use adaptive designs that allow for modifications based on interim data. This can include changes to the dosage, the addition or removal of patient cohorts, or adjustments to the study's primary endpoint based on preliminary results.

Participant Selection:

- **Inclusion Criteria**: Participants must have the specific condition or disease the drug is targeting, often within a particular stage of the disease or with certain genetic markers that the drug is designed to interact with.
- **Exclusion Criteria**: Excludes patients who might have conditions or be taking medications that could interfere with the study's outcomes or increase the risk of adverse effects.

Safety Monitoring:

- **Ongoing Assessment**: Regular monitoring for any adverse effects, which is critical as the drug is being tested in a larger group than in Phase I. This includes frequent physical exams, laboratory tests, and sometimes additional safety monitoring boards.
- **Ethical Considerations**: Ensuring informed consent, maintaining patient safety, and the ethical handling of any adverse events are paramount. Ethical oversight continues to be provided by institutional review boards or ethics committees.

Data Handling and Analysis:

- **Blinding and Randomization**: To minimize bias, blinding is often employed, where neither the participants nor the study staff know which treatment each participant receives. Randomization helps ensure that the groups are comparable at the start of the trial.
- **Statistical Analysis**: Robust statistical methods are used to analyze the data collected, to ensure the results are valid and reliable. This might include interim analyses that can prompt changes in the trial conduct based on early findings.

By the end of a Phase II trial, researchers should have a clear understanding of the drug's efficacy and a more refined view of its safety profile, guiding decisions about advancing to Phase III testing. These trials are critical for eliminating ineffective treatments before larger scale and more costly Phase III trials are undertaken.

4.2.2.2 Selection of Participants

The selection of participants for Phase II clinical trials is a process that is meticulously designed to ensure that the study population can provide reliable and relevant data regarding the efficacy and safety of the drug under investigation. This selection process is critical not only for achieving the scientific objectives of the trial but also for ensuring the ethical treatment of participants.

Criteria for Selection:

- **Disease-Specific Criteria:** Participants must have the specific disease or condition the drug is intended to treat. The criteria might specify the stage of the disease, prior treatment history, and whether certain biomarkers or genetic markers are present, depending on the drug's mechanism of action.
- **Health and Demographic Factors:** While Phase I trials often use healthy volunteers, Phase II trials select patients with the disease. However, their overall health, apart from the disease in question, should be stable. Demographic factors such as age, gender, and ethnicity may also be considered to ensure that the trial results are applicable to the broader population.
- **Exclusion Criteria:** Potential participants who have other serious health issues that could confound the results or who are taking medications that might interact with the investigational drug are typically excluded. This helps in reducing the risk of adverse effects and ensures clearer interpretation of the drug's efficacy and safety.

Screening Process:

- **Medical Evaluation:** Includes detailed assessments through physical examinations, medical history, laboratory tests, and sometimes advanced diagnostics to confirm the disease and its stage, and to assess the eligibility based on health criteria.

- **Informed Consent**: Before participation, individuals must be thoroughly informed about the trial's purposes, risks, benefits, and their rights as participants. This process ensures they understand their involvement and consent voluntarily.

Ethical Considerations:

- **Protection of Vulnerable Groups**: Extra care is taken to protect vulnerable populations, such as those with severe disease, elderly patients, or those with cognitive impairments, ensuring they are not unduly burdened or exposed to excessive risk.
- **Voluntary Participation**: Ensuring that participation is voluntary and based on full and comprehensible information is key. Participants must be free to withdraw at any time without any penalty or loss of benefits to which they are otherwise entitled.

Ongoing Assessment:

- **Reassessment of Eligibility**: Participants' health status may be reassessed throughout the trial to ensure continued eligibility. Changes in health or new medications might necessitate their withdrawal from the study to protect their safety and maintain the integrity of the trial data.
- **Adaptive Enrollment**: Based on interim results, the enrollment criteria may be adjusted to narrow or expand the participant pool. This adaptive approach can help focus on subsets of patients who are more likely to benefit from the drug.

The rigorous selection and ongoing assessment of participants are crucial to the success of Phase II trials, helping to ensure that the findings are both scientifically valid and ethically obtained. These trials are fundamental in determining the potential for a drug to proceed to larger-scale Phase III studies.

4.2.3 Phase III: Efficacy and Monitoring Adverse Reactions

4.2.3.1 Objectives and Study Design

Objectives of Phase III Trials: The primary objective of Phase III clinical trials is to confirm the efficacy of the drug observed in Phase II trials and to monitor adverse reactions from a larger, more diverse population.

This phase is critical for ensuring the drug's safety and effectiveness across different demographics and various medical conditions. The comprehensive data collected during Phase III trials are used to support regulatory approval applications.

Study Design:

- **Trial Types:**
  - **Randomized Controlled Trials (RCTs):** These are the most common design in Phase III trials, where participants are randomly assigned to receive either the study drug or a control, which may be a placebo or a current standard treatment. This design helps to eliminate bias and provides a clear comparison between the new drug and existing treatments.
  - **Multi-center Trials:** Phase III trials are often conducted at multiple sites and in various countries to ensure the findings are generalizable to a broad population. This also allows the drug's performance to be evaluated under different healthcare systems and patient care standards.
- **Sample Size:** Typically involves a large number of participants, often ranging from several hundred to thousands, to detect any rare side effects and to provide statistically significant data on the drug's efficacy.
- **Endpoints:**
  - **Primary Endpoints:** These are directly related to the efficacy of the drug, such as disease remission rates, survival rates, or significant improvement in the quality of life, depending on the drug's intended use.
  - **Secondary Endpoints:** Include additional efficacy measures, long-term effects, and more comprehensive safety data.
- **Duration:** Phase III trials usually last longer than earlier phases, often spanning several years, to gather adequate data on the drug's long-term efficacy and side effects.
- **Blinding and Randomization:** To prevent bias, most Phase III trials are double-blinded, meaning neither the participants nor the study staff (including researchers and healthcare providers) know which treatment

the participants are receiving.

Participant Selection:

- **Inclusion Criteria:** Participants typically include a wide range of patients who have the disease or condition the drug is intended to treat, reflecting various stages of the disease, different subtypes of the condition, and coexisting health issues.
- **Exclusion Criteria:** While the criteria are designed to be inclusive, certain conditions that could skew the efficacy results or pose significant health risks to participants are grounds for exclusion.

Safety Monitoring:

- **Adverse Event Reporting:** All potential adverse events are meticulously documented and analyzed to determine any possible link to the drug. Safety monitoring is a critical component of Phase III trials.
- **Independent Data Monitoring Committees (IDMC):** These committees periodically review the data to ensure patient safety, study integrity, and if necessary, make recommendations regarding the continuation, modification, or termination of the trial based on preliminary findings.

Regulatory Oversight:

- **Interim Analyses:** Conducted to assess early data, which can be used to adjust trial parameters if necessary to improve safety or efficacy outcomes.
- **Ethical Compliance:** All aspects of the trial are conducted in accordance with ethical standards and regulatory requirements to protect participant welfare and ensure credible results.

The results from Phase III trials are crucial for determining whether a drug should be approved for widespread use. They provide the robust data needed to ensure that the benefits of the drug outweigh the risks, meeting the stringent requirements set by regulatory authorities.

4.2.3.2 Large Scale Implementation

Large-scale implementation in the context of Phase III clinical trials refers to the execution of the trial across multiple sites and possibly multiple countries to evaluate the drug's efficacy and safety in a diverse population. This scale-up is crucial for assessing the generalizability of the trial results and ensuring that the drug performs consistently across different demographic and geographical settings.

Key Aspects of Large Scale Implementation:

- **Multi-Center Coordination:** Coordination across various clinical trial sites requires robust management practices to ensure consistency in how the trial is conducted. This includes uniform training for all site staff on the trial protocol, data collection methods, and handling of adverse events.
- **Logistical Management:** Managing the logistics of a large-scale trial involves the distribution of the drug and control substances, maintaining the blinding where necessary, and handling the substantial amounts of data generated. This requires a well-organized supply chain and sophisticated data management systems to track progress and manage information securely.
- **Recruitment Strategies:** Effective recruitment strategies are critical to enroll a sufficient number of participants in a timely manner. These strategies might include public awareness campaigns, collaboration with patient advocacy groups, and leveraging electronic health records to identify potential participants who meet the trial criteria.
- **Diversity and Inclusion:** Ensuring diversity in the trial population is essential to test the drug's efficacy and safety across various subgroups, including different ages, races, ethnicities, genders, and comorbid conditions. This helps in understanding any variable drug responses and safety concerns that might arise in different demographic groups.
- **Regulatory Compliance:** Each country or region may have its own regulatory requirements concerning clinical trials. Large-scale trials must comply with international regulations and standards, such as those from the International Council for Harmonisation of Technical Requirements for Pharmaceuticals for Human Use (ICH), as well as local laws and guidelines.
- **Data Integrity and Monitoring:** To maintain the integrity of the trial data, rigorous monitoring is necessary. This includes regular audits and checks by independent monitors who visit the trial sites to ensure that the trial is conducted according to the protocol and good clinical practice (GCP) guidelines.

- **Adaptive Trial Designs**: Sometimes, adaptive trial designs are employed to make adjustments based on interim data. These adaptations might include modifying the dosage, changing the recruitment criteria, or even stopping the trial early for efficacy or safety reasons.
- **Stakeholder Engagement**: Engaging with various stakeholders, including healthcare professionals, patient groups, and regulatory bodies, is crucial for the smooth execution of the trial. Their input can provide valuable insights into the practical aspects of the drug's application and potential market needs.
- **Ethical Considerations**: Upholding high ethical standards is paramount, especially in diverse and sometimes vulnerable populations. Ensuring informed consent, respecting participant rights, and maintaining transparency about trial results are all essential components.

The successful large-scale implementation of a Phase III clinical trial is vital for generating reliable data on a drug's efficacy and safety, ultimately supporting its approval for public use. This stage not only tests the drug's therapeutic effects but also its real-world application across a broad and varied patient population.

4.2.4 Phase IV: Post-Marketing Surveillance

4.2.4.1 Objectives and Regulatory Requirements

Objectives of Phase IV Trials: Phase IV trials, also known as post-marketing surveillance, are conducted after a drug has been approved for use by regulatory authorities and is available on the market. The primary objectives of these trials are to monitor the drug's long-term effectiveness and safety, to identify any rare or long-term adverse effects, and to evaluate the drug's performance in a broader, more diverse population than was possible during the controlled environments of earlier trial phases.

Key Objectives:

- **Safety Monitoring**: Continuously assess the safety profile of the drug with a focus on detecting rare, delayed, or long-term adverse effects that may not have been apparent in earlier phases.
- **Effectiveness**: Evaluate the real-world effectiveness of the drug, which may differ from controlled trial conditions due to varied patient compliance, dosing regimens, and co-treatments.
- **Identification of New Therapeutic Uses**: Sometimes, additional benefits of the drug, not originally anticipated, are discovered through

widespread use.

- **Comparative Effectiveness**: Compare the drug's effectiveness and side effects with other drugs available on the market.

Regulatory Requirements:

- **Reporting Adverse Events**: There is a mandatory requirement to report all serious adverse events to the regulatory authorities. This includes both new events and those previously noted, but now appearing with greater frequency or severity.
- **Periodic Safety Update Reports (PSURs)**: Drug manufacturers are required to submit regular updates to regulatory bodies. These reports summarize the data collected from global marketing experience, including exposure, adverse effects, and risk-benefit evaluations.
- **Risk Management Plans (RMPs)**: Companies must develop and maintain a plan to manage identified risks associated with the drug, which may include measures to minimize potential risks to patients.

Compliance and Oversight:

- **Regulatory Audits and Inspections**: Regulatory authorities conduct periodic audits and inspections to ensure compliance with post-marketing surveillance obligations.
- **Labeling Changes**: Based on new safety and efficacy data, regulatory authorities may require updates to the drug's labeling to include new side effects, warnings, or contraindications.
- **Post-Marketing Commitments**: Sometimes, as a condition of approval, drug manufacturers are required to conduct specific post-marketing studies to further assess risks or benefits. These are legally enforceable commitments.

Ethical Considerations:

- **Informed Consent in Ongoing Studies**: For any ongoing trials that occur in the post-marketing phase, maintaining informed consent is crucial, especially when new information about the drug emerges.
- **Transparency and Reporting**: Maintaining transparency in reporting and communication with healthcare providers, patients, and regulatory

bodies is essential to uphold public trust and ensure patient safety.

The role of Phase IV trials is critical in the lifecycle of a drug, providing essential data that can refine or confirm the therapeutic use of the drug, guide healthcare providers, and protect patients. This phase ensures that the benefits of a drug continue to outweigh the risks in the general population and under routine healthcare conditions.

4.2.4.2 Monitoring Long-Term Effects and Efficacy

Monitoring the long-term effects and efficacy of a drug in Phase IV of clinical trials is a critical aspect of post-marketing surveillance. This process helps to ensure that the benefits of a drug observed in controlled clinical settings are sustained over time and across a broader patient base in real-world conditions.

Key Aspects of Monitoring:

- **Long-Term Safety Surveillance**: Ongoing surveillance is conducted to observe adverse effects that may appear only after prolonged use of the drug or with cumulative exposure. This includes tracking both known side effects to assess their frequency and severity over time, and identifying new side effects that were not previously detected. Regularly updating safety profiles is crucial for maintaining an up-to-date understanding of the drug's risk factors.
- **Assessment of Real-World Efficacy**: Monitoring efficacy in the post-marketing phase involves evaluating how well the drug works when used by the general population under less controlled conditions than in clinical trials. This includes assessing:
  - **Therapeutic outcomes**: Are the intended health benefits consistently achieved across different subgroups and varied patient adherence levels?
  - **Quality of life improvements**: Does the drug contribute to overall enhancements in patient well-being and functionality?
  - **Comparison with other therapies**: How does the drug perform in comparison with other available treatments in terms of effectiveness and preference?
- **Patient Population Diversity**: Phase IV trials can involve a more diverse patient population than earlier phases, including individuals with

different comorbidities, ages, ethnic backgrounds, and concomitant medications. This diversity helps to identify variations in drug efficacy and safety profiles across different groups, which can be critical for personalized medicine approaches.

- **Data Collection Methods**:

  - **Patient registries and databases**: These tools are used to collect data from a large number of patients who are using the drug. They provide valuable insights into long-term outcomes and side effects.
  - **Electronic health records (EHRs)**: Leveraging EHRs allows researchers to passively collect comprehensive data on drug usage patterns, health outcomes, and adverse events.
  - **Direct patient reporting**: Systems that enable patients to report their experiences directly can be a valuable source of information on drug efficacy and adverse reactions.

- **Analytical Techniques**:

  - **Data mining**: Advanced statistical methods and data mining techniques are used to analyze large datasets to identify patterns, trends, and correlations that might indicate potential issues or benefits with the drug.
  - **Longitudinal studies**: These studies track patients over time to observe the long-term effects and sustainability of the drug's therapeutic benefits.

- **Regulatory Interaction and Compliance**:

  - **Updating labeling and marketing materials**: Based on new safety and efficacy information, manufacturers may need to update the drug's labeling, packaging, and promotional materials to include new findings or instructions.
  - **Regular reporting to authorities**: Drug manufacturers are required to periodically report to regulatory authorities with comprehensive updates on the drug's long-term safety and efficacy, fulfilling ongoing regulatory compliance obligations.

The focus on monitoring long-term effects and efficacy in Phase IV ensures that the healthcare community remains informed about the drug's performance and that patients continue to receive safe and effective treatment. This phase not only helps to safeguard public health but also supports the optimization of therapeutic strategies and drug usage guidelines in clinical practice.

4.3 Designing Clinical Study Documents

4.3.1 Study Protocol

4.3.1.1 Structure and Components of a Protocol

The study protocol is a fundamental document in clinical trials, outlining the rationale, objectives, design, methodology, statistical considerations, and organization of a study. It ensures that the trial is conducted and reported in accordance with rigorous scientific and ethical standards. Here is a breakdown of the essential structure and components of a typical clinical study protocol:

Title Page: The title page includes the title of the study, trial number, and names and contact information of the principal investigator(s), the sponsor, and other key personnel.

Table of Contents: A detailed table of contents allows readers to easily navigate through the document.

1. Background and Rationale:

- **Introduction**: Describes the scientific background, the rationale for the study, and the theoretical framework.
- **Literature Review**: Summarizes relevant research that supports the trial's premise and design.

2. Objectives:

- **Primary Objectives**: Clear statement of the primary question the study intends to answer.
- **Secondary Objectives**: Any secondary endpoints the study aims to assess.

3. Trial Design:

- **Type of Trial**: Describes whether it is interventional or observational, randomized, blinded, placebo-controlled, etc.

- **Study Setting**: Outlines where the study will take place, such as hospitals, clinics, community settings, etc.
- **Phases of Study**: If applicable, the phase of the clinical trial (I-IV).

4. Participant Information:

- **Inclusion Criteria**: Specifies the characteristics that must be present for participants to join the study.
- **Exclusion Criteria**: Lists conditions or characteristics that disqualify potential participants.
- **Withdrawal Criteria**: Conditions under which participants may be withdrawn from the study.

5. Intervention(s):

- **Details of Intervention**: Describes the drug, device, or procedure being tested, including administration, dosage, and duration.
- **Control/Comparator Description**: Details the control or comparator group treatments, if applicable.

6. Outcomes:

- **Primary Outcomes**: The main results being measured to evaluate the intervention's effect.
- **Secondary Outcomes**: Additional outcomes to be measured to provide further understanding.

7. Sample Size Calculation:

- **Justification**: Explains the basis for the number of participants needed to achieve statistically significant results.
- **Power Analysis**: Details the statistical power of the study, often necessary to detect a pre-specified effect size.

8. Data Collection Methods:

- **Data Sources**: Specifies where and how data will be collected (e.g., medical records, direct assessments).

- **Data Management**: Outlines the procedures for data entry, coding, security, and storage.

9. Statistical Analysis:

- **Descriptive Statistics**: How the data will be summarized and reported.
- **Inferential Statistics**: Statistical tests that will be used to interpret the data.

10. Ethical Considerations:

- **Ethical Approval**: Details of the ethical review board approval.
- **Informed Consent Process**: Describes how informed consent will be obtained from participants.

11. Funding and Sponsorship:

- **Funding Source**: Identifies the source of funding and any potential conflicts of interest.
- **Role of Sponsor**: Specifies the sponsor's role in study design, data analysis, and publication.

12. Appendices:

- **Consent Forms**: Copies of informed consent forms and other participant-related documents.
- **Study Tools**: Questionnaires, assessment tools, and other instruments used in the study.

Each element of the protocol is designed to ensure that the study can be thoroughly and reproducibly conducted by any team of qualified researchers, providing a clear and complete blueprint of the trial's conduct and intentions.

4.3.1.2 Example of a Protocol Layout

To illustrate how a clinical study protocol is structured, here's an example layout of a hypothetical protocol for a clinical trial investigating the efficacy of a new medication for hypertension. This example will include annotations explaining the purpose of each section and how it contributes to the overall design and conduct of the study.

Title Page

- **Trial Title**: "A Phase III, Randomized, Double-Blind, Placebo-Controlled Study of Hypertensinol in Adults with Stage 2 Hypertension"
- **Protocol Version**: Include the date and version number.
- **Trial Registration Number**: A unique identifier for the trial.
- **Principal Investigator**: Name and contact information.
- **Sponsor**: Name of the pharmaceutical company or research institution sponsoring the trial.
- **Approval Date**: Date when the protocol was last reviewed and approved by an ethics committee.

Table of Contents

- Lists all sections and sub-sections with page numbers for easy navigation.

1. Introduction and Background

- **Overview of Condition**: Brief description of hypertension, its impact, current treatments, and the need for new solutions.
- **Rationale for the Study**: Explanation of why this new drug, Hypertensinol, might be beneficial based on preclinical or Phase I and II data.

2. Study Objectives

- **Primary Objective**: To evaluate the efficacy of Hypertensinol in reducing systolic and diastolic blood pressure.
- **Secondary Objectives:** To assess the safety profile and impact on quality of life.

3. Study Design

- **Description of the Study Design**: Details on it being a randomized, double-blind, placebo-controlled trial.

- **Study Phases**: Explanation of the different stages of the trial including screening, treatment, follow-up, and analysis phases.

4. Study Population

- **Inclusion Criteria**: Age 18-65, diagnosed with Stage 2 hypertension, etc.
- **Exclusion Criteria**: Pregnancy, severe concurrent illness, prior adverse reaction to similar drugs, etc.

5. Treatment Plan

- **Intervention**: Detailed dosing regimen for Hypertensinol and the placebo.
- **Administration**: Information on how the medication is to be administered.
- **Duration of Treatment**: Duration participants will receive the treatment and follow-up periods.

6. Assessment of Efficacy

- **Primary Endpoints**: Specific measures, e.g., reduction in systolic and diastolic blood pressure after 12 weeks.
- **Secondary Endpoints**: Safety assessments, quality of life surveys, etc.

7. Safety Assessments

- **Adverse Events Monitoring**: Procedures for monitoring, recording, and reporting adverse events.
- **Data Safety Monitoring Board (DSMB)**: Details about the independent committee overseeing trial safety.

8. Data Collection and Management

- **Data Collection Methods**: Use of electronic data capture systems, paper case report forms, etc.
- **Data Management**: Description of data management practices, including data privacy measures and audit trails.

9. Statistical Analysis

- **Statistical Methods**: Detailed description of statistical tests and models to be used for analyzing the primary and secondary endpoints.
- **Interim Analysis**: Plans for any interim analysis to be conducted by the DSMB.

10. Ethical Considerations

- **Ethical Approval**: Documentation of approval from relevant ethics committees.
- **Informed Consent Process**: Description of how informed consent will be obtained, including sample consent forms.

11. Study Timelines

- **Key Milestones**: Estimated start and end dates, timelines for enrollment, intervention, follow-up, and data analysis.

12. Appendices

- **Relevant Documents**: Consent forms, investigator brochures, patient information sheets, and any other supplementary documents.

This example layout provides a comprehensive overview of how a clinical study protocol is structured to guide the execution and management of a clinical trial, ensuring that all regulatory, ethical, and scientific standards are met.

4.3.2 Case Report Forms (CRF)

4.3.2.1 Purpose and Types of CRFs

Purpose of Case Report Forms (CRFs): Case Report Forms (CRFs) are crucial tools in clinical trials, designed to systematically capture data on each trial participant according to the protocol. The primary purposes of CRFs are:

- **Data Collection**: CRFs provide a standardized method for collecting and structuring data from clinical trials. This standardization ensures consistency in data capture, making it easier to compare and analyze data across different participants and sites.

- **Regulatory Compliance**: Accurate and thorough completion of CRFs is essential for meeting the regulatory requirements set by authorities like the FDA or EMA. CRFs help ensure that the data collected is reliable, traceable, and verifiable.
- **Quality Control**: CRFs are designed to minimize errors in data collection by providing predefined choices and structured input fields, which enhance the accuracy of the data collected.
- **Research Integrity**: Well-designed CRFs support the integrity of the research by ensuring that the data collected are comprehensive and directly aligned with the study's objectives.

Types of CRFs:

- **Paper CRFs**: Traditionally, CRFs were paper-based, where data were entered manually. This type involves physical forms that investigators fill out during patient visits. Although increasingly less common, paper CRFs are still used, particularly in smaller or resource-limited study environments.
- **Electronic CRFs (eCRFs)**: These are the digital version of paper CRFs, used in electronic data capture (EDC) systems. eCRFs offer several advantages over paper forms, including:
    - **Real-time Data Entry**: Data can be entered and validated in real-time, reducing the time between data collection and analysis.
    - **Error Reduction**: Built-in validations and skip patterns reduce the likelihood of entry errors.
    - **Remote Monitoring**: Allows data monitors to review and query data without being physically present at the study site.
- **Patient-Reported Outcome Forms (PROs)**: These CRFs are designed to capture data directly from patients about their health condition, treatment response, and quality of life, often using surveys or diaries. PROs can be both paper-based or electronic.
- **Source Data Verification Forms**: These are used to verify that the data entered into the CRF aligns with the original data sources such as medical records, laboratory results, or diagnostic reports. This form is crucial for ensuring data quality and integrity.

- **Pharmacokinetic (PK) and Pharmacodynamic (PD) CRFs**: Specifically designed to capture data related to the pharmacokinetics (how the body processes a drug) and pharmacodynamics (how a drug affects the body) of a medication. These are essential in early-phase trials where dosing and drug behavior are critical outcomes.

Each type of CRF is tailored to meet the specific needs of the clinical trial, whether it be capturing complex laboratory data, simple health status updates, or detailed demographic information. The design and implementation of CRFs must be meticulously planned to ensure they meet the study's needs while maintaining compliance with regulatory standards.

4.3.2 Case Report Forms (CRF)

4.3.2.2 Designing Effective CRFs

Designing an effective Case Report Form (CRF) is critical for ensuring that the data collected in clinical trials are accurate, complete, and verifiable. Effective CRFs facilitate the precise capturing of data required to meet the study objectives while adhering to regulatory standards. Here are key considerations and steps involved in designing effective CRFs:

1. Define the Study Requirements:

- **Identify Data Needs**: Start by defining what data are necessary to meet the study's objectives. This includes demographic data, clinical data, lab results, and any other data points relevant to the study endpoints.
- **Protocol Alignment**: Ensure the CRF design is aligned with the clinical study protocol. Every data point collected should have a clear purpose and be directly related to a study question or requirement.

2. Layout and Organization:

- **Logical Flow**: Arrange the sections of the CRF in a logical order that follows the workflow of data collection, typically mirroring the sequence of patient visits or assessments.
- **Clear Sectioning**: Use sections and subsections to group related data fields, making the CRF easier to navigate and complete.

3. Question Design:

- **Clarity in Wording**: Use clear, unambiguous language to avoid misinterpretation of the questions by those filling out the form.
- **Appropriate Field Types**: Choose the right type of input field (e.g., text box, checkbox, radio button, dropdown list) based on the kind of response expected. This helps in standardizing responses and facilitating data entry and analysis.
- **Mandatory Fields**: Clearly indicate which fields are mandatory, ensuring critical data are not missed.

4. Instructions for Completing the CRF:

- **Embedded Instructions**: Include concise instructions directly on the CRF for how to fill out each section, especially for complex or unusual data collection points.
- **Training Materials**: Develop comprehensive training materials and conduct training sessions for all personnel involved in data collection to ensure they understand how to complete the CRF correctly.

5. Validation Rules:

- **Error Checking**: Implement validation rules in electronic CRFs (eCRFs) to check for data entry errors such as out-of-range values, inconsistent data entries, and missing data for mandatory fields.
- **Consistency Checks**: Include checks for consistency across related data fields to catch discrepancies (e.g., ensuring dates of subsequent visits are after initial visits).

6. Pilot Testing:

- **Testing the CRF**: Before full deployment, conduct a pilot test of the CRF with a small subset of users to identify any issues with the design, layout, or understanding of the questions.
- **Feedback and Revisions**: Collect feedback from the pilot users and make necessary adjustments to improve the usability and effectiveness of the CRF.

7. Integration with Data Management Systems:

- **Data Capture Compatibility**: Ensure that the CRF is compatible with the electronic data capture (EDC) systems used in the trial for seamless data integration and management.
- **Audit Trails**: For eCRFs, ensure that the system maintains an audit trail for all data entries and changes, as required by regulatory guidelines.

8. Regulatory Compliance:

- **Adherence to Standards**: Design CRFs to comply with regulatory standards and guidelines, such as those from the FDA or EMA, which might include specific requirements for data collection and reporting.

Effective CRF design is a crucial step in the planning and execution of clinical trials, impacting the quality of the data collected and the efficiency of the trial. Well-designed CRFs not only support accurate data collection but also facilitate compliance with regulatory standards, contributing to the overall success of the clinical study.

4.3.3 Informed Consent Forms (ICF)

4.3.3.1 Elements of Informed Consent

Informed Consent Forms (ICFs) are vital documents used in clinical trials to ensure that participants are fully aware of the study's nature, its risks, benefits, and their rights before agreeing to participate. The ethical principle underlying informed consent is respect for the autonomy and dignity of participants. A well-structured ICF should include the following key elements to ensure comprehensive understanding and voluntary participation:

1. Introduction to the Study:

- **Study Title and Purpose**: Clear description of the study's title, purpose, and why it is being conducted.
- **Sponsor**: Information about the organization or institution sponsoring the research.

2. Description of Procedures:

- **Study Procedures**: Detailed explanation of what will be done during the study, including all medical interventions and visits.

- **Time Commitment**: The expected duration of the study for participants, including the length and number of visits.

3. Risks and Discomforts:

- **Potential Risks**: Description of any known risks, discomforts, side effects, or inconveniences that might occur as a result of participation in the study.
- **Risk Severity and Likelihood**: Information about the severity and likelihood of potential risks.

4. Benefits:

- **Potential Benefits**: Outline of any potential benefits to the participant or to others, which may reasonably be expected from the research.
- **No Guarantee of Benefits**: It should be clearly stated that while potential benefits can be hoped for, they cannot be guaranteed.

5. Alternatives to Participation:

- **Available Alternatives**: Information on any appropriate alternative procedures or courses of treatment, if any, that might be advantageous to the participant.

6. Confidentiality:

- **Privacy of Records**: Assurance that the participant's records will be kept confidential and details about who will have access to these records.
- **Data Handling**: Explanation of how data will be collected, stored, and protected.

7. Compensation and Treatment in case of Injury:

- **Compensation**: If applicable, details about compensation or any benefits to which participants might be entitled in case of trial-related injuries.
- **Medical Treatment**: Information regarding what treatment will be available in case of any trial-related injuries and who will bear the cost of such treatment.

8. Voluntary Participation and Withdrawal:

- **Right to Refuse or Withdraw**: Statement that participation is voluntary and that participants can withdraw from the study at any time without penalty or loss of benefits to which they are otherwise entitled.
- **Consequences of Withdrawal**: Explanation of any consequences or effects if a participant decides to withdraw from the study.

9. Contacts for Questions or Problems:

- **Contact Information**: Details of whom to contact for answers to pertinent questions about the research and research participants' rights, and whom to contact in the event of a research-related injury.

10. Consent Statement:

- **Affirmation of Understanding**: Participants affirm that they have read the consent form (or it has been read to them), they have had the opportunity to ask questions and have them answered satisfactorily, and they understand the information provided.
- **Signature Line**: Space for the participant's signature and date, confirming their consent to participate, as well as lines for the signatures of witnesses or study personnel as required.

These elements ensure that all participants are well-informed about the nature and implications of the study, thereby upholding the ethical standards of research and protecting participant rights and welfare.

4.3.3 Informed Consent Forms (ICF)

4.3.3.1 Elements of Informed Consent

Informed Consent Forms (ICFs) are vital documents used in clinical trials to ensure that participants are fully aware of the study's nature, its risks, benefits, and their rights before agreeing to participate. The ethical principle underlying informed consent is respect for the autonomy and dignity of participants. A well-structured ICF should include the following key elements to ensure comprehensive understanding and voluntary participation:

1. Introduction to the Study:

- **Study Title and Purpose**: Clear description of the study's title, purpose, and why it is being conducted.
- **Sponsor**: Information about the organization or institution sponsoring the research.

2. Description of Procedures:

- **Study Procedures**: Detailed explanation of what will be done during the study, including all medical interventions and visits.
- **Time Commitment**: The expected duration of the study for participants, including the length and number of visits.

3. Risks and Discomforts:

- **Potential Risks**: Description of any known risks, discomforts, side effects, or inconveniences that might occur as a result of participation in the study.
- **Risk Severity and Likelihood**: Information about the severity and likelihood of potential risks.

4. Benefits:

- **Potential Benefits**: Outline of any potential benefits to the participant or to others, which may reasonably be expected from the research.
- **No Guarantee of Benefits**: It should be clearly stated that while potential benefits can be hoped for, they cannot be guaranteed.

5. Alternatives to Participation:

- **Available Alternatives**: Information on any appropriate alternative procedures or courses of treatment, if any, that might be advantageous to the participant.

6. Confidentiality:

- **Privacy of Records**: Assurance that the participant's records will be kept confidential and details about who will have access to these records.

- **Data Handling**: Explanation of how data will be collected, stored, and protected.

7. Compensation and Treatment in case of Injury:

- **Compensation**: If applicable, details about compensation or any benefits to which participants might be entitled in case of trial-related injuries.
- **Medical Treatment**: Information regarding what treatment will be available in case of any trial-related injuries and who will bear the cost of such treatment.

8. Voluntary Participation and Withdrawal:

- **Right to Refuse or Withdraw**: Statement that participation is voluntary and that participants can withdraw from the study at any time without penalty or loss of benefits to which they are otherwise entitled.
- **Consequences of Withdrawal**: Explanation of any consequences or effects if a participant decides to withdraw from the study.

9. Contacts for Questions or Problems:

- **Contact Information**: Details of whom to contact for answers to pertinent questions about the research and research participants‘ rights, and whom to contact in the event of a research-related injury.

10. Consent Statement:

- **Affirmation of Understanding**: Participants affirm that they have read the consent form (or it has been read to them), they have had the opportunity to ask questions and have them answered satisfactorily, and they understand the information provided.
- **Signature Line**: Space for the participant's signature and date, confirming their consent to participate, as well as lines for the signatures of witnesses or study personnel as required.

These elements ensure that all participants are well-informed about the nature and implications of the study, thereby upholding the ethical standards of research and protecting participant rights and welfare.

4.3.3 Informed Consent Forms (ICF)

4.3.3.1 Elements of Informed Consent

4.3.3 Informed Consent Forms (ICF)

4.3.3.1 Elements of Informed Consent

Informed Consent Forms (ICFs) are vital documents used in clinical trials to ensure that participants are fully aware of the study's nature, its risks, benefits, and their rights before agreeing to participate. The ethical principle underlying informed consent is respect for the autonomy and dignity of participants. A well-structured ICF should include the following key elements to ensure comprehensive understanding and voluntary participation:

1. Introduction to the Study:

- **Study Title and Purpose**: Clear description of the study's title, purpose, and why it is being conducted.
- **Sponsor**: Information about the organization or institution sponsoring the research.

2. Description of Procedures:

- **Study Procedures**: Detailed explanation of what will be done during the study, including all medical interventions and visits.
- **Time Commitment**: The expected duration of the study for participants, including the length and number of visits.

3. Risks and Discomforts:

- **Potential Risks**: Description of any known risks, discomforts, side effects, or inconveniences that might occur as a result of participation in the study.
- **Risk Severity and Likelihood**: Information about the severity and likelihood of potential risks.

4. Benefits:

- **Potential Benefits**: Outline of any potential benefits to the participant or to others, which may reasonably be expected from the research.
- **No Guarantee of Benefits**: It should be clearly stated that while potential benefits can be hoped for, they cannot be guaranteed.

5. Alternatives to Participation:

- **Available Alternatives**: Information on any appropriate alternative procedures or courses of treatment, if any, that might be advantageous to the participant.

6. Confidentiality:

- **Privacy of Records**: Assurance that the participant's records will be kept confidential and details about who will have access to these records.
- **Data Handling**: Explanation of how data will be collected, stored, and protected.

7. Compensation and Treatment in case of Injury:

- **Compensation**: If applicable, details about compensation or any benefits to which participants might be entitled in case of trial-related injuries.
- **Medical Treatment**: Information regarding what treatment will be available in case of any trial-related injuries and who will bear the cost of such treatment.

8. Voluntary Participation and Withdrawal:

- **Right to Refuse or Withdraw**: Statement that participation is voluntary and that participants can withdraw from the study at any time without penalty or loss of benefits to which they are otherwise entitled.
- **Consequences of Withdrawal**: Explanation of any consequences or effects if a participant decides to withdraw from the study.

9. Contacts for Questions or Problems:

- **Contact Information**: Details of whom to contact for answers to pertinent questions about the research and research participants' rights, and whom to contact in the event of a research-related injury.

10. Consent Statement:

- **Affirmation of Understanding**: Participants affirm that they have read the consent form (or it has been read to them), they have had the opportunity to ask questions and have them answered satisfactorily, and they understand the information provided.
- **Signature Line**: Space for the participant's signature and date, confirming their consent to participate, as well as lines for the signatures of witnesses or study personnel as required.

These elements ensure that all participants are well-informed about the nature and implications of the study, thereby upholding the ethical standards of research and protecting participant rights and welfare.

CHAPTER FIVE

GOOD CLINICAL PRACTICE AND GUIDELINES

5.1 Introduction to Clinical Practice Guidelines

5.1.1 Definition and Purpose of Clinical Practice Guidelines

Clinical Practice Guidelines (CPGs) represent systematically developed statements to assist practitioners and patient decisions about appropriate healthcare for specific clinical circumstances. These guidelines aim to optimize patient care by providing evidence-based recommendations derived from rigorous analysis of current research, expert consensus, and consideration of patient values and preferences. They serve as a tool to standardize healthcare practices, promote consistency in clinical decision-making, and improve the quality and efficiency of patient care delivery across diverse healthcare settings. Importantly, CPGs are not rigid protocols but rather flexible frameworks intended to guide rather than dictate clinical practice. They facilitate the translation of scientific evidence into actionable recommendations tailored to individual patient needs while also accounting for variations in healthcare resources, patient populations, and clinical contexts.

5.1.2 Development Process of Clinical Practice Guidelines

The development of Clinical Practice Guidelines (CPGs) typically involves a systematic and transparent process to ensure credibility, reliability, and relevance. This process begins with the identification of a specific clinical topic or area of healthcare practice that warrants guideline development. Stakeholder involvement, including healthcare professionals, patients, researchers, and policymakers, is integral throughout the guideline development process to ensure diverse perspectives and expertise are considered.

Next, systematic reviews of the existing evidence are conducted to evaluate the benefits and risks of different healthcare interventions relevant to the clinical topic. This evidence synthesis serves as the foundation for formulating recommendations, which are typically graded based on the strength of the evidence and the degree of consensus among experts.

The formulation of recommendations involves weighing the quality of evidence, clinical relevance, potential harms and benefits, patient preferences, and feasibility of implementation. Recommendations are then drafted and subjected to peer review and external validation to enhance their validity and applicability.

Finally, dissemination and implementation strategies are employed to promote awareness and uptake of the guidelines among healthcare providers and organizations. Regular updates and revisions are also necessary to ensure that guidelines remain current and reflective of evolving evidence and clinical practice standards.

practice of Adherence to Guidelines in Clinical Research

Adherence to Clinical Practice Guidelines (CPGs) is paramount in clinical research as it ensures the integrity, quality, and ethical conduct of studies while safeguarding the well-being of research participants. These guidelines serve as a blueprint for conducting research ethically, transparently, and rigorously, thereby fostering trust in the scientific community and among regulatory authorities, sponsors, and the public.

First and foremost, adherence to CPGs promotes consistency and standardization in research methodologies, data collection, and analysis techniques. By following established guidelines, researchers can minimize variability in study protocols, procedures, and outcomes, thereby enhancing the reliability, reproducibility, and comparability of research findings across different studies and settings.

Furthermore, adherence to CPGs helps ensure the safety and welfare of research participants by outlining ethical principles and standards for the recruitment, enrollment, and treatment of human subjects. These guidelines mandate the informed consent process, risk assessment, and monitoring procedures to minimize potential harm and maximize the benefits of participation in clinical research. By adhering to CPGs, researchers demonstrate their commitment to upholding the rights, dignity, and well-being of research participants, thereby fostering public trust and confidence in the research enterprise.

5.1.3 Role of Regulatory Authorities in Developing Guidelines

Regulatory authorities play a pivotal role in the development, dissemination, and oversight of Clinical Practice Guidelines (CPGs), ensuring that healthcare practices adhere to established standards, regulations, and ethical principles. These authorities, which may include government agencies, professional organizations, and international consortia, collaborate with stakeholders from various sectors to develop evidence-based guidelines that promote patient safety, quality of care, and public health.

One of the primary roles of regulatory authorities in guideline development is to identify areas of healthcare practice that require standardization, improvement, or regulation. By conducting comprehensive assessments of public health needs, epidemiological trends, and gaps in clinical care, regulatory authorities can prioritize the development of guidelines for specific disease areas, conditions, or interventions where evidence-based recommendations are lacking or inconsistent.

Regulatory authorities also contribute to the formulation of CPGs by providing expertise, guidance, and resources throughout the guideline development process. They may establish expert panels, working groups, or advisory committees composed of healthcare professionals, researchers, patient advocates, and other stakeholders to review existing evidence, assess the quality of research studies, and synthesize recommendations based on the best available evidence.

Moreover, regulatory authorities ensure that CPGs adhere to methodological standards, ethical principles, and regulatory requirements to uphold the credibility, validity, and applicability of the guidelines. They may establish criteria for evaluating the quality of evidence, grading the strength of recommendations, and addressing conflicts of interest among guideline developers to minimize bias and ensure transparency in the guideline development process.

Once developed, regulatory authorities play a crucial role in disseminating and implementing CPGs to healthcare providers, organizations, and policymakers. They may use various channels, such as websites, publications, conferences, and educational programs, to promote awareness, adoption, and adherence to guidelines, thereby facilitating their integration into clinical practice and healthcare policy.

Furthermore, regulatory authorities provide oversight and monitoring of guideline implementation to ensure compliance with established standards and regulations. They may conduct audits, evaluations, and reviews of healthcare practices, protocols, and outcomes to assess the effectiveness, impact, and adherence to CPGs, identifying areas for improvement and addressing barriers to guideline implementation.

5.2 ICH-GCP Guidelines

5.2.1 Overview of ICH-GCP Guidelines

The International Council for Harmonisation of Technical Requirements for Pharmaceuticals for Human Use (ICH) Good Clinical Practice (GCP) guidelines represent a globally recognized framework for the design, conduct, monitoring, auditing, recording, and reporting of clinical trials involving human subjects. These guidelines aim to ensure the ethical and scientific integrity of clinical research while protecting the rights, safety, and well-being of study participants.

At its core, the ICH-GCP guidelines provide a set of principles and standards that govern the conduct of clinical trials, emphasizing the importance of quality, transparency, and accountability throughout the research process. These guidelines are applicable to all parties involved in clinical research, including sponsors, investigators, ethics committees, regulatory authorities, and contract research organizations (CROs), regardless of geographic location or jurisdiction.

Key components of the ICH-GCP guidelines include:

1. **Ethical Principles:** The guidelines emphasize the primacy of protecting the rights, safety, and well-being of human subjects participating in clinical trials. They require adherence to ethical principles outlined in internationally recognized documents, such as the Declaration of Helsinki and the Belmont Report, which govern the conduct of research involving human participants.
2. **Scientific Integrity:** ICH-GCP guidelines promote the scientific validity and reliability of clinical trial data by emphasizing the importance of robust study design, methodology, and data collection procedures. They require the use of scientifically sound and justified study protocols that address research objectives, endpoints, eligibility criteria, treatment regimens, and statistical analysis plans.
3. **Quality Assurance and Quality Control:** The guidelines emphasize the implementation of quality assurance and quality control measures to

ensure the accuracy, completeness, and reliability of clinical trial data. They require sponsors and investigators to establish and maintain quality management systems, including standard operating procedures (SOPs), document control, training programs, and internal audits, to monitor and evaluate compliance with regulatory requirements and study protocols.

4. **Risk Management:** ICH-GCP guidelines emphasize the importance of risk management throughout the lifecycle of clinical trials, from study design and planning to data analysis and reporting. They require sponsors and investigators to identify, assess, mitigate, and communicate risks associated with the research protocol, study interventions, and participant safety, taking into account factors such as the nature of the investigational product, study population, and anticipated benefits and risks.

5.2.2 Key Principles of ICH-GCP Guidelines

The ICH-GCP guidelines are founded on several key principles aimed at ensuring the ethical conduct, scientific integrity, and quality of clinical trials involving human subjects. These principles serve as a framework for sponsors, investigators, ethics committees, regulatory authorities, and other stakeholders involved in clinical research. Understanding and adhering to these principles are essential for the successful planning, execution, and reporting of clinical trials.

1. **Protection of Human Subjects:** The paramount principle of ICH-GCP guidelines is the protection of the rights, safety, and well-being of human subjects participating in clinical trials. This principle emphasizes the need for informed consent, voluntary participation, confidentiality, and respect for the individual's dignity and autonomy. Researchers must ensure that potential risks to participants are minimized and that the potential benefits outweigh the risks.
2. **Ethical Conduct:** ICH-GCP guidelines mandate adherence to ethical principles outlined in internationally recognized documents, such as the Declaration of Helsinki and the Belmont Report. Researchers must conduct clinical trials in accordance with these principles, which include honesty, integrity, transparency, and accountability in all aspects of research conduct.

3. **Scientific Integrity:** Clinical trials conducted in accordance with ICH-GCP guidelines must adhere to rigorous scientific standards to ensure the validity and reliability of the data generated. This principle emphasizes the importance of sound study design, methodology, and data collection procedures that are scientifically justified and capable of addressing research objectives and hypotheses.
4. **Protocol Compliance:** ICH-GCP guidelines require adherence to the study protocol, which serves as a detailed plan outlining the objectives, methodology, eligibility criteria, treatment regimens, and data analysis procedures for the clinical trial. Researchers must strictly adhere to the protocol to ensure the consistency and reliability of study results and to minimize bias and variability in study conduct.
5. **Quality Assurance and Control:** Ensuring the quality and integrity of clinical trial data is essential for generating reliable and credible results. ICH-GCP guidelines emphasize the implementation of quality assurance and quality control measures throughout the research process, including the establishment of standard operating procedures, document control systems, training programs, and internal audits to monitor and evaluate compliance with regulatory requirements and study protocols.
6. **Risk Management:** Clinical trials involve inherent risks to participants, researchers, and the integrity of the study data. ICH-GCP guidelines require sponsors and investigators to identify, assess, mitigate, and communicate risks associated with the research protocol, study interventions, and participant safety. Risk management strategies should be integrated into the study design, planning, execution, and monitoring to ensure the safety and well-being of all involved parties.

By adhering to these key principles, stakeholders can ensure the ethical conduct, scientific integrity, and quality of clinical trials conducted in accordance with ICH-GCP guidelines, thereby contributing to the generation of reliable and credible data to support regulatory decisions, healthcare policy, and medical practice.

5.2.3 Implementation Challenges of ICH-GCP Guidelines

Despite their importance in ensuring the ethical conduct and scientific integrity of clinical trials, the implementation of International Council for Harmonisation of Technical Requirements for Pharmaceuticals for Human Use – Good Clinical Practice (ICH-GCP) guidelines is often fraught with challenges. These challenges arise from various factors related to regulatory requirements, organizational practices, resource constraints, and cultural differences. Addressing these challenges is crucial for promoting compliance with ICH-GCP guidelines and enhancing the quality and credibility of clinical research.

1. **Regulatory Complexity:** The regulatory landscape governing clinical trials is complex and constantly evolving, with differences in requirements among countries and regions. Sponsors and investigators must navigate diverse regulatory frameworks, guidelines, and documentation requirements, which can lead to confusion, delays, and compliance issues.
2. **Resource Constraints:** Conducting clinical trials in accordance with ICH-GCP guidelines requires significant resources, including financial, human, and infrastructural resources. However, many research institutions, particularly in low- and middle-income countries, face challenges in accessing adequate funding, expertise, and research infrastructure, which can hinder their ability to comply with ICH-GCP standards.
3. **Training and Capacity Building:** Ensuring that researchers, investigators, and other stakeholders have the necessary knowledge, skills, and expertise to conduct clinical trials in compliance with ICH-GCP guidelines is essential. However, there may be gaps in training and capacity building initiatives, particularly in resource-constrained settings, leading to inadequate understanding and implementation of ICH-GCP standards.
4. **Ethical Considerations:** Adhering to ethical principles outlined in ICH-GCP guidelines, such as obtaining informed consent, protecting participant confidentiality, and ensuring voluntary participation, can present challenges in culturally diverse contexts. Differences in cultural norms, beliefs, and attitudes towards research participation may influence the informed consent process and raise ethical concerns that must be addressed appropriately.
5. **Data Management and Quality Assurance:** Maintaining the integrity, confidentiality, and accuracy of clinical trial data is critical for ensuring the reliability and credibility of study results. However, challenges may arise in implementing robust data management systems, ensuring data quality, and complying with data protection regulations, particularly in multicenter trials involving diverse stakeholders and data sources.

6. **Compliance Monitoring and Auditing:** Monitoring and auditing are essential components of ensuring compliance with ICH-GCP guidelines throughout the lifecycle of clinical trials. However, challenges may arise in conducting timely and effective monitoring visits, addressing non-compliance issues, and implementing corrective and preventive actions to mitigate risks and ensure study integrity.
7. **Globalization of Clinical Trials:** The globalization of clinical trials has led to increased complexity and diversity in study populations, research settings, and regulatory requirements. Sponsors and investigators must navigate cultural, linguistic, and logistical challenges associated with conducting trials in diverse geographical regions, which can impact the implementation of ICH-GCP guidelines and the generalizability of study findings.

Addressing these implementation challenges requires concerted efforts from stakeholders at all levels, including regulatory authorities, sponsors, investigators, ethics committees, and research institutions. Strategies for overcoming these challenges may include enhancing regulatory harmonization and collaboration, investing in training and capacity building initiatives, strengthening ethical review processes, improving data management systems, and fostering transparency and accountability in clinical research practices. By addressing these challenges, stakeholders can promote compliance with ICH-GCP guidelines and enhance the quality, integrity, and credibility of clinical trials conducted worldwide.

5.2.4 Case Study: Adherence to ICH-GCP Guidelines in a Multi-center Clinical Trial

Introduction: In this case study, we examine the implementation of International Council for Harmonisation of Technical Requirements for Pharmaceuticals for Human Use – Good Clinical Practice (ICH-GCP) guidelines in a multi-center clinical trial investigating the efficacy and safety of a novel treatment for a rare genetic disorder. The trial involves collaboration between academic research centers and pharmaceutical companies across multiple countries.

Background: The clinical trial aims to evaluate the efficacy and safety of a gene therapy intervention for patients with a rare genetic disorder characterized by progressive neurodegeneration. The study protocol, developed in accordance with ICH-GCP guidelines, outlines the eligibility criteria, treatment regimen, outcome measures, and monitoring procedures for the trial.

Challenges Faced:

1. **Regulatory Hurdles:** Obtaining regulatory approvals from multiple national regulatory authorities posed a significant challenge due to differences in regulatory requirements, documentation, and timelines. Delays in regulatory approval processes impacted the initiation and timeline of the trial.
2. **Logistical Complexity:** Coordinating activities across multiple study sites in different countries presented logistical challenges related to study coordination, communication, and standardization of procedures. Language barriers, cultural differences, and time zone variations further compounded logistical complexities.
3. **Resource Constraints:** Some study sites, particularly those in low- and middle-income countries, faced resource constraints in terms of funding, infrastructure, and personnel. Limited access to specialized equipment, trained personnel, and research support services impacted the conduct and quality of the trial.

Strategies Implemented:

1. **Regulatory Harmonization:** The study team engaged in proactive communication and collaboration with regulatory authorities to facilitate alignment of regulatory requirements and streamline approval processes. Regular updates, clarification requests, and submission of comprehensive documentation expedited regulatory approvals.
2. **Centralized Study Coordination:** A centralized study coordination center was established to oversee and coordinate activities across study sites, ensuring consistency in study conduct, data collection, and monitoring procedures. Standard operating procedures (SOPs) were developed and disseminated to ensure uniformity in study implementation.
3. **Capacity Building:** Training and capacity building initiatives were conducted to enhance the knowledge and skills of investigators, research coordinators, and study personnel involved in the trial. Training sessions covered ICH-GCP guidelines, study protocol procedures, data collection techniques, adverse event reporting, and ethical considerations.

Outcome: Despite the challenges encountered, adherence to ICH-GCP guidelines was maintained throughout the trial, resulting in the successful completion of patient recruitment, treatment administration, and data collection. The trial yielded valuable insights into the safety and efficacy of the gene therapy intervention, contributing to the advancement of scientific knowledge and potential therapeutic options for patients with the rare genetic disorder.

Conclusion: This case study highlights the importance of adherence to ICH-GCP guidelines in ensuring the ethical conduct, scientific integrity, and quality of multi-center clinical trials. Despite the complexities and challenges encountered, proactive strategies, collaboration, and capacity building efforts enabled successful implementation of the trial, underscoring the value of standardized guidelines in guiding clinical research practices and improving patient outcomes.

5.3 CDSCO Guidelines

5.3.1 Overview of CDSCO Guidelines

The Central Drugs Standard Control Organization (CDSCO) guidelines represent a set of regulatory standards and requirements established by the regulatory authority in India for the regulation and oversight of pharmaceuticals, medical devices, and clinical research. These guidelines aim to ensure the safety, efficacy, and quality of healthcare products and practices in India, aligning with international standards while addressing the specific needs and priorities of the Indian healthcare system.

At its core, the CDSCO guidelines encompass a wide range of regulatory areas, including drug approval, manufacturing practices, clinical trials, pharmacovigilance, and post-market surveillance. They serve as a comprehensive framework for governing the entire lifecycle of healthcare products, from research and development to marketing authorization, distribution, and post-market monitoring.

Key components of the CDSCO guidelines include:

1. **Drug Approval Process:** The CDSCO guidelines outline the regulatory requirements and procedures for the approval of new drugs, biological products, and generic drugs in India. They specify the data requirements for preclinical and clinical studies, as well as the criteria for demonstrating safety, efficacy, and quality of pharmaceutical products.
2. **Manufacturing Standards:** The CDSCO guidelines establish Good Manufacturing Practices (GMP) and quality standards for

pharmaceutical manufacturing facilities to ensure the consistent production of safe, effective, and high-quality drugs. These standards encompass various aspects of manufacturing, including facility design, equipment validation, raw material sourcing, production processes, quality control, and packaging.

3. **Clinical Trial Regulations:** In line with international standards, the CDSCO guidelines provide regulatory requirements and procedures for the conduct of clinical trials in India. They specify the responsibilities of sponsors, investigators, ethics committees, and regulatory authorities in ensuring the ethical conduct, scientific integrity, and quality of clinical research.
4. **Pharmacovigilance:** The CDSCO guidelines mandate the establishment of pharmacovigilance systems to monitor and assess the safety of marketed drugs and medical devices in India. They outline the requirements for adverse event reporting, risk assessment, signal detection, and risk management, as well as the responsibilities of manufacturers, regulatory authorities, healthcare professionals, and consumers in pharmacovigilance activities.
5. **Post-Market Surveillance:** The CDSCO guidelines require ongoing monitoring and surveillance of marketed drugs and medical devices to detect and address potential safety concerns, quality issues, and regulatory violations. They specify the procedures for conducting inspections, audits, and investigations of manufacturing facilities, distribution channels, and adverse event reports.

Overall, the CDSCO guidelines play a crucial role in safeguarding public health and promoting access to safe, effective, and quality healthcare products in India. By establishing regulatory standards and requirements, the CDSCO guidelines contribute to the regulation and oversight of the pharmaceutical and healthcare industry, ensuring compliance with applicable laws,

5.3.2 Comparison with ICH-GCP Guidelines

The Central Drugs Standard Control Organization (CDSCO) guidelines and the International Council for Harmonisation of Technical Requirements for Pharmaceuticals for Human Use – Good Clinical Practice (ICH-GCP) guidelines are both regulatory frameworks aimed at ensuring the ethical conduct, scientific integrity, and quality of clinical research. While they share common objectives, there are notable differences between the two sets of guidelines in terms of scope, applicability, and regulatory requirements.

1. **Scope and Applicability:**

   - **CDSCO Guidelines:** The CDSCO guidelines primarily focus on regulatory standards and requirements specific to India's healthcare system and pharmaceutical industry. They encompass a wide range of regulatory areas, including drug approval, manufacturing practices, clinical trials, pharmacovigilance, and post-market surveillance, and are applicable to pharmaceutical companies, research institutions, healthcare professionals, and regulatory authorities operating within India.
   - **ICH-GCP Guidelines:** In contrast, the ICH-GCP guidelines are internationally recognized standards developed through a collaborative effort between regulatory authorities and pharmaceutical industry representatives from different regions, including the United States, Europe, and Japan. These guidelines provide a harmonized framework for the design, conduct, monitoring, and reporting of clinical trials globally, irrespective of geographic location or jurisdiction. They are applicable to sponsors, investigators, ethics committees, and regulatory authorities involved in clinical research worldwide.

1. **Regulatory Requirements:**

   - **CDSCO Guidelines:** The CDSCO guidelines are tailored to meet the specific regulatory requirements and priorities of the Indian healthcare system. They outline the procedures and criteria for drug approval, manufacturing practices, clinical trial regulations, pharmacovigilance, and post-market surveillance in India, taking into account local epidemiological factors, healthcare infrastructure, and regulatory frameworks.
   - **ICH-GCP Guidelines:** The ICH-GCP guidelines provide a standardized framework for the ethical conduct and quality assurance of clinical trials across different countries and regions. They emphasize principles such as patient safety, informed consent, data integrity, and regulatory compliance, while allowing for

flexibility in implementation to accommodate local regulations and cultural considerations.

3. **Harmonization with International Standards:**

    - **CDSCO Guidelines:** While the CDSCO guidelines are aligned with international best practices and standards, they may incorporate specific requirements and procedures tailored to the Indian context. Collaborative efforts are made to harmonize CDSCO guidelines with relevant international guidelines, including ICH-GCP guidelines, to facilitate global regulatory convergence and mutual recognition of regulatory decisions.
    - **ICH-GCP Guidelines:** The ICH-GCP guidelines serve as a global benchmark for the ethical conduct and quality assurance of clinical trials, providing a common framework for sponsors, investigators, and regulatory authorities worldwide. They promote harmonization of regulatory standards and facilitate the acceptance of clinical trial data across different regulatory jurisdictions, thereby accelerating the development and approval of new therapies and treatments.

5.3.3 Unique Features of CDSCO Guidelines

The Central Drugs Standard Control Organization (CDSCO) guidelines incorporate several unique features that distinguish them from other regulatory frameworks and contribute to their effectiveness in regulating pharmaceuticals, medical devices, and clinical research in India. These features address the specific needs, priorities, and challenges of India's healthcare system and pharmaceutical industry, ensuring the safety, efficacy, and quality of healthcare products and practices.

1. **Tailored to Indian Healthcare System:** The CDSCO guidelines are specifically tailored to meet the regulatory requirements and priorities of India's healthcare system, taking into account factors such as disease burden, healthcare infrastructure, epidemiological trends, and regulatory frameworks. They are designed to address the unique challenges and opportunities associated with healthcare delivery and pharmaceutical regulation in India, promoting access to safe, effective, and affordable healthcare products for the Indian population.

2. **Focus on Access to Medicines:** A key emphasis of the CDSCO guidelines is to promote access to essential medicines and healthcare products for the Indian population, particularly for diseases prevalent in low- and middle-income countries. The guidelines prioritize the approval and availability of affordable generic drugs and biosimilars, facilitating competition, price reduction, and increased access to essential therapies for patients.
3. **Emphasis on Traditional Medicines:** Recognizing the importance of traditional systems of medicine in India, the CDSCO guidelines incorporate provisions for the regulation of traditional medicines, herbal products, and traditional healthcare practices. They establish standards and requirements for the safety, efficacy, and quality of traditional medicines, ensuring their appropriate use and integration into the mainstream healthcare system.
4. **Promotion of Innovation:** While ensuring regulatory compliance and quality assurance, the CDSCO guidelines also aim to foster innovation and research in the pharmaceutical and healthcare sectors. They provide pathways and incentives for the development and approval of new drugs, biological products, medical devices, and innovative therapies, supporting India's emergence as a hub for pharmaceutical research, innovation, and manufacturing.
5. **Collaborative Approach:** The CDSCO guidelines promote collaboration and partnership among various stakeholders, including government agencies, pharmaceutical companies, research institutions, healthcare professionals, patient groups, and civil society organizations. Collaborative efforts are made to develop, implement, and review regulatory standards, guidelines, and policies, ensuring stakeholder engagement, transparency, and accountability in regulatory decision-making.
6. **Adaptability and Flexibility:** Recognizing the dynamic nature of healthcare and pharmaceutical regulation, the CDSCO guidelines are designed to be adaptable and flexible, allowing for updates, revisions, and amendments in response to emerging trends, scientific advancements, and regulatory developments. They incorporate mechanisms for continuous improvement, feedback, and stakeholder consultation to ensure relevance, effectiveness, and responsiveness to changing healthcare needs and challenges.

5.3.4 Challenges in Harmonizing CDSCO Guidelines with International Standards

Harmonizing Central Drugs Standard Control Organization (CDSCO) guidelines with international standards presents several challenges due to differences in regulatory frameworks, healthcare systems, and priorities between India and other countries. These challenges can hinder efforts to align regulatory requirements and promote mutual recognition of regulatory decisions, potentially impacting the efficiency, consistency, and effectiveness of global pharmaceutical regulation.

1. **Regulatory Variability:** One of the primary challenges in harmonizing CDSCO guidelines with international standards is the variability in regulatory requirements and practices among different countries and regions. Regulatory frameworks, approval processes, documentation requirements, and quality standards may differ significantly, making it challenging to achieve alignment and mutual recognition of regulatory decisions.
2. **Diversity of Healthcare Systems:** Differences in healthcare systems, infrastructure, and resources between India and other countries can complicate efforts to harmonize CDSCO guidelines with international standards. Healthcare delivery models, patient populations, disease burdens, and epidemiological profiles may vary, necessitating tailored regulatory approaches and standards to address country-specific needs and priorities.
3. **Resource Constraints:** Resource constraints, particularly in low- and middle-income countries, can pose challenges in implementing and complying with international standards and requirements. Limited funding, infrastructure, technical expertise, and regulatory capacity may hinder efforts to harmonize CDSCO guidelines with international standards, leading to disparities in regulatory practices and outcomes.
4. **Cultural and Sociopolitical Factors:** Cultural norms, sociopolitical dynamics, and public health priorities may influence regulatory decision-making and implementation in different countries. Variations in attitudes towards healthcare, patient preferences, ethical considerations, and public perception of pharmaceutical regulation may impact the alignment of CDSCO guidelines with international standards and the acceptance of regulatory harmonization initiatives.

5. **Complexity of Global Supply Chains:** The globalization of pharmaceutical manufacturing and supply chains introduces complexity and challenges in ensuring compliance with international standards and regulations. Supply chain integrity, product quality, manufacturing practices, and distribution networks may vary across different countries and regions, posing risks to regulatory harmonization efforts and patient safety.
6. **Data Requirements and Standards:** Differences in data requirements, documentation standards, and data submission formats between CDSCO guidelines and international standards can create barriers to regulatory harmonization. Harmonizing data requirements for clinical trials, drug approval applications, and post-market surveillance activities requires alignment of data standards, terminology, and reporting formats across regulatory jurisdictions.

5.4 Challenges in Guideline Implementation

5.4.1 Lack of Awareness and Training

One of the primary challenges in the implementation of clinical practice guidelines is the lack of awareness and adequate training among healthcare professionals. This challenge arises due to several factors:

1. **Complexity of Guidelines:** Clinical practice guidelines often contain detailed recommendations based on the latest evidence, which may be complex and difficult to understand for healthcare professionals without specialized training. The sheer volume of guidelines across different specialties and subspecialties further complicates the dissemination and understanding of these recommendations.
2. **Limited Access to Guidelines:** Healthcare professionals may face challenges in accessing up-to-date clinical practice guidelines, particularly in resource-constrained settings or in regions where electronic resources are not readily available. Lack of access to guidelines hinders their adoption and implementation in clinical practice.
3. **Inadequate Training Programs:** Healthcare professionals may not receive adequate training on how to interpret and apply clinical practice guidelines in their day-to-day practice. Training programs on guideline implementation, evidence-based medicine, and critical appraisal skills may be lacking or insufficiently integrated into medical education and continuing professional development.

4. **Resistance to Change:** Healthcare professionals may be resistant to change and reluctant to adopt new guidelines, especially if they perceive them as conflicting with their clinical judgment or established practices. Overcoming resistance to change requires effective communication, engagement, and leadership to foster a culture of evidence-based practice within healthcare organizations.
5. **Resource Constraints:** Implementation of clinical practice guidelines often requires additional resources, including time, personnel, technology, and financial support. Healthcare settings with limited resources may struggle to allocate sufficient resources for guideline implementation, leading to gaps in awareness, training, and infrastructure needed to support guideline adherence.

Addressing the challenge of lack of awareness and training in guideline implementation requires multifaceted strategies:

- **Education and Training Programs:** Developing and implementing educational programs and training initiatives to enhance healthcare professionals‘ awareness, knowledge, and skills in guideline interpretation, application, and implementation.
- **Guideline Dissemination:** Utilizing diverse channels for disseminating clinical practice guidelines, including online platforms, academic journals, professional societies, and continuing medical education activities, to improve accessibility and awareness among healthcare professionals.
- **Clinical Decision Support Systems:** Integrating clinical decision support systems (CDSS) into electronic health records (EHRs) and healthcare workflows to provide real-time access to evidence-based recommendations and support guideline adherence at the point of care.
- **Quality Improvement Initiatives:** Implementing quality improvement initiatives, audit and feedback mechanisms, and performance metrics to monitor guideline adherence, identify barriers to implementation, and drive continuous improvement in clinical practice.
- **Multidisciplinary Collaboration:** Engaging multidisciplinary teams, including physicians, nurses, pharmacists, allied health professionals, and administrators, in guideline implementation efforts to foster collaboration, communication, and shared responsibility for improving patient care outcomes.

5.4.2 Resource Constraints

Resource constraints pose a significant challenge to the effective implementation of clinical practice guidelines in healthcare settings. These constraints may manifest in various forms, including:

1. **Financial Limitations:** Healthcare organizations, particularly those in low-resource settings or underfunded healthcare systems, may face financial constraints that limit their ability to invest in guideline implementation initiatives. Lack of funding for staff training, infrastructure development, technology upgrades, and quality improvement efforts can impede the adoption and adherence to clinical practice guidelines.
2. **Human Resources:** Shortages of healthcare professionals, such as physicians, nurses, pharmacists, and allied health workers, can strain healthcare delivery systems and limit the capacity to implement clinical practice guidelines effectively. High patient-to-provider ratios, staff turnover, and workforce shortages can compromise the availability of personnel needed to adhere to guidelines and deliver evidence-based care.
3. **Infrastructure and Equipment:** Inadequate infrastructure, outdated facilities, and insufficient medical equipment can hinder the implementation of clinical practice guidelines. Lack of access to essential resources, such as diagnostic tools, medications, medical supplies, and supportive technologies, may prevent healthcare providers from delivering guideline-recommended care and interventions.
4. **Information Technology:** Limited access to information technology (IT) infrastructure, electronic health records (EHRs), clinical decision support systems (CDSS), and health information exchange (HIE) platforms can hamper the integration and dissemination of clinical practice guidelines into routine clinical workflows. Inadequate IT systems may impede the electronic delivery of guideline recommendations and real-time decision support to healthcare providers at the point of care.
5. **Training and Education:** Insufficient opportunities for staff training, continuing medical education (CME), and professional development can hinder healthcare professionals' awareness, knowledge, and skills in implementing clinical practice guidelines. Lack of access to evidence-based medicine (EBM) training programs, guideline dissemination

activities, and peer learning opportunities may limit the ability of providers to stay updated on best practices and guidelines.

Addressing resource constraints in guideline implementation requires a multifaceted approach:

- **Advocacy and Funding:** Advocating for increased funding and resource allocation for healthcare organizations, particularly in underserved communities and low-resource settings, to support guideline implementation initiatives, infrastructure upgrades, and workforce development efforts.
- **Strategic Planning:** Developing strategic plans and resource allocation strategies that prioritize guideline implementation as a core component of quality improvement and patient safety initiatives. Aligning resource allocation decisions with organizational priorities, performance metrics, and patient outcomes goals.
- **Collaboration and Partnerships:** Leveraging collaborations and partnerships with government agencies, non-profit organizations, academic institutions, and private sector stakeholders to mobilize resources, share best practices, and support guideline implementation efforts through joint initiatives and resource-sharing agreements.
- **Capacity Building:** Investing in workforce development programs, staff training initiatives, and professional education opportunities to enhance healthcare professionals' knowledge, skills, and competencies in guideline interpretation, application, and implementation.
- **Technology Adoption:** Investing in information technology infrastructure, EHR systems, CDSS platforms, telemedicine solutions, and digital health tools to facilitate the integration and dissemination of clinical practice guidelines into routine clinical workflows and decision-making processes.
- **Quality Improvement:** Implementing quality improvement methodologies, performance measurement systems, and audit and feedback mechanisms to monitor guideline adherence, identify resource gaps, and drive continuous improvement in guideline implementation efforts.

5.4.3 Interpretation Variability

Interpretation variability poses a significant challenge to the effective implementation of clinical practice guidelines in healthcare settings. This challenge arises due to several factors:

1. **Subjectivity in Guidelines:** Clinical practice guidelines often contain recommendations that are open to interpretation, allowing for flexibility in application based on individual patient characteristics, clinician expertise, and clinical judgment. However, this subjectivity can lead to variability in how guidelines are interpreted and applied in practice, resulting in inconsistent adherence to recommended practices.
2. **Complexity of Recommendations:** Some clinical practice guidelines may contain complex or ambiguous recommendations that are difficult to interpret and apply in real-world clinical scenarios. Guidelines that lack clarity, specificity, or actionable guidance may be subject to misinterpretation or varying interpretations among healthcare providers, leading to inconsistency in care delivery.
3. **Clinician Knowledge and Experience:** Variability in clinician knowledge, experience, training, and familiarity with clinical practice guidelines can influence how guidelines are interpreted and implemented in clinical practice. Healthcare providers with different backgrounds, specialties, and levels of expertise may interpret guidelines differently based on their individual understanding and clinical judgment.
4. **Patient Factors:** Patient-specific factors, including demographics, comorbidities, preferences, values, and social determinants of health, can influence how guidelines are interpreted and applied in clinical practice. Clinicians may tailor guideline recommendations based on individual patient needs and preferences, leading to variability in care delivery and treatment decisions.
5. **Healthcare Setting Differences:** Variability in healthcare settings, practice settings, and organizational cultures can impact how guidelines are interpreted and implemented across different institutions, specialties, and regions. Variations in resources, infrastructure, workflows, and clinical pathways may contribute to differences in guideline adherence and interpretation among healthcare providers.

Addressing interpretation variability in guideline implementation requires multifaceted strategies:

- **Guideline Clarity and Consistency:** Developing clinical practice guidelines that are clear, concise, evidence-based, and actionable can help reduce interpretation variability among healthcare providers. Guidelines should provide specific recommendations, algorithms, decision trees, and clinical scenarios to guide practice and minimize ambiguity.
- **Education and Training:** Providing comprehensive education, training, and continuing medical education (CME) programs to healthcare providers on guideline interpretation, application, and implementation can enhance consistency and adherence to recommended practices. Training initiatives should focus on evidence-based medicine (EBM), critical appraisal skills, guideline dissemination, and clinical decision-making.
- **Clinical Decision Support Systems (CDSS):** Integrating clinical decision support systems (CDSS) into electronic health records (EHRs) and clinical workflows can help standardize guideline implementation and reduce interpretation variability by providing real-time guidance, alerts, reminders, and decision support to healthcare providers at the point of care.
- **Peer Collaboration and Feedback:** Facilitating peer collaboration, multidisciplinary team discussions, and case-based learning opportunities can promote consensus building, shared decision-making, and peer review of guideline interpretation and implementation practices. Peer feedback mechanisms and quality improvement initiatives can help identify and address variability in care delivery.
- **Quality Assurance and Monitoring:** Implementing quality assurance mechanisms, audit and feedback processes, performance metrics, and benchmarking initiatives can help monitor and evaluate guideline adherence, interpretation variability, and clinical outcomes. Regular review of adherence rates, clinical outcomes, and patient satisfaction can inform continuous quality improvement efforts.

5.4.4 Case Study: Overcoming Implementation Challenges in a Resource-Limited Setting

Introduction: This case study examines the successful implementation of clinical practice guidelines in a resource-limited healthcare setting, highlighting strategies employed to overcome common implementation challenges.

Background: The healthcare facility, located in a rural area with limited financial resources and infrastructure, aimed to improve the quality of care for patients with chronic diseases, such as diabetes and hypertension. However, implementation barriers, including lack of awareness, limited staff training, and inadequate infrastructure, initially hindered guideline adherence and quality improvement efforts.

Challenges Faced:

1. **Limited Financial Resources:** The healthcare facility faced budget constraints, limiting investments in staff training, infrastructure upgrades, and technology adoption needed for guideline implementation.
2. **Staff Training and Awareness:** Healthcare providers lacked awareness and training on evidence-based practices and clinical guidelines, leading to inconsistent adherence and interpretation of recommended practices.
3. **Infrastructure Deficiencies:** Inadequate infrastructure, including outdated equipment, limited access to electronic health records (EHRs), and absence of clinical decision support systems (CDSS), hampered guideline implementation and data-driven decision-making.
4. **Patient Education and Engagement:** Limited patient education resources and community outreach initiatives hindered efforts to engage and empower patients in self-management of chronic diseases and adherence to guideline-recommended treatments.

Strategies Implemented:

1. **Training and Capacity Building:** The healthcare facility prioritized staff training and capacity building initiatives, offering regular workshops, seminars, and online courses on evidence-based medicine, clinical guidelines, and chronic disease management.
2. **Guideline Adaptation and Simplification:** Clinical practice guidelines were adapted and simplified to align with the facility's resources, patient population, and clinical workflows, ensuring relevance and feasibility of implementation.
3. **Technology Integration:** Despite resource limitations, the facility leveraged existing technology, such as mobile health (mHealth) applications and telemedicine platforms, to facilitate guideline implementation, patient monitoring, and remote consultations.

4. **Community Partnerships:** Collaborating with community organizations, local governments, and non-profit groups, the facility implemented community-based education programs, health fairs, and outreach initiatives to raise awareness and engage patients in self-management of chronic diseases.
5. **Quality Improvement Initiatives:** Implementing quality improvement methodologies, such as Plan-Do-Study-Act (PDSA) cycles and continuous quality improvement (CQI) projects, the facility monitored guideline adherence, identified barriers to implementation, and implemented targeted interventions to address gaps in care delivery.

Outcomes: Despite resource constraints, the healthcare facility achieved significant improvements in guideline adherence, patient outcomes, and quality of care for chronic diseases. Key outcomes included:

- Increased staff awareness and adherence to clinical practice guidelines.
- Improved patient education and engagement in self-management of chronic diseases.
- Enhanced infrastructure and technology integration to support guideline implementation.
- Reduction in disease complications, hospital admissions, and healthcare costs.
- Recognition as a model of best practices in guideline implementation and quality improvement in resource-limited settings.

Conclusion: This case study demonstrates that with strategic planning, innovative solutions, and community partnerships, healthcare facilities in resource-limited settings can overcome implementation challenges and achieve meaningful improvements in guideline adherence and patient care outcomes. By prioritizing staff training, guideline adaptation, technology integration, and community engagement, healthcare organizations can enhance the quality, effectiveness, and sustainability of guideline implementation efforts, ultimately improving the health and well-being of underserved populations.

5.4.5 Strategies for Effective Guideline Implementation

Effective implementation of clinical practice guidelines requires a multifaceted approach that addresses various challenges and barriers. The following strategies can enhance the uptake, adherence, and impact of guidelines in healthcare settings:

1. **Multidisciplinary Stakeholder Engagement:** Engage diverse stakeholders, including clinicians, administrators, policymakers, patients, and community representatives, in the guideline implementation process. Collaborative decision-making, shared accountability, and stakeholder involvement promote buy-in, ownership, and sustainability of implementation efforts.
2. **Leadership and Organizational Culture:** Cultivate strong leadership support and foster a culture of quality improvement, evidence-based practice, and continuous learning within healthcare organizations. Leadership commitment, clear communication, and alignment of organizational priorities with guideline implementation goals are essential for driving change and promoting a culture of excellence.
3. **Tailored Implementation Strategies:** Customize implementation strategies to the specific needs, context, and resources of healthcare settings. Adapt guidelines to local practice environments, patient populations, and available resources, and tailor implementation plans to address unique challenges and barriers to adherence.
4. **Education and Training:** Provide comprehensive education, training, and support to healthcare providers on guideline interpretation, application, and implementation. Offer continuing medical education (CME) programs, workshops, seminars, and online resources to enhance clinicians' knowledge, skills, and confidence in following guideline recommendations.
5. **Clinical Decision Support Systems (CDSS):** Integrate clinical decision support systems (CDSS) into electronic health records (EHRs) and clinical workflows to provide real-time guidance, reminders, and alerts to healthcare providers at the point of care. CDSS can facilitate adherence to guideline-recommended practices, streamline decision-making, and promote evidence-based care delivery.
6. **Quality Improvement Initiatives:** Implement quality improvement methodologies, such as Plan-Do-Study-Act (PDSA) cycles, audit and feedback, and performance metrics, to monitor guideline adherence, identify gaps in care delivery, and implement targeted interventions for improvement. Continuous monitoring, evaluation, and feedback mechanisms are essential for driving practice change and sustaining improvements over time.

7. **Patient Engagement and Shared Decision-Making:** Engage patients as partners in care by providing education, resources, and support to empower them in self-management of their health conditions. Foster shared decision-making, open communication, and collaboration between patients and healthcare providers to ensure that guideline recommendations align with patients' values, preferences, and goals of care.
8. **Health Information Technology (HIT) Solutions:** Leverage health information technology (HIT) solutions, such as electronic health records (EHRs), telemedicine platforms, mobile health (mHealth) applications, and remote monitoring devices, to support guideline implementation, data-driven decision-making, and patient engagement. HIT solutions can enhance communication, coordination, and continuity of care across healthcare settings.
9. **Continuous Learning and Adaptation:** Foster a culture of continuous learning, adaptation, and improvement by regularly reviewing and updating clinical practice guidelines based on new evidence, emerging best practices, and feedback from frontline clinicians and patients. Encourage ongoing quality improvement efforts and learning collaboratives to promote innovation and excellence in care delivery.

5.5 Ensuring Compliance and Quality Assurance

5.5.1 Monitoring and Auditing Procedures

Monitoring and auditing procedures are essential components of ensuring compliance with clinical practice guidelines and maintaining quality assurance in healthcare settings. These procedures involve systematic assessment, evaluation, and review of clinical practices, processes, and outcomes to identify areas for improvement, ensure adherence to guidelines, and mitigate risks to patient safety. Key elements of monitoring and auditing procedures include:

1. **Establishment of Performance Metrics:** Define clear performance metrics, quality indicators, and benchmarks aligned with clinical practice guidelines and organizational goals. Performance metrics may include measures of guideline adherence, clinical outcomes, patient satisfaction, and process efficiency to assess the quality and effectiveness of care delivery.

2. **Regular Data Collection and Analysis:** Collect relevant data on clinical practices, processes, and outcomes using standardized data collection tools, electronic health records (EHRs), and clinical registries. Analyze data systematically to identify trends, patterns, variations, and areas of concern that require further investigation or quality improvement interventions.
3. **Peer Review and Clinical Feedback:** Conduct peer review and clinical feedback sessions to review clinical cases, treatment decisions, and adherence to guidelines among healthcare providers. Collaborative discussions, case presentations, and feedback from peers can promote learning, knowledge sharing, and consensus building on best practices and guideline adherence.
4. **Internal Audits and Quality Reviews:** Perform regular internal audits, quality reviews, and compliance assessments to evaluate adherence to clinical practice guidelines, regulatory requirements, and organizational policies. Use audit findings to identify areas of non-compliance, root causes of deviations, and opportunities for corrective action and quality improvement.
5. **External Audits and Accreditation Surveys:** Participate in external audits, accreditation surveys, and regulatory inspections conducted by accrediting bodies, government agencies, or third-party organizations. External audits provide independent validation of compliance with standards, guidelines, and quality assurance requirements and may identify areas for improvement and benchmarking against peers.
6. **Feedback Mechanisms and Performance Reporting:** Establish feedback mechanisms and performance reporting systems to communicate audit findings, quality metrics, and performance indicators to stakeholders, including healthcare providers, administrators, governing bodies, and patients. Transparent reporting promotes accountability, transparency, and continuous improvement in care delivery.
7. **Root Cause Analysis and Corrective Action:** Conduct root cause analysis (RCA) and corrective action planning to address identified deficiencies, deviations, or adverse events. Implement corrective actions, process improvements, and quality assurance measures to prevent recurrence of errors, enhance patient safety, and optimize clinical outcomes.
8. **Continuous Quality Improvement (CQI) Initiatives:** Integrate monitoring and auditing procedures into a continuous quality

improvement (CQI) framework that emphasizes ongoing assessment, feedback, learning, and adaptation. CQI initiatives promote a culture of excellence, innovation, and continuous improvement in healthcare delivery.

5.5.2 Role of Quality Management Systems

Quality management systems (QMS) play a crucial role in ensuring compliance with clinical practice guidelines and maintaining high standards of quality assurance in healthcare settings. QMS encompasses a set of policies, procedures, processes, and resources designed to monitor, evaluate, and improve the quality and safety of patient care delivery. The role of QMS in ensuring compliance and quality assurance includes the following aspects:

1. **Standardization of Processes:** QMS establishes standardized processes and procedures for clinical operations, documentation, and quality control measures. Standardization ensures consistency, reliability, and reproducibility in healthcare practices, reducing variability and minimizing the risk of errors or deviations from clinical practice guidelines.
2. **Documentation and Recordkeeping:** QMS facilitates comprehensive documentation and recordkeeping of clinical activities, patient encounters, treatment plans, and outcomes. Accurate and complete documentation ensures transparency, traceability, and accountability in healthcare delivery, supporting compliance with regulatory requirements and accreditation standards.
3. **Risk Management:** QMS incorporates risk management principles and methodologies to identify, assess, and mitigate risks to patient safety, quality of care, and regulatory compliance. Risk assessment, hazard analysis, and mitigation strategies are integral components of QMS implementation, aiming to prevent adverse events, errors, and non-conformities.
4. **Performance Measurement and Monitoring:** QMS establishes mechanisms for performance measurement, monitoring, and evaluation of key quality indicators, clinical outcomes, and process metrics. Performance data are systematically collected, analyzed, and reported to track progress, identify areas for improvement, and drive evidence-based decision-making in healthcare delivery.

5. **Continuous Quality Improvement (CQI):** QMS fosters a culture of continuous quality improvement (CQI) by promoting ongoing assessment, feedback, learning, and adaptation in healthcare organizations. CQI initiatives involve systematic review of processes, root cause analysis of deficiencies, implementation of corrective actions, and monitoring of outcomes to drive improvement in patient care quality and safety.
6. **Training and Education:** QMS supports staff training, education, and competency assessment programs to ensure that healthcare providers possess the knowledge, skills, and competencies required to deliver high-quality, guideline-concordant care. Training initiatives focus on evidence-based practices, clinical guidelines, patient safety, and quality improvement methodologies.
7. **Compliance and Accreditation:** QMS facilitates compliance with regulatory requirements, accreditation standards, and industry best practices by providing a framework for systematic adherence to guidelines, policies, and quality assurance protocols. Accreditation bodies and regulatory agencies evaluate QMS implementation as part of accreditation surveys, inspections, and audits to assess organizational compliance and quality performance.
8. **Patient-Centered Care:** QMS emphasizes patient-centered care principles by promoting patient engagement, empowerment, and involvement in decision-making processes. Patient feedback, preferences, and outcomes are integrated into QMS processes to ensure that healthcare services are responsive to patient needs, values, and preferences.

5.5.3 Continuous Improvement Strategies

Continuous improvement strategies are vital for ensuring ongoing adherence to clinical practice guidelines and enhancing quality assurance in healthcare settings. These strategies involve systematic approaches to identify, evaluate, and address opportunities for improvement in clinical practices, processes, and outcomes. Key continuous improvement strategies include:

1. **Plan-Do-Study-Act (PDSA) Cycles:** Implement Plan-Do-Study-Act (PDSA) cycles to test and implement changes in clinical practices and workflows. PDSA cycles involve planning a change, implementing it on

a small scale, studying its effects, and acting on lessons learned to refine and scale up successful interventions. This iterative approach promotes rapid-cycle testing, learning, and adaptation to drive continuous improvement.

2. **Root Cause Analysis (RCA):** Conduct root cause analysis (RCA) to investigate the underlying causes of errors, adverse events, or deviations from clinical practice guidelines. RCA involves identifying contributing factors, systemic issues, and process failures that led to the problem, implementing corrective actions to address root causes, and preventing recurrence of similar events in the future.
3. **Quality Improvement Teams:** Establish multidisciplinary quality improvement teams composed of healthcare providers, administrators, quality assurance experts, and frontline staff. Quality improvement teams collaborate to identify improvement opportunities, develop action plans, implement changes, and monitor outcomes to drive continuous improvement in patient care quality and safety.
4. **Performance Feedback and Review:** Provide regular performance feedback and review mechanisms to healthcare providers and teams on adherence to clinical practice guidelines, quality indicators, and patient outcomes. Feedback loops enable timely recognition of achievements, identification of areas for improvement, and alignment of performance with organizational goals and standards.
5. **Lean and Six Sigma Methodologies:** Apply Lean and Six Sigma methodologies to streamline processes, reduce waste, and optimize efficiency in healthcare delivery. Lean focuses on eliminating non-value-added activities, improving flow, and enhancing patient throughput, while Six Sigma aims to minimize variation, defects, and errors in clinical processes to achieve high-quality outcomes.
6. **Benchmarking and Best Practices Sharing:** Benchmark performance metrics, clinical outcomes, and quality indicators against peer institutions, industry benchmarks, and best practices. Sharing best practices, success stories, and lessons learned with other healthcare organizations fosters collaboration, learning, and adoption of evidence-based practices to drive continuous improvement across the healthcare system.
7. **Patient Engagement and Feedback:** Engage patients as partners in care by soliciting their feedback, preferences, and experiences with healthcare services. Patient feedback mechanisms, satisfaction surveys,

and patient advisory councils provide valuable insights into areas for improvement, enhance patient-centered care, and drive quality improvement efforts aligned with patient needs and priorities.

8. **Continuing Education and Training:** Provide ongoing education, training, and professional development opportunities to healthcare providers on clinical practice guidelines, evidence-based practices, and quality improvement methodologies. Continuous learning ensures that clinicians remain updated on the latest guidelines, best practices, and innovations in healthcare delivery, enabling them to deliver high-quality, guideline-concordant care.

By implementing these continuous improvement strategies, healthcare organizations can foster a culture of excellence, innovation, and continuous learning, driving ongoing adherence to clinical practice guidelines and quality assurance standards. Continuous improvement efforts contribute to better patient outcomes, enhanced safety, and greater efficiency in healthcare delivery, ultimately improving the overall quality of care provided to patients.

CHAPTER SIX

ETHICAL CONSIDERATIONS IN CLINICAL RESEARCH

6.1 Understanding Ethical Guidelines

6.1.1 Introduction to Ethical Principles in Research

Ethical principles form the cornerstone of responsible conduct in clinical research, guiding the actions and decisions of investigators, sponsors, and institutions involved in the process. At its core, ethical research upholds values such as respect for individual autonomy, beneficence, non-maleficence, and justice. Respect for autonomy entails recognizing individuals' rights to make informed decisions about their participation in research, emphasizing the importance of obtaining voluntary and informed consent. Beneficence emphasizes the obligation to maximize benefits and minimize harm to research participants, ensuring that potential risks are justified by potential benefits. Similarly, the principle of non-maleficence underscores the duty to avoid causing harm or injury to participants, necessitating careful risk assessment and mitigation strategies. Moreover, the principle of justice demands fair distribution of the benefits and burdens of research, addressing issues of equity in participant selection, access to benefits, and fair allocation of resources. These ethical principles serve as guiding frameworks, balancing the pursuit of scientific knowledge with the protection of human subjects' rights and welfare. Through adherence to these principles, researchers uphold the integrity and credibility of their work, fostering trust among stakeholders and the broader community.

6.1.2 Historical Context: Development of Ethical Guidelines

The development of ethical guidelines in clinical research reflects a historical evolution shaped by notable ethical lapses and landmark events. One pivotal moment was the Nuremberg Code of 1947, established in response to the egregious human experimentation conducted by Nazi physicians during World War II. This foundational document emphasized the primacy of voluntary consent, informed participation, and avoidance of unnecessary harm in research involving human subjects. Building upon this framework, the Declaration of Helsinki, first adopted in 1964 and subsequently revised, provided further guidance on ethical principles and standards for biomedical research. The Declaration emphasized the need for independent review of research protocols by ethics committees and underscored the importance of protecting vulnerable populations, including children, prisoners, and the mentally impaired. Additionally, the Belmont Report, published in 1979 in the United States, outlined three fundamental ethical principles—respect for persons, beneficence, and justice—and articulated guidelines for the ethical conduct of research involving human subjects. These foundational documents, along with subsequent revisions and international collaborations, have contributed to the development of comprehensive ethical guidelines and regulatory frameworks governing clinical research worldwide. They serve as enduring pillars, guiding researchers, institutional review boards, and regulatory bodies in upholding ethical standards and safeguarding the rights and well-being of research participants.

6.1.3 Key Ethical Principles in Clinical Research

Ethical conduct in clinical research is underpinned by several key principles that serve as guiding imperatives for researchers, sponsors, and oversight bodies.

Respect for Autonomy: This principle acknowledges individuals' right to self-determination and underscores the importance of obtaining voluntary and informed consent from research participants. Respect for autonomy necessitates transparent disclosure of relevant information about the research study, including its purpose, procedures, risks, and potential benefits, enabling individuals to make autonomous decisions about their participation.

Beneficence: Central to the ethical framework of clinical research is the principle of beneficence, which emphasizes the obligation to maximize benefits and minimize harms to research participants. Researchers have a duty to ensure that potential risks are justified by the expected benefits of the research, and to prioritize the well-being of participants throughout the research process.

Non-Maleficence: Complementary to beneficence, the principle of non-maleficence enjoins researchers to avoid causing harm or injury to research participants. This principle underscores the importance of conducting thorough risk assessments and implementing appropriate measures to mitigate potential harms, thereby minimizing the likelihood of adverse outcomes.

Justice: The principle of justice requires fair distribution of the benefits and burdens of research, as well as equitable access to research opportunities. Researchers must strive to ensure that the selection of research participants is based on scientific merit and relevance to the research aims, rather than arbitrary or discriminatory criteria. Moreover, justice entails addressing disparities in access to research benefits, resources, and outcomes, particularly among vulnerable and marginalized populations.

These ethical principles provide a normative framework for responsible conduct in clinical research, guiding decision-making processes and shaping the ethical review and oversight of research protocols. By upholding these principles, researchers demonstrate their commitment to ethical integrity, accountability, and the protection of human subjects' rights and welfare.

6.2 The Informed Consent Process

In clinical research, the informed consent process serves as a critical ethical and legal requirement, ensuring that individuals understand the nature of the research study and voluntarily agree to participate. This process involves conveying essential information about the study to potential participants and obtaining their voluntary agreement to participate without coercion or undue influence. The informed consent process encompasses two key components: understanding the importance and purpose of informed consent, and delineating the essential elements that comprise a valid informed consent document.

6.2.1 Importance and Purpose of Informed Consent

The importance and purpose of informed consent in clinical research cannot be overstated. At its core, informed consent is a foundational principle rooted in respect for individual autonomy, dignity, and rights. It serves as a mechanism to uphold participants‘ rights to make autonomous decisions about their involvement in research, ensuring that they have the necessary information to make informed choices. Additionally, informed consent functions as a safeguard against potential exploitation, coercion, or harm, protecting participants' welfare and minimizing risks associated with research participation. From an ethical standpoint, obtaining valid informed consent is imperative for upholding the principles of beneficence, non-maleficence, and justice, and maintaining the integrity and credibility of the research process. Furthermore, informed consent is a legal requirement in many jurisdictions, serving as evidence of ethical conduct and compliance with regulatory standards. Overall, the informed consent process plays a vital role in promoting transparency, trust, and accountability in clinical research, while safeguarding participants‘ rights, welfare, and well-being.

6.2.2 Elements of Informed Consent

Informed consent comprises several essential elements that must be included in the consent document to ensure that participants have a thorough understanding of the research study and its implications before agreeing to participate. These elements are designed to facilitate informed decision-making and protect participants' rights and welfare throughout the research process. Key elements of informed consent include:

- Disclosure of Information: Providing participants with clear and understandable details about the purpose, procedures, risks, potential benefits, and alternatives to participation in the research study.
- Voluntariness: Ensuring that participation is voluntary and free from coercion, undue influence, or external pressures.
- Competence: Verifying that participants have the capacity to understand the information presented and make autonomous decisions about their participation.
- Understanding: Confirming that participants comprehend the information provided and appreciate the implications of their decision to participate.
- Documentation: Obtaining written documentation of participants‘ informed consent, signed voluntarily after they have been adequately informed and have had the opportunity to ask questions or seek clarification.
- Continued Consent: Informing participants that they have the right to withdraw from the study at any time without penalty or adverse consequences, and providing mechanisms for addressing concerns or questions throughout the research process.

By incorporating these essential elements into the informed consent process, researchers can ensure that participants are fully informed, empowered to make autonomous decisions, and protected from potential harms or exploitation.

6.2.2.1 Disclosure of Information

Disclosure of information is a foundational element of the informed consent process in clinical research, ensuring that participants are provided with comprehensive details about the research study to make informed decisions about their participation. This element entails transparent communication of essential information related to the purpose, procedures, risks, potential benefits, and alternatives to participation in the study.

Central to the disclosure of information is the principle of transparency, which requires researchers to provide clear and understandable explanations of the research study, avoiding technical jargon or language that may obscure key concepts. Participants should be informed about the overarching goals and objectives of the study, including its rationale and significance within the broader scientific context. Additionally, researchers must describe the specific procedures involved in the study, such as diagnostic tests, interventions, or data collection methods, ensuring that participants understand what will be required of them if they choose to participate.

Equally important is the disclosure of potential risks and benefits associated with participation in the research study. Researchers have a duty to communicate honestly and accurately about foreseeable risks or discomforts that participants may experience, as well as any potential benefits or advancements that may result from the study. This includes discussing the likelihood and severity of potential adverse events, as well as any measures in place to minimize or mitigate risks.

Moreover, participants should be informed about any alternatives to participation in the research study, such as standard treatment options or alternative research studies, allowing them to weigh the potential benefits and risks of each option and make an informed decision based on their preferences and values.

Effective disclosure of information requires researchers to tailor their communication to the individual needs, preferences, and level of understanding of participants, ensuring that information is presented in a manner that is accessible and culturally sensitive. Additionally, researchers should provide ample opportunity for participants to ask questions, seek clarification, and express any concerns or reservations they may have about the research study.

By prioritizing comprehensive disclosure of information, researchers uphold the ethical principles of respect for autonomy, beneficence, and transparency, empowering participants to make informed decisions about their involvement in clinical research while safeguarding their rights and welfare.

6.2.2.2 Competence of Participants

Another crucial element of the informed consent process in clinical research is ensuring the competence of participants to understand the information presented and make autonomous decisions about their participation. Competence refers to individuals' ability to comprehend the relevant information, appreciate the implications of their decision to participate, and communicate their preferences effectively.

Assessing participants' competence involves evaluating their cognitive abilities, decision-making capacity, and communication skills. While competence is presumed for adult individuals, certain factors such as cognitive impairment, psychiatric disorders, or language barriers may affect participants' capacity to understand and engage in the informed consent process. In such cases, researchers have a responsibility to take additional steps to assess and support participants' decision-making capacity.

Researchers should employ appropriate techniques to assess participants' competence, such as conducting interviews, using standardized assessment tools, or consulting with qualified healthcare professionals, such as psychologists or psychiatrists. These assessments should be conducted in a respectful and non-coercive manner, taking into account participants' cultural backgrounds, preferences, and individual circumstances.

If concerns arise about a participant's competence to provide informed consent, researchers should take steps to ensure that the participant's rights and welfare are protected. This may involve providing additional information or support to enhance understanding, involving legally authorized representatives or surrogate decision-makers, or seeking guidance from institutional review boards or ethics committees.

Ultimately, the goal of assessing competence is to ensure that participants are capable of making informed decisions about their participation in research, based on a thorough understanding of the relevant information and their own values, preferences, and interests. By addressing concerns about competence proactively and respectfully, researchers uphold the ethical principle of respect for persons and safeguard participants' autonomy and well-being throughout the informed consent process.

6.2.2.3 Voluntariness

Voluntariness is a fundamental principle of the informed consent process in clinical research, emphasizing the importance of participants' freedom to choose whether or not to participate without coercion, undue influence, or external pressures. Ensuring voluntariness requires researchers to create an environment that respects participants' autonomy and allows them to make decisions free from manipulation or coercion.

Participants must be given the opportunity to consider their participation in the research study without feeling obligated or pressured to do so. Researchers should clearly communicate that participation is voluntary and that individuals are free to decline or withdraw from the study at any time without facing negative consequences or reprisals. This includes informing participants that their decision regarding participation will not affect their access to medical care or other benefits to which they are entitled.

Moreover, researchers should take steps to minimize potential sources of undue influence or coercion, particularly in vulnerable populations or situations where participants may feel pressured to participate due to social, economic, or interpersonal factors. This may involve providing assurances of confidentiality, anonymity, and privacy, as well as ensuring that participants are not offered incentives or inducements that could compromise their ability to make autonomous decisions.

It is essential for researchers to establish clear boundaries and maintain a neutral stance when discussing the research study with potential participants, refraining from exerting undue influence or using persuasive tactics to encourage participation. Additionally, researchers should be attentive to power differentials that may exist between themselves and participants, taking care to avoid situations where participants may feel compelled to comply with requests due to perceived authority or influence.

By upholding the principle of voluntariness, researchers demonstrate their commitment to respecting participants' autonomy, dignity, and rights, while promoting trust, transparency, and ethical conduct in clinical research. Voluntary participation ensures that research findings are based on the genuine consent of individuals who have freely chosen to contribute to scientific knowledge, thereby enhancing the integrity and credibility of the research process.

6.2.3 Obtaining Informed Consent

Obtaining informed consent is a critical step in the ethical conduct of clinical research, ensuring that participants understand the nature of the study and voluntarily agree to participate. This process involves a series of procedures and documentation designed to facilitate informed decision-making and protect participants' rights and welfare.

6.2.3.1 Procedures and Documentation

The procedures for obtaining informed consent typically begin with the researcher providing potential participants with detailed information about the research study, including its purpose, procedures, risks, potential benefits, and alternatives to participation. This information should be presented in a clear, understandable manner, tailored to the participants' level of comprehension and cultural background. Researchers should allow participants sufficient time to review the information, ask questions, and discuss any concerns or reservations they may have.

Once participants have had the opportunity to consider the information provided, researchers must ensure that they have the capacity to understand the information and make autonomous decisions about their participation. This may involve assessing participants' competence through interviews, standardized assessment tools, or consultation with qualified healthcare professionals, particularly in cases where concerns about decision-making capacity arise.

After ensuring that participants are adequately informed and competent to provide consent, researchers must obtain their voluntary agreement to participate in the study. This typically involves presenting participants with a written consent form that outlines the key details of the research study and provides space for participants to indicate their willingness to participate by signing or providing their consent electronically.

The consent form should include all essential elements required for informed consent, such as disclosure of information, voluntariness, competence, and documentation of consent. Additionally, the consent form should clearly state that participation is voluntary and that participants have the right to withdraw from the study at any time without penalty or adverse consequences.

Researchers are responsible for ensuring that participants fully understand the information presented in the consent form and have the opportunity to ask questions or seek clarification before providing consent. This may involve using plain language, visual aids, or interpreter services to enhance participants' understanding, particularly in multicultural or multilingual settings.

Once participants have provided consent, researchers should provide them with a copy of the signed consent form for their records and retain the original document in accordance with regulatory requirements. Additionally, researchers should maintain ongoing communication with participants throughout the research study, addressing any concerns or questions that may arise and obtaining re-consent if significant changes to the study protocol occur.

By following these procedures and documenting the informed consent process appropriately, researchers uphold ethical standards, protect participants' rights, and ensure the integrity and credibility of the research study.

6.2.3.2 Special Considerations (e.g., Vulnerable Populations)

In the informed consent process for clinical research, special considerations must be given to vulnerable populations to ensure their rights, autonomy, and welfare are protected. Vulnerable populations include individuals who may be at increased risk of harm or exploitation due to factors such as age, cognitive impairment, socioeconomic status, or institutionalization. These populations require additional safeguards to mitigate potential risks and ensure that they can provide informed consent voluntarily and autonomously.

When obtaining informed consent from vulnerable populations, researchers should take into account the unique challenges and vulnerabilities that may affect participants' ability to understand the information presented and make autonomous decisions about their participation. This may involve adapting the consent process to accommodate participants' cognitive, linguistic, or sensory impairments, ensuring that information is presented in a manner that is accessible, understandable, and culturally sensitive.

Furthermore, researchers must be mindful of power dynamics and potential sources of coercion or undue influence that may impact vulnerable populations' decision-making processes. This includes avoiding situations where participants feel pressured to participate due to perceived authority figures, familial expectations, or economic incentives. Researchers should strive to create a supportive and empowering environment that encourages participants to exercise their autonomy and make decisions based on their own values, preferences, and interests.

In some cases, vulnerable populations may lack the capacity to provide informed consent independently, requiring the involvement of legally authorized representatives or surrogate decision-makers. Researchers must follow established procedures for obtaining proxy consent, ensuring that the individual acting on behalf of the participant is well-informed about the research study and can make decisions that align with the participant's best interests.

Moreover, researchers should engage in proactive outreach and collaboration with community stakeholders, advocacy groups, and healthcare providers to ensure that the informed consent process is culturally competent, respectful, and responsive to the needs and concerns of vulnerable populations. This may involve providing education and training to research staff on working with vulnerable populations, establishing partnerships with community organizations, or incorporating community feedback into the development of consent materials and procedures.

6.3 Role and Function of Institutional Review Boards (IRBs) / Independent Ethics Committees (IECs)

Institutional Review Boards (IRBs) and Independent Ethics Committees (IECs) play a crucial role in ensuring the ethical conduct of clinical research and the protection of research participants' rights, safety, and welfare. These oversight bodies are responsible for reviewing and approving research protocols, monitoring ongoing studies, and safeguarding the rights and interests of research participants.

6.3.1 Composition of IRBs/IECs

The composition of IRBs and IECs is carefully structured to ensure diverse expertise and perspectives are represented in the review and oversight process. The members of these committees are selected based on their professional qualifications, experience, and expertise in relevant disciplines, as well as their commitment to ethical principles and protection of human subjects in research.

6.3.1.1 Members and Expertise

IRBs and IECs typically comprise multidisciplinary teams of individuals with diverse backgrounds and expertise, including:

1. **Scientific Experts**: These members possess specialized knowledge and expertise in the scientific and technical aspects of the research being reviewed. They may include physicians, scientists, statisticians, and other healthcare professionals with expertise in the relevant field of study.
2. **Ethical Experts**: Ethicists or philosophers with expertise in bioethics, medical ethics, or research ethics provide critical insights into the ethical considerations and implications of the research. They help ensure that research protocols adhere to ethical principles and guidelines, including respect for autonomy, beneficence, non-maleficence, and justice.
3. **Community Representatives**: Community members or laypersons who represent the interests of the broader community served by the research institution or organization bring valuable perspectives and insights into the review process. They help ensure that research protocols are responsive to community needs, values, and concerns, and that research benefits are distributed equitably.
4. **Legal Experts**: Legal professionals, such as attorneys or legal advisors, may be included on IRBs or IECs to provide guidance on legal requirements, regulatory compliance, and liability issues related to the conduct of clinical research. They help ensure that research protocols adhere to applicable laws, regulations, and institutional policies.
5. **Patient Advocates**: Individuals with personal or professional experience as patient advocates or representatives of patient advocacy organizations contribute valuable perspectives on the interests, rights, and well-being of research participants. They advocate for participant-centered approaches and ensure that participant voices are heard and respected in the review process.
6. **Institutional Representatives**: Institutional officials or administrators responsible for research oversight and compliance, such as research directors, compliance officers, or legal counsel, may serve as ex officio members or liaisons to the IRB or IEC. They provide institutional support, resources, and guidance to ensure effective IRB/IEC operations and adherence to institutional policies and procedures.

6.3.1.2 Conflicts of Interest

Conflicts of interest represent a significant concern in the composition and functioning of Institutional Review Boards (IRBs) and Independent Ethics Committees (IECs), as they have the potential to undermine the impartiality and integrity of the review process. Conflicts of interest occur when IRB/IEC members have competing personal, professional, financial, or institutional interests that may influence their judgment or decision-making regarding research protocols.

To mitigate conflicts of interest, IRBs and IECs typically implement policies and procedures to identify, disclose, manage, and, when necessary, mitigate or eliminate conflicts of interest among their members. Key strategies include:

1. **Disclosure Requirements**: Members are required to disclose any relevant financial interests, professional affiliations, or personal relationships that may pose a conflict of interest with respect to specific research protocols under review. Transparent disclosure enables IRBs and IECs to assess potential conflicts and take appropriate action to address them.
2. **Recusal and Abstention**: Members with identified conflicts of interest are typically required to recuse themselves from the review and decision-making process for the affected research protocol. This ensures that individuals with potential biases or conflicts do not participate in the evaluation or approval of protocols where their interests may unduly influence their judgment.
3. **Independent Review and Oversight**: IRBs and IECs may establish independent review mechanisms or oversight committees tasked with evaluating conflicts of interest disclosures, assessing their potential impact on the review process, and determining appropriate mitigation strategies. Independent oversight helps ensure objectivity, fairness, and transparency in conflict resolution.
4. **Decision-Making Protocols**: IRBs and IECs may adopt formal decision-making protocols or voting procedures to address conflicts of interest and ensure that decisions regarding research protocols are made impartially and based on the merits of the protocol and its ethical considerations, rather than personal interests or biases.
5. **Training and Education**: Members of IRBs and IECs receive training and education on conflicts of interest, ethical principles, and regulatory requirements governing research review and oversight. Training programs help raise awareness of potential conflicts, enhance members' understanding of their ethical responsibilities, and promote adherence to best practices in conflict management and resolution.

6. **Regular Monitoring and Review**: IRBs and IECs conduct regular monitoring and review of their members' disclosures and conflict management processes to ensure compliance with established policies and procedures. Ongoing evaluation helps identify areas for improvement, strengthen conflict management mechanisms, and maintain public trust and confidence in the integrity of the review process.

6.3.2 Responsibilities of IRBs/IECs

Institutional Review Boards (IRBs) and Independent Ethics Committees (IECs) are entrusted with a range of critical responsibilities to ensure the ethical conduct of clinical research and the protection of research participants' rights, safety, and welfare. One of their primary responsibilities is the review of research protocols.

6.3.2.1 Review of Research Protocols

The review of research protocols is a core function of IRBs and IECs, involving a comprehensive evaluation of the scientific, ethical, and regulatory aspects of proposed research studies. The review process typically includes the following key components:

1. **Scientific Merit**: IRBs and IECs assess the scientific merit and validity of research protocols to ensure that they are based on sound scientific principles and have the potential to contribute valuable knowledge to the field. This involves evaluating the study design, methodology, feasibility, and scientific rationale, as well as the qualifications and expertise of the research team.
2. **Ethical Considerations**: IRBs and IECs evaluate the ethical aspects of research protocols to ensure that they adhere to ethical principles and guidelines governing the conduct of research involving human participants. This includes assessing the risks and potential benefits of the research, the adequacy of informed consent procedures, protections for vulnerable populations, and plans for ensuring privacy, confidentiality, and data security.
3. **Regulatory Compliance**: IRBs and IECs ensure that research protocols comply with applicable laws, regulations, and institutional policies governing the conduct of clinical research. This includes compliance with regulatory requirements related to human subjects protection, data privacy and security, informed consent, and reporting of adverse events

or protocol deviations.

4. **Protection of Participants**: A primary focus of IRB and IEC review is the protection of research participants' rights, safety, and welfare. Committees carefully evaluate the risks and potential benefits of the research to ensure that participants are not exposed to undue harm or exploitation. Additionally, IRBs and IECs assess the adequacy of measures to protect the confidentiality, privacy, and dignity of participants, as well as provisions for monitoring participant safety and responding to adverse events or unanticipated problems.
5. **Informed Consent**: IRBs and IECs review informed consent documents and procedures to ensure that participants are provided with clear, understandable information about the research study and have the opportunity to make informed decisions about their participation. This includes evaluating the adequacy of the information provided, the voluntariness of participants' consent, and the procedures for obtaining and documenting consent.
6. **Continuing Review**: IRBs and IECs conduct ongoing review and oversight of approved research studies to ensure compliance with approved protocols, regulatory requirements, and ethical standards. This includes monitoring study progress, reviewing amendments or modifications to the protocol, and assessing reports of adverse events or protocol deviations.

Ongoing Oversight and Monitoring

In addition to the initial review of research protocols, Institutional Review Boards (IRBs) and Independent Ethics Committees (IECs) are responsible for providing ongoing oversight and monitoring of approved research studies. This continuous evaluation ensures that research protocols remain in compliance with ethical principles, regulatory requirements, and institutional policies throughout the duration of the study.

Key aspects of ongoing oversight and monitoring include:

1. **Study Progress Monitoring**: IRBs and IECs regularly monitor the progress of approved research studies to ensure that they are being conducted in accordance with the approved protocol, informed consent procedures, and applicable regulations. This involves reviewing study reports, progress updates, and any amendments or modifications to the protocol to assess compliance and identify any issues or concerns that

may arise during the course of the study.

2. **Adverse Event Reporting**: Research teams are required to promptly report any adverse events, unanticipated problems, or protocol deviations to the IRB or IEC overseeing the study. Committees review these reports to assess the severity of the events, their relationship to the research intervention or procedures, and the adequacy of measures to protect participant safety. Depending on the nature and severity of the events, IRBs and IECs may recommend changes to the protocol, additional safety monitoring, or suspension or termination of the study if warranted.
3. **Protocol Amendments**: If significant changes to the research protocol are proposed during the course of the study, such as modifications to study procedures, eligibility criteria, or informed consent documents, IRBs and IECs must review and approve these amendments to ensure that they comply with ethical principles and regulatory requirements. Amendments may be submitted by the research team for review and approval before implementation to ensure ongoing compliance and participant protection.
4. **Participant Enrollment and Retention**: IRBs and IECs monitor participant enrollment and retention rates to ensure that recruitment efforts are conducted ethically and transparently, and that participants are not unduly coerced or incentivized to participate. Committees may review recruitment materials, enrollment logs, and retention strategies to assess compliance with ethical guidelines and ensure that participants' rights and welfare are protected throughout the study.
5. **Data and Safety Monitoring**: Some research studies, particularly clinical trials involving investigational drugs or devices, may require independent data and safety monitoring committees (DSMCs) to oversee participant safety and data integrity. IRBs and IECs collaborate with DSMCs to ensure that appropriate safety monitoring plans are in place, adverse events are promptly reported and evaluated, and data quality and integrity are maintained throughout the study.

By providing ongoing oversight and monitoring of approved research studies, IRBs and IECs fulfill their responsibility to protect research participants, uphold ethical standards, and ensure the integrity and credibility of clinical research. Their proactive approach to monitoring study progress, addressing issues as they arise, and promoting continuous improvement helps to maintain public trust and confidence in the research enterprise.

6.3.2.3 Continuing Review of Approved Research

Institutional Review Boards (IRBs) and Independent Ethics Committees (IECs) are tasked with conducting continuing reviews of approved research studies to ensure ongoing compliance with ethical principles, regulatory requirements, and institutional policies. These reviews are essential for maintaining the integrity of research protocols and safeguarding the rights, safety, and welfare of research participants throughout the duration of the study.

Key aspects of the continuing review process include:

1. **Scheduled Reviews**: IRBs and IECs establish policies and procedures for conducting scheduled continuing reviews of approved research studies at regular intervals, as mandated by regulatory guidelines or institutional policies. The frequency and timing of these reviews may vary depending on factors such as the level of risk associated with the study, the duration of participant involvement, and the requirements of the funding agency or regulatory authority.
2. **Review of Study Progress**: During continuing reviews, IRBs and IECs evaluate the progress of approved research studies to ensure that they are being conducted in accordance with the approved protocol, informed consent procedures, and applicable regulations. This involves reviewing study reports, progress updates, and any amendments or modifications to the protocol since the last review to assess compliance and identify any issues or concerns that may have arisen during the course of the study.
3. **Assessment of Participant Safety**: IRBs and IECs pay particular attention to the safety and well-being of research participants during continuing reviews, monitoring adverse events, unanticipated problems, or protocol deviations that may have occurred since the last review. Committees assess the severity of these events, their relationship to the research intervention or procedures, and the adequacy of measures to protect participant safety. Based on their findings, IRBs and IECs may recommend changes to the protocol, additional safety monitoring, or suspension or termination of the study if warranted.
4. **Informed Consent Updates**: If changes to the informed consent documents or procedures are proposed during the course of the study,

IRBs and IECs review and approve these updates to ensure that participants continue to be adequately informed about the research study and their rights and responsibilities. Amendments to informed consent documents may be submitted by the research team for review and approval before implementation to ensure ongoing compliance and participant protection.

5. **Protocol Amendments**: Significant changes to the research protocol may require formal amendments and review by the IRB or IEC to ensure that they comply with ethical principles and regulatory requirements. Committees assess proposed protocol amendments to determine their impact on participant safety, study integrity, and ethical considerations, and may require modifications or additional information before granting approval.
6. **Continued Approval**: Following the completion of the continuing review process, IRBs and IECs issue a determination regarding the continued approval of the research study. If the study is found to be in compliance with ethical and regulatory standards, approval is granted for a specified period, and researchers are authorized to continue conducting the study as approved. If concerns or issues are identified during the review process, IRBs and IECs may require modifications to the protocol, additional monitoring, or suspension or termination of the study until the issues are addressed satisfactorily.

6.3.3.1 Case Presentation

The case involves a clinical trial investigating the efficacy and safety of an experimental drug for the treatment of a rare neurological disorder affecting children. The research protocol has been approved by the IRB/IEC, and the study is ongoing. However, during the course of the trial, several ethical concerns arise regarding participant recruitment, informed consent, and participant safety.

The research team is facing challenges in recruiting an adequate number of participants due to the rarity of the condition and the stringent eligibility criteria outlined in the protocol. Concerns are raised that the recruitment efforts may be overly aggressive, potentially leading to coercion or undue influence on vulnerable participants and their families. Additionally, there are questions about the adequacy of the informed consent process, particularly regarding the complexity of the information presented and the comprehension levels of participants and their guardians.

Furthermore, reports of adverse events and serious complications among participants receiving the experimental drug have raised concerns about participant safety. Some members of the research team advocate for suspending the study until the safety issues are fully investigated and addressed, while others argue that halting the trial prematurely may deprive participants of potentially life-saving treatment and compromise the scientific validity of the study.

The IRB/IEC convenes to review the ethical dilemmas presented by the case and to determine the appropriate course of action. Committee members carefully evaluate the concerns raised, taking into account ethical principles such as respect for autonomy, beneficence, non-maleficence, and justice. They consider the potential risks and benefits of the research study, the adequacy of participant protections, and the feasibility of addressing the ethical concerns within the context of the ongoing trial.

Through a comprehensive review process, the IRB/IEC collaborates with the research team to develop strategies for addressing the ethical dilemmas identified, which may include:

- Enhancing informed consent procedures to ensure that participants and their guardians fully understand the risks, benefits, and alternatives to participation in the study.
- Implementing additional safeguards to protect the rights and welfare of vulnerable participants, such as independent advocates or support services.
- Conducting further investigations into the safety concerns raised, including data monitoring and analysis, and implementing corrective measures as needed to minimize risks to participants.
- Providing ongoing oversight and monitoring of the trial to ensure compliance with ethical principles and regulatory requirements and to address any new ethical dilemmas that may arise during the course of the study.

By engaging in a collaborative and systematic review process, the IRB/IEC strives to uphold ethical standards, protect research participants, and promote the integrity and credibility of clinical research, even in the face of complex ethical dilemmas.

6.3.3.2 IRB/IEC Decision-Making Process

The decision-making process of Institutional Review Boards (IRBs) or Independent Ethics Committees (IECs) involves a systematic and collaborative approach to evaluating ethical dilemmas and determining the appropriate course of action. This process ensures that research studies adhere to ethical principles and regulatory requirements while protecting the rights, safety, and welfare of research participants. Below is an outline of the IRB/IEC decision-making process:

1. **Case Presentation and Discussion**: The IRB/IEC begins by reviewing the case presentation, including the background information, ethical concerns, and relevant details of the research study. Committee members engage in a thorough discussion of the ethical dilemmas presented, seeking clarification, sharing perspectives, and identifying key issues that require further consideration.
2. **Ethical Analysis**: The committee conducts a systematic ethical analysis of the case, considering the ethical principles and guidelines that govern the conduct of research involving human participants. This analysis involves evaluating the potential risks and benefits of the research study, the adequacy of participant protections, and the implications of different courses of action for the welfare of research participants and the integrity of the research enterprise.
3. **Review of Relevant Information**: Committee members review all available information relevant to the case, including the research protocol, informed consent documents, participant enrollment and safety data, and reports of adverse events or protocol deviations. This comprehensive review ensures that decisions are based on a thorough understanding of the facts and circumstances surrounding the case.
4. **Deliberation and Consensus-Building**: The IRB/IEC engages in deliberative discussions aimed at reaching a consensus on the appropriate course of action. Committee members share their perspectives, raise concerns, and explore potential solutions to the ethical dilemmas presented. Through open and respectful dialogue, the committee works towards consensus on key decisions and recommendations.
5. **Decision-Making**: Based on the ethical analysis and deliberations, the IRB/IEC makes decisions regarding the case, which may include approving, modifying, or suspending the research study, implementing additional safeguards for participant protection, or recommending

further investigations or corrective actions. Decisions are guided by the principles of respect for autonomy, beneficence, non-maleficence, and justice, as well as the ethical and legal requirements governing research conduct.

6. **Documentation and Reporting**: The decisions of the IRB/IEC are documented in meeting minutes, decision letters, or other official documents, detailing the rationale for the decisions made, any conditions or requirements imposed, and the actions to be taken by the research team or institution. This documentation ensures transparency, accountability, and compliance with regulatory requirements.
7. **Communication of Decisions**: The decisions of the IRB/IEC are communicated to the research team, relevant stakeholders, and institutional officials responsible for research oversight and compliance. Clear and timely communication of decisions ensures that all parties understand their responsibilities and obligations and facilitates implementation of approved actions.

6.3.3.3 Outcome and Lessons Learned

After thorough deliberation and decision-making, the Institutional Review Board (IRB) or Independent Ethics Committee (IEC) arrives at a resolution regarding the ethical dilemmas presented in the case study. The outcome of this process may vary depending on the specific circumstances of the case and the ethical considerations involved. Below are potential outcomes and lessons learned from the IRB/IEC review process:

1. **Outcome**:

    - The IRB/IEC may approve the research study with certain conditions or modifications to address the ethical concerns identified. This decision reflects the committee's determination that the study can proceed ethically and in accordance with regulatory requirements, provided that specific safeguards are implemented to protect participant rights, safety, and welfare.
    - Alternatively, the IRB/IEC may require significant revisions to the research protocol or informed consent procedures before granting approval. This decision indicates that the committee has identified substantial ethical issues or deficiencies that must be addressed before the study can proceed responsibly.

- In some cases, the IRB/IEC may determine that the ethical concerns raised are too significant or cannot be adequately addressed within the existing framework of the study. As a result, the committee may recommend suspension or termination of the research study until the ethical dilemmas are resolved satisfactorily.

1. **Lessons Learned:**

- The IRB/IEC review process provides valuable insights into the complexities and challenges of conducting ethical research, particularly in cases involving vulnerable populations, rare diseases, or novel interventions. Committee members gain a deeper understanding of ethical principles, regulatory requirements, and best practices in research oversight.
- Collaboration and communication among committee members, researchers, and other stakeholders are essential for addressing ethical dilemmas effectively. Through open dialogue and consensus-building, the IRB/IEC fosters a culture of transparency, accountability, and ethical decision-making.
- Continuous learning and improvement are inherent in the IRB/IEC review process. Each case presents unique ethical considerations and opportunities for reflection, evaluation, and refinement of policies, procedures, and practices. By documenting outcomes and lessons learned, the IRB/IEC contributes to ongoing quality improvement and enhancement of research ethics oversight.
- Ethical dilemmas in clinical research underscore the importance of balancing scientific advancement with ethical considerations and participant protections. The IRB/IEC plays a critical role in ensuring that research studies uphold ethical standards, promote participant welfare, and contribute to the advancement of knowledge in a responsible and ethical manner.

CHAPTER SEVEN

GLOBAL REGULATORY ENVIRONMENTS

7.1 Regulatory Landscape Overview

7.1 Regulatory Landscape Overview

7.1.1 Introduction to Regulatory Frameworks

Regulatory frameworks form the backbone of governance structures in virtually every sector, encompassing a spectrum of rules, guidelines, and standards designed to ensure compliance, safety, and ethical conduct. At their core, these frameworks serve as guardians of public interest, aiming to mitigate risks, promote fairness, and foster trust within industries. Within the global context, regulatory landscapes vary significantly due to diverse political, economic, and social factors influencing the formulation and implementation of regulations. Moreover, the dynamism of technological advancements continually challenges regulators to adapt and evolve frameworks to address emerging complexities and risks. Consequently, understanding the nuances of regulatory environments becomes imperative for businesses, policymakers, and stakeholders alike, as they navigate through an increasingly interconnected and regulated world.

7.1.2 Evolution of Regulatory Frameworks

The evolution of regulatory frameworks mirrors the trajectory of human civilization, shaped by historical events, socio-economic developments, and technological revolutions. Early regulatory efforts were often reactive responses to crises, such as industrial accidents or financial meltdowns, aimed at preventing recurrences through prescriptive rules and inspections. Over time, however, the focus shifted towards proactive risk management strategies, incorporating principles of risk assessment, transparency, and stakeholder engagement. This evolutionary journey underscores the transition from command-and-control regulatory approaches towards more flexible, adaptive governance models capable of accommodating rapid changes and uncertainties inherent in contemporary globalized markets.

7.1.3 Key Components of Regulatory Frameworks

Regulatory frameworks typically comprise several interconnected components, each fulfilling distinct yet complementary roles in ensuring effective governance. Central to these components are legislative statutes, which delineate the legal boundaries and mandates of regulatory agencies, empowering them to enforce rules and sanctions. Additionally, regulatory frameworks encompass administrative mechanisms, including licensing procedures, permit approvals, and regulatory reporting requirements, facilitating compliance and oversight. Furthermore, oversight bodies play a pivotal role in monitoring regulatory performance, evaluating effectiveness, and recommending reforms to address systemic deficiencies or emerging challenges. Lastly, public participation mechanisms, such as public consultations and stakeholder engagement forums, foster transparency, accountability, and legitimacy in regulatory decision-making processes, enhancing public trust and confidence in governance systems.

7.1.4 Importance of Regulatory Compliance

Regulatory compliance stands as a cornerstone of responsible corporate behavior and sustainable business operations within the global marketplace. Upholding regulatory requirements not only safeguards against legal liabilities and financial penalties but also fosters a culture of integrity, transparency, and trustworthiness. Moreover, compliance with regulatory mandates enhances operational efficiency by streamlining processes, minimizing risks, and optimizing resource allocation. Beyond mere adherence to legal obligations, regulatory compliance serves as a catalyst for innovation and competitiveness, prompting organizations to adopt best practices, invest in research and development, and pursue continuous improvement initiatives. Furthermore, adherence to ethical and regulatory standards cultivates positive relationships with stakeholders, including customers, investors, and communities, thereby bolstering corporate reputation and brand loyalty. Ultimately, the commitment to regulatory compliance transcends mere regulatory obligations, reflecting a commitment to ethical conduct, corporate citizenship, and sustainable development in the pursuit of long-term organizational success.

7.1.5 Key Regulatory Agencies in the USA, Europe, and India

Regulatory agencies play a pivotal role in overseeing compliance with laws and regulations, ensuring consumer protection, market stability, and public health. In the United States, several key agencies hold significant regulatory authority across various sectors. The Securities and Exchange Commission (SEC) regulates securities markets, aiming to protect investors and maintain fair, orderly, and efficient markets. The Food and Drug Administration (FDA) oversees the safety and efficacy of food, drugs, medical devices, and cosmetics, safeguarding public health. Additionally, the Environmental Protection Agency (EPA) sets and enforces environmental regulations to mitigate pollution and promote sustainable practices.

In Europe, regulatory oversight is primarily coordinated by the European Union (EU) institutions, including the European Commission, the European Parliament, and the European Council. The European Medicines Agency (EMA) plays a crucial role in evaluating and authorizing medicines for the EU market, ensuring their safety, efficacy, and quality. Similarly, the European Banking Authority (EBA) supervises and regulates banking activities to maintain financial stability and protect consumers. Furthermore, the European Securities and Markets Authority (ESMA) oversees securities markets, promoting investor protection and market integrity.

In India, regulatory functions are dispersed among various government agencies at the national and state levels. The Securities and Exchange Board of India (SEBI) regulates securities markets, aiming to protect investor interests and promote market transparency. The Reserve Bank of India (RBI) oversees monetary policy, banking regulation, and currency issuance, ensuring financial stability and economic growth. Additionally, the Food Safety and Standards Authority of India (FSSAI) sets standards for food safety and regulates the food industry, safeguarding public health and consumer interests.

These regulatory agencies, through their mandates and enforcement mechanisms, play critical roles in shaping regulatory environments and fostering trust, stability, and accountability within their respective jurisdictions.

7.2 Regulatory Frameworks in the USA

7.2.1 FDA Regulations

The Food and Drug Administration (FDA) stands as a cornerstone of regulatory oversight in the United States, charged with safeguarding public health by regulating a vast array of products, including food, drugs, medical devices, cosmetics, and tobacco. FDA regulations are characterized by a comprehensive framework designed to ensure the safety, efficacy, and quality of these products, thereby minimizing risks to consumers and promoting public welfare.

FDA regulations encompass diverse aspects of product development, manufacturing, distribution, and marketing, with the overarching goal of balancing innovation with risk management. For pharmaceuticals, the FDA employs a rigorous approval process, requiring manufacturers to demonstrate the safety and effectiveness of their products through extensive preclinical and clinical trials before they can be marketed and sold to the public. Similarly, medical devices are subject to stringent regulatory requirements, ranging from premarket notification submissions to quality system regulations governing manufacturing practices.

Moreover, the FDA exercises authority over food safety, implementing regulations to prevent contamination, adulteration, and misbranding of food products. Through initiatives such as the Food Safety Modernization Act (FSMA), the FDA seeks to modernize food safety practices, enhance traceability, and prevent foodborne illnesses.

In addition to product regulation, the FDA plays a crucial role in regulating advertising, labeling, and promotional activities to ensure accuracy, transparency, and fair marketing practices. This includes reviewing and approving labeling for prescription drugs and overseeing direct-to-consumer advertising to prevent false or misleading claims.

Furthermore, the FDA has expanded its regulatory purview to address emerging challenges and technologies, such as biotechnology, nanotechnology, and digital health. By adapting regulations to reflect scientific advancements and evolving market trends, the FDA aims to foster innovation while upholding its public health mandate.

7.2.1.1 Drug Approval Process

The drug approval process regulated by the Food and Drug Administration (FDA) in the United States is a multifaceted and stringent procedure designed to ensure the safety, efficacy, and quality of pharmaceutical products before they are made available to the public. This process involves several stages, each characterized by rigorous scientific evaluation and regulatory scrutiny.

The journey begins with preclinical studies, where pharmaceutical companies conduct extensive laboratory and animal testing to assess the biological activity, pharmacokinetics, and toxicology of potential drug candidates. Data from these studies are submitted to the FDA in an Investigational New Drug (IND) application, which outlines the proposed clinical trial protocols and safety profiles of the investigational drug.

Upon IND approval, the drug moves into clinical trials, which are conducted in three phases. Phase I trials involve a small number of healthy volunteers to evaluate safety, dosage, and initial pharmacological effects. Phase II trials expand the study to a larger group of patients to assess efficacy and identify potential side effects. Finally, Phase III trials enroll a larger patient population to confirm efficacy, monitor adverse reactions, and compare the new drug with existing treatments or placebos.

Following successful completion of clinical trials, the pharmaceutical company submits a New Drug Application (NDA) to the FDA, which includes comprehensive data on the drug's safety, efficacy, manufacturing processes, and labeling. The FDA reviews the NDA to determine whether the benefits of the drug outweigh its risks and whether it meets regulatory standards for approval.

If the FDA approves the NDA, the drug is granted marketing authorization, allowing it to be marketed and sold to the public. However, the regulatory process does not end there. The FDA continues to monitor the safety and effectiveness of approved drugs through post-market surveillance programs, adverse event reporting systems, and ongoing review of scientific literature.

Moreover, the FDA has mechanisms in place to expedite the development and review of drugs for serious or life-threatening conditions, such as Fast Track designation, Breakthrough Therapy designation, and Accelerated Approval pathway. These initiatives aim to facilitate timely access to innovative treatments while maintaining rigorous standards of safety and efficacy.

7.2.1.2 Medical Device Regulation

Medical device regulation in the United States is overseen by the Food and Drug Administration (FDA), which is responsible for ensuring the safety and effectiveness of medical devices before they are marketed and sold to healthcare providers and consumers. The regulatory framework for medical devices encompasses a broad range of products, including diagnostic equipment, surgical instruments, implants, and software applications used in healthcare settings.

The regulatory pathway for medical devices is determined by the level of risk associated with the device, with three main classifications: Class I, Class II, and Class III. Class I devices are considered low risk and are subject to general controls, such as labeling requirements and adherence to good manufacturing practices. Class II devices pose moderate risk and typically require special controls, such as performance standards, post-market surveillance, and premarket notification (510(k)) submissions demonstrating substantial equivalence to a legally marketed device. Class III devices, which present the highest risk, undergo the most rigorous regulatory scrutiny and require premarket approval (PMA) applications demonstrating safety and effectiveness based on clinical data.

The regulatory process for medical devices begins with premarket submissions to the FDA, which provide detailed information on the device's design, intended use, manufacturing processes, and performance characteristics. Depending on the device class and regulatory pathway, submissions may include clinical data, bench testing results, and risk assessments to demonstrate compliance with regulatory requirements.

Upon receipt of a premarket submission, the FDA conducts a comprehensive review to assess the device's safety and effectiveness in accordance with regulatory standards. This review may involve evaluation of clinical data, device labeling, manufacturing practices, and compliance with quality system regulations. For Class III devices requiring premarket approval, the FDA convenes expert panels to provide independent assessment and recommendations on the device's risks and benefits.

If the FDA determines that a medical device meets regulatory requirements, it grants marketing authorization, allowing the device to be commercialized and distributed in the United States. However, the regulatory process does not end there. The FDA continues to oversee post-market surveillance activities, including adverse event reporting, device tracking systems, and periodic inspections of manufacturing facilities, to monitor device performance, identify safety concerns, and take appropriate regulatory action if necessary.

In addition to premarket review and post-market surveillance, the FDA collaborates with international regulatory agencies and standards organizations to harmonize regulatory requirements, facilitate global market access, and promote interoperability of medical devices. By fostering innovation, protecting public health, and ensuring regulatory compliance, the FDA plays a crucial role in promoting patient safety and advancing healthcare delivery in the United States.

7.3 Regulatory Frameworks in Europe

7.3.1 European Medicines Agency (EMA)

The European Medicines Agency (EMA) serves as a central regulatory authority responsible for the evaluation, supervision, and approval of medicines within the European Union (EU) and European Economic Area (EEA). Established in 1995, the EMA plays a pivotal role in ensuring the safety, efficacy, and quality of medicinal products, thereby safeguarding public health and facilitating access to innovative therapies across member states.

The regulatory framework overseen by the EMA encompasses a wide range of activities, including the evaluation of marketing authorization applications, pharmacovigilance monitoring, scientific advice provision, and harmonization of regulatory standards. Central to its operations is the centralized procedure, which enables the EMA to coordinate the assessment of medicinal products on behalf of all EU member states, resulting in a single marketing authorization valid throughout the EU/EEA.

The process of obtaining marketing authorization through the centralized procedure involves several key steps. Pharmaceutical companies submit a marketing authorization application to the EMA, providing comprehensive data on the quality, safety, and efficacy of the medicinal product. The EMA's Committee for Medicinal Products for Human Use (CHMP) conducts a thorough scientific assessment of the application, evaluating preclinical and clinical data to determine whether the benefits of the medicine outweigh its risks.

Following the CHMP's recommendation, the European Commission issues a marketing authorization decision, granting the medicine access to the EU/EEA market. However, the regulatory process does not end there. The EMA continues to monitor the safety and effectiveness of authorized medicines through pharmacovigilance activities, including adverse drug reaction reporting, periodic safety update assessments, and risk management plan evaluations.

In addition to its role in human medicines, the EMA also oversees the regulation of veterinary medicines through the Committee for Medicinal Products for Veterinary Use (CVMP). This includes the evaluation of marketing authorization applications for veterinary drugs, as well as the monitoring of their safety and efficacy post-approval.

Furthermore, the EMA actively collaborates with regulatory agencies and international organizations worldwide to harmonize regulatory standards, share scientific expertise, and facilitate global access to medicines. By promoting regulatory convergence and scientific excellence, the EMA contributes to the efficient development, evaluation, and regulation of medicines, ultimately benefiting patients, healthcare professionals, and the pharmaceutical industry across Europe and beyond.

7.3.1.1 Marketing Authorization Process

The marketing authorization process overseen by the European Medicines Agency (EMA) is a comprehensive and rigorous procedure designed to evaluate the quality, safety, and efficacy of medicinal products intended for use within the European Union (EU) and European Economic Area (EEA). This process, governed by the centralized procedure, enables the EMA to coordinate the assessment of marketing authorization applications on behalf of all EU member states, resulting in a single marketing authorization valid throughout the EU/EEA.

The marketing authorization process involves several key steps:

1. **Submission of Marketing Authorization Application (MAA):** Pharmaceutical companies seeking marketing authorization for a medicinal product submit a comprehensive MAA to the EMA. This application includes detailed data on the product's quality, safety, and efficacy, derived from preclinical and clinical studies conducted in accordance with regulatory requirements.
2. **Validation:** Upon receipt of the MAA, the EMA conducts an initial validation check to ensure that the application is complete and meets regulatory requirements. This includes verifying the submission of all required documents and supporting data.
3. **Scientific Assessment:** The EMA's Committee for Medicinal Products for Human Use (CHMP) conducts a thorough scientific assessment of the MAA, evaluating the quality, safety, and efficacy of the medicinal product based on the data submitted by the applicant. This assessment involves review of preclinical and clinical study results, as well as consideration of risk-benefit profiles and relevant pharmacovigilance data.
4. **CHMP Opinion:** Following the scientific assessment, the CHMP provides an opinion on whether the medicinal product should be granted marketing authorization. This opinion takes into account the overall

benefit-risk balance of the product and may include recommendations for specific conditions of use, risk management measures, or post-authorization commitments.

5. **European Commission Decision:** Based on the CHMP's opinion, the European Commission issues a decision on whether to grant marketing authorization for the medicinal product. If the decision is positive, the European Commission issues a marketing authorization, allowing the product to be marketed and sold within the EU/EEA.
6. **Post-Authorization Monitoring:** After marketing authorization is granted, the EMA continues to monitor the safety and effectiveness of the authorized medicinal product through pharmacovigilance activities. This includes ongoing surveillance of adverse drug reactions, periodic safety update assessments, and evaluation of risk management plans.

7.3.1.2 Pharmacovigilance

Pharmacovigilance is a crucial component of the regulatory framework overseen by the European Medicines Agency (EMA) and plays a fundamental role in monitoring the safety of medicinal products throughout their lifecycle. Pharmacovigilance encompasses the detection, assessment, understanding, and prevention of adverse effects or any other drug-related problems.

The pharmacovigilance system in Europe operates on several levels:

1. **Adverse Event Reporting:** Healthcare professionals, patients, and pharmaceutical companies are encouraged to report any suspected adverse reactions associated with medicinal products to national competent authorities or directly to the EMA through the EudraVigilance database. Adverse event reports are systematically collected, evaluated, and analyzed to identify potential safety signals and trends.
2. **Signal Detection:** Pharmacovigilance experts analyze adverse event data to detect potential safety signals, which may indicate previously unrecognized risks or emerging safety concerns associated with medicinal products. Signal detection activities involve statistical analyses, data mining techniques, and qualitative assessments to prioritize signals for further investigation.
3. **Risk Assessment and Evaluation:** Once a potential safety signal is identified, the EMA conducts a comprehensive risk assessment to

evaluate the likelihood, severity, and impact of the safety concern on public health. This assessment involves review of available evidence, including clinical trial data, real-world observational studies, and regulatory actions taken in other jurisdictions.

4. **Risk Management:** Based on the outcome of risk assessment, the EMA may implement risk management measures to mitigate identified safety risks and optimize the benefit-risk balance of medicinal products. These measures may include updates to product labeling, implementation of risk minimization strategies, or post-authorization safety studies to further characterize the safety profile of the product.
5. **Communication and Transparency:** The EMA promotes transparency and communication of pharmacovigilance findings to healthcare professionals, patients, and the public through various channels, including safety alerts, public statements, and regulatory guidance documents. Timely dissemination of safety information enables informed decision-making and enhances patient safety.
6. **Collaboration and Exchange of Information:** The EMA collaborates with national competent authorities, international regulatory agencies, and stakeholders to facilitate the exchange of pharmacovigilance information, harmonize regulatory approaches, and promote global collaboration in safeguarding public health.

7.3.1.2 Pharmacovigilance

Pharmacovigilance is a pivotal aspect of the regulatory framework governed by the European Medicines Agency (EMA) within the European Union (EU) and European Economic Area (EEA). It encompasses a systematic and proactive approach to monitoring the safety of medicinal products throughout their lifecycle, from pre-market clinical trials to post-market surveillance.

Adverse Event Reporting: Pharmacovigilance relies on the continuous reporting of suspected adverse drug reactions (ADRs) by healthcare professionals, patients, and pharmaceutical companies. These reports are submitted to national competent authorities and collated in the EudraVigilance database, which serves as a central repository for pharmacovigilance data in the EU/EEA.

Signal Detection and Analysis: Pharmacovigilance experts analyze the collected ADR reports to detect potential safety signals, which may indicate previously unrecognized risks or emerging safety concerns associated with medicinal products. Statistical methods, data mining techniques, and qualitative assessments are employed to prioritize signals for further investigation.

Risk Assessment and Evaluation: Upon identification of a potential safety signal, the EMA conducts a comprehensive risk assessment to evaluate the likelihood, severity, and impact of the safety concern on public health. This assessment involves the review of available evidence, including clinical trial data, real-world observational studies, and regulatory actions taken in other jurisdictions.

Risk Management: Based on the outcome of risk assessment, the EMA may implement risk management measures to mitigate identified safety risks and optimize the benefit-risk balance of medicinal products. These measures may include updates to product labeling, implementation of risk minimization strategies, or post-authorization safety studies.

Communication and Transparency: The EMA prioritizes transparency and communication of pharmacovigilance findings to healthcare professionals, patients, and the public. Safety alerts, public statements, and regulatory guidance documents are utilized to disseminate safety information in a timely and accessible manner, enabling informed decision-making and enhancing patient safety.

Collaboration and Exchange of Information: The EMA collaborates closely with national competent authorities, international regulatory agencies, and stakeholders to facilitate the exchange of pharmacovigilance information, harmonize regulatory approaches, and promote global collaboration in safeguarding public health.

7.3.2 Contrasts with FDA Regulations

Regulatory frameworks in Europe, overseen by the European Medicines Agency (EMA), exhibit notable differences from those administered by the Food and Drug Administration (FDA) in the United States. These distinctions arise from variances in legislative mandates, procedural requirements, and cultural approaches to healthcare regulation. Here, we delineate key contrasts between EMA regulations and FDA regulations:

1. Centralized vs. Decentralized Approval Procedures:

- **EMA (Europe):** Operates a centralized procedure where marketing authorization for medicinal products is granted by the EMA on behalf of all EU member states, resulting in a single authorization valid throughout the EU/EEA.

- **FDA (USA):** Utilizes a decentralized approach where marketing approval is granted by the FDA independently, with separate applications required for each jurisdiction within the United States.

2. Pharmacovigilance Systems:

- **EMA (Europe):** Establishes a robust pharmacovigilance system involving centralized reporting of adverse drug reactions (ADRs) through the EudraVigilance database, enabling systematic monitoring and analysis of safety signals.
- **FDA (USA):** Operates the FDA Adverse Event Reporting System (FAERS) for the collection and analysis of ADR reports, facilitating post-market surveillance and signal detection.

3. Clinical Trial Requirements:

- **EMA (Europe):** Adheres to stringent requirements for clinical trial authorization, emphasizing the need for ethical review, patient safety, and scientific validity.
- **FDA (USA):** Implements regulations governing investigational new drug (IND) applications, outlining procedures for the conduct of clinical trials, including requirements for informed consent, institutional review board (IRB) oversight, and data integrity.

4. Risk Management Strategies:

- **EMA (Europe):** Emphasizes risk management strategies to mitigate identified safety risks associated with medicinal products, including updates to product labeling, risk minimization measures, and post-authorization safety studies.
- **FDA (USA):** Implements risk evaluation and mitigation strategies (REMS) to manage known or potential risks associated with certain drugs, including elements to assure safe use (ETASU) and communication plans.

5. Approval Timelines and Flexibility:

- **EMA (Europe):** Generally adopts a standardized timeline for regulatory review, providing predictability in the approval process. Offers conditional marketing authorization and accelerated assessment for medicines addressing unmet medical needs.
- **FDA (USA):** Exhibits flexibility in approval timelines, with expedited pathways such as Fast Track, Breakthrough Therapy, and Priority Review designations to facilitate access to innovative therapies for serious or life-threatening conditions.

6. Legal Framework and Jurisdiction:

- **EMA (Europe):** Operates within the legal framework of EU regulations and directives, with jurisdiction extending to all EU member states and European Economic Area (EEA) countries.
- **FDA (USA):** Governed by the Federal Food, Drug, and Cosmetic Act (FD&C Act) and other relevant statutes, with jurisdiction limited to the United States and its territories.

7.3.3 Case Study: EMA Approval for a Biologic Therapy

This case study explores the regulatory journey of a hypothetical biologic therapy, "BioXcel," from initial development to approval by the European Medicines Agency (EMA) for marketing authorization within the European Union (EU).

Discovery and Preclinical Development:

The journey begins with researchers identifying a novel therapeutic target implicated in a chronic autoimmune disease. Preclinical studies are conducted to assess the safety, efficacy, and mechanism of action of BioXcel in cellular and animal models. These studies provide compelling evidence of BioXcel's ability to modulate the immune response and ameliorate disease symptoms.

Investigational New Drug (IND) Application:

Based on promising preclinical data, the pharmaceutical company sponsoring BioXcel's development submits an Investigational New Drug (IND) application to the EMA. The IND application includes comprehensive data on BioXcel's pharmacological properties, manufacturing processes, and proposed clinical trial protocols.

Clinical Trials:

BioXcel progresses through a series of clinical trials, conducted in accordance with Good Clinical Practice (GCP) guidelines:

1. **Phase I:** Phase I trials involve a small number of healthy volunteers to evaluate BioXcel's safety, tolerability, and pharmacokinetics. These trials establish an appropriate dosing regimen for further study.
2. **Phase II:** Phase II trials expand the study to a larger group of patients with the target autoimmune disease to assess BioXcel's preliminary efficacy and safety profile. These trials provide valuable insights into the optimal patient population and dosage.
3. **Phase III:** Phase III trials enroll a larger patient population to confirm BioXcel's efficacy, safety, and tolerability in comparison to standard-of-care treatments or placebo. These pivotal trials generate robust clinical data to support regulatory submission.

Marketing Authorization Application (MAA):

Following successful completion of clinical trials, the pharmaceutical company submits a Marketing Authorization Application (MAA) to the EMA. The MAA includes comprehensive data on BioXcel's safety, efficacy, quality, and risk management measures, derived from preclinical and clinical studies.

EMA Review and Approval:

The EMA's Committee for Medicinal Products for Human Use (CHMP) conducts a thorough scientific assessment of the MAA, reviewing the clinical data and risk-benefit profile of BioXcel. After extensive evaluation, the CHMP provides a positive opinion recommending marketing authorization for BioXcel within the EU.

European Commission Decision:

Based on the CHMP's positive opinion, the European Commission issues a decision granting marketing authorization for BioXcel, allowing the pharmaceutical company to market and distribute the biologic therapy within the EU/EEA. This approval represents a significant milestone in providing patients with a novel treatment option for their chronic autoimmune disease.

7.4 Regulatory Frameworks in India

7.4.1 Central Drugs Standard Control Organization (CDSCO)

In India, the Central Drugs Standard Control Organization (CDSCO) stands as the apex regulatory body responsible for the regulation and control of pharmaceuticals, medical devices, cosmetics, and diagnostics. Established under the Drugs and Cosmetics Act, 1940, and the Drugs and Cosmetics Rules, 1945, the CDSCO plays a pivotal role in ensuring the safety, efficacy, and quality of healthcare products available in the Indian market.

The regulatory framework administered by the CDSCO encompasses various functions and responsibilities:

1. **Regulatory Approvals:** The CDSCO evaluates applications for the approval of new drugs, clinical trials, import and export licenses, and manufacturing licenses for pharmaceuticals, medical devices, and cosmetics. It conducts thorough reviews to ensure compliance with regulatory requirements and standards.
2. **Quality Control:** The CDSCO conducts inspections and assessments of manufacturing facilities, testing laboratories, and distribution channels to verify compliance with Good Manufacturing Practices (GMP), Good Laboratory Practices (GLP), and Good Distribution Practices (GDP). It also oversees the testing and analysis of pharmaceutical products to ascertain their quality and safety.
3. **Pharmacovigilance:** The CDSCO monitors the safety of medicinal products through pharmacovigilance activities, including the collection, assessment, and reporting of adverse drug reactions (ADRs). It collaborates with healthcare professionals, pharmaceutical companies, and regulatory agencies to identify and mitigate potential safety risks.
4. **Medical Devices Regulation:** In recent years, the CDSCO has expanded its regulatory purview to include medical devices, aiming to enhance patient safety and promote innovation in the healthcare sector. It establishes regulatory requirements for the registration, import, manufacture, and sale of medical devices in India.
5. **International Collaboration:** The CDSCO collaborates with international regulatory agencies, such as the World Health Organization (WHO), the United States Food and Drug Administration (FDA), and the European Medicines Agency (EMA), to harmonize regulatory standards, exchange best practices, and facilitate global access to safe and effective healthcare products.
6. **Public Awareness and Education:** The CDSCO engages in public awareness campaigns and educational initiatives to inform healthcare professionals, consumers, and industry stakeholders about regulatory

requirements, drug safety issues, and the importance of regulatory compliance. It fosters transparency and accountability in the regulatory process.

7.4.1.1 Drug Approval Procedures

The Central Drugs Standard Control Organization (CDSCO) in India implements drug approval procedures to ensure the safety, efficacy, and quality of pharmaceutical products before they are marketed and distributed within the country. The regulatory framework includes several key procedures:

1. **New Drug Approval:** Pharmaceutical companies seeking approval for new drugs in India must submit an application to the CDSCO. This application includes comprehensive data on the drug's pharmacological properties, preclinical and clinical studies, manufacturing processes, and proposed labeling. The CDSCO evaluates the application to determine whether the new drug meets regulatory standards for safety, efficacy, and quality.
2. **Clinical Trials Approval:** Before conducting clinical trials in India, pharmaceutical companies must obtain approval from the CDSCO's Drug Controller General of India (DCGI). The approval process involves submission of a clinical trial application, which includes detailed study protocols, informed consent forms, investigator brochures, and other relevant documents. The CDSCO reviews the application to ensure that the proposed clinical trials comply with ethical and regulatory requirements.
3. **Import and Export Licenses:** The CDSCO regulates the import and export of pharmaceutical products through the issuance of import and export licenses. Pharmaceutical companies must obtain licenses from the CDSCO to import or export drugs, ensuring compliance with regulatory standards for quality, safety, and labeling.
4. **Manufacturing Licenses:** Pharmaceutical manufacturers operating in India must obtain manufacturing licenses from the CDSCO to produce and distribute pharmaceutical products. The CDSCO conducts inspections of manufacturing facilities to verify compliance with Good Manufacturing Practices (GMP) and other regulatory requirements. Manufacturing licenses are issued to companies that demonstrate adherence to quality standards and regulatory compliance.

5. **Abbreviated New Drug Application (ANDA):** In addition to new drug approvals, the CDSCO reviews Abbreviated New Drug Applications (ANDAs) for generic drugs. Pharmaceutical companies seeking approval for generic versions of existing drugs must submit ANDAs containing bioequivalence data, formulation details, and other relevant information. The CDSCO evaluates ANDAs to ensure that generic drugs are therapeutically equivalent to their brand-name counterparts and meet regulatory standards for safety and quality.

7.4.1.2 Challenges and Criticisms

Despite its efforts to regulate pharmaceuticals and ensure public safety, the Central Drugs Standard Control Organization (CDSCO) faces several challenges and criticisms:

1. **Regulatory Delays:** One of the primary criticisms leveled against the CDSCO is the issue of regulatory delays in the approval process for new drugs and clinical trials. Lengthy delays in the review and approval of applications can significantly impede patient access to innovative treatments and hinder research and development efforts within the pharmaceutical industry.
2. **Insufficient Resources and Capacity:** The CDSCO grapples with resource constraints and staffing shortages, which can hamper its ability to effectively carry out regulatory functions. Inadequate funding, limited infrastructure, and a shortage of trained personnel contribute to inefficiencies in the regulatory system, leading to backlogs and delays in processing applications.
3. **Quality Control and Enforcement:** Despite regulatory oversight, instances of substandard and counterfeit medicines continue to pose significant challenges in India. Weak enforcement of quality control measures, including inspections of manufacturing facilities and surveillance of the supply chain, undermines public confidence in the safety and efficacy of pharmaceutical products.
4. **Conflicts of Interest and Corruption:** The CDSCO has faced allegations of conflicts of interest and corruption, with reports of regulatory officials colluding with pharmaceutical companies for favorable treatment or financial gain. These allegations raise concerns about the integrity and impartiality of the regulatory decision-making process, eroding trust in the regulatory authority.

5. **Lack of Transparency and Accountability:** Transparency and accountability issues persist within the CDSCO, with limited public access to regulatory decisions, data, and proceedings. The lack of transparency hampers scrutiny of regulatory processes, impedes public participation, and diminishes accountability for regulatory actions.
6. **Harmonization with International Standards:** India's regulatory framework for pharmaceuticals may not always align with international standards and best practices, leading to challenges in harmonization and mutual recognition of regulatory approvals with other countries. Divergent regulatory requirements can create barriers to trade and hinder the global competitiveness of Indian pharmaceutical products.

Addressing these challenges and criticisms requires concerted efforts from the CDSCO, government authorities, industry stakeholders, and civil society organizations. Enhancing regulatory efficiency, strengthening quality control mechanisms, promoting transparency and accountability, and fostering international collaboration are essential steps toward ensuring a robust and effective regulatory framework for pharmaceuticals in India.

7.4.2 Unique Aspects of Indian Regulatory Landscape

The regulatory landscape for pharmaceuticals in India exhibits several unique aspects that distinguish it from regulatory frameworks in other countries:

1. **Large Generic Drug Market:** India has a thriving generic drug industry, characterized by the production and export of affordable generic medicines to both domestic and international markets. The Indian regulatory framework emphasizes the approval of generic drugs, with a focus on bioequivalence studies to demonstrate therapeutic equivalence with brand-name counterparts.
2. **Regulation of Traditional Medicines:** India has a rich tradition of traditional medicines, including Ayurveda, Siddha, and Unani systems, which are regulated under separate regulatory frameworks. The Ayurveda, Yoga & Naturopathy, Unani, Siddha, and Homoeopathy (AYUSH) ministry oversees the regulation of traditional medicines, ensuring quality, safety, and efficacy.
3. **Compulsory Licensing and Patent Challenges:** India has provisions for compulsory licensing, allowing the government to grant licenses to manufacture patented drugs in certain circumstances, such as public

health emergencies or unmet medical needs. This unique aspect of the regulatory landscape enables access to essential medicines at affordable prices and has led to legal battles with multinational pharmaceutical companies over patent protection.

4. **Price Control Mechanisms:** India implements price control mechanisms to regulate the prices of essential medicines and ensure affordability for patients. The National Pharmaceutical Pricing Authority (NPPA) establishes and monitors prices of essential drugs through the Drug Price Control Orders (DPCO), contributing to equitable access to medicines.
5. **Pharmacovigilance Initiatives:** India has made efforts to strengthen pharmacovigilance systems to monitor the safety of medicines post-market. The Pharmacovigilance Programme of India (PvPI) facilitates the reporting, collection, and analysis of adverse drug reactions (ADRs), enhancing patient safety and regulatory oversight.
6. **Harmonization with International Standards:** While India maintains its regulatory independence, efforts are underway to harmonize regulatory standards with international guidelines and practices. Collaboration with international regulatory agencies and participation in initiatives such as the International Council for Harmonisation of Technical Requirements for Pharmaceuticals for Human Use (ICH) demonstrate India's commitment to aligning with global standards.
7. **Promotion of Clinical Research:** India has emerged as a preferred destination for clinical research due to its large and diverse patient population, cost-effectiveness, and skilled healthcare professionals. The regulatory framework encourages clinical research while ensuring adherence to ethical and scientific standards to protect participant rights and safety.

These unique aspects of the Indian regulatory landscape reflect the country's diverse pharmaceutical industry, public health priorities, and commitment to promoting access to affordable healthcare. By addressing the specific needs and challenges of the Indian context, the regulatory framework seeks to balance innovation, affordability, and patient safety in the pharmaceutical sector.

7.4.3 Comparison with US and EU Regulations

When comparing the regulatory frameworks for pharmaceuticals in India with those in the United States (US) and the European Union (EU), several key differences and similarities emerge:

1. **Regulatory Authority:**

- **India:** The Central Drugs Standard Control Organization (CDSCO) is the primary regulatory authority overseeing pharmaceuticals in India.
- **US:** The Food and Drug Administration (FDA) is responsible for regulating pharmaceuticals in the US.
- **EU:** The European Medicines Agency (EMA) serves as the central regulatory authority for pharmaceuticals within the EU.

2. **Approval Processes:**

- **India:** India follows a drug approval process that emphasizes the approval of generic drugs, with a focus on bioequivalence studies.
- **US:** The US FDA implements rigorous approval processes for new drugs, including preclinical and clinical trials, before granting marketing authorization.
- **EU:** The EU regulatory framework includes centralized, decentralized, and mutual recognition procedures for marketing authorization, allowing for streamlined approval across member states.

3. **Generic Drug Market:**

- **India:** India has a robust generic drug industry, with a significant portion of pharmaceutical production focused on generic medicines.
- **US:** The US also has a substantial generic drug market, with generic drugs accounting for a significant share of prescription drug consumption.
- **EU:** Generic drugs play a vital role in the EU pharmaceutical market, contributing to cost savings and improving access to essential medicines.

4. **Patent Protection and Compulsory Licensing:**

- **India:** India has provisions for compulsory licensing, allowing for the manufacture of patented drugs under certain conditions to address public health needs.
- **US:** The US has strong patent protection laws and limited provisions for compulsory licensing.

- **EU:** Patent protection in the EU is governed by national laws and the European Patent Convention, with limited provisions for compulsory licensing.

5. Price Control Mechanisms:

- **India:** India implements price control mechanisms to regulate the prices of essential medicines through the National Pharmaceutical Pricing Authority (NPPA).
- **US:** The US does not have centralized price control mechanisms for pharmaceuticals, relying instead on market forces to determine drug prices.
- **EU:** Some EU member states implement price control measures for pharmaceuticals, while others rely on negotiated pricing agreements with manufacturers.

6. Pharmacovigilance Systems:

- **India:** India has made efforts to strengthen pharmacovigilance systems through initiatives like the Pharmacovigilance Programme of India (PvPI).
- **US:** The US FDA operates the FDA Adverse Event Reporting System (FAERS) to monitor the safety of pharmaceutical products.
- **EU:** The EMA oversees pharmacovigilance activities in the EU, including the collection and analysis of adverse drug reaction reports.

While India, the US, and the EU share common goals of ensuring the safety, efficacy, and quality of pharmaceutical products, differences in regulatory approaches reflect unique healthcare systems, priorities, and legal frameworks in each region. Understanding these variations is essential for pharmaceutical companies operating in global markets and seeking regulatory approval for their products.

7.5 Cross-Border Regulatory Considerations

7.5.1 Harmonization Efforts

Cross-border regulatory considerations play a crucial role in fostering collaboration, enhancing regulatory efficiency, and promoting global access to safe and effective healthcare products. Harmonization efforts aim to align regulatory standards, processes, and requirements across different jurisdictions, thereby facilitating the development, evaluation, and regulation of pharmaceuticals, medical devices, and other healthcare products. Several initiatives and organizations contribute to harmonization efforts on a global scale:

1. **International Council for Harmonisation of Technical Requirements for Pharmaceuticals for Human Use (ICH):** The ICH brings together regulatory authorities and pharmaceutical industry representatives from around the world to develop harmonized guidelines for the pharmaceutical sector. These guidelines cover various aspects of drug development, including quality, safety, efficacy, and multidisciplinary topics such as pharmacovigilance and regulatory communication.
2. **World Health Organization (WHO):** The WHO plays a pivotal role in promoting global health and harmonizing regulatory standards for pharmaceuticals and medical products. It collaborates with member states to develop international guidelines and standards, facilitate capacity-building initiatives, and provide technical assistance to strengthen regulatory systems in low- and middle-income countries.
3. **Transatlantic Cooperation:** Collaboration between regulatory agencies in the United States (FDA) and the European Union (EMA) aims to harmonize regulatory approaches and streamline regulatory processes for pharmaceuticals and medical devices. Initiatives such as the Mutual Recognition Agreement (MRA) between the US and the EU facilitate the acceptance of inspections and product approvals, reducing duplication of efforts and enhancing regulatory efficiency.
4. **Asia-Pacific Economic Cooperation (APEC):** APEC member economies work together to promote regulatory convergence and harmonization in the Asia-Pacific region. Initiatives such as the APEC Harmonization Center facilitate the exchange of regulatory information, capacity-building activities, and alignment of regulatory standards to support trade and public health goals.
5. **Regional Harmonization Initiatives:** Regional harmonization efforts, such as those led by the Association of Southeast Asian Nations (ASEAN) and the African Medicines Regulatory Harmonization (AMRH) initiative, aim to strengthen regulatory systems and promote alignment of standards within specific geographic regions. These initiatives enhance regulatory cooperation, facilitate access to medicines, and support regional integration efforts.

7.5.2 Impact of Trade Agreements

Trade agreements have a significant impact on cross-border regulatory considerations in the pharmaceutical and healthcare sectors. These agreements can influence regulatory harmonization, market access, intellectual property rights, and other aspects of regulatory frameworks. The impact of trade agreements on regulatory considerations includes:

1. **Harmonization of Standards:** Trade agreements often include provisions aimed at harmonizing regulatory standards and promoting mutual recognition of regulatory approvals between participating countries. This can streamline regulatory processes, reduce duplication of efforts, and facilitate market access for pharmaceuticals and medical devices across borders.
2. **Market Access:** Trade agreements may facilitate market access by reducing tariffs, trade barriers, and regulatory barriers to entry. This can expand market opportunities for pharmaceutical companies and increase access to healthcare products for consumers in participating countries.
3. **Intellectual Property Protection:** Trade agreements often include provisions related to intellectual property rights, including patent protection for pharmaceuticals and medical devices. Stronger intellectual property protections may incentivize innovation and investment in research and development but can also impact access to affordable medicines through measures such as patent extensions and data exclusivity.
4. **Regulatory Cooperation:** Trade agreements may promote regulatory cooperation and information sharing between regulatory authorities in participating countries. This can enhance regulatory capacity, facilitate alignment of regulatory standards, and improve coordination on issues such as pharmacovigilance, quality control, and post-market surveillance.
5. **Dispute Resolution Mechanisms:** Trade agreements typically include dispute resolution mechanisms to address conflicts or disputes related to regulatory issues, intellectual property rights, or market access. These mechanisms provide a forum for resolving disputes and ensuring compliance with the terms of the agreement.

CHAPTER EIGHT

ROLES IN CLINICAL RESEARCH

8.1 Sponsor Responsibilities

8.1.1 Definition and Overview of Sponsorship

Sponsorship within clinical research embodies a pivotal role defined by multifaceted responsibilities crucial for the progression and integrity of medical investigations. At its core, sponsorship represents an entity, often an organization or institution, which assumes the overarching responsibility for the initiation, management, and financing of a clinical trial. This role encompasses a spectrum of duties that encompass financial support, protocol development, regulatory compliance, and ethical adherence. The sponsor serves as the primary architect of the trial, orchestrating its design, implementation, and monitoring to ensure adherence to rigorous scientific standards and regulatory requirements. Through sponsorship, stakeholders undertake a commitment to safeguarding participant welfare, scientific rigor, and data integrity throughout the research process.

Underpinning the concept of sponsorship lies a dedication to fostering transparency, accountability, and ethical conduct within clinical research endeavors. Sponsors are entrusted with the obligation to uphold the principles outlined in various regulatory frameworks, including Good Clinical Practice (GCP) guidelines and relevant local and international regulations. By assuming sponsorship, organizations pledge to navigate the intricate landscape of clinical research with unwavering integrity, upholding the rights, safety, and well-being of research participants as paramount. This entails comprehensive oversight of trial conduct, from the initial planning stages through to the dissemination of results, with meticulous attention to detail to mitigate potential risks and ensure the reliability and validity of study findings.

Critical to the sponsor's mandate is the facilitation of effective communication and collaboration among all stakeholders involved in the clinical trial process. This necessitates clear and open lines of communication with investigators, regulatory authorities, ethics committees, and other relevant entities to streamline operational processes and address any emerging challenges promptly. Moreover, sponsors bear the responsibility of providing adequate resources and support to investigators to enable the seamless execution of research protocols while adhering to predefined timelines and milestones. By fostering a culture of collaboration and support, sponsors contribute to the advancement of scientific knowledge and the translation of research findings into tangible benefits for patients and society at large.

8.1.2 Regulatory Compliance

Regulatory compliance constitutes a cornerstone of sponsor responsibilities within clinical research, necessitating meticulous adherence to a myriad of local and international regulations governing the conduct of clinical trials. At its essence, regulatory compliance entails the sponsor's commitment to aligning trial conduct with the principles delineated in various regulatory frameworks, including but not limited to the International Council for Harmonisation of Technical Requirements for Pharmaceuticals for Human Use (ICH) guidelines, the Declaration of Helsinki, and applicable national and regional regulations. Central to regulatory compliance is the assurance of participant safety, data integrity, and ethical conduct throughout all phases of the clinical trial.

The sponsor assumes a pivotal role in navigating the complex regulatory landscape, ensuring that trial protocols are developed, implemented, and monitored in accordance with established regulatory standards. This encompasses the submission of comprehensive trial protocols and supporting documentation to regulatory authorities for approval, as well as ongoing reporting of adverse events, protocol deviations, and other pertinent information throughout the duration of the trial. Moreover, sponsors are tasked with facilitating regulatory inspections and audits, providing regulators with access to essential trial documentation and data to verify compliance with regulatory requirements.

In addition to regulatory oversight, sponsors bear the responsibility of ensuring that all investigational sites and personnel involved in the trial adhere to relevant regulatory guidelines and requirements. This may involve providing training and support to investigators and site staff on protocol-specific procedures, Good Clinical Practice (GCP) guidelines, and regulatory obligations to uphold the highest standards of research conduct. Furthermore, sponsors are obligated to monitor trial conduct closely, employing risk-based monitoring strategies to identify and mitigate potential compliance issues proactively.

A cornerstone of regulatory compliance is the ethical conduct of clinical research, with sponsors acting as stewards of participant rights and welfare. This entails obtaining informed consent from all trial participants in accordance with regulatory guidelines and ensuring that their rights, safety, and privacy are protected throughout the duration of the trial. Sponsors must also adhere to stringent requirements for the collection, handling, and storage of participant data, safeguarding confidentiality and integrity to uphold the trust and confidence of both participants and regulatory authorities.

8.1.3 Financial Obligations and Support

Financial obligations and support constitute integral components of sponsor responsibilities in clinical research, reflecting a commitment to providing the necessary resources and financial backing to ensure the successful planning, execution, and completion of clinical trials. At the outset, sponsors assume the responsibility for financing all aspects of the trial, including but not limited to protocol development, site selection and activation, participant recruitment and retention, data collection and management, regulatory submissions, and monitoring activities. This financial support encompasses a broad spectrum of expenses, ranging from personnel salaries and study-related materials to investigational product costs and overhead expenses associated with trial conduct.

In addition to providing direct financial support, sponsors are tasked with ensuring the fair and equitable distribution of financial resources among all stakeholders involved in the clinical trial process. This includes compensating investigators and research staff for their time and effort in conducting the trial, as well as reimbursing participating sites for expenses incurred in the delivery of trial-related services, such as laboratory tests, imaging studies, and participant reimbursements. Furthermore, sponsors may offer financial incentives or compensation to participants for their involvement in the trial, subject to regulatory guidelines and ethical considerations.

Beyond financial backing, sponsors play a critical role in offering logistical and operational support to investigators and trial sites to facilitate the smooth implementation of research protocols. This may involve providing infrastructure support, such as access to study-related equipment and facilities, as well as logistical assistance in coordinating site visits, monitoring activities, and regulatory submissions. Moreover, sponsors may offer technical expertise and guidance to investigators in protocol development, data collection methodologies, and regulatory compliance to enhance the quality and efficiency of trial conduct.

Throughout the duration of the trial, sponsors maintain a fiduciary responsibility to ensure the effective management and allocation of financial resources in accordance with predefined budgets and financial plans. This necessitates robust financial oversight mechanisms, including budget monitoring, expenditure tracking, and financial reporting, to ensure transparency, accountability, and compliance with regulatory requirements. By exercising prudent financial stewardship, sponsors uphold the integrity and credibility of clinical research endeavors, fostering trust and confidence among stakeholders and regulatory authorities.

8.1.4 Study Oversight and Monitoring

Study oversight and monitoring constitute essential facets of sponsor responsibilities in clinical research, entailing the systematic evaluation and supervision of trial conduct to ensure adherence to protocol requirements, regulatory standards, and ethical principles. As stewards of research integrity, sponsors assume a central role in overseeing all aspects of trial implementation, from initial planning and site selection to data analysis and dissemination of results. This oversight encompasses a spectrum of activities aimed at safeguarding participant welfare, data integrity, and the validity of study findings throughout the research process.

At the outset, sponsors are tasked with establishing robust systems and processes for monitoring trial conduct, encompassing both centralized and site-specific monitoring strategies. Centralized monitoring involves the review and analysis of trial data collected from multiple sites to identify trends, discrepancies, and potential protocol deviations that may necessitate further investigation. Site-specific monitoring, on the other hand, entails periodic visits to investigational sites by qualified monitors to assess compliance with protocol requirements, Good Clinical Practice (GCP) guidelines, and regulatory obligations.

Central to study oversight is the implementation of risk-based monitoring approaches tailored to the specific characteristics and complexity of each clinical trial. By identifying and prioritizing areas of potential risk, sponsors can allocate monitoring resources efficiently, focusing on critical data points, high-risk procedures, and vulnerable participant populations to ensure the integrity and reliability of study data. This risk-based approach enables sponsors to optimize monitoring activities while minimizing unnecessary burden on investigators and trial sites, fostering a more streamlined and cost-effective approach to study oversight.

In addition to monitoring trial conduct, sponsors are responsible for responding promptly to emerging issues and deviations from protocol requirements, implementing corrective and preventive actions as necessary to mitigate risks and ensure ongoing compliance with regulatory standards. This may involve providing guidance and support to investigators and site staff, conducting additional training or education sessions, or revising study protocols and procedures in response to evolving circumstances or emerging safety concerns.

Throughout the duration of the trial, sponsors maintain continuous vigilance over study progress and data quality, conducting regular reviews of interim data and safety reports to assess trial performance and inform decision-making processes. This ongoing monitoring enables sponsors to identify and address issues proactively, ensuring that the trial remains on track to achieve its objectives within predefined timelines and budgetary constraints. By exercising diligent oversight and monitoring, sponsors uphold the highest standards of research conduct, fostering trust, transparency, and accountability in the pursuit of scientific knowledge and medical advancement.

8.2 Investigator Responsibilities

8.2.1 Role of the Principal Investigator

The principal investigator (PI) holds a pivotal role in the conduct of clinical research, serving as the linchpin between the sponsor, study participants, and investigational site personnel. As the primary leader and coordinator of the study team, the PI assumes overall responsibility for the scientific and ethical integrity of the research endeavor. This encompasses a diverse array of duties and obligations aimed at ensuring the successful planning, execution, and completion of the clinical trial while upholding the highest standards of research conduct and participant welfare.

Leadership and Oversight: At the outset, the PI assumes leadership responsibility for the design and implementation of the study protocol, collaborating with the sponsor and study team to develop a scientifically rigorous and ethically sound research plan. The PI oversees all aspects of trial conduct, including participant recruitment, enrollment, and follow-up, as well as data collection, management, and analysis. Through effective leadership and communication, the PI fosters a collaborative and cohesive team environment, ensuring that all study personnel are adequately trained and motivated to fulfill their respective roles and responsibilities.

Protocol Adherence and Compliance: The PI plays a central role in ensuring adherence to the study protocol, regulatory requirements, and Good Clinical Practice (GCP) guidelines throughout the duration of the trial. This entails thorough familiarization with the protocol and associated study documents, as well as ongoing monitoring and enforcement of protocol-specific procedures and requirements at the investigational site. The PI collaborates closely with study coordinators, research staff, and other site personnel to ensure that all aspects of trial conduct are conducted in accordance with applicable regulations and ethical principles.

Participant Safety and Welfare: Central to the PI's responsibilities is the protection of participant rights, safety, and well-being throughout the course of the clinical trial. The PI is responsible for obtaining informed consent from all study participants in accordance with regulatory guidelines and ethical principles, ensuring that participants are fully informed about the nature of the study, its potential risks and benefits, and their rights as research subjects. In the event of adverse events or safety concerns, the PI assumes responsibility for promptly reporting and managing these events in accordance with regulatory requirements and study protocols, taking appropriate measures to mitigate risks and safeguard participant welfare.

Data Integrity and Quality: The PI maintains rigorous oversight of data collection, management, and quality assurance processes to ensure the integrity and reliability of study data. This includes implementing standardized data collection procedures, training study personnel on data entry and documentation requirements, and conducting regular reviews of study data to identify errors, discrepancies, or deviations from protocol. The PI collaborates with the study team to address any data-related issues promptly, implementing corrective actions and ensuring that data integrity is maintained throughout the duration of the trial.

8.2.2 Study Conduct and Compliance

The conduct of a clinical trial rests heavily on the shoulders of the investigators, who are tasked with ensuring adherence to protocols, regulations, and ethical standards throughout the study's duration. Study conduct and compliance, therefore, constitute core responsibilities for investigators, demanding meticulous attention to detail, unwavering commitment to participant welfare, and stringent adherence to regulatory guidelines.

Adherence to Protocol: Investigators are entrusted with the responsibility of executing the study protocol with precision and accuracy. This involves ensuring that all aspects of the protocol, including eligibility criteria, treatment interventions, data collection procedures, and follow-up assessments, are implemented as specified. By meticulously adhering to the protocol, investigators uphold the scientific validity and integrity of the study, enabling meaningful interpretation of study findings and conclusions.

Regulatory Compliance: Investigators are obligated to conduct the clinical trial in compliance with applicable regulatory requirements, including but not limited to Good Clinical Practice (GCP) guidelines, local regulations, and institutional policies. This entails obtaining necessary approvals from regulatory authorities and ethics committees prior to study initiation, as well as maintaining ongoing compliance with regulatory obligations throughout the trial. Investigators must adhere to regulatory standards for participant recruitment, informed consent, data collection, safety reporting, and study documentation, ensuring that all activities are conducted in accordance with established guidelines and regulations.

Participant Safety and Welfare: Central to the investigator's role is the protection of participant rights, safety, and well-being. Investigators are responsible for obtaining informed consent from study participants, ensuring that they fully understand the nature of the study, its potential risks and benefits, and their rights as research subjects. Throughout the trial, investigators monitor participant safety closely, promptly reporting and managing adverse events or other safety concerns in accordance with regulatory requirements and study protocols. By prioritizing participant welfare, investigators uphold the ethical principles of beneficence and nonmaleficence, fostering trust and confidence in the research process.

Data Integrity and Quality: Investigators are tasked with maintaining the integrity and quality of study data through rigorous data collection, management, and quality assurance practices. This involves implementing standardized data collection procedures, training study personnel on data entry and documentation requirements, and conducting regular reviews of study data to identify errors, discrepancies, or deviations from protocol. Investigators collaborate with the study team to address any data-related issues promptly, implementing corrective actions to ensure that data integrity is preserved and study conclusions are based on accurate and reliable information.

8.2.3 Patient Safety and Informed Consent

Patient safety and informed consent are foundational principles in clinical research, and investigators play a crucial role in upholding these principles throughout the course of a study. Ensuring the safety and well-being of study participants and obtaining their informed consent are paramount responsibilities that demand careful consideration and adherence to ethical and regulatory guidelines.

Patient Safety: Investigators bear a profound responsibility for safeguarding the safety and welfare of study participants. This obligation encompasses several key aspects, including the identification and mitigation of potential risks associated with the investigational intervention, the implementation of measures to minimize harm, and the prompt reporting and management of adverse events. Investigators must conduct thorough assessments of participant eligibility and suitability for inclusion in the study, taking into account medical history, concomitant medications, and other relevant factors that may impact safety. Throughout the trial, investigators monitor participants closely for any signs of adverse events or unexpected reactions, promptly intervening as necessary to ensure their safety and well-being. By prioritizing patient safety, investigators uphold the ethical imperative of beneficence and contribute to the integrity and credibility of the research endeavor.

Informed Consent: Obtaining informed consent from study participants is a fundamental ethical requirement that underscores respect for individual autonomy and decision-making. Investigators are responsible for ensuring that participants receive comprehensive information about the nature of the study, its purpose, procedures, potential risks and benefits, and alternatives to participation. This information must be presented in a clear, understandable manner, allowing participants to make informed decisions about their involvement in the research. Investigators must also ensure that participants have adequate time and opportunity to ask questions, seek clarification, and deliberate on their decision without coercion or undue influence. Additionally, investigators must document the informed consent process thoroughly, including the provision of written consent forms signed by participants or their legally authorized representatives. By adhering to principles of informed consent, investigators uphold ethical standards of respect for persons and promote transparency and trust in the research enterprise.

8.2.4 Data Integrity and Record Keeping

In the realm of clinical research, maintaining data integrity and comprehensive record-keeping practices are essential responsibilities for investigators. Upholding the highest standards of data integrity and documentation not only ensures the reliability and validity of study findings but also facilitates regulatory compliance and transparency in research conduct.

Data Integrity: Investigators are entrusted with the task of ensuring the integrity of study data from its collection through to analysis and reporting. This entails implementing robust data collection procedures that are standardized, consistent, and aligned with the study protocol. Investigators must also establish rigorous quality control measures to verify the accuracy, completeness, and reliability of collected data, detecting and addressing errors or discrepancies promptly. By maintaining data integrity, investigators uphold the scientific rigor and credibility of the research, enabling meaningful interpretation and dissemination of study findings.

Record Keeping: Comprehensive record-keeping practices are essential for documenting all aspects of the research process, from protocol development and participant recruitment to data collection, analysis, and regulatory submissions. Investigators must maintain organized and detailed records that provide a clear and accurate account of study activities, including correspondence with regulatory authorities, ethics committees, and sponsors, as well as documentation of informed consent procedures, adverse events, protocol deviations, and participant demographics. These records serve as a critical source of documentation for regulatory inspections, audits, and reviews, ensuring accountability, transparency, and compliance with regulatory requirements.

Data Management: Effective data management practices are crucial for organizing, storing, and safeguarding study data throughout the duration of the trial. Investigators must implement secure data storage systems and procedures to protect the confidentiality and integrity of participant data, adhering to applicable data privacy laws and regulations. Additionally, investigators should establish clear protocols for data access, sharing, and retention, ensuring that data are accessible to authorized personnel for analysis and review while maintaining confidentiality and privacy protections for study participants. By implementing robust data management practices, investigators enhance the efficiency, accuracy, and reliability of data collection and analysis, facilitating the generation of high-quality evidence to support scientific conclusions.

8.2.5 Case Study: Investigator Challenges in Patient Recruitment

In the context of clinical research, patient recruitment is a critical aspect of study conduct that can significantly impact the timeline, cost, and feasibility of a trial. Investigators often encounter various challenges and barriers in recruiting eligible participants, which can pose significant obstacles to the successful completion of the study. This case study examines some common challenges faced by investigators in patient recruitment and explores strategies to address these challenges effectively.

Challenge 1: Limited Patient Pool

One of the primary challenges investigators may encounter is a limited pool of eligible patients who meet the study's inclusion criteria. This can be particularly challenging for rare diseases or conditions with a small patient population, making it difficult to recruit a sufficient number of participants within a reasonable timeframe.

Strategy: To address this challenge, investigators can collaborate with multiple clinical sites or research networks to expand the reach and access to potential participants. Additionally, leveraging patient registries, advocacy groups, and social media platforms can help raise awareness of the study among eligible patients and facilitate recruitment efforts.

Challenge 2: Competition with Standard of Care

In some cases, patients may be hesitant to participate in a clinical trial due to concerns about deviating from standard-of-care treatments or interventions they are currently receiving. This reluctance can pose a significant barrier to recruitment, particularly if the perceived benefits of participating in the trial are not clearly communicated or understood.

Strategy: Investigators can overcome this challenge by emphasizing the potential benefits of participating in the trial, such as access to novel treatments, closer monitoring and follow-up, and the opportunity to contribute to scientific knowledge and medical advancements. Providing clear and transparent information about the study protocol, including the rationale for the research and the potential risks and benefits, can help alleviate patient concerns and enhance recruitment rates.

Challenge 3: Logistic and Practical Barriers

Logistic and practical barriers, such as transportation issues, scheduling conflicts, and financial constraints, can also hinder patient recruitment efforts. These barriers may disproportionately affect vulnerable populations or individuals with limited access to healthcare resources, further exacerbating disparities in research participation.

Strategy: Investigators can address logistic and practical barriers by offering flexible scheduling options, providing transportation assistance or reimbursement for travel expenses, and offering financial incentives or compensation to offset the costs associated with study participation. Additionally, collaborating with community organizations, healthcare providers, and local stakeholders can help identify and address barriers to recruitment within specific populations or communities.

Challenge 4: Lack of Awareness and Education

Many potential participants may be unaware of the availability of clinical trials or may have misconceptions about research participation, leading to low awareness and interest in participating in clinical research studies.

Strategy: Investigators can enhance awareness and education about clinical trials through targeted outreach and educational campaigns aimed at both patients and healthcare providers. This may involve disseminating informational materials, hosting educational seminars or webinars, and engaging in community outreach activities to raise awareness of the importance of clinical research and the opportunities available for participation.

8.3 Other Trial Personnel

8.3.1 Clinical Research Associates (CRAs)

Clinical Research Associates (CRAs) play a vital role in the execution and management of clinical trials, serving as the primary liaison between the sponsor and investigational sites. CRAs are responsible for ensuring that clinical trials are conducted in compliance with protocol requirements, regulatory standards, and Good Clinical Practice (GCP) guidelines. Their responsibilities encompass a wide range of activities aimed at facilitating site initiation, monitoring trial conduct, and ensuring data integrity throughout the duration of the study.

Site Initiation: CRAs are involved in the site initiation process, which involves assessing the readiness of investigational sites to conduct the trial. This includes reviewing essential documents such as the investigator's brochure, protocol, and informed consent form, ensuring that all regulatory and ethical requirements are met prior to study initiation. CRAs also provide training and support to site personnel on protocol-specific procedures, data collection methods, and regulatory obligations to ensure that sites are adequately prepared to initiate trial activities.

Monitoring Trial Conduct: One of the primary responsibilities of CRAs is to conduct regular monitoring visits to investigational sites to ensure compliance with protocol requirements, GCP guidelines, and regulatory standards. During these visits, CRAs review study documents, including informed consent forms, case report forms, and source documents, to verify the accuracy and completeness of data collection. CRAs also assess site adherence to protocol procedures, participant recruitment and enrollment, and safety reporting requirements, identifying any deviations or issues that may impact study conduct or data integrity.

Data Management: CRAs play a critical role in data management, ensuring the accuracy, completeness, and integrity of study data throughout the duration of the trial. This involves reviewing and verifying data entered into electronic data capture systems or case report forms against source documents to identify discrepancies or errors. CRAs also collaborate with site personnel to resolve data queries, discrepancies, or missing information promptly, ensuring that data are accurate and reliable for analysis and reporting purposes.

Regulatory Compliance: CRAs are responsible for ensuring regulatory compliance at investigational sites, including adherence to local and international regulations, institutional policies, and study-specific requirements. This includes maintaining up-to-date regulatory documentation, such as investigator CVs, site approvals, and regulatory submissions, and ensuring that all regulatory requirements are met throughout the duration of the trial. CRAs also assist sites in preparing for regulatory inspections and audits, providing support and guidance to address any findings or deficiencies identified during inspections.

8.3.1.1 Duties and Responsibilities

Clinical Research Associates (CRAs) shoulder a spectrum of duties and responsibilities crucial for the effective execution and management of clinical trials. Their multifaceted role encompasses various tasks aimed at ensuring compliance with protocol requirements, regulatory standards, and Good Clinical Practice (GCP) guidelines. Below are the key duties and responsibilities of CRAs:

1. **Site Initiation:** CRAs participate in site initiation visits, where they assess the readiness of investigational sites to conduct the trial. They review essential documents, such as the investigator's brochure, protocol, and informed consent form, to ensure regulatory and ethical compliance prior to study initiation. CRAs provide training and support to site personnel on protocol-specific procedures, data collection methods, and regulatory obligations.
2. **Monitoring Trial Conduct:** CRAs conduct regular monitoring visits to investigational sites to monitor compliance with protocol requirements, GCP guidelines, and regulatory standards. They review study documents, including informed consent forms, case report forms, and source documents, to verify data accuracy and completeness. CRAs assess site adherence to protocol procedures, participant recruitment, enrollment, and safety reporting requirements, identifying and addressing any deviations or issues that may impact study conduct or data integrity.
3. **Data Management:** CRAs oversee data management activities to ensure the accuracy, completeness, and integrity of study data. They review and verify data entered into electronic data capture systems or case report forms against source documents, identifying discrepancies or errors. CRAs collaborate with site personnel to resolve data queries, discrepancies, or missing information promptly, ensuring that data are accurate and reliable for analysis and reporting purposes.
4. **Regulatory Compliance:** CRAs ensure regulatory compliance at investigational sites, including adherence to local and international regulations, institutional policies, and study-specific requirements. They maintain up-to-date regulatory documentation, such as investigator CVs, site approvals, and regulatory submissions, throughout the trial. CRAs assist sites in preparing for regulatory inspections and audits, providing support and guidance to address any findings or deficiencies identified during inspections.

8.3.1.2 Monitoring and Site Visits

Monitoring and site visits constitute integral components of the Clinical Research Associate's (CRA) role in ensuring the quality, compliance, and integrity of clinical trials. These activities are essential for assessing site performance, verifying data accuracy, and addressing any issues or deviations promptly. Below are the key aspects of monitoring and site visits conducted by CRAs:

1. **Preparation and Planning:** Prior to site visits, CRAs meticulously prepare by reviewing study protocols, essential documents, and regulatory requirements. They develop a monitoring plan outlining the objectives, scope, and activities to be conducted during the site visit. CRAs coordinate with site personnel to schedule visits and ensure availability of necessary study documents and resources.
2. **On-Site Monitoring:** During on-site visits, CRAs conduct various activities to assess site compliance with protocol requirements, regulatory standards, and GCP guidelines. They review study documents, including informed consent forms, case report forms, and source documents, to verify data accuracy and completeness. CRAs observe study procedures, participant interactions, and data collection processes to ensure adherence to protocol specifications. They also interview site personnel to assess their understanding of protocol procedures and provide guidance or training as needed.
3. **Data Verification:** CRAs perform data verification activities to ensure the accuracy and reliability of study data. They compare data recorded in case report forms or electronic data capture systems with source documents, such as medical records and laboratory reports, to identify discrepancies or errors. CRAs query site personnel about any inconsistencies or missing information and collaborate with them to resolve data discrepancies promptly.
4. **Adherence to Regulatory Requirements:** CRAs assess site compliance with regulatory requirements, including documentation of regulatory approvals, adherence to institutional policies, and reporting of adverse events and protocol deviations. They ensure that site personnel maintain accurate and up-to-date regulatory documentation, such as investigator CVs, ethics committee approvals, and study-related communications. CRAs provide guidance and support to address any regulatory issues or deficiencies identified during site visits.
5. **Communication and Reporting:** Following site visits, CRAs communicate findings, observations, and recommendations to site personnel and relevant stakeholders. They prepare detailed monitoring reports documenting site visit activities, data verification results, protocol deviations, and regulatory compliance issues. CRAs collaborate with site personnel to develop corrective and preventive action plans

to address identified deficiencies and ensure ongoing compliance with study requirements.

8.3.1.3 Ensuring Protocol Adherence

Ensuring protocol adherence is paramount for maintaining the scientific validity, integrity, and regulatory compliance of clinical trials. Clinical Research Associates (CRAs) play a pivotal role in monitoring and enforcing protocol adherence across investigational sites. Below are the key strategies employed by CRAs to ensure protocol adherence:

1. **Protocol Familiarization:** CRAs thoroughly familiarize themselves with the study protocol, including all protocol-specific procedures, requirements, and timelines. They ensure that site personnel are equally familiar with the protocol and understand their roles and responsibilities in adhering to its specifications.
2. **Training and Education:** CRAs provide comprehensive training and education to site personnel on protocol-specific procedures, Good Clinical Practice (GCP) guidelines, and regulatory requirements. They conduct training sessions and workshops to ensure that all personnel involved in the study are equipped with the knowledge and skills necessary to adhere to the protocol effectively.
3. **Site Initiation Visits:** During site initiation visits, CRAs review the study protocol with site personnel, clarifying any ambiguities and addressing questions or concerns. They ensure that site personnel understand the protocol requirements related to participant eligibility, informed consent procedures, study assessments, data collection, and safety reporting.
4. **Ongoing Monitoring:** CRAs conduct regular monitoring visits to investigational sites to assess protocol adherence throughout the duration of the trial. They review study documents, including case report forms, source documents, and regulatory files, to verify that data collection procedures are conducted in accordance with the protocol. CRAs observe study procedures and participant interactions to ensure that protocol-specific assessments are performed correctly and consistently.
5. **Data Verification:** CRAs perform data verification activities to ensure that data recorded in case report forms or electronic data capture systems accurately reflect protocol-specified assessments and outcomes. They compare data entered by site personnel with source documents,

such as medical records and laboratory reports, to identify discrepancies or errors that may indicate protocol deviations.

6. **Protocol Amendments:** CRAs assist site personnel in implementing protocol amendments by ensuring that all changes are communicated effectively and implemented in a timely manner. They provide guidance on the revised protocol procedures and ensure that site personnel receive appropriate training and education to adhere to the amended protocol requirements.
7. **Documentation and Reporting:** CRAs maintain detailed documentation of protocol adherence assessments, deviations, and corrective actions taken to address non-compliance issues. They communicate findings and observations to site personnel and sponsors through monitoring reports and other documentation, facilitating transparency and accountability in protocol adherence.

By employing these strategies, CRAs play a critical role in ensuring protocol adherence across investigational sites, thereby contributing to the overall success and integrity of clinical trials. Their diligence, attention to detail, and commitment to regulatory compliance help to mitigate risks, uphold participant safety, and generate reliable data for scientific analysis and interpretation.

8.3.2 Auditors

8.3.2.1 Purpose and Scope of Audits

Audits play a crucial role in the quality assurance and regulatory compliance of clinical trials, ensuring that research activities adhere to established protocols, regulations, and ethical standards. The purpose of audits is multifaceted, encompassing various objectives aimed at evaluating the integrity, reliability, and compliance of trial conduct. The scope of audits extends across the entire spectrum of clinical trial activities, from protocol development and participant recruitment to data collection, analysis, and reporting. Below are the key purposes and scope of audits in clinical research:

Purpose of Audits:

1. **Quality Assurance:** Audits serve as a quality assurance mechanism to verify that clinical trial activities are conducted in accordance with protocol requirements, Good Clinical Practice (GCP) guidelines, and regulatory standards. By assessing the quality and reliability of study

data, procedures, and documentation, audits help identify deficiencies, deviations, or discrepancies that may compromise the integrity or validity of research findings.

2. **Regulatory Compliance:** Audits ensure compliance with applicable regulatory requirements, including local and international regulations, institutional policies, and study-specific obligations. By evaluating adherence to regulatory standards for participant recruitment, informed consent, data collection, safety reporting, and record-keeping, audits help mitigate regulatory risks and ensure that trials are conducted ethically and transparently.
3. **Risk Management:** Audits help identify and mitigate risks associated with clinical trial conduct, including operational, procedural, and data-related risks. By assessing potential vulnerabilities, gaps, or weaknesses in trial processes and procedures, audits enable sponsors, investigators, and regulatory authorities to implement corrective and preventive actions to mitigate risks and enhance the overall quality and integrity of trial conduct.
4. **Continuous Improvement:** Audits provide opportunities for continuous improvement and optimization of clinical trial processes and practices. By identifying areas for enhancement or refinement, audits inform best practices, standard operating procedures, and quality management systems, fostering a culture of continuous learning and improvement within the research enterprise.

Scope of Audits:

1. **Protocol Compliance:** Audits assess adherence to protocol requirements, including participant eligibility criteria, treatment interventions, study procedures, assessments, and endpoints. Auditors review study documents, case report forms, and source documents to verify that data collection and management procedures are conducted in accordance with the protocol.
2. **Regulatory Compliance:** Audits evaluate compliance with regulatory requirements, including local and international regulations, institutional policies, and ethical standards. Auditors review regulatory documentation, informed consent forms, ethics committee approvals, and safety reporting procedures to ensure that trial conduct adheres to applicable regulations and guidelines.

3. **Data Integrity:** Audits verify the integrity and reliability of study data by assessing data collection, management, and reporting processes. Auditors review data entry accuracy, completeness, and consistency across study documents and electronic data capture systems, comparing data against source documents to identify discrepancies or errors that may indicate data manipulation or fraud.
4. **Participant Safety:** Audits assess the adequacy and effectiveness of measures to protect participant rights, safety, and well-being. Auditors review adverse event reporting procedures, informed consent processes, and safety monitoring protocols to ensure that participant safety is prioritized throughout the trial.

8.3.2.2 Conducting Audits and Evaluating Compliance

The process of conducting audits in clinical research involves meticulous planning, thorough execution, and comprehensive evaluation to ensure compliance with protocol requirements, regulatory standards, and ethical guidelines. Auditors employ a systematic approach to assess various aspects of trial conduct and identify areas for improvement or corrective action. Below are the key steps involved in conducting audits and evaluating compliance:

1. Audit Planning:

- **Objective Setting:** Auditors define the objectives and scope of the audit, outlining specific areas of focus, key processes, and regulatory requirements to be evaluated.
- **Audit Plan Development:** Auditors develop a detailed audit plan, specifying the audit methodology, sampling strategy, audit schedule, and resources required for the audit.
- **Document Review:** Auditors review relevant study documents, including the protocol, informed consent forms, case report forms, regulatory submissions, and site-specific documentation, to familiarize themselves with the study and identify areas of potential non-compliance.

2. On-Site Audit Activities:

- **Site Visits:** Auditors conduct on-site visits to investigational sites to assess trial conduct and compliance with protocol requirements, GCP guidelines, and regulatory standards.

- **Document Review:** Auditors review study documents, including participant medical records, source documents, and regulatory files, to verify data accuracy, completeness, and consistency.
- **Interviews:** Auditors interview site personnel, including investigators, study coordinators, and research staff, to assess their understanding of protocol procedures, regulatory requirements, and roles and responsibilities.

3. Compliance Evaluation:

- **Protocol Adherence:** Auditors evaluate compliance with protocol requirements, including participant eligibility criteria, treatment interventions, study procedures, assessments, and endpoints.
- **Regulatory Compliance:** Auditors assess adherence to regulatory requirements, including local and international regulations, institutional policies, and study-specific obligations.
- **Data Integrity:** Auditors verify the integrity and reliability of study data by assessing data collection, management, and reporting processes.
- **Participant Safety:** Auditors evaluate the adequacy and effectiveness of measures to protect participant rights, safety, and well-being, including informed consent processes, adverse event reporting, and safety monitoring protocols.

4. Findings and Recommendations:

- **Non-Compliance Identification:** Auditors document findings of non-compliance or deviations from protocol requirements, regulatory standards, or GCP guidelines.
- **Root Cause Analysis:** Auditors conduct a root cause analysis to identify the underlying causes of non-compliance and assess the potential impact on participant safety, data integrity, and study outcomes.
- **Recommendations:** Auditors provide recommendations for corrective and preventive actions to address identified deficiencies, mitigate risks, and improve compliance with protocol requirements and regulatory standards.

5. Reporting and Follow-Up:

- **Audit Report:** Auditors prepare a comprehensive audit report documenting audit findings, observations, recommendations, and corrective action plans.
- **Follow-Up:** Auditors collaborate with sponsors, investigators, and site personnel to implement corrective and preventive actions in response to audit findings. They conduct follow-up activities to verify the effectiveness of corrective actions and ensure ongoing compliance with protocol requirements and regulatory standards.

8.3.2.3 Corrective Actions and Follow-Up

After conducting audits and identifying areas of non-compliance or deficiencies in clinical trial conduct, it is essential to implement corrective actions promptly to address these issues and prevent recurrence. Corrective actions are measures taken to rectify identified deficiencies, mitigate risks, and improve compliance with protocol requirements, regulatory standards, and ethical guidelines. Additionally, follow-up activities are crucial for verifying the effectiveness of corrective actions and ensuring ongoing compliance with regulatory requirements. Below are the key steps involved in corrective actions and follow-up:

1. Corrective Action Planning:

- **Identification of Deficiencies:** Based on audit findings and observations, deficiencies and areas of non-compliance are identified, including deviations from protocol requirements, regulatory standards, or Good Clinical Practice (GCP) guidelines.
- **Root Cause Analysis:** A thorough root cause analysis is conducted to determine the underlying causes of identified deficiencies. This involves examining the processes, procedures, and factors contributing to non-compliance to address the root causes effectively.
- **Development of Corrective Action Plans:** Corrective action plans are developed to address identified deficiencies and prevent recurrence. These plans outline specific actions, responsibilities, timelines, and resources required to implement corrective measures effectively.

2. Implementation of Corrective Actions:

- **Assignment of Responsibilities:** Responsibilities for implementing corrective actions are assigned to relevant individuals or departments, including sponsors, investigators, study coordinators, and site personnel.

- **Timely Execution:** Corrective actions are implemented promptly to address identified deficiencies and mitigate associated risks. This may involve revising study procedures, providing additional training, updating study documents, or improving data management practices.

3. Monitoring and Verification:

- **Follow-Up Activities:** Follow-up activities are conducted to monitor the implementation of corrective actions and verify their effectiveness in addressing identified deficiencies. This may involve additional site visits, document reviews, or data audits to assess compliance with corrective measures.
- **Verification of Compliance:** Auditors or quality assurance personnel verify compliance with corrective actions by reviewing documentation, conducting interviews, and assessing adherence to revised procedures and protocols.

4. Documentation and Reporting:

- **Documentation of Corrective Actions:** All corrective actions taken in response to audit findings are documented thoroughly, including details of actions implemented, responsible parties, timelines, and outcomes.
- **Reporting:** A summary report of corrective actions and follow-up activities is prepared, documenting the results of verification efforts and any ongoing compliance issues or residual risks.

5. Continuous Improvement:

- **Lessons Learned:** Lessons learned from audit findings, corrective actions, and follow-up activities are documented and shared within the organization to facilitate continuous improvement and optimization of clinical trial processes.
- **Process Optimization:** Identified deficiencies and corrective actions inform process optimization initiatives aimed at enhancing quality, compliance, and efficiency in clinical trial conduct.

8.3.2.3 Corrective Actions and Follow-Up

Following the identification of any discrepancies or non-compliance issues during audits in clinical trials, it's imperative to initiate corrective actions swiftly to rectify the problems and prevent their recurrence. Corrective actions are steps taken to address the root causes of identified issues and ensure adherence to protocol requirements, regulatory standards, and ethical guidelines. Additionally, robust follow-up procedures are essential to verify the effectiveness of corrective measures and maintain ongoing compliance. Here's an outline of the process:

1. Identification of Deficiencies:

- Once audit findings are documented, deficiencies or areas of non-compliance are identified clearly and comprehensively.
- These may include deviations from the study protocol, regulatory violations, data integrity concerns, or procedural discrepancies.

2. Root Cause Analysis:

- A thorough root cause analysis is conducted to delve into the underlying reasons for the identified deficiencies.
- This involves examining the processes, systems, or human factors contributing to the non-compliance.

3. Development of Corrective Action Plans:

- Corrective action plans are formulated to address the root causes of the identified issues effectively.
- These plans outline specific actions to be taken, responsibilities assigned to relevant parties, timelines for implementation, and resources required.

4. Implementation of Corrective Actions:

- Responsible individuals or teams execute the corrective actions according to the predetermined plan.
- Timeliness and effectiveness are crucial in implementing the corrective measures to mitigate risks promptly.

5. Monitoring and Verification:

- Follow-up procedures are established to monitor the progress and effectiveness of the corrective actions.
- Verification activities are conducted to ensure that the implemented measures have successfully addressed the identified deficiencies.

6. Documentation and Reporting:

- All corrective actions taken, along with their outcomes, are thoroughly documented.
- A comprehensive report detailing the corrective actions and their verification results is prepared for documentation purposes and regulatory compliance.

7. Continuous Improvement:

- Lessons learned from the audit findings and corrective actions are used to enhance processes and systems continuously.
- Regular reviews and evaluations are conducted to identify opportunities for improvement and optimize trial conduct.

8.3.3 Coordinators

8.3.3.1 Role in Study Management

Clinical research coordinators (CRCs) are integral members of the research team, playing a central role in the management and coordination of clinical trials. Their responsibilities encompass various aspects of study management aimed at ensuring the smooth conduct of the trial and compliance with protocol requirements, regulatory standards, and ethical guidelines. Below are the key roles and responsibilities of CRCs in study management:

1. Protocol Implementation:

- CRCs are responsible for implementing the study protocol at investigational sites, ensuring that all procedures and activities are conducted in accordance with protocol requirements.
- They coordinate with investigators and other site personnel to facilitate protocol-specific assessments, interventions, and data collection procedures.

2. Participant Recruitment and Enrollment:

- CRCs oversee participant recruitment and enrollment activities, including screening, eligibility assessment, and informed consent processes.
- They liaise with healthcare providers, referral networks, and community organizations to identify and enroll eligible participants into the study.

3. Study Coordination and Logistics:

- CRCs coordinate study-related logistics, including scheduling participant visits, arranging study assessments and procedures, and coordinating study supplies and materials.
- They ensure that study visits are conducted efficiently, participants are adequately informed and prepared, and all necessary resources are available.

4. Data Collection and Management:

- CRCs are responsible for collecting, recording, and managing study data in accordance with protocol requirements and regulatory standards.
- They ensure the accuracy, completeness, and integrity of study data by adhering to standardized data collection procedures and documentation practices.

5. Regulatory Compliance:

- CRCs ensure compliance with regulatory requirements, including obtaining and maintaining regulatory approvals, reporting adverse events, and maintaining essential study documentation.
- They assist investigators in preparing regulatory submissions, ethics committee applications, and other regulatory documents as required.

6. Participant Safety and Well-being:

- CRCs prioritize participant safety and well-being throughout the trial, ensuring that participants receive appropriate care, monitoring, and follow-up.

- They promptly report adverse events, protocol deviations, and other safety concerns to investigators and regulatory authorities, as required.

7. Communication and Collaboration:

- CRCs serve as the primary point of contact for study participants, investigators, sponsors, and other stakeholders, facilitating communication and collaboration among team members.
- They provide ongoing support, guidance, and training to site personnel to ensure that study procedures are conducted correctly and consistently.

8.3.3.2 Patient Recruitment and Screening

Patient recruitment and screening are pivotal components of clinical trials, and clinical research coordinators (CRCs) are instrumental in managing these processes effectively. Their role in patient recruitment and screening involves various responsibilities aimed at identifying eligible participants and ensuring their suitability for inclusion in the study. Here's an overview of the key tasks performed by CRCs in patient recruitment and screening:

1. Developing Recruitment Strategies:

- CRCs collaborate with investigators and study teams to develop comprehensive recruitment strategies tailored to the study's target population and recruitment goals.
- They identify potential recruitment sources, including healthcare providers, patient registries, community organizations, and online platforms, to maximize outreach and engagement.

2. Outreach and Engagement:

- CRCs engage in outreach activities to raise awareness of the study among potential participants and healthcare providers.
- They develop promotional materials, such as flyers, brochures, and online advertisements, to disseminate information about the study and its eligibility criteria.

3. Screening Eligibility Criteria:

- CRCs screen potential participants to assess their eligibility for inclusion in the study based on predefined criteria outlined in the study protocol.
- They conduct initial screenings to gather basic demographic and medical history information and assess participants' suitability for further evaluation.

4. Informed Consent Process:

- CRCs facilitate the informed consent process, explaining the study purpose, procedures, risks, and benefits to potential participants and obtaining their voluntary consent to participate.
- They ensure that participants have a clear understanding of the study requirements, their rights as research subjects, and the voluntary nature of participation.

5. Assessing Participant Suitability:

- CRCs assess participants' suitability for inclusion in the study based on medical history, demographic characteristics, and other eligibility criteria specified in the protocol.
- They conduct physical examinations, laboratory tests, and other assessments to confirm participants' eligibility and ensure their safety throughout the trial.

6. Managing Participant Databases:

- CRCs maintain databases of potential participants, including contact information, screening outcomes, and study eligibility status.
- They track participant recruitment progress, screening results, and enrollment numbers to monitor recruitment goals and timelines.

7. Coordination with Investigational Sites:

- CRCs coordinate with investigational sites to facilitate participant screening visits, ensuring that screening procedures are conducted consistently and according to protocol requirements.
- They communicate screening outcomes and participant eligibility status to investigators and study teams, coordinating further assessment and

enrollment as necessary.

8. Follow-Up and Retention Strategies:

- CRCs implement follow-up strategies to maintain communication with potential participants and encourage their continued participation in the study.
- They develop retention strategies to minimize participant attrition and maximize retention rates throughout the duration of the trial.

8.3.3.3 Liaising with Investigators and Sponsors

Clinical research coordinators (CRCs) serve as vital intermediaries between investigators, sponsors, and other stakeholders involved in clinical trials. Their role in liaising with investigators and sponsors is essential for ensuring effective communication, collaboration, and coordination throughout the trial process. Here's an overview of the key responsibilities of CRCs in this aspect:

1. Facilitating Communication:

- CRCs facilitate communication between investigators, sponsors, and study teams, ensuring that all parties are informed of relevant study updates, protocol amendments, and regulatory requirements.
- They serve as the primary point of contact for inquiries, feedback, and communication between investigators and sponsors, relaying messages and coordinating responses as needed.

2. Protocol Adherence and Compliance:

- CRCs work closely with investigators to ensure adherence to the study protocol, including protocol-specific procedures, assessments, and timelines.
- They collaborate with sponsors to address protocol-related queries, resolve discrepancies, and implement protocol amendments in a timely manner.

3. Study Oversight and Monitoring:

- CRCs assist investigators in coordinating study oversight and monitoring activities, including scheduling monitoring visits, providing access to study documents and data, and facilitating site inspections.
- They liaise with sponsors to ensure that study monitoring activities are conducted according to regulatory requirements and sponsor-specific procedures.

4. Regulatory Compliance and Documentation:

- CRCs collaborate with investigators and sponsors to ensure regulatory compliance throughout the trial, including obtaining and maintaining regulatory approvals, ethics committee submissions, and informed consent documentation.
- They assist investigators in preparing regulatory documents, study reports, and submissions to regulatory authorities as required by the sponsor.

5. Study Progress and Reporting:

- CRCs provide regular updates on study progress, participant recruitment, enrollment numbers, and data collection to investigators and sponsors.
- They assist in preparing study reports, progress summaries, and milestone achievements for sponsors, ensuring timely and accurate reporting of study activities.

6. Investigator Meetings and Trainings:

- CRCs coordinate investigator meetings, site initiation visits, and training sessions organized by sponsors, facilitating attendance, scheduling, and logistical arrangements.
- They assist investigators in preparing presentations, training materials, and documentation for investigator meetings and trainings as required by the sponsor.

7. Issue Resolution and Escalation:

- CRCs serve as intermediaries in resolving issues, conflicts, or challenges that arise during the course of the trial, escalating critical issues to investigators and sponsors for resolution.
- They collaborate with sponsors to address site-specific issues, protocol deviations, data discrepancies, and participant concerns, ensuring timely resolution and follow-up.

8.4 Ensuring Compliance and Ethical Conduct

8.4.1 Regulatory Framework and Guidelines

Ensuring compliance with regulatory requirements and ethical standards is paramount in clinical research to safeguard participant rights, welfare, and data integrity. The regulatory framework governing clinical trials encompasses a myriad of laws, regulations, and guidelines established by national and international regulatory authorities and ethical review bodies. Here's an overview of the key components of the regulatory framework and guidelines:

1. International Regulations:

- **International Conference on Harmonisation (ICH) Guidelines:** ICH guidelines provide harmonized standards for the conduct of clinical trials, covering topics such as Good Clinical Practice (GCP), safety reporting, and data management. These guidelines are endorsed by regulatory authorities from the US, EU, Japan, and other countries.
- **Declaration of Helsinki:** The Declaration of Helsinki outlines ethical principles for medical research involving human participants, emphasizing principles such as voluntary informed consent, participant rights, and risk minimization.

2. National Regulations:

- **Food and Drug Administration (FDA) Regulations (US):** The FDA regulates clinical trials in the United States, enforcing regulations such as Title 21 of the Code of Federal Regulations (CFR) Part 50 (Protection of Human Subjects) and Part 56 (Institutional Review Boards). These regulations govern informed consent, institutional review board (IRB) oversight, and regulatory submissions.
- **European Medicines Agency (EMA) Regulations (EU):** The EMA oversees clinical trials in the European Union, enforcing regulations

such as Directive 2001/20/EC and Regulation (EU) No 536/2014. These regulations govern clinical trial authorization, GCP compliance, and pharmacovigilance requirements.

3. Ethical Guidelines:

- **Council for International Organizations of Medical Sciences (CIOMS) Guidelines:** CIOMS guidelines provide ethical guidance for biomedical research, addressing topics such as research ethics committees, research on vulnerable populations, and benefit-risk assessment.
- **World Medical Association (WMA) Guidelines:** The WMA issues ethical guidelines for medical research, including the Declaration of Helsinki, WMA Declaration of Taipei on Ethical Considerations Regarding Health Databases and Biobanks, and WMA Declaration of Reykjavik on Ethical Considerations Regarding Health Databases.

4. Institutional Policies and Standard Operating Procedures (SOPs):

- Research institutions and organizations develop internal policies and SOPs to ensure compliance with regulatory requirements and ethical standards.
- These policies cover various aspects of clinical trial conduct, including protocol development, participant recruitment, informed consent procedures, data management, and adverse event reporting.

5. Oversight and Compliance Mechanisms:

- Regulatory authorities and ethical review bodies, such as IRBs/ethics committees, monitor and oversee clinical trials to ensure compliance with regulatory requirements and ethical standards.
- They review study protocols, informed consent forms, investigator qualifications, and safety monitoring plans to assess compliance and ethical conduct.

8.4.2 Institutional Review Board (IRB) Oversight

Institutional Review Boards (IRBs) play a pivotal role in ensuring the ethical conduct and regulatory compliance of clinical research involving human participants. Their oversight is critical for safeguarding participant rights, welfare, and confidentiality throughout the research process. Here's an overview of the key aspects of IRB oversight in clinical research:

1. Protocol Review and Approval:

- IRBs review research protocols to assess the scientific merit, ethical soundness, and methodological rigor of proposed studies.
- They evaluate the risks and benefits of participation, adequacy of informed consent procedures, and protections for vulnerable populations.
- Upon review, IRBs may approve, require modifications to, or disapprove research protocols based on their findings.

2. Informed Consent Process:

- IRBs review and approve informed consent documents to ensure that participants are provided with clear, comprehensible information about the study purpose, procedures, risks, and benefits.
- They assess the adequacy of consent forms in conveying information to participants and obtaining voluntary informed consent.
- IRBs may require revisions to consent forms to enhance clarity, readability, and comprehension for participants.

3. Ongoing Study Oversight:

- IRBs provide ongoing oversight of approved studies to monitor compliance with protocol requirements, regulatory standards, and ethical guidelines.
- They review and approve amendments to study protocols, including changes to study procedures, participant eligibility criteria, or data collection methods.
- IRBs may conduct periodic reviews of ongoing studies to assess participant safety, data integrity, and continued ethical acceptability.

4. Participant Safety Monitoring:

- IRBs oversee the monitoring of participant safety throughout the duration of clinical trials, including the reporting and management of adverse events and unanticipated problems.

- They review and evaluate safety monitoring plans, data safety monitoring reports, and serious adverse event reports to ensure appropriate participant protection measures are in place.

5. Confidentiality and Data Protection:

- IRBs assess the adequacy of measures to protect participant confidentiality and privacy, including data security protocols and access controls.
- They review data management plans, including data collection, storage, and sharing procedures, to ensure compliance with regulatory requirements and ethical standards.

6. Compliance Reporting and Documentation:

- IRBs require researchers to submit regular progress reports, adverse event reports, and other study-related documentation for review and monitoring.
- They maintain comprehensive records of protocol reviews, approvals, modifications, and adverse event reports to ensure transparency and accountability in the research process.

8.4.3 Good Clinical Practice (GCP) Standards

Good Clinical Practice (GCP) standards are a set of international ethical and scientific quality standards for designing, conducting, recording, and reporting clinical trials involving human participants. Compliance with GCP ensures that the rights, safety, and well-being of trial participants are protected and that clinical trial data are credible and accurate. Here's an overview of the key aspects of GCP standards:

1. Ethical Conduct:

- GCP emphasizes the importance of conducting clinical trials in accordance with ethical principles outlined in international guidelines such as the Declaration of Helsinki.
- Trials must be based on the ethical principles of respect for individuals, beneficence, justice, and respect for vulnerable populations.

2. Investigator Responsibilities:

- GCP outlines the responsibilities of investigators, including ensuring that trials are conducted in compliance with the protocol, obtaining informed consent from participants, and ensuring the accuracy and integrity of data collected.
- Investigators are responsible for the conduct of the trial at their site and for ensuring that all trial-related activities are conducted by qualified personnel.

3. Protocol Compliance:

- GCP emphasizes the importance of adhering to the study protocol to ensure the validity and integrity of trial results.
- Any deviations from the protocol must be documented and justified, and their impact on participant safety and data integrity must be assessed.

4. Informed Consent:

- GCP requires that informed consent be obtained from all trial participants prior to their participation in the study.
- Informed consent must be voluntary, based on adequate information provided to participants, and documented appropriately in written form.

5. Safety Reporting:

- GCP mandates the reporting of adverse events and serious adverse events occurring during the trial to regulatory authorities, ethics committees, and sponsors.
- Investigators are responsible for promptly reporting adverse events, assessing their severity and relationship to the investigational product, and taking appropriate action to ensure participant safety.

6. Data Integrity and Record Keeping:

- GCP emphasizes the importance of maintaining accurate, complete, and reliable records of trial data.
- Trial data must be recorded contemporaneously, accurately transcribed, and stored securely to prevent loss, tampering, or unauthorized access.

7. Monitoring and Quality Assurance:

- GCP requires that clinical trials be subject to regular monitoring and quality assurance activities to ensure compliance with protocol requirements and GCP standards.
- Monitoring activities include site visits, source data verification, and review of trial documentation to assess protocol adherence, data accuracy, and participant safety.

8. Regulatory Compliance:

- GCP mandates compliance with applicable regulatory requirements and guidelines governing clinical research, including those issued by regulatory authorities and ethical review bodies.
- Trials must be conducted in accordance with local regulatory requirements, and all necessary approvals must be obtained before the trial commences.

8.4.4 Handling Adverse Events and Reporting Requirements

In clinical research, the identification, assessment, and management of adverse events (AEs) are critical components of ensuring participant safety and regulatory compliance. Adverse events are any untoward medical occurrences that happen during a clinical trial, whether or not they are related to the investigational product. Here's an overview of handling adverse events and reporting requirements in clinical trials:

1. Adverse Event Identification:

- Clinical trial personnel, including investigators and clinical research coordinators (CRCs), are responsible for promptly identifying and documenting adverse events reported by trial participants or observed during study visits.
- Adverse events may include symptoms, signs, laboratory abnormalities, or other medical occurrences, regardless of their severity or relationship to the investigational product.

2. Adverse Event Assessment:

- Investigators assess the severity, causality, and expectedness of adverse events to determine appropriate management and reporting actions.
- Severity is classified based on the impact of the adverse event on the participant's daily activities, with categories ranging from mild to severe.
- Causality refers to the likelihood that the adverse event is related to the investigational product, with assessments ranging from unrelated to definitely related.
- Expectedness refers to whether the adverse event is a known risk associated with the investigational product or is unexpected based on its known safety profile.

3. Adverse Event Management:

- Investigators and study personnel manage adverse events by providing appropriate medical care and interventions to participants, as necessary, to alleviate symptoms and ensure participant safety.
- Management strategies may include dose adjustments, treatment modifications, temporary or permanent discontinuation of the investigational product, or referral to medical specialists for further evaluation and management.

4. Adverse Event Reporting Requirements:

- Investigators are required to report adverse events to regulatory authorities, ethics committees, and sponsors in accordance with regulatory requirements and reporting timelines.
- Reporting requirements vary by jurisdiction but generally include expedited reporting of serious adverse events (SAEs) and unexpected adverse reactions that occur during the trial.
- SAEs are adverse events that result in death, are life-threatening, require hospitalization or prolongation of existing hospitalization, result in persistent or significant disability or incapacity, or are otherwise considered medically significant.

5. Expedited Reporting:

- Serious adverse events and unexpected adverse reactions are subject to expedited reporting requirements, typically requiring notification to regulatory authorities and ethics committees within a specified timeframe (e.g., 7 to 15 calendar days).

- Investigators and sponsors must submit comprehensive reports detailing the nature, severity, timing, and outcome of the adverse event, along with an assessment of causality and potential implications for participant safety and trial conduct.

6. Documentation and Record Keeping:

- Adverse events and their management are documented meticulously in the participant's medical records and the trial's case report forms (CRFs).
- Detailed records of adverse events, including their description, severity, management, outcome, and follow-up, are maintained throughout the trial to ensure accurate reporting and documentation.

8.4.5 Case Study: Ethical Dilemmas in Clinical Research

In a multicenter clinical trial evaluating the efficacy of a new treatment for a rare neurological disorder, several ethical dilemmas arose, challenging the integrity of the research and the well-being of trial participants. Here's an overview of the ethical dilemmas encountered and potential strategies for resolution:

1. Informed Consent Issues:

- Dilemma: Some trial participants, particularly those with severe cognitive impairment due to their neurological condition, struggled to comprehend the study information provided during the informed consent process.
- Strategy: Researchers and clinical research coordinators (CRCs) should employ alternative approaches to ensure that participants with cognitive impairments understand the study risks, benefits, and procedures. This may include the use of simplified consent forms, multimedia presentations, and extended discussions with family members or legal representatives to facilitate informed decision-making.

2. Participant Vulnerability:

- Dilemma: Trial participants with a rare neurological disorder may be vulnerable due to their medical condition, limited treatment options, and potential for exploitation.
- Strategy: Researchers and study personnel must implement additional safeguards to protect the rights and welfare of vulnerable participants. This may include enhanced monitoring, regular assessments of decision-making capacity, and proactive measures to address participant concerns or distress throughout the trial.

3. Equity and Access:

- Dilemma: Access to investigational treatments may be limited for participants from disadvantaged socioeconomic backgrounds or underserved communities, raising concerns about equity and fairness in research participation.
- Strategy: Researchers should strive to promote equity and inclusivity in clinical trial recruitment by actively engaging with diverse communities, addressing barriers to participation, and providing support services to ensure equal access to research opportunities. Collaboration with community organizations and patient advocacy groups can facilitate outreach efforts and promote diversity in trial enrollment.

4. Transparency and Disclosure:

- Dilemma: Trial participants may have unrealistic expectations about the potential benefits of the investigational treatment or the likelihood of personal benefit, leading to misunderstandings or dissatisfaction with study outcomes.
- Strategy: Researchers should maintain transparency and open communication with participants throughout the trial, providing clear and accurate information about the study objectives, risks, and uncertainties. Managing participant expectations through ongoing education and dialogue can help foster realistic understanding and acceptance of trial outcomes.

5. Data Integrity and Reporting:

- Dilemma: Pressure to achieve favorable study results or meet enrollment targets may compromise the integrity of data collection and reporting, leading to biased or unreliable study outcomes.
- Strategy: Researchers and sponsors must prioritize scientific rigor and adherence to ethical principles in all aspects of trial conduct. Implementing robust data management practices, independent monitoring, and peer review mechanisms can mitigate potential biases and ensure the reliability and validity of study findings.

8.5 Quality Control and Assurance

8.5.1 Data Management and Quality Assurance

In clinical research, robust data management practices and quality assurance processes are essential for ensuring the accuracy, integrity, and reliability of study data. Data management encompasses the collection, storage, processing, and analysis of clinical trial data, while quality assurance involves systematic monitoring and evaluation to identify and address errors or discrepancies. Here's an overview of data management and quality assurance in clinical research:

1. Data Collection and Standardization:

- Clinical research coordinators (CRCs) are responsible for collecting study data using standardized data collection forms and procedures.
- Data collection tools should be designed to capture relevant study variables accurately and consistently across all study sites.
- Standardization ensures that data collected are comparable and can be analyzed effectively to meet study objectives.

2. Data Entry and Validation:

- Collected data are entered into electronic databases or case report forms (CRFs) by study personnel.
- Data entry is subjected to validation checks to identify errors or inconsistencies, such as missing data, out-of-range values, or data entry errors.
- Validation checks help ensure data accuracy and completeness before analysis.

3. Data Cleaning and Query Resolution:

- Data managers review entered data to identify discrepancies or inconsistencies that require clarification.
- Queries are generated to resolve discrepancies, and study personnel respond with corrections or explanations.
- Data cleaning involves resolving queries and ensuring that all data are accurate, consistent, and ready for analysis.

4. Data Security and Confidentiality:

- Measures are implemented to safeguard the security and confidentiality of study data.
- Access to study databases is restricted to authorized personnel, and data encryption and password protection are used to prevent unauthorized access.
- Data anonymization techniques may be employed to protect participant confidentiality when sharing data for analysis or publication.

5. Quality Control Checks:

- Quality control checks are performed throughout the data management process to ensure adherence to protocol requirements and data quality standards.
- Checks may include regular review of data entry accuracy, completeness of documentation, and compliance with data management procedures.
- Any deviations or discrepancies are addressed promptly through corrective actions and retraining as necessary.

6. Audits and Inspections:

- Internal and external audits may be conducted to evaluate the quality and integrity of study data and processes.
- Auditors review study documentation, data management procedures, and adherence to regulatory requirements and GCP standards.
- Findings from audits are used to identify areas for improvement and implement corrective actions to enhance data quality and compliance.

7. Continuous Monitoring and Improvement:

- Continuous monitoring of data management processes is essential to identify trends, detect potential issues, and implement preventive measures.
- Feedback mechanisms are established to solicit input from study personnel and stakeholders for ongoing process improvement.
- Lessons learned from data management experiences are used to refine procedures, optimize workflows, and enhance overall data quality and efficiency.

8.5.2 Protocol Deviations and Non-Compliance

In clinical research, protocol deviations and non-compliance with study protocols can have significant implications for data integrity, participant safety, and regulatory compliance. Protocol deviations refer to departures from the study protocol's predefined procedures, while non-compliance involves failure to adhere to regulatory requirements, Good Clinical Practice (GCP) standards, or institutional policies. Here's an overview of how protocol deviations and non-compliance are managed and mitigated in clinical research:

1. Identification and Documentation:

- Clinical trial personnel, including investigators and clinical research coordinators (CRCs), are responsible for identifying and documenting protocol deviations and instances of non-compliance as they occur.
- Deviations may include missed study visits, deviations from the dosing schedule, incomplete data collection, or deviations from inclusion/exclusion criteria.
- Non-compliance may involve failure to obtain informed consent, inadequate documentation of study procedures, or failure to report adverse events as required.

2. Assessment of Severity and Impact:

- Upon identification, protocol deviations and instances of non-compliance are assessed to determine their severity, impact on participant safety, and implications for data integrity.
- Deviations are categorized based on severity, ranging from minor deviations with minimal impact to major deviations that could compromise participant safety or data quality.

- Non-compliance is assessed in terms of its potential consequences for study conduct, participant rights, and regulatory compliance.

3. Corrective Actions and Documentation:

- For minor protocol deviations, corrective actions may involve remedial training, re-education of study personnel, or additional monitoring to prevent recurrence.
- Major deviations and instances of non-compliance require more significant corrective actions, including protocol amendments, participant re-consent, data corrections, or suspension of study activities.
- All corrective actions taken in response to protocol deviations or non-compliance are documented thoroughly, including the rationale for the action, the individuals involved, and the outcomes of corrective measures.

4. Reporting and Documentation:

- Protocol deviations and instances of non-compliance are reported to regulatory authorities, ethics committees, and sponsors as required by regulatory guidelines and reporting obligations.
- Detailed documentation of protocol deviations, corrective actions, and outcomes is maintained in the trial's documentation, including the trial master file (TMF) and adverse event reports.
- Reporting timelines and requirements for protocol deviations and non-compliance vary depending on the severity and impact of the deviation, as well as local regulatory requirements.

5. Preventive Measures and Training:

- To prevent protocol deviations and non-compliance, comprehensive training and education programs are provided to study personnel involved in trial conduct.
- Training covers protocol requirements, GCP standards, regulatory obligations, and procedures for documenting and reporting deviations.
- Ongoing monitoring and quality assurance activities are conducted to identify potential areas of non-compliance and implement preventive

measures before deviations occur.

6. Continuous Improvement:

- Lessons learned from protocol deviations and instances of non-compliance are used to refine study protocols, enhance training programs, and improve monitoring and oversight mechanisms.
- Continuous improvement efforts aim to strengthen adherence to protocol requirements, mitigate risks, and enhance overall quality and integrity of clinical research conduct.

8.5.3 Training and Education of Trial Personnel

Training and education of trial personnel are essential components of ensuring the successful conduct of clinical trials, maintaining data integrity, and upholding ethical standards. Properly trained personnel are equipped with the knowledge and skills necessary to adhere to study protocols, regulatory requirements, and Good Clinical Practice (GCP) standards. Here's an overview of training and education practices for trial personnel:

1. Initial Training:

- Trial personnel, including investigators, clinical research coordinators (CRCs), nurses, and other study staff, undergo comprehensive initial training before participating in clinical trials.
- Training programs cover essential topics such as study protocol requirements, GCP guidelines, regulatory obligations, and specific procedures relevant to the trial.

2. Study-Specific Training:

- In addition to general training, trial personnel receive study-specific training tailored to the requirements and procedures of each clinical trial.
- Study-specific training sessions may include detailed instruction on protocol-specific procedures, data collection techniques, investigational product administration, and safety monitoring.

3. Role-Specific Training:

- Training programs are customized based on the roles and responsibilities of trial personnel within the study team.
- Investigators receive training on their responsibilities for study oversight, participant recruitment, informed consent procedures, and adverse event reporting.
- CRCs and other study coordinators receive training on data collection, participant management, regulatory compliance, and documentation requirements.

4. GCP Training:

- GCP training is a fundamental component of trial personnel education, emphasizing the principles of ethical conduct, participant protection, and data integrity in clinical research.
- GCP training programs cover topics such as the history and principles of GCP, roles and responsibilities of trial personnel, informed consent requirements, safety reporting, and regulatory compliance.

5. Continuing Education:

- Trial personnel engage in ongoing continuing education activities to stay updated on advancements in clinical research, regulatory changes, and best practices.
- Continuing education may include attendance at conferences, workshops, webinars, and online courses related to clinical research, GCP, and specialized areas of study.

6. Assessment and Certification:

- Trial personnel may be required to undergo formal assessment and certification processes to demonstrate competency in key areas of clinical trial conduct.
- Certification programs may be offered by professional organizations, academic institutions, or industry associations and typically involve written examinations or practical assessments of knowledge and skills.

7. Refresher Training:

- Periodic refresher training sessions are conducted to reinforce key concepts, address common challenges, and update trial personnel on any changes to study protocols or regulatory requirements.
- Refresher training helps ensure that trial personnel maintain proficiency and compliance throughout the duration of the trial.

8. Documentation and Records:

- Documentation of training activities and personnel qualifications is maintained as part of the trial's documentation, including training logs, certificates of completion, and personnel files.
- Records of training and education activities provide evidence of compliance with regulatory requirements and GCP standards during regulatory inspections and audits.

8.5.4 Implementing Corrective and Preventive Actions

In clinical research, the implementation of corrective and preventive actions (CAPA) is crucial for addressing deficiencies, mitigating risks, and improving quality processes. Corrective actions are taken to address existing issues or non-conformities identified through audits, inspections, or quality control checks, while preventive actions aim to prevent recurrence of similar issues in the future. Here's an overview of implementing corrective and preventive actions in clinical trials:

1. Root Cause Analysis:

- Before implementing corrective actions, a thorough root cause analysis is conducted to identify the underlying causes of the issue or non-conformity.
- Root cause analysis techniques, such as the 5 Whys, fishbone diagrams, or fault tree analysis, are used to systematically identify contributing factors and root causes.

2. Corrective Action Plan (CAP):

- Based on the findings of the root cause analysis, a corrective action plan (CAP) is developed to address the identified issues effectively.
- The CAP outlines specific corrective actions to be taken, responsible parties, timelines for implementation, and criteria for verification of

effectiveness.

3. Implementation of Corrective Actions:

- Corrective actions are implemented promptly and effectively according to the CAP.
- This may involve process improvements, procedural changes, retraining of personnel, or revisions to study protocols or documentation.

4. Monitoring and Verification:

- The effectiveness of corrective actions is monitored and verified to ensure that the identified issues have been adequately addressed.
- Verification activities may include follow-up audits, inspections, or quality control checks to assess compliance with corrective measures and determine whether the issue has been resolved satisfactorily.

5. Preventive Action Plan (PAP):

- In addition to addressing existing issues, preventive action plans (PAPs) are developed to proactively identify and mitigate potential risks and non-conformities.
- PAPs may involve risk assessments, process improvements, additional training, or implementation of preventive controls to minimize the likelihood of recurrence.

6. Continuous Improvement:

- Corrective and preventive actions are integral components of a continuous improvement process in clinical research.
- Lessons learned from the implementation of CAPAs are used to refine processes, enhance quality management systems, and prevent future occurrences of similar issues.

7. Documentation and Record Keeping:

- All corrective and preventive actions taken, including the root cause analysis, CAP, and verification activities, are documented thoroughly.

- Documentation provides a record of the actions taken, rationale for decision-making, and evidence of compliance with regulatory requirements and quality standards.

8. Communication and Transparency:

- Clear communication channels are maintained throughout the CAPA process to ensure that stakeholders are informed of actions taken and progress made.
- Transparency in the CAPA process fosters accountability, trust, and collaboration among trial personnel, sponsors, regulatory authorities, and other stakeholders.

By implementing effective corrective and preventive actions, clinical trial sponsors and investigators can address quality issues, minimize risks, and enhance the integrity and reliability of clinical research processes and outcomes.

8.5.5 Case Study: Maintaining Data Integrity in a Large-Scale Clinical Trial

In a large-scale clinical trial evaluating the efficacy and safety of a novel treatment for a prevalent chronic condition, maintaining data integrity posed significant challenges due to the complexity and scale of the study. Here's an overview of the strategies employed to ensure data integrity throughout the trial:

1. Robust Data Management Infrastructure:

- A comprehensive data management infrastructure was established to support data collection, storage, and analysis across multiple study sites.
- Electronic data capture (EDC) systems were implemented to facilitate real-time data entry, validation, and monitoring, minimizing the risk of data transcription errors and ensuring data accuracy.

2. Standardized Data Collection Procedures:

- Standardized data collection procedures and case report forms (CRFs) were developed to ensure consistent data capture across all study sites.
- Training sessions were conducted to educate study personnel on proper data collection techniques, protocol adherence, and regulatory

requirements.

3. Quality Control Checks and Monitoring:

- Regular quality control checks were performed to monitor data integrity and identify discrepancies or inconsistencies.
- Data management teams conducted routine data reviews, source data verification, and query resolution to address any issues promptly and maintain data accuracy.

4. Adherence to Good Clinical Practice (GCP) Standards:

- Trial personnel received comprehensive training on GCP standards, emphasizing the importance of ethical conduct, participant protection, and data integrity.
- Adherence to GCP standards was reinforced through ongoing monitoring, audits, and compliance assessments throughout the trial.

5. Risk-Based Monitoring Approach:

- A risk-based monitoring approach was implemented to prioritize monitoring activities based on the level of risk to data quality and participant safety.
- Higher-risk study activities and critical data points were subject to more intensive monitoring, while low-risk activities received less frequent monitoring.

6. Proactive Issue Identification and Resolution:

- Proactive measures were taken to identify and address potential issues before they escalated into major concerns.
- Data management teams conducted regular data reviews and trend analyses to detect emerging patterns or anomalies, allowing for timely intervention and corrective action.

7. Stakeholder Collaboration and Communication:

- Effective communication channels were established among study stakeholders, including investigators, study coordinators, data managers, and sponsors.
- Regular meetings and updates were provided to ensure alignment on data management processes, protocol adherence, and resolution of any data-related issues.

8. Continuous Improvement and Lessons Learned:

- Lessons learned from ongoing data management experiences were used to refine processes, optimize workflows, and enhance data quality throughout the trial.
- Feedback mechanisms were established to solicit input from study personnel and stakeholders, driving continuous improvement efforts to maintain data integrity.

By implementing these strategies, the clinical trial successfully maintained data integrity, ensuring the reliability and validity of study outcomes. The proactive approach to data management, adherence to GCP standards, and collaborative efforts among stakeholders contributed to the overall success of the trial and the generation of high-quality data for analysis and interpretation.

CHAPTER NINE

DATA MANAGEMENT IN CLINICAL TRIALS

9.1 Components of Data Management

9.1 Components of Data Management

Data management in clinical trials involves various components aimed at ensuring the accuracy, completeness, and integrity of study data. These components encompass data collection, processing, storage, and analysis, among other aspects essential for maintaining data quality throughout the trial. Here, we delve into the key components of data management:

9.1.1 Data Collection Methods

9.1.1.1 Electronic Data Capture (EDC) Systems

Electronic Data Capture (EDC) systems represent a pivotal advancement in clinical trial data collection methods, revolutionizing the way data are captured, stored, and managed. EDC systems replace traditional paper-based methods with electronic platforms, offering numerous advantages in terms of efficiency, accuracy, and data quality. Here's an in-depth exploration of EDC systems:

1. Streamlined Data Entry:

- EDC systems allow for direct electronic data entry by study personnel, eliminating the need for manual transcription from paper source documents.
- Data can be entered directly into electronic case report forms (eCRFs) via user-friendly interfaces, reducing the likelihood of data entry errors and transcription discrepancies.

2. Real-Time Data Capture:

- With EDC systems, data are captured in real-time as study visits and assessments are conducted, enabling immediate access to up-to-date study data.
- Real-time data capture facilitates timely data review, query generation, and resolution, enhancing overall data quality and trial efficiency.

3. Data Validation and Error Checks:

- EDC systems incorporate built-in validation checks and error detection algorithms to ensure data accuracy and completeness.
- Automated data validation rules can flag inconsistencies, out-of-range values, and missing data fields, prompting study personnel to address issues promptly.

4. Remote Data Entry and Monitoring:

- EDC systems support remote data entry and monitoring capabilities, allowing study personnel to access and enter data from any location with internet connectivity.
- Remote monitoring features enable sponsors and monitors to review study data in real-time, facilitating ongoing data quality oversight and compliance monitoring.

5. Data Security and Compliance:

- EDC systems employ robust security measures to safeguard sensitive study data and protect participant confidentiality.
- Encryption, access controls, and audit trails are implemented to ensure data security and compliance with regulatory requirements, such as Health Insurance Portability and Accountability Act (HIPAA) and General Data Protection Regulation (GDPR).

6. Efficient Data Management Workflows:

- EDC systems streamline data management workflows by automating data cleaning, query management, and data export processes.

- Data management teams can track and manage data discrepancies more efficiently, reducing the time and resources required for data cleaning and reconciliation.

7. Scalability and Flexibility:

- EDC systems offer scalability and flexibility to accommodate the evolving needs of clinical trials, including multi-center studies, adaptive trial designs, and complex data collection requirements.
- Customizable eCRFs and data capture templates can be tailored to specific study protocols and endpoints, ensuring compatibility with diverse study designs and therapeutic areas.

8. Integration with Other Systems:

- EDC systems can integrate with other clinical trial management systems (CTMS), electronic health record (EHR) systems, and laboratory information management systems (LIMS) to streamline data exchange and interoperability.
- Integration capabilities enhance data traceability, reduce data duplication, and facilitate seamless data flow between different stakeholders and systems involved in the trial.

Electronic Data Capture (EDC) systems offer significant advantages over traditional paper-based data collection methods, enhancing data quality, efficiency, and compliance in clinical trials. By leveraging EDC technology, researchers and sponsors can optimize data management processes, improve study oversight, and accelerate the pace of clinical research, ultimately benefiting patients and advancing medical knowledge.

9.1.1 Data Collection Methods

9.1.1.2 Paper Case Report Forms (CRFs)

Paper Case Report Forms (CRFs) have been a traditional method for collecting data in clinical trials, offering a tangible format for documenting study observations and participant information. While Electronic Data Capture (EDC) systems have become increasingly prevalent, paper CRFs still hold significance in certain contexts. Here's an exploration of paper CRFs in clinical trial data collection:

1. Familiarity and Accessibility:

- Paper CRFs provide a familiar format for study personnel, particularly in settings where electronic infrastructure may be limited or unfamiliar.
- Study sites with limited access to electronic devices or internet connectivity may rely on paper CRFs as a practical and accessible data collection method.

2. Flexibility and Adaptability:

- Paper CRFs offer flexibility in data collection, allowing study personnel to customize forms based on the unique requirements of each study.
- CRFs can be tailored to accommodate specific study protocols, data fields, and assessments, providing flexibility to capture diverse data types and study endpoints.

3. Immediate Data Capture:

- With paper CRFs, data can be captured immediately during study visits and assessments, without the need for electronic devices or connectivity.
- Study personnel can record data directly onto paper forms, facilitating real-time data capture and documentation without delays or reliance on technology.

4. Cost-Effectiveness:

- Paper CRFs may offer cost advantages in certain situations, particularly for small-scale studies or research conducted in resource-limited settings.
- The initial setup costs for paper CRFs are often lower compared to EDC systems, making them a cost-effective option for studies with limited budgets or infrastructure.

5. Participant Privacy and Confidentiality:

- Paper CRFs provide a level of participant privacy and confidentiality, as study data are physically stored and transported in sealed envelopes or secure containers.

- Concerns about data security and electronic breaches are minimized with paper CRFs, reducing the risk of unauthorized access to sensitive participant information.

6. Regulatory Acceptance and Compliance:

- Paper CRFs remain widely accepted by regulatory authorities for data collection in clinical trials, with established guidelines and standards for paper-based data capture.
- Studies conducted using paper CRFs must adhere to regulatory requirements for data accuracy, completeness, and documentation, ensuring compliance with Good Clinical Practice (GCP) standards.

7. Data Entry and Management Challenges:

- Paper CRFs introduce challenges in data entry and management, requiring manual transcription of data into electronic databases for analysis.
- Data entry errors, transcription discrepancies, and delays in data processing are common issues associated with paper CRFs, necessitating rigorous quality control measures and validation checks.

8. Limited Data Accessibility and Sharing:

- Paper CRFs may limit data accessibility and sharing compared to electronic data capture methods, as data must be physically transported or mailed to central data management centers for processing and analysis.
- Delays in data availability and limited real-time access to study data may impact study oversight, decision-making, and collaboration among study stakeholders.

While Electronic Data Capture (EDC) systems have become the preferred method for data collection in many clinical trials, paper Case Report Forms (CRFs) remain relevant in certain contexts. Paper CRFs offer familiarity, flexibility, and cost-effectiveness, particularly in settings with limited electronic infrastructure or resource constraints. However, challenges in data entry, management, and accessibility underscore the importance of evaluating the suitability of paper CRFs relative to the specific needs and requirements of each clinical trial.

9.1.2 Data Entry and Cleaning Processes

In clinical trials, ensuring the accuracy and integrity of collected data is paramount for reliable study outcomes. Data entry and cleaning processes play a crucial role in this regard, involving meticulous procedures to identify and rectify errors or inconsistencies in the dataset. Here's an exploration of these processes:

9.1.2.1 Double Data Entry

Double data entry is a method used to enhance data accuracy and reliability by independently entering study data twice and comparing the two entries for discrepancies. Here's an overview of the double data entry process:

1. Independent Data Entry:

- Two separate data entry operators independently transcribe the same set of study data into electronic databases or case report forms (CRFs) without consulting each other.
- Each operator works with a copy of the original source documents to ensure consistency and accuracy in data entry.

2. Comparison and Discrepancy Identification:

- After both data entry operators have completed their entries, the two datasets are compared systematically to identify any discrepancies or inconsistencies between them.
- Discrepancies may include differences in data values, missing data fields, or data entry errors such as typographical mistakes.

3. Resolution of Discrepancies:

- Discrepancies identified during the comparison process are reviewed and resolved through a structured reconciliation process.
- Operators may refer back to the original source documents to verify data accuracy and determine the correct values for discrepancies.

4. Consensus and Consistency Checks:

- In cases where discrepancies cannot be resolved easily, a consensus decision is reached through discussion between data entry operators or involvement of a third-party arbitrator.
- Consistency checks are performed to ensure that discrepancies are resolved consistently across all instances of double data entry.

5. Quality Control and Assurance:

- Double data entry serves as a quality control measure to enhance data accuracy and reliability in clinical trials.
- The process helps identify and correct data entry errors, transcription mistakes, and other inconsistencies that could compromise the integrity of the dataset.

6. Resource Intensiveness:

- Double data entry is resource-intensive and time-consuming, requiring the involvement of multiple data entry operators and additional quality control measures.
- The increased workload and personnel requirements associated with double data entry may impact study timelines and resource allocation.

7. Validation and Verification:

- Following resolution of discrepancies, the final dataset undergoes validation and verification to ensure that data integrity has been restored.
- Validation checks may include range checks, logic checks, and consistency checks to identify any remaining errors or anomalies in the dataset.

8. Considerations for Implementation:

- Double data entry is typically employed in studies where data accuracy is critical, such as pivotal clinical trials or studies involving high-stakes outcomes.
- The decision to use double data entry should consider factors such as study complexity, resource availability, and regulatory requirements for

data quality assurance.

Double data entry is a rigorous method for enhancing data accuracy and reliability in clinical trials, involving independent entry of study data by two operators followed by comparison and resolution of discrepancies. While resource-intensive, double data entry serves as an effective quality control measure to ensure the integrity of study datasets and support reliable study outcomes.

9.1.2.2 Data Validation Checks

Data validation checks are essential components of the data cleaning process in clinical trials, aimed at identifying and rectifying errors, inconsistencies, and outliers in the dataset. These checks help ensure the accuracy, completeness, and integrity of collected data. Here's an overview of data validation checks in clinical trial data management:

1. Range Checks:

- Range checks verify that data values fall within predefined acceptable ranges or limits specified in the study protocol.
- For example, range checks may ensure that vital signs, laboratory values, or demographic data are within physiologically plausible ranges for study participants.

2. Consistency Checks:

- Consistency checks assess the logical coherence of data across different variables or data fields within the dataset.
- These checks identify inconsistencies or contradictions in data entries that violate predefined logical relationships or rules.
- For instance, consistency checks may flag instances where a participant's age contradicts their date of birth or enrollment date.

3. Format Checks:

- Format checks validate data entries based on specified formats or data types, ensuring adherence to predefined formatting rules.
- Format checks may verify the correct formatting of dates, numerical values, text fields, or categorical variables according to study requirements.

4. Completeness Checks:

- Completeness checks assess whether all required data fields or variables have been adequately populated for each study participant or observation.
- These checks identify missing data entries or incomplete records that may compromise the integrity and interpretability of the dataset.

5. Logic Checks:

- Logic checks evaluate the logical consistency of data entries based on predefined rules or algorithms.
- Logic checks identify implausible or contradictory data patterns that may indicate data entry errors, data manipulation, or protocol deviations.
- For example, logic checks may flag instances where a participant's reported medication dosage exceeds the maximum allowable dose specified in the study protocol.

6. Referential Integrity Checks:

- Referential integrity checks verify the consistency and accuracy of data relationships or links between related data tables or datasets.
- These checks ensure that data references, identifiers, or key fields are valid and consistent across different data sources or tables.
- Referential integrity checks prevent data inconsistencies that could arise from incomplete or incorrect data linkage.

7. Duplicate Checks:

- Duplicate checks identify and flag duplicate or redundant entries within the dataset, including duplicate participant records, observations, or data points.
- Duplicate checks help maintain data accuracy and prevent data duplication, ensuring that each participant or observation is represented uniquely in the dataset.

8. Automated Validation Tools:

- Automated validation tools and software applications are often used to facilitate data validation checks, streamlining the process and reducing manual effort.
- These tools can perform predefined validation checks automatically, generate error reports, and flag data anomalies for review and resolution by data management teams.

In summary, data validation checks are integral to the data cleaning process in clinical trials, helping ensure the accuracy, completeness, and integrity of study data. By implementing a comprehensive set of validation checks, researchers and data managers can identify and rectify errors or inconsistencies promptly, supporting reliable study outcomes and data interpretation.

9.1.3 Data Storage and Security

Data storage and security are critical aspects of clinical trial data management, ensuring the confidentiality, integrity, and availability of study data throughout the trial lifecycle. Electronic data storage systems play a central role in facilitating secure storage and management of clinical trial data. Let's explore electronic data storage systems in more detail:

9.1.3.1 Electronic Data Storage Systems

Electronic data storage systems provide centralized repositories for securely storing and managing clinical trial data in digital format. These systems offer numerous features and capabilities to support data storage, access, retrieval, and security. Here's an overview of electronic data storage systems in clinical trial data management:

1. Centralized Data Repository:

- Electronic data storage systems serve as centralized repositories for storing all types of clinical trial data, including participant demographics, study visits, laboratory results, and adverse events.
- Centralized data storage facilitates efficient data management, collaboration among study personnel, and data sharing across multiple study sites or stakeholders.

2. Scalability and Flexibility:

- Electronic data storage systems are scalable and flexible, capable of accommodating large volumes of data and adapting to evolving study requirements.

- These systems can handle diverse data formats, variable data structures, and complex data models, supporting a wide range of clinical research studies and protocols.

3. Data Accessibility and Retrieval:

- Electronic data storage systems enable rapid and secure access to study data by authorized users, regardless of their geographic location.
- Study personnel can retrieve and query data efficiently using intuitive user interfaces, search functionalities, and data visualization tools.

4. Version Control and Audit Trails:

- Electronic data storage systems incorporate version control mechanisms and audit trails to track changes to study data over time.
- Version control ensures that data modifications are documented, timestamped, and traceable, maintaining data integrity and compliance with regulatory requirements.

5. Data Encryption and Access Controls:

- Data encryption techniques, such as encryption algorithms and secure socket layer (SSL) protocols, are employed to protect sensitive study data during transmission and storage.
- Access controls, including user authentication, role-based permissions, and access restrictions, safeguard data against unauthorized access or disclosure.

6. Backup and Disaster Recovery:

- Electronic data storage systems implement robust backup and disaster recovery mechanisms to prevent data loss and ensure business continuity.
- Regular data backups, offsite storage, and redundant data storage facilities minimize the risk of data loss due to hardware failures, natural disasters, or cyberattacks.

7. Compliance with Regulatory Standards:

- Electronic data storage systems adhere to regulatory standards and guidelines for data security, privacy, and confidentiality in clinical research.
- Compliance certifications, such as Health Insurance Portability and Accountability Act (HIPAA) compliance or International Organization for Standardization (ISO) certifications, attest to the system's adherence to industry best practices and regulatory requirements.

8. Data Lifecycle Management:

- Electronic data storage systems support comprehensive data lifecycle management, including data capture, storage, archiving, and eventual disposal or retention.
- Data retention policies, data archiving procedures, and data purging mechanisms ensure compliance with regulatory requirements and data governance standards.

Electronic data storage systems provide secure, scalable, and flexible solutions for storing and managing clinical trial data. By leveraging advanced features such as encryption, access controls, version control, and audit trails, these systems help ensure data integrity, confidentiality, and compliance throughout the trial lifecycle, ultimately supporting high-quality research outcomes and regulatory submissions.

9.1.3.2 Regulatory Compliance and Data Protection Measures

In clinical trial data management, regulatory compliance and data protection measures are paramount to safeguarding the confidentiality, integrity, and availability of sensitive participant data. Adherence to regulatory requirements and implementation of robust data protection measures are essential components of maintaining data security throughout the trial lifecycle. Here's an exploration of regulatory compliance and data protection measures in clinical trial data storage:

1. Regulatory Framework Compliance:

- Clinical trial data storage systems must comply with relevant regulatory frameworks, including guidelines set forth by regulatory authorities such as the Food and Drug Administration (FDA), European Medicines

Agency (EMA), and International Council for Harmonisation of Technical Requirements for Pharmaceuticals for Human Use (ICH).

- Compliance with regulatory standards ensures that data storage practices adhere to established guidelines for data security, privacy, and confidentiality in clinical research.

2. Data Encryption:

- Data encryption is a fundamental data protection measure used to safeguard sensitive participant data stored within electronic data storage systems.
- Encryption algorithms and protocols are employed to encrypt data at rest and in transit, rendering it unreadable to unauthorized users or malicious actors.

3. Access Controls and Authentication:

- Access controls and user authentication mechanisms are implemented to restrict access to study data to authorized personnel only.
- Role-based access controls (RBAC), multi-factor authentication (MFA), and strong password policies help prevent unauthorized access to sensitive data and maintain data confidentiality.

4. Data Minimization:

- Data minimization principles are applied to limit the collection, storage, and retention of personal data to only what is necessary for the purpose of the clinical trial.
- Reducing the volume of stored data minimizes the risk of data breaches and unauthorized access while enhancing data privacy and compliance with data protection regulations.

5. Data Integrity and Audit Trails:

- Data integrity measures ensure the accuracy, completeness, and reliability of study data stored within electronic data storage systems.
- Audit trails track and record all interactions with study data, including data access, modifications, and deletions, providing a comprehensive

record of data activities for regulatory compliance and accountability purposes.

6. Data Transfer and Sharing Protocols:

- Protocols for data transfer and sharing are established to ensure secure transmission of study data between study sites, collaborators, and regulatory authorities.
- Secure file transfer protocols (e.g., Secure File Transfer Protocol (SFTP), HTTPS) and encryption techniques are employed to protect data during transit and maintain data confidentiality.

7. Regulatory Reporting Requirements:

- Data storage systems must support compliance with regulatory reporting requirements for adverse events, safety data, and study outcomes.
- Timely and accurate reporting of study data to regulatory authorities ensures transparency, accountability, and compliance with regulatory obligations throughout the trial.

8. Data Retention and Disposal Policies:

- Data retention and disposal policies are established to govern the retention period and eventual disposal of study data in accordance with regulatory requirements.
- Clear policies and procedures for data retention, archiving, and destruction help mitigate the risk of data breaches, unauthorized access, and non-compliance with data protection regulations.

Regulatory compliance and data protection measures are essential considerations in clinical trial data storage to ensure the confidentiality, integrity, and security of participant data. By implementing robust data encryption, access controls, audit trails, and compliance protocols, electronic data storage systems can support regulatory compliance and data protection objectives, ultimately safeguarding the rights and privacy of study participants and maintaining the integrity of clinical trial data.

9.2 Importance of Data Integrity and Accuracy

Data integrity and accuracy are foundational principles in clinical trial data management, essential for ensuring the reliability, validity, and trustworthiness of study findings. Maintaining high standards of data integrity and accuracy is crucial throughout the trial lifecycle to support evidence-based decision-making, regulatory compliance, and ultimately, the safety and well-being of study participants. Here, we delve into the significance of data integrity and accuracy, with a focus on ensuring data quality and reliability:

9.2.1 Ensuring Data Quality and Reliability

9.2.1.1 Source Data Verification

Source data verification (SDV) is a critical process in clinical trial data management aimed at confirming the accuracy and completeness of data recorded in source documents against data entered into the trial database. SDV plays a pivotal role in ensuring data quality and reliability by validating the integrity of study data throughout the trial. Here's an exploration of source data verification in clinical trial data management:

1. Confirming Data Accuracy:

- Source data verification involves comparing data entered into the trial database with the original source documents, such as medical records, laboratory reports, and participant diaries.
- By confirming data accuracy through SDV, discrepancies, errors, or inconsistencies between source documents and trial data can be identified and rectified promptly.

2. Validating Data Completeness:

- SDV verifies the completeness of data recorded in source documents by ensuring that all required data fields and variables are adequately documented.
- Incomplete or missing data entries can be identified through SDV, enabling study personnel to follow up with site staff or study participants to obtain the necessary information for data completeness.

3. Detecting Data Errors and Discrepancies:

- SDV helps detect data errors, discrepancies, or outliers that may compromise the integrity and reliability of study data.

- Discrepancies identified during source data verification, such as transcription errors, data entry mistakes, or protocol deviations, are flagged for resolution through query generation and data clarification processes.

4. Enhancing Data Quality Assurance:

- Source data verification serves as a quality assurance measure to ensure the accuracy, completeness, and reliability of clinical trial data.
- By validating data integrity at the source, SDV helps maintain high standards of data quality throughout the trial, supporting regulatory compliance and data integrity objectives.

5. Risk-Based Approach to Source Data Verification:

- A risk-based approach may be employed to prioritize source data verification activities based on the level of risk to data quality and participant safety.
- Higher-risk data elements, critical study endpoints, or key safety variables may undergo more intensive source data verification, while low-risk data elements may receive less frequent verification.

6. Efficient Resource Allocation:

- Source data verification optimizes resource allocation by focusing verification efforts on data elements or study sites where data quality concerns are most likely to arise.
- Targeted source data verification helps maximize the effectiveness of data monitoring activities while minimizing resource burdens on study personnel and sponsors.

7. Compliance with Regulatory Requirements:

- Source data verification is mandated by regulatory authorities as part of Good Clinical Practice (GCP) standards and guidelines for ensuring data quality and integrity in clinical trials.
- Compliance with regulatory requirements for source data verification demonstrates adherence to best practices in data management and

supports the credibility and acceptability of study findings.

Source data verification is a critical component of ensuring data quality and reliability in clinical trial data management. By validating data accuracy, completeness, and consistency against original source documents, SDV helps maintain high standards of data integrity throughout the trial, supporting regulatory compliance, evidence-based decision-making, and the generation of reliable study outcomes.

9.2.1.2 Query Resolution Processes

Query resolution processes are essential components of clinical trial data management, designed to address discrepancies, errors, and missing information identified during data review and verification. Efficient query resolution is crucial for ensuring the accuracy, completeness, and integrity of study data. Here's an exploration of query resolution processes in clinical trial data management:

1. Query Identification:

- Query resolution begins with the identification of discrepancies, errors, or missing information detected during data review, source data verification, or data validation checks.
- Queries may be generated automatically by data management systems or identified manually by data reviewers, monitors, or study personnel.

2. Query Generation and Documentation:

- Queries are generated to flag discrepancies between source documents and trial data or to request clarification or additional information from study sites or participants.
- Each query is documented systematically, including details such as query description, data field, query status, priority level, and resolution deadline.

3. Query Assignment and Management:

- Queries are assigned to designated personnel responsible for query resolution, typically data managers, clinical research associates (CRAs), or site coordinators.

- Query management systems or tracking tools are used to assign, track, and monitor the status of queries throughout the resolution process.

4. Communication with Study Sites:

- Queries are communicated to study sites promptly through query letters, query forms, or electronic query management systems.
- Clear instructions and guidance are provided to study sites on how to address queries, including requirements for providing supporting documentation or explanations.

5. Timely Resolution and Follow-Up:

- Study sites are expected to respond to queries in a timely manner, typically within specified resolution deadlines established in the query management system.
- Data management teams conduct regular follow-up with study sites to track query resolution progress, provide assistance or clarification as needed, and ensure timely resolution of outstanding queries.

6. Query Resolution Documentation:

- Upon resolution of queries, documentation is maintained to capture the actions taken, explanations provided, and any modifications made to the trial data.
- Resolved queries are documented with clear audit trails, including timestamps, user IDs, and details of the resolution outcome.

7. Escalation of Unresolved Queries:

- Queries that remain unresolved beyond the specified resolution deadline may be escalated to higher-level personnel, such as clinical trial managers, principal investigators, or sponsor representatives.
- Escalation procedures ensure that unresolved queries receive appropriate attention and follow-up to facilitate timely resolution and data clarification.

8. Quality Control and Oversight:

- Query resolution processes are subject to quality control measures and oversight to ensure consistency, accuracy, and adherence to predefined resolution protocols.
- Quality control checks may include periodic reviews of query resolution activities, audit trail verification, and validation of resolved query outcomes.

Query resolution processes are integral to maintaining data quality and integrity in clinical trial data management. By promptly identifying and addressing discrepancies, errors, and missing information, query resolution ensures the accuracy, completeness, and reliability of study data, supporting evidence-based decision-making, regulatory compliance, and the generation of high-quality study outcomes.

9.2.2 Regulatory Requirements for Data Integrity

Data integrity is a cornerstone of clinical trial conduct, ensuring that study data is accurate, complete, and reliable. Regulatory authorities such as the Food and Drug Administration (FDA) and the European Medicines Agency (EMA) provide guidelines and regulations to uphold data integrity standards in clinical research. Let's explore the FDA and EMA guidelines pertaining to data integrity:

9.2.2.1 FDA and EMA Guidelines

FDA Guidelines:

- The FDA emphasizes the importance of data integrity in ensuring the reliability and credibility of clinical trial data submitted to support regulatory submissions.
- The FDA's guidance documents, including "Guidance for Industry: Data Integrity and Compliance with Drug CGMP" and "Guidance for Industry: Electronic Source Data in Clinical Investigations," outline expectations for data integrity practices in pharmaceutical manufacturing and clinical research.
- Key principles emphasized by the FDA include ensuring that data is attributable, legible, contemporaneous, original, and accurate (ALCOA), as well as adherence to good documentation practices (GDP) and electronic records management principles.

EMA Guidelines:

- The EMA also places significant emphasis on data integrity in clinical trial conduct and regulatory submissions.
- EMA guidelines such as "Reflection Paper on GCP Compliance in Relation to Trial Master Files (Paper and/or Electronic)" and "Reflection Paper on Expectations for Electronic Source Data and Data Transcribed to Electronic Data Collection Tools in Clinical Trials" provide guidance on maintaining data integrity throughout the clinical trial lifecycle.
- The EMA expects sponsors, investigators, and other stakeholders to implement robust data management systems, procedures, and controls to ensure data integrity, reliability, and traceability.

Key Components of FDA and EMA Guidelines:

- Both FDA and EMA guidelines stress the importance of implementing effective data management systems and controls to prevent data manipulation, falsification, or unauthorized access.
- Requirements for electronic data capture (EDC) systems, electronic signatures, audit trails, and data validation are outlined to ensure the integrity and security of electronic trial data.
- FDA and EMA guidelines mandate that sponsors, investigators, and clinical research organizations (CROs) maintain comprehensive documentation, including source documents, case report forms (CRFs), and trial master files (TMFs), to support the accuracy and reliability of trial data.
- The guidelines emphasize the need for training and oversight to ensure that all personnel involved in clinical trial conduct understand their responsibilities for maintaining data integrity and compliance with regulatory requirements.

Compliance and Enforcement:

- Compliance with FDA and EMA guidelines for data integrity is essential for obtaining regulatory approval and market authorization for investigational drugs and medical devices.
- Regulatory inspections, audits, and assessments are conducted by FDA and EMA inspectors to verify compliance with data integrity standards and identify any deficiencies or non-compliance issues.

- Failure to comply with data integrity requirements can result in regulatory actions, including warning letters, enforcement actions, product recalls, or rejection of regulatory submissions.

In summary, both the FDA and EMA provide guidelines and regulations to ensure data integrity in clinical trial conduct and regulatory submissions. Adherence to these guidelines is essential for maintaining the reliability, credibility, and regulatory compliance of clinical trial data, ultimately supporting patient safety and public health.

9.2.2.2 ICH GCP Standards

The International Council for Harmonisation of Technical Requirements for Pharmaceuticals for Human Use (ICH) provides globally recognized standards for the conduct of clinical trials, including guidelines on data integrity. The ICH Good Clinical Practice (GCP) guidelines outline principles and standards for ensuring the integrity, reliability, and quality of clinical trial data. Let's delve into the key aspects of ICH GCP standards related to data integrity:

ICH GCP Standards:

- The ICH GCP guidelines establish a framework for the design, conduct, monitoring, and reporting of clinical trials to ensure the protection of trial participants and the generation of credible data for regulatory submissions.
- Data integrity is a fundamental principle of ICH GCP, emphasizing the importance of accurate, complete, and reliable data collection, recording, and reporting throughout the trial.

Key Components of ICH GCP Standards for Data Integrity:

- **Source Data Verification (SDV):** ICH GCP recommends that sponsors and investigators conduct appropriate monitoring activities, including source data verification (SDV), to ensure the accuracy and reliability of trial data. SDV involves comparing data recorded in source documents with data entered into case report forms (CRFs) or electronic data capture (EDC) systems to identify discrepancies or errors.
- **Data Management Systems and Procedures:** ICH GCP guidelines require sponsors to establish and maintain effective data management systems and procedures to ensure data integrity and compliance with

regulatory requirements. This includes implementing robust data validation processes, electronic data capture (EDC) systems, and quality control measures to prevent data manipulation, falsification, or unauthorized access.

- **Clinical Trial Documentation:** ICH GCP emphasizes the importance of comprehensive documentation practices to support the accuracy, reliability, and traceability of trial data. Sponsors are required to maintain complete and accurate trial documentation, including protocol documents, case report forms (CRFs), source documents, and trial master files (TMFs), throughout the trial.
- **Training and Oversight:** ICH GCP guidelines mandate that all personnel involved in the conduct of clinical trials receive adequate training on data integrity principles and regulatory requirements. Sponsors and investigators are responsible for providing ongoing oversight and supervision to ensure that trial personnel understand their roles and responsibilities for maintaining data integrity and compliance with GCP standards.

Compliance and Enforcement:

- Compliance with ICH GCP standards for data integrity is essential for obtaining regulatory approval and market authorization for investigational drugs and medical devices.
- Regulatory authorities may conduct inspections and audits to assess compliance with ICH GCP standards and identify any deficiencies or non-compliance issues.
- Failure to comply with ICH GCP standards for data integrity can result in regulatory actions, including warning letters, enforcement actions, or rejection of regulatory submissions.

The ICH GCP guidelines provide internationally recognized standards for ensuring data integrity in clinical trial conduct. Adherence to these standards is essential for maintaining the reliability, credibility, and regulatory compliance of clinical trial data, ultimately supporting patient safety and the advancement of medical knowledge.

9.3.1.2 Reporting Timelines and Requirements

In clinical trials, the timely and accurate reporting of adverse events (AEs) is crucial for ensuring participant safety, regulatory compliance, and the integrity of study data. Adverse event reporting timelines and requirements are defined by regulatory authorities and study protocols to facilitate the prompt identification, documentation, and evaluation of adverse events. Here's an exploration of reporting timelines and requirements for adverse events in clinical trials:

1. Adverse Event Reporting Timelines:

- Adverse event reporting timelines specify the timeframe within which study personnel must report adverse events to the appropriate authorities, such as the sponsor, regulatory agencies, and ethics committees.
- Timelines for reporting adverse events are typically delineated in the study protocol, investigator's brochure, and regulatory guidelines, such as Good Clinical Practice (GCP) standards and regulatory submissions requirements.

2. Immediate Reporting Requirements:

- Some adverse events, particularly serious adverse events (SAEs) or unexpected adverse reactions, may require immediate reporting to regulatory authorities and ethics committees.
- Immediate reporting requirements are triggered when an adverse event is considered serious, unexpected, or life-threatening, necessitating urgent action to protect participant safety and welfare.

3. Standard Reporting Timelines:

- Standard reporting timelines specify the timeframe for reporting non-serious adverse events and other adverse reactions that do not meet the criteria for immediate reporting.
- These timelines typically range from within 24 to 72 hours for non-serious adverse events, depending on the severity, nature, and context of the event.

4. Follow-Up Reporting:

- Follow-up reporting may be required for adverse events that persist, worsen, or require additional investigation or medical intervention

beyond the initial reporting period.
- Follow-up reports provide updated information on the status, management, and outcome of adverse events, ensuring ongoing monitoring and evaluation of participant safety.

5. Documentation and Record-Keeping:

- Adverse event reports must be documented accurately and comprehensively, including details such as the event description, onset date, severity, outcome, relationship to study intervention, and action taken.
- Records of adverse event reports, including original case report forms (CRFs), source documents, and adverse event narratives, must be maintained in the trial master file (TMF) and sponsor's records for regulatory inspection and review.

6. Regulatory Submission Requirements:

- Adverse event reports are submitted to regulatory authorities, such as the Food and Drug Administration (FDA) or European Medicines Agency (EMA), as part of regulatory submissions, including investigational new drug applications (INDs), new drug applications (NDAs), or marketing authorization applications (MAAs).
- Regulatory submission requirements specify the format, content, and timing of adverse event reports, ensuring consistency, transparency, and compliance with regulatory standards.

7. Investigator Responsibilities:

- Investigators are responsible for promptly reporting adverse events occurring at their study sites to the sponsor, ethics committees, and regulatory authorities in accordance with protocol-specified timelines and requirements.
- Investigators must ensure accurate and timely documentation of adverse events in the trial records, including CRFs, medical records, and adverse event narratives.

In summary, reporting timelines and requirements for adverse events in clinical trials are defined to ensure the timely identification, documentation, and evaluation of adverse events, supporting participant safety and regulatory compliance. Adherence to reporting timelines and accurate documentation of adverse events are essential responsibilities of investigators, sponsors, and study personnel to maintain the integrity and validity of clinical trial data.

9.3.2 Serious Adverse Event (SAE) Reporting

In clinical trials, Serious Adverse Event (SAE) reporting is a critical aspect of safety monitoring and regulatory compliance. SAEs are defined by specific criteria that help differentiate them from other adverse events (AEs) based on their severity and potential impact on participant safety. Let's explore the criteria for determining SAEs:

9.3.2.1 Criteria for SAE Determination

The determination of whether an adverse event qualifies as a Serious Adverse Event (SAE) is based on predefined criteria established in the study protocol, regulatory guidelines, and International Council for Harmonisation of Technical Requirements for Pharmaceuticals for Human Use (ICH) Good Clinical Practice (GCP) standards. Here are the key criteria for SAE determination:

1. Severity:

- SAEs are events that result in death, are life-threatening, require hospitalization or prolongation of existing hospitalization, result in persistent or significant disability/incapacity, or are congenital anomalies/birth defects.
- The severity of an adverse event is assessed based on its impact on the participant's health, functional status, or clinical outcome, with an emphasis on events that pose immediate or long-term risks to the participant's well-being.

2. Immediate Medical Intervention:

- Adverse events that require immediate medical intervention to prevent death, serious injury, or irreversible harm are considered SAEs.
- Examples of events requiring immediate medical intervention include myocardial infarction, stroke, anaphylaxis, respiratory arrest, and severe allergic reactions.

3. Hospitalization or Prolongation of Hospitalization:

- Adverse events that necessitate hospitalization or result in the prolongation of existing hospitalization beyond what is expected for the underlying condition are classified as SAEs.
- Hospitalization may be required for medical observation, diagnostic evaluation, treatment, or surgical intervention related to the adverse event.

4. Persistent or Significant Disability/Incapacity:

- Adverse events that result in persistent or significant disability, impairment of physical or cognitive function, or loss of capacity to perform activities of daily living are considered SAEs.
- Disabilities or incapacities that substantially affect the participant's quality of life, functional independence, or ability to engage in usual activities qualify as SAEs.

5. Congenital Anomalies/Birth Defects:

- Adverse events occurring in the offspring of participants, such as congenital anomalies or birth defects, are classified as SAEs.
- Events observed in newborns or infants that are medically significant, clinically relevant, or require medical intervention are reported as SAEs, regardless of their severity or outcome.

6. Other Medically Significant Events:

- Adverse events that are deemed medically significant, clinically relevant, or have the potential to cause substantial harm to the participant's health or well-being may be classified as SAEs.
- Criteria for SAE determination may vary depending on the nature of the study, the population under investigation, and regulatory requirements specific to the jurisdiction in which the trial is conducted.

The criteria for determining Serious Adverse Events (SAEs) in clinical trials are based on predefined thresholds for severity, immediate medical intervention, hospitalization, disability/incapacity, congenital anomalies/

birth defects, and other medically significant events. Adherence to established criteria for SAE determination is essential for ensuring consistent and accurate reporting of serious adverse events, supporting participant safety, regulatory compliance, and the integrity of clinical trial data.

9.3.2.2 Expedited Reporting to Regulatory Authorities

In clinical trials, expedited reporting of Serious Adverse Events (SAEs) to regulatory authorities is essential for ensuring prompt evaluation of participant safety and regulatory oversight. Expedited reporting timelines and requirements are established to facilitate the timely communication of SAEs to regulatory agencies, enabling regulatory review and assessment of potential risks associated with investigational products. Here's an overview of expedited reporting to regulatory authorities for SAEs:

1. Definition of Expedited Reporting:

- Expedited reporting refers to the prompt submission of Serious Adverse Event (SAE) reports to regulatory authorities, such as the Food and Drug Administration (FDA) in the United States or the European Medicines Agency (EMA) in Europe, within specified timelines.

2. Criteria for Expedited Reporting:

- Regulatory guidelines define criteria for expedited reporting of SAEs based on the severity, seriousness, and potential causal relationship to the investigational product.
- SAEs meeting predefined criteria for seriousness, such as death, life-threatening events, hospitalization, disability, or congenital anomalies, typically require expedited reporting to regulatory authorities.

3. Timelines for Expedited Reporting:

- Expedited reporting timelines specify the timeframe within which sponsors, investigators, or clinical research organizations (CROs) must submit SAE reports to regulatory authorities.
- Timelines for expedited reporting vary depending on the severity and nature of the adverse event, as well as regulatory requirements specific to the jurisdiction in which the trial is conducted.

4. Immediate Reporting Requirements:

- Some SAEs, particularly those considered life-threatening, require immediate reporting to regulatory authorities within a very short timeframe, often within 24 hours of the sponsor or investigator becoming aware of the event.
- Immediate reporting ensures that regulatory agencies receive timely notification of critical safety issues requiring urgent regulatory action or intervention.

5. Standard Reporting Timelines:

- For SAEs that do not meet the criteria for immediate reporting but are still considered serious, expedited reporting timelines typically range from within 7 to 15 calendar days, depending on regulatory requirements and the nature of the event.

6. Reporting Requirements and Documentation:

- Expedited reporting to regulatory authorities involves submitting comprehensive SAE reports that include detailed information about the event, participant characteristics, medical history, concomitant medications, clinical course, outcome, and assessment of causality.
- SAE reports must be documented accurately, with clear and concise narratives describing the event and its potential relationship to the investigational product.

7. Investigator Responsibilities:

- Investigators are responsible for promptly notifying sponsors of SAEs occurring at their study sites and providing all relevant information required for expedited reporting to regulatory authorities.
- Investigators must ensure that SAE reports are submitted within the specified timelines and comply with regulatory requirements for content, format, and documentation.

8. Regulatory Oversight and Review:

- Regulatory authorities review expedited SAE reports to assess the safety profile of investigational products, evaluate potential risks to trial participants, and determine the need for regulatory action, such as protocol amendments, safety alerts, or product labeling changes.
- Regulatory oversight of expedited reporting ensures that sponsors and investigators fulfill their obligations to monitor and report adverse events in accordance with regulatory requirements and ethical standards.

Expedited reporting to regulatory authorities for Serious Adverse Events (SAEs) is a critical aspect of safety monitoring in clinical trials. Adherence to expedited reporting timelines and requirements ensures timely communication of safety information, facilitates regulatory oversight, and supports the protection of trial participants' rights and welfare.

9.3.3 Data and Safety Monitoring Boards (DSMBs)

Data and Safety Monitoring Boards (DSMBs) play a crucial role in safeguarding the interests and safety of participants in clinical trials. These independent expert committees are responsible for monitoring trial data and ensuring that the study is conducted with integrity and in adherence to ethical and regulatory standards. Let's delve into the role and function of DSMBs:

9.3.3.1 Role and Function of DSMBs

1. Independent Oversight:

- DSMBs provide independent oversight of clinical trials, separate from the sponsor, investigator, and regulatory authorities. This independence ensures unbiased evaluation of trial data and recommendations for participant safety.

2. Safety Monitoring:

- One of the primary functions of DSMBs is to monitor the safety of participants enrolled in clinical trials. DSMBs review safety data, including adverse events, serious adverse events, and other safety-related information, to assess the risk-benefit profile of the investigational intervention.

3. Interim Data Analysis:

- DSMBs conduct interim data analyses to assess the accumulating trial data for efficacy, safety, and futility. These analyses may involve reviewing interim endpoints, efficacy outcomes, and safety parameters to determine whether the trial should continue as planned, be modified, or terminated early.

4. Risk-Benefit Assessment:

- DSMBs evaluate the risk-benefit ratio of the investigational intervention based on emerging trial data. They assess whether the potential benefits of the intervention outweigh the risks and whether participant safety is adequately protected throughout the trial.

5. Protocol Adherence:

- DSMBs assess protocol adherence and compliance with study procedures to ensure that the trial is conducted according to the predefined protocol. Any deviations from the protocol are reviewed, and recommendations may be made to address protocol violations or discrepancies.

6. Trial Continuation or Modification:

- Based on their safety and efficacy assessments, DSMBs provide recommendations regarding the continuation, modification, or termination of the trial. These recommendations are communicated to the sponsor, investigator, and relevant regulatory authorities for consideration and action.

7. Unblinded Safety Review:

- In blinded trials, DSMBs typically have access to unblinded safety data to facilitate their safety assessments. However, they are blinded to treatment assignment to prevent bias in their evaluations.

8. Communication and Reporting:

- DSMBs communicate their findings and recommendations to the sponsor, investigator, and relevant stakeholders through formal reports and meetings. They provide regular updates on safety issues, interim analyses, and trial progress to ensure transparency and accountability.

9. Expertise and Composition:

- DSMBs comprise a multidisciplinary panel of experts with expertise in clinical research methodology, biostatistics, ethics, and relevant medical specialties. The composition of DSMBs is carefully selected to ensure that members possess the necessary qualifications and experience to fulfill their roles effectively.

10. Ethical Considerations:

- DSMBs adhere to ethical principles and guidelines, including those outlined in the Declaration of Helsinki and Good Clinical Practice (GCP) standards. They prioritize participant safety and welfare while upholding the scientific integrity and validity of the trial.

Data and Safety Monitoring Boards (DSMBs) play a vital role in overseeing the conduct of clinical trials and ensuring the safety and welfare of trial participants. Through independent safety monitoring, interim data analysis, protocol adherence assessment, and risk-benefit evaluation, DSMBs contribute to the integrity, validity, and ethical conduct of clinical research. Their recommendations guide decision-making regarding trial continuation, modification, or termination, ultimately advancing the scientific understanding of investigational interventions while protecting participant rights and safety.

9.3.3.2 Case Study: Role of DSMB in a Phase III Clinical Trial

In a Phase III clinical trial evaluating the safety and efficacy of a novel vaccine candidate for a viral infection, a Data and Safety Monitoring Board (DSMB) was established to provide independent oversight and ensure participant safety throughout the trial. The DSMB's role and actions in this case study illustrate the critical importance of their involvement in safeguarding the integrity and ethical conduct of the trial:

Trial Background:

- The Phase III clinical trial enrolled thousands of participants across multiple study sites to assess the vaccine candidate's effectiveness in preventing the target viral infection.
- Participants were randomized to receive either the investigational vaccine or placebo according to the study protocol.

DSMB Composition:

- The DSMB comprised a multidisciplinary panel of experts, including clinical researchers, biostatisticians, vaccinologists, and ethicists, with extensive experience in vaccine development and safety monitoring.

DSMB Activities and Role:

1. **Safety Monitoring:** Throughout the trial, the DSMB conducted ongoing safety monitoring to assess the occurrence of adverse events and serious adverse events (SAEs) in vaccine recipients compared to placebo recipients. Adverse event data were reviewed regularly to detect any safety signals or unexpected findings.
2. **Interim Data Analysis:** The DSMB performed interim data analyses at predefined intervals to evaluate the accumulating efficacy data and safety profile of the vaccine candidate. Interim analyses focused on efficacy endpoints, vaccine effectiveness, and safety outcomes to inform decision-making regarding trial continuation or modification.
3. **Risk-Benefit Assessment:** Based on safety and efficacy data, the DSMB conducted a rigorous risk-benefit assessment to determine whether the potential benefits of the vaccine outweighed the risks. The DSMB considered factors such as vaccine efficacy, safety profile, participant demographics, and disease prevalence in their assessments.
4. **Protocol Adherence:** The DSMB monitored protocol adherence and compliance with study procedures to ensure that the trial was conducted according to the predefined protocol. Any deviations or protocol violations were reviewed, and recommendations were made to address non-compliance issues.
5. **Recommendations and Reporting:** Following each DSMB meeting, the board provided recommendations to the trial sponsor and regulatory authorities regarding trial continuation, modification, or termination. Recommendations were communicated through formal reports

summarizing safety data, interim analyses, and risk-benefit assessments.

DSMB Findings and Recommendations:

- Throughout the trial, the DSMB reviewed safety data and efficacy outcomes to assess the vaccine candidate's performance and safety profile. The DSMB found no evidence of significant safety concerns or adverse events related to the vaccine.
- Interim efficacy analyses indicated promising results, with preliminary evidence of vaccine effectiveness in preventing the target viral infection.
- Based on their evaluations, the DSMB recommended the continuation of the trial without modification, emphasizing the importance of ongoing safety monitoring and data collection to further evaluate the vaccine's long-term safety and efficacy.

Conclusion:

- The DSMB's proactive involvement and independent oversight played a critical role in ensuring the integrity, safety, and ethical conduct of the Phase III clinical trial. Through rigorous safety monitoring, interim data analysis, and risk-benefit assessment, the DSMB provided valuable insights and recommendations to guide decision-making and advance the development of the vaccine candidate. Their contributions were instrumental in maintaining participant trust, regulatory compliance, and scientific rigor throughout the trial process.

9.3.3.2 Case Study: Role of DSMB in a Phase III Clinical Trial

In a Phase III clinical trial assessing the efficacy and safety of a novel drug for treating a rare autoimmune disorder, the Data and Safety Monitoring Board (DSMB) played a pivotal role in overseeing the trial's progress and ensuring participant safety. Here's a detailed case study illustrating the DSMB's involvement and contributions:

Trial Background:

- The Phase III clinical trial aimed to evaluate the efficacy and safety of the investigational drug in reducing disease activity and improving clinical outcomes among patients with the autoimmune disorder.

- The trial enrolled hundreds of participants across multiple study sites worldwide, following a randomized, double-blind, placebo-controlled design.

DSMB Composition:

- The DSMB comprised a diverse panel of independent experts, including clinicians specialized in autoimmune diseases, biostatisticians, pharmacologists, and ethicists.
- Members of the DSMB were selected based on their expertise, experience, and independence from the trial sponsor and investigators.

DSMB Activities and Role:

1. **Safety Monitoring:** The DSMB conducted ongoing safety monitoring to review adverse events (AEs) reported by trial participants. They assessed the frequency, severity, and relationship of AEs to the investigational drug to identify any safety concerns or emerging trends.
2. **Interim Data Analysis:** Interim analyses were performed by the DSMB at predefined intervals to evaluate the accumulating efficacy and safety data. These analyses focused on primary and secondary endpoints, including disease activity scores, biomarker levels, and patient-reported outcomes.
3. **Risk-Benefit Assessment:** Based on safety and efficacy data, the DSMB conducted a comprehensive risk-benefit assessment to evaluate the overall benefit-risk profile of the investigational drug. They considered factors such as treatment efficacy, safety profile, and potential risks associated with long-term use.
4. **Protocol Adherence:** The DSMB monitored protocol adherence and compliance with study procedures to ensure that the trial was conducted in accordance with ethical and regulatory standards. They reviewed protocol deviations, amendments, and data quality to maintain the trial's integrity.
5. **Recommendations and Reporting:** Following each review, the DSMB provided recommendations to the trial sponsor regarding trial continuation, modification, or termination. These recommendations were communicated through formal reports summarizing safety data, interim analyses, and risk-benefit assessments.

DSMB Findings and Recommendations:

- Throughout the trial, the DSMB reviewed safety and efficacy data to assess the investigational drug's performance and safety profile. They found no evidence of significant safety concerns related to the drug.
- Interim efficacy analyses showed promising results, with a significant reduction in disease activity and improvements in clinical outcomes observed in patients receiving the investigational drug compared to placebo.
- Based on their evaluations, the DSMB recommended the continuation of the trial without modification, emphasizing the drug's potential therapeutic benefit and favorable safety profile.

Conclusion:

- The DSMB's diligent oversight and independent review were instrumental in ensuring the safety, integrity, and ethical conduct of the Phase III clinical trial. Their contributions helped to safeguard participant welfare, maintain regulatory compliance, and advance the development of the investigational drug for the treatment of the autoimmune disorder. Through rigorous safety monitoring and data analysis, the DSMB provided valuable insights and recommendations that guided decision-making and contributed to the trial's successful outcome.

CHAPTER TEN

POST-MARKETING SURVEILLANCE

10.1 Methods of Post-Marketing Surveillance

10.1.1 Spontaneous Reporting Systems

10.1.1.1 Overview and Purpose

Spontaneous reporting systems (SRS) represent a cornerstone of post-marketing surveillance, serving as vital tools for the detection and assessment of adverse events (AEs) associated with pharmaceutical products following their approval and widespread use. These systems rely on voluntary reporting from healthcare professionals, patients, and consumers to collect information on suspected adverse reactions, allowing regulatory authorities and pharmaceutical companies to monitor product safety comprehensively. The overview and purpose of spontaneous reporting systems encompass several key aspects:

1. Passive Surveillance Mechanism:

- Spontaneous reporting systems operate as passive surveillance mechanisms, relying on the voluntary submission of adverse event reports by healthcare professionals, patients, and consumers. Participants are encouraged to report any suspected adverse reactions associated with pharmaceutical products, regardless of severity or causality.

2. Early Detection of Safety Signals:

- The primary purpose of spontaneous reporting systems is to facilitate the early detection of safety signals and emerging risks associated with pharmaceutical products in real-world settings. By collecting and analyzing spontaneous reports of adverse events, regulatory authorities and pharmaceutical companies can identify potential safety concerns that may not have been evident during pre-market clinical trials.

3. Signal Detection and Signal Evaluation:

- Spontaneous reporting systems play a crucial role in signal detection and signal evaluation, allowing regulatory authorities to prioritize and investigate safety signals based on the frequency, severity, and plausibility of reported adverse events. Signal detection involves identifying potential safety concerns, while signal evaluation involves assessing the strength of the evidence and determining the need for further regulatory action.

4. Post-Marketing Risk Assessment:

- Spontaneous reporting systems contribute to post-marketing risk assessment by providing valuable data on the incidence, nature, and severity of adverse events associated with pharmaceutical products in real-world clinical practice. This information helps regulatory authorities and pharmaceutical companies evaluate the overall safety profile of marketed products and make informed decisions regarding risk mitigation strategies, labeling changes, or product withdrawals, if necessary.

5. Pharmacovigilance Activities:

- Spontaneous reporting systems are integral to pharmacovigilance activities aimed at monitoring and improving the safety of pharmaceutical products throughout their lifecycle. By promoting the continuous monitoring of adverse events and facilitating the exchange of safety information between healthcare stakeholders, spontaneous reporting systems enhance the early detection and management of potential safety risks associated with marketed products.

Spontaneous reporting systems represent a fundamental component of post-marketing surveillance, providing a mechanism for the passive collection and analysis of adverse event reports from healthcare professionals, patients, and consumers. By facilitating the early detection of safety signals, supporting post-marketing risk assessment, and enhancing pharmacovigilance activities, spontaneous reporting systems play a critical role in ensuring the ongoing safety and effectiveness of pharmaceutical products in real-world clinical practice.

10.1.1.2 Reporting Mechanisms and Data Collection

Reporting mechanisms and data collection processes are fundamental aspects of spontaneous reporting systems (SRS), enabling the systematic collection, collation, and analysis of adverse event reports from various sources. These mechanisms facilitate the timely submission of adverse event information and ensure the quality and integrity of pharmacovigilance data. Here's an overview of reporting mechanisms and data collection processes within spontaneous reporting systems:

1. Healthcare Professionals (HCPs) Reporting:

- Healthcare professionals, including physicians, pharmacists, nurses, and other allied healthcare providers, serve as primary reporters within spontaneous reporting systems. They are encouraged to report suspected adverse reactions encountered in clinical practice or during patient care.
- Reporting mechanisms for healthcare professionals typically include dedicated online reporting portals, telephone hotlines, fax-based reporting forms, and electronic reporting systems integrated into electronic health records (EHRs) or pharmacovigilance software.

2. Consumers and Patients Reporting:

- Consumers and patients also play a crucial role in spontaneous reporting by reporting adverse events they experience or observe after using pharmaceutical products. Direct patient reporting contributes to the detection of adverse events not always captured by healthcare professionals.
- Reporting mechanisms for consumers and patients include online reporting forms, toll-free telephone numbers, patient support programs, mobile applications, and patient advocacy groups facilitating adverse

event reporting.

3. Pharmaceutical Companies Reporting:

- Pharmaceutical companies are obligated to collect and submit adverse event reports received from healthcare professionals, consumers, and other sources to regulatory authorities as part of their pharmacovigilance responsibilities.
- Reporting mechanisms for pharmaceutical companies include dedicated safety departments responsible for receiving and processing adverse event reports, as well as electronic reporting systems for submission to regulatory authorities in compliance with regulatory requirements.

4. Regulatory Authorities and Health Agencies:

- Regulatory authorities and health agencies play a central role in coordinating and managing spontaneous reporting systems at the national and international levels. They receive, review, and analyze adverse event reports submitted by healthcare professionals, consumers, and pharmaceutical companies.
- Reporting mechanisms for regulatory authorities include centralized pharmacovigilance databases, electronic reporting portals, and regulatory reporting forms for the submission and analysis of adverse event data.

5. Data Collection and Analysis:

- Adverse event data collected through spontaneous reporting systems undergo systematic data collection and analysis processes to identify potential safety signals, trends, and patterns. Data elements typically include the type of adverse event, patient demographics, suspected product(s), concomitant medications, and outcome.
- Data analysis involves signal detection algorithms, statistical methods, and qualitative assessments to prioritize and evaluate potential safety concerns. Trends in adverse event reporting are monitored over time to detect emerging risks and inform regulatory decisions.

Reporting mechanisms and data collection processes are integral components of spontaneous reporting systems, facilitating the systematic collection, collation, and analysis of adverse event reports from healthcare professionals, consumers, and pharmaceutical companies. These mechanisms enable timely reporting of suspected adverse reactions, enhance pharmacovigilance activities, and support the continuous monitoring and evaluation of pharmaceutical product safety in real-world clinical practice.

10.1.2 Electronic Health Records (EHRs) Analysis

10.1.2.1 Utilization of Real-World Data

Electronic Health Records (EHRs) offer a wealth of real-world data that can be harnessed for post-marketing surveillance and pharmacovigilance purposes. The utilization of real-world data from EHRs provides valuable insights into the safety and effectiveness of pharmaceutical products in routine clinical practice. Here's an exploration of how real-world data from EHRs is utilized for post-marketing surveillance:

1. Comprehensive Patient Information:

- EHRs contain comprehensive patient information, including demographics, medical history, diagnoses, procedures, medications prescribed, laboratory results, and clinical notes. This wealth of data offers a holistic view of patients‘ healthcare journeys and enables the identification of potential adverse events associated with pharmaceutical products.

2. Longitudinal Follow-Up:

- EHRs provide longitudinal follow-up data, allowing for the continuous monitoring of patients' health outcomes over time. Longitudinal data from EHRs enable the detection of adverse events that may occur after prolonged exposure to pharmaceutical products, including rare or long-term safety concerns.

3. Real-World Treatment Patterns:

- Analysis of EHR data allows for the assessment of real-world treatment patterns, including medication prescribing practices, dosing regimens, treatment duration, and adherence. Understanding real-world treatment patterns provides insights into the use of pharmaceutical products in diverse patient populations and clinical settings.

4. Signal Detection and Hypothesis Generation:

- Real-world data from EHRs are used for signal detection and hypothesis generation in post-marketing surveillance. Analysis of EHR data can identify potential safety signals or unexpected associations between pharmaceutical products and adverse events, prompting further investigation through targeted pharmacovigilance studies.

5. Comparative Effectiveness Research:

- EHR data facilitate comparative effectiveness research by comparing the safety and effectiveness of different treatment options in real-world clinical practice. Comparative effectiveness studies leverage EHR data to evaluate the relative benefits and risks of pharmaceutical products compared to standard of care or alternative treatments.

6. Patient-Centered Outcomes Research:

- EHR data support patient-centered outcomes research by assessing patient-reported outcomes, quality of life measures, and treatment satisfaction. Patient-centered research conducted using EHR data provides insights into the impact of pharmaceutical products on patients' health-related quality of life and treatment preferences.

7. Post-Authorization Safety Studies (PASS):

- Real-world data from EHRs are utilized in post-authorization safety studies (PASS) to fulfill regulatory requirements for post-marketing surveillance. PASS studies leverage EHR data to evaluate the safety profile of pharmaceutical products in real-world clinical practice, complementing data from clinical trials.

8. Regulatory Decision-Making:

- Regulatory authorities utilize real-world data from EHRs to inform regulatory decision-making regarding the approval, labeling, and risk management of pharmaceutical products. EHR data contribute to the assessment of product safety, effectiveness, and benefit-risk profile in real-world clinical settings.

The utilization of real-world data from Electronic Health Records (EHRs) plays a vital role in post-marketing surveillance and pharmacovigilance. EHR data provide valuable insights into the safety and effectiveness of pharmaceutical products in routine clinical practice, supporting signal detection, hypothesis generation, comparative effectiveness research, patient-centered outcomes research, and regulatory decision-making. Leveraging real-world data from EHRs enhances post-marketing surveillance efforts and promotes the continuous monitoring of pharmaceutical product safety in diverse patient populations and healthcare settings.

10.1.2 Electronic Health Records (EHRs) Analysis

10.1.2.1 Utilization of Real-World Data

Electronic Health Records (EHRs) represent a rich source of real-world data that can be leveraged for various purposes, including post-marketing surveillance. The utilization of real-world data from EHRs offers valuable insights into the safety, effectiveness, and utilization of pharmaceutical products in routine clinical practice. Here's a closer look at how real-world data from EHRs is utilized:

1. Comprehensive Patient Information:

- EHRs contain comprehensive patient information, including demographic data, medical history, diagnoses, medications, laboratory results, and treatment outcomes. This wealth of data provides a holistic view of patients' health status and treatment journeys.

2. Longitudinal Data Collection:

- EHRs enable the collection of longitudinal data, allowing for the tracking of patients' health over time. Longitudinal data capture provides insights into the long-term effects of pharmaceutical products and facilitates the detection of adverse events that may occur after prolonged exposure.

3. Signal Detection and Safety Surveillance:

- Real-world data from EHRs are used for signal detection and safety surveillance, enabling the identification of potential adverse events associated with pharmaceutical products in real-world clinical practice. Analysis of EHR data helps detect safety signals early, prompting further investigation or regulatory action if necessary.

4. Comparative Effectiveness Research:

- EHR data support comparative effectiveness research by comparing the outcomes of different treatment strategies or pharmaceutical products in real-world clinical settings. Comparative effectiveness studies using EHR data help assess the relative benefits and risks of treatment options and inform clinical decision-making.

5. Pharmacovigilance and Post-Marketing Studies:

- EHRs are valuable sources of data for pharmacovigilance activities and post-marketing studies. Pharmaceutical companies, regulatory agencies, and research organizations utilize EHR data to assess the safety and effectiveness of pharmaceutical products in larger patient populations and diverse clinical settings.

6. Real-World Treatment Patterns:

- Analysis of EHR data allows for the evaluation of real-world treatment patterns, including medication prescribing practices, dosing regimens, treatment adherence, and medication switching. Understanding real-world treatment patterns helps optimize healthcare delivery and improve patient outcomes.

7. Regulatory Decision-Making:

- Regulatory authorities use real-world data from EHRs to inform regulatory decision-making processes, such as drug approval, labeling updates, and risk management strategies. EHR data provide real-world evidence of pharmaceutical product safety and effectiveness, complementing data from clinical trials.

8. Quality Improvement Initiatives:

- Healthcare organizations leverage EHR data for quality improvement initiatives aimed at enhancing patient care and safety. Analysis of EHR data helps identify areas for improvement in healthcare delivery, medication management, and patient outcomes.

The utilization of real-world data from Electronic Health Records (EHRs) plays a critical role in post-marketing surveillance, pharmacovigilance, comparative effectiveness research, and regulatory decision-making. EHR data offer valuable insights into the safety, effectiveness, and utilization of pharmaceutical products in real-world clinical practice, supporting evidence-based healthcare decision-making and continuous improvement in patient care.

10.1.2.2 Identification of Adverse Events and Patterns

In the realm of post-marketing surveillance, the analysis of Electronic Health Records (EHRs) serves as a potent tool for identifying adverse events (AEs) and discerning underlying patterns. By scrutinizing the vast troves of patient data contained within EHR systems, healthcare professionals, researchers, and regulatory bodies can pinpoint potential safety concerns associated with pharmaceutical products. Here's an exploration of how EHR analysis aids in the identification of adverse events and patterns:

1. Adverse Event Detection:

- EHR analysis enables the systematic detection of adverse events recorded in patient records. By mining EHR data for indications of adverse reactions, healthcare providers can identify instances where patients experienced unexpected or harmful responses to medications or treatments.

2. Signal Detection and Pharmacovigilance:

- Through sophisticated data analysis techniques, EHR systems aid in signal detection for pharmacovigilance purposes. Algorithms and data mining methods sift through EHR databases to flag potential safety signals, drawing attention to adverse events that warrant further investigation or monitoring.

3. Temporal Associations and Causality Assessment:

- EHR analysis facilitates the examination of temporal associations between medication use and adverse events. Tracking the timing of drug administration and subsequent adverse reactions allows for a more nuanced understanding of potential causal relationships, aiding in the assessment of drug safety profiles.

4. Identification of Rare and Unexpected Events:

- EHR data offer insights into rare and unexpected adverse events that may not have been apparent during pre-market clinical trials due to limited sample sizes or short study durations. By aggregating data from diverse patient populations, EHR analysis enhances the detection of rare adverse events that require closer scrutiny.

5. Pattern Recognition and Clustering:

- Advanced analytics applied to EHR datasets facilitate pattern recognition and clustering of adverse events. By identifying clusters of similar adverse reactions or symptom patterns across patient records, healthcare professionals can discern potential drug-related effects and investigate underlying mechanisms.

6. Risk Factor Analysis:

- EHR analysis allows for the identification of patient-specific risk factors associated with adverse events. By analyzing demographic characteristics, medical history, comorbidities, and concomitant medications, researchers can pinpoint factors that predispose certain individuals to adverse reactions, informing personalized risk assessment strategies.

7. Comparative Analysis and Benchmarking:

- Comparative analysis of EHR data enables benchmarking of adverse event rates across different patient cohorts, treatment modalities, or healthcare settings. By comparing adverse event frequencies and severity levels, healthcare organizations can identify areas for improvement in patient safety and medication management practices.

8. Real-Time Surveillance and Alerting:

- Integration of EHR systems with real-time surveillance tools enables proactive monitoring of adverse events and automated alerting mechanisms. Healthcare providers receive timely notifications of potential safety concerns, allowing for prompt intervention and mitigation strategies to minimize patient harm.

The analysis of Electronic Health Records (EHRs) plays a pivotal role in identifying adverse events and discerning underlying patterns that may signal safety concerns associated with pharmaceutical products. By leveraging EHR data for signal detection, temporal analysis, pattern recognition, and risk factor assessment, healthcare stakeholders can enhance pharmacovigilance efforts and improve patient safety outcomes in real-world clinical practice.

10.1.3 Prescription Event Monitoring

10.1.3.1 Prospective Monitoring of Newly Marketed Drugs

Prescription Event Monitoring (PEM) is a form of post-marketing surveillance designed for the prospective monitoring of newly marketed drugs. This method involves the systematic collection of data on adverse events associated with recently introduced medications. Here's an exploration of the pros and cons of prospective monitoring of newly marketed drugs through PEM:

Pros:

1. **Early Detection of Safety Signals:** PEM enables the early detection of potential safety signals or adverse reactions associated with newly marketed drugs. By actively monitoring adverse events in real-time, healthcare authorities can promptly respond to emerging safety concerns and take appropriate regulatory actions.
2. **Focused Data Collection:** Unlike spontaneous reporting systems that rely on voluntary reporting, PEM involves structured data collection

from prescribers and patients. This focused approach ensures the systematic capture of adverse event data, enhancing the reliability and completeness of pharmacovigilance information.

3. **Longitudinal Follow-Up:** PEM allows for longitudinal follow-up of patients prescribed newly marketed drugs, enabling the assessment of long-term safety outcomes and the detection of delayed adverse reactions. Continuous monitoring over an extended period enhances the understanding of the drug's safety profile beyond initial clinical trials.
4. **Detailed Data Collection:** The structured nature of PEM facilitates the collection of detailed patient information, including demographic data, medical history, concomitant medications, and clinical outcomes. This comprehensive data capture enables thorough safety assessments and enhances the ability to identify potential risk factors.
5. **Customized Study Designs:** PEM studies can be tailored to specific drug products, therapeutic indications, or patient populations, allowing for customized study designs based on the drug's characteristics and anticipated safety concerns. This flexibility enables targeted monitoring and hypothesis-driven research.

Cons:

1. **Resource Intensive:** Conducting PEM studies requires significant resources, including personnel, infrastructure, and funding. The need for dedicated monitoring systems, data collection tools, and trained staff can impose logistical and financial burdens on healthcare organizations and regulatory agencies.
2. **Limited Generalizability:** PEM studies may have limited generalizability due to selective patient recruitment and specialized monitoring procedures. Patients enrolled in PEM may not fully represent the broader population of drug users, leading to potential biases in safety assessments and outcomes.
3. **Delayed Results:** The prospective nature of PEM studies means that safety data may not be available until after the drug has been on the market for some time. Unlike retrospective analyses that can leverage existing data, PEM requires time for data collection, analysis, and interpretation, leading to potential delays in safety assessments.
4. **Underreporting and Bias:** Despite structured data collection protocols, PEM studies may still be susceptible to underreporting of adverse events

and reporting bias. Prescribers and patients may be less inclined to report adverse reactions, particularly if they perceive them as minor or unrelated to the medication.

5. **Regulatory Compliance Challenges:** Compliance with PEM protocols and data reporting requirements may pose challenges for prescribers, healthcare facilities, and regulatory authorities. Ensuring consistent adherence to study protocols and data submission timelines requires ongoing communication, training, and monitoring efforts.

Prospective monitoring of newly marketed drugs through Prescription Event Monitoring (PEM) offers several advantages, including early safety signal detection, focused data collection, longitudinal follow-up, detailed data capture, and customized study designs. However, PEM studies also face challenges related to resource intensity, limited generalizability, delayed results, underreporting, reporting bias, and regulatory compliance. Balancing these pros and cons is essential for optimizing the effectiveness of PEM in post-marketing surveillance and ensuring the continued safety of newly introduced medications.

10.1.3.2 Longitudinal Data Collection and Analysis

Longitudinal data collection and analysis are integral components of Prescription Event Monitoring (PEM), facilitating the systematic assessment of safety outcomes associated with newly marketed drugs over extended periods. Here's an exploration of how longitudinal data collection and analysis are conducted within the context of PEM:

Longitudinal Data Collection:

1. **Prospective Patient Follow-Up:** PEM involves the prospective follow-up of patients prescribed newly marketed drugs for a specified period after initiation of treatment. Patients are typically enrolled at the time of prescription, and their clinical outcomes and adverse events are monitored longitudinally over time.
2. **Structured Data Collection:** During the follow-up period, structured data collection tools, such as patient questionnaires or electronic reporting forms, are utilized to capture relevant information on adverse events, treatment adherence, and clinical outcomes. Prescribers and patients are encouraged to report any suspected adverse reactions promptly.

3. **Regular Monitoring and Assessment:** Healthcare professionals responsible for PEM conduct regular monitoring and assessment of patient data to identify and document adverse events and other safety outcomes. Data collection intervals may vary based on the drug's characteristics, therapeutic indications, and anticipated safety concerns.
4. **Comprehensive Patient Information:** Longitudinal data collection in PEM studies allows for the capture of comprehensive patient information, including demographic data, medical history, concomitant medications, and treatment outcomes. This rich dataset enables thorough safety assessments and facilitates the identification of potential risk factors or confounding variables.

Longitudinal Data Analysis:

1. **Temporal Analysis of Adverse Events:** Longitudinal data analysis involves the temporal examination of adverse events and clinical outcomes observed over the follow-up period. Researchers assess the timing of adverse reactions relative to drug exposure to determine potential causal relationships and temporal trends.
2. **Cumulative Incidence of Adverse Events:** Researchers calculate the cumulative incidence of adverse events over time to quantify the risk of experiencing specific adverse reactions associated with the newly marketed drug. This analysis provides insights into the drug's safety profile and helps prioritize adverse events for further investigation.
3. **Time-to-Event Analysis:** Longitudinal data analysis may include time-to-event analysis techniques, such as Kaplan-Meier survival curves or Cox proportional hazards models, to assess the time until the occurrence of adverse events or treatment discontinuation. These methods account for varying follow-up durations and censoring of patient data.
4. **Subgroup Analyses and Stratification:** Researchers may conduct subgroup analyses and stratification based on patient characteristics, treatment regimens, or disease severity to explore potential effect modifiers and identify patient populations at higher risk of adverse events. Stratified analyses enhance the understanding of treatment effects and safety outcomes across different subgroups.
5. **Signal Detection and Risk Assessment:** Longitudinal data analysis enables signal detection and risk assessment by identifying emerging safety signals, trends, or patterns associated with the newly marketed

drug. Researchers evaluate the strength of associations between drug exposure and adverse events to inform regulatory decisions and risk mitigation strategies.

Longitudinal data collection and analysis are essential components of Prescription Event Monitoring (PEM), allowing for the systematic assessment of safety outcomes associated with newly marketed drugs over extended follow-up periods. Through structured data collection, regular monitoring, and sophisticated analytical techniques, PEM studies enhance the understanding of drug safety profiles, facilitate early detection of adverse events, and support evidence-based regulatory decision-making.

10.1.4 Active Surveillance Systems

10.1.4.1 Sentinel Systems and Distributed Data Networks

Active surveillance systems, such as Sentinel Systems and Distributed Data Networks, represent innovative approaches to post-marketing surveillance that leverage real-time data from diverse healthcare sources to monitor drug safety and effectiveness. Here's an exploration of Sentinel Systems and Distributed Data Networks:

Sentinel Systems:

1. **Real-Time Monitoring:** Sentinel Systems are active surveillance networks established by regulatory agencies, such as the U.S. Food and Drug Administration (FDA), to monitor the safety of medical products in real time. These systems continuously collect and analyze electronic health data from a network of healthcare organizations to detect and assess adverse events associated with pharmaceutical products.
2. **Large-Scale Data Infrastructure:** Sentinel Systems utilize large-scale data infrastructure, including electronic health records (EHRs), insurance claims databases, and registries, to access comprehensive patient information across diverse populations. By aggregating and standardizing electronic health data, Sentinel Systems enable robust pharmacovigilance activities and signal detection efforts.
3. **Signal Detection and Evaluation:** Sentinel Systems employ sophisticated analytical methods, such as data mining algorithms, statistical modeling, and Bayesian approaches, to detect and evaluate potential safety signals associated with drugs and medical devices. Rapid signal detection capabilities allow regulatory agencies to promptly investigate emerging safety concerns and implement risk mitigation

strategies.

4. **Collaborative Partnerships:** Sentinel Systems foster collaborative partnerships between regulatory agencies, healthcare organizations, academic institutions, and industry stakeholders. By leveraging multidisciplinary expertise and resources, Sentinel Systems enhance the efficiency and effectiveness of post-marketing surveillance efforts and promote transparency and accountability in drug safety monitoring.

Distributed Data Networks:

1. **Decentralized Data Infrastructure:** Distributed Data Networks consist of interconnected healthcare organizations that share electronic health data through a decentralized infrastructure. Unlike centralized databases, distributed networks maintain data ownership and control within individual healthcare entities while enabling secure data sharing and collaboration.
2. **Interoperable Data Standards:** Distributed Data Networks rely on interoperable data standards and common data models to facilitate seamless data exchange and integration across disparate healthcare systems. Standardized data formats ensure consistency and compatibility, allowing for harmonized data analysis and aggregation across participating organizations.
3. **Multi-Center Collaborations:** Distributed Data Networks facilitate multi-center collaborations and research initiatives by pooling electronic health data from diverse patient populations and healthcare settings. These networks enable large-scale epidemiological studies, comparative effectiveness research, and safety surveillance activities that leverage real-world data to inform clinical practice and regulatory decision-making.
4. **Privacy and Security Protections:** Distributed Data Networks prioritize patient privacy and data security through robust encryption, anonymization techniques, and access controls. Data governance policies and regulatory compliance frameworks ensure adherence to ethical and legal standards for the protection of patient health information and confidentiality.

Sentinel Systems and Distributed Data Networks represent cutting-edge approaches to active surveillance in post-marketing pharmacovigilance.

These systems harness the power of real-time electronic health data to monitor drug safety and effectiveness, detect adverse events, and facilitate evidence-based decision-making in healthcare. Through collaborative partnerships, interoperable data standards, and stringent privacy protections, Sentinel Systems and Distributed Data Networks contribute to the advancement of patient safety and public health initiatives on a national and global scale.

10.1.4.2 Cohort Event Monitoring

Cohort Event Monitoring (CEM) is an active surveillance method utilized in pharmacovigilance to assess the safety of newly marketed drugs in real-world clinical practice. This approach involves the systematic monitoring of predefined patient cohorts to detect and evaluate adverse events associated with the use of specific medications. Here's an overview of Cohort Event Monitoring:

1. **Patient Cohort Identification:** CEM begins with the identification and enrollment of a defined patient cohort prescribed the newly marketed drug of interest. Cohort selection criteria may include specific demographics, clinical characteristics, or indications for drug use, ensuring a representative sample of patients who are likely to receive the medication.
2. **Prospective Data Collection:** Once the patient cohort is established, prospective data collection begins, typically through structured data collection tools, such as patient questionnaires, diaries, or electronic reporting forms. Patients are followed longitudinally over a specified period, and information on adverse events, medication adherence, and clinical outcomes is systematically collected.
3. **Active Surveillance:** Unlike passive surveillance systems that rely on spontaneous reporting, CEM involves active surveillance methodologies to actively monitor adverse events among the enrolled patient cohort. Healthcare professionals may conduct regular follow-up visits, telephone interviews, or electronic communications to gather information on adverse reactions and treatment outcomes.
4. **Structured Data Analysis:** Data collected through CEM undergo structured analysis to identify and evaluate adverse events associated with the newly marketed drug. Researchers employ statistical methods, such as incidence rate calculations, relative risk assessments, and signal detection algorithms, to quantify the frequency, severity, and potential

causality of adverse reactions.

5. **Signal Detection and Risk Assessment:** CEM enables the detection of safety signals and the assessment of drug-related risks through systematic data analysis. Researchers compare observed adverse event rates with expected rates based on pre-defined benchmarks or reference populations, allowing for the identification of potential safety concerns and the estimation of relative risk levels.
6. **Risk Communication and Management:** Findings from CEM studies are communicated to healthcare stakeholders, regulatory authorities, and pharmaceutical companies to facilitate risk communication and management strategies. Timely dissemination of safety information enables informed decision-making regarding drug labeling updates, risk mitigation measures, and regulatory interventions to safeguard patient health.
7. **Longitudinal Follow-Up:** CEM studies involve longitudinal follow-up of patient cohorts to assess the persistence of adverse events, treatment discontinuation rates, and long-term safety outcomes associated with the newly marketed drug. Continued surveillance over an extended period enhances the understanding of the drug's safety profile and enables the detection of rare Cohort Event Monitoring (CEM) is an active surveillance method employed in pharmacovigilance to assess the safety of newly marketed drugs through systematic data collection, analysis, and monitoring of predefined patient cohorts. By combining prospective data collection with structured analysis techniques, CEM enables the early detection of safety signals, risk assessment, and informed decision-making to protect patient safety and optimize healthcare outcomes.

10.2 Importance for Ongoing Drug Safety

10.2.1 Detection of Rare Adverse Events

10.2.1.1 Challenges in Pre-Market Clinical Trials

While pre-market clinical trials are essential for assessing the safety and efficacy of new drugs, they may not always detect rare adverse events due to several inherent challenges. Here's an exploration of the challenges associated with detecting rare adverse events in pre-market clinical trials:

1. **Sample Size Limitations:** Pre-market clinical trials typically involve a limited number of participants, often recruited from homogeneous populations under controlled conditions. The small sample sizes may

not adequately represent the diverse patient populations encountered in real-world clinical practice, making it challenging to detect rare adverse events that occur infrequently.

2. **Selection Bias:** Participants enrolled in pre-market clinical trials may not fully reflect the characteristics of the broader patient population due to strict eligibility criteria and exclusion of certain patient groups, such as those with comorbidities or concomitant medications. Selection bias can hinder the generalizability of trial results and obscure the detection of rare adverse events that predominantly affect excluded populations.
3. **Short Duration of Exposure:** Pre-market clinical trials typically have relatively short durations of exposure to the investigational drug, often ranging from weeks to months. Rare adverse events that manifest after prolonged or cumulative exposure may go undetected during the limited trial period, leading to underestimation of long-term safety risks associated with the drug.
4. **Low Event Rates:** Rare adverse events by definition occur infrequently, with low event rates that may not be captured within the small sample sizes of pre-market clinical trials. The low prevalence of rare adverse events diminishes statistical power and increases the likelihood of type II errors, wherein true safety signals are missed due to insufficient data.
5. **Heterogeneity of Patient Responses:** Patients exhibit variability in their response to drugs due to genetic factors, underlying diseases, concomitant medications, and environmental influences. The heterogeneity of patient responses complicates the detection of rare adverse events, as individual susceptibility may vary, making it challenging to identify consistent patterns across study participants.
6. **Detection Bias and Reporting Artifacts:** Detection bias may arise in pre-market clinical trials due to heightened awareness of potential adverse events among investigators, leading to increased vigilance and over-reporting of symptoms. Additionally, reporting artifacts, such as differential ascertainment and documentation practices, can introduce bias and confound the accurate assessment of adverse event frequencies.
7. **Post-Marketing Experience:** Despite rigorous pre-market evaluation, some rare adverse events may only become apparent once the drug is widely used in clinical practice. Post-marketing surveillance systems, such as spontaneous reporting databases, active surveillance networks, and cohort studies, play a crucial role in detecting rare adverse events that were not identified during pre-market clinical trials.

Detecting rare adverse events in pre-market clinical trials poses significant challenges due to sample size limitations, selection bias, short duration of exposure, low event rates, patient heterogeneity, detection bias, and post-marketing experience. Addressing these challenges requires a comprehensive approach that integrates pre-market clinical trial data with post-marketing surveillance efforts to ensure ongoing drug safety monitoring and risk assessment throughout the product lifecycle.

10.2.1.2 Real-World Experience and Signal Detection

Real-world experience plays a pivotal role in complementing pre-market clinical trial data by providing insights into the occurrence of rare adverse events and facilitating signal detection for new drugs. Here's an exploration of how real-world experience contributes to signal detection and ongoing drug safety:

1. **Diverse Patient Populations:** Real-world experience encompasses a broader spectrum of patient populations than pre-market clinical trials, including individuals with diverse demographic characteristics, comorbidities, and concomitant medications. The heterogeneous nature of real-world patient populations allows for the identification of rare adverse events that may disproportionately affect specific subgroups not adequately represented in clinical trials.
2. **Longitudinal Follow-Up:** Real-world experience provides longitudinal follow-up of patients exposed to drugs over extended periods, enabling the detection of rare adverse events that manifest after prolonged or cumulative exposure. Continuous monitoring of patients in routine clinical practice facilitates the identification of delayed adverse reactions, gradual onset events, and long-term safety risks that may not have been evident during short-term clinical trials.
3. **Large-Scale Data Capture:** Real-world data sources, such as electronic health records (EHRs), claims databases, registries, and spontaneous reporting systems, capture a vast volume of patient information from diverse healthcare settings and geographic regions. The large-scale data capture capacity of real-world sources enhances signal detection capabilities by providing comprehensive coverage of drug utilization patterns and adverse event frequencies across populations.
4. **Naturalistic Treatment Settings:** Real-world experience reflects the complexities of healthcare delivery and medication use in naturalistic treatment settings, where patients receive drugs under routine clinical

conditions. The pragmatic nature of real-world practice allows for the observation of real-time prescribing patterns, off-label use, medication errors, drug interactions, and other factors that influence the occurrence of adverse events in everyday clinical practice.

5. **Data Mining and Surveillance Tools:** Advanced data mining algorithms, statistical methods, and surveillance tools are employed to analyze real-world data sources for signal detection purposes. These analytical techniques enable the systematic identification of potential safety signals, temporal associations, dose-response relationships, and patterns of adverse event clustering that warrant further investigation and risk assessment.
6. **Post-Marketing Studies:** Post-marketing studies, including cohort studies, case-control studies, and observational research, leverage real-world data to assess the safety and effectiveness of drugs in large patient populations. These studies supplement pre-market clinical trial findings by providing real-world evidence of drug-related adverse events, treatment outcomes, and comparative effectiveness in diverse clinical settings.
7. **Regulatory Pharmacovigilance:** Regulatory agencies, pharmaceutical companies, and healthcare stakeholders actively monitor real-world data sources for pharmacovigilance purposes to ensure ongoing drug safety monitoring and risk management. Real-world experience informs regulatory decision-making processes, including drug labeling updates, risk communication strategies, post-approval safety studies, and regulatory actions to protect public health.

Real-world experience serves as a valuable resource for signal detection and ongoing drug safety monitoring by providing insights into the occurrence of rare adverse events, long-term safety outcomes, and drug utilization patterns in diverse patient populations and clinical settings. Leveraging real-world data sources and analytical tools enhances pharmacovigilance efforts, facilitates evidence-based decision-making, and fosters continuous improvement in patient care and drug safety throughout the product lifecycle.

10.2.2 Assessment of Drug Effectiveness

10.2.2.1 Monitoring Real-World Treatment Outcomes

Monitoring real-world treatment outcomes is integral to assessing the effectiveness of drugs in routine clinical practice beyond the controlled settings of pre-market clinical trials. Here's an exploration of how monitoring real-world treatment outcomes contributes to the assessment of drug effectiveness:

1. **Patient-Centered Outcomes:** Real-world treatment outcomes reflect the impact of drugs on patient health, well-being, and quality of life in everyday clinical practice. Monitoring patient-centered outcomes, such as symptom improvement, functional status, treatment satisfaction, and adherence to therapy, provides valuable insights into the real-world effectiveness of drugs from the patient's perspective.
2. **Clinical Endpoints:** Real-world treatment outcomes encompass a broad spectrum of clinical endpoints relevant to disease management and therapeutic goals. These endpoints may include disease remission, symptom control, disease progression, hospitalization rates, healthcare utilization, and mortality outcomes. Monitoring clinical endpoints in routine clinical practice allows for the assessment of drug effectiveness in real-world patient populations over time.
3. **Comparative Effectiveness:** Real-world treatment outcomes facilitate comparative effectiveness research by comparing the effectiveness of different drugs or treatment modalities in real-world clinical settings. Comparative effectiveness studies leverage real-world data sources, such as electronic health records (EHRs), claims databases, and registries, to evaluate the relative benefits, risks, and cost-effectiveness of alternative treatment options for specific patient populations or therapeutic indications.
4. **Longitudinal Follow-Up:** Monitoring real-world treatment outcomes involves longitudinal follow-up of patients exposed to drugs over extended periods in routine clinical practice. Longitudinal data capture enables the assessment of treatment durability, long-term effectiveness, and persistence of treatment benefits beyond the initial phases of drug therapy. Continuous monitoring facilitates the identification of changes in treatment response, disease progression, or adverse events over time.
5. **Real-Time Surveillance:** Real-world treatment outcomes contribute to real-time surveillance efforts aimed at monitoring drug effectiveness and safety in real-world clinical practice. Advanced data analytics, surveillance tools, and electronic reporting systems enable the systematic monitoring of treatment outcomes, adverse events, and drug utilization patterns across diverse patient populations and healthcare

settings. Real-time surveillance enhances the early detection of emerging safety signals, treatment failures, or unexpected treatment responses that may require intervention or further investigation.

6. **Quality Improvement Initiatives:** Real-world treatment outcomes inform quality improvement initiatives aimed at optimizing patient care, treatment protocols, and clinical decision-making in healthcare settings. Analyzing real-world data allows healthcare organizations to identify opportunities for practice improvement, guideline adherence, and evidence-based interventions to enhance patient outcomes and healthcare delivery efficiency.
7. **Regulatory Evaluation:** Regulatory agencies, such as the U.S. Food and Drug Administration (FDA) and the European Medicines Agency (EMA), consider real-world treatment outcomes as part of their regulatory evaluation process for new drugs and therapeutic interventions. Real-world evidence of drug effectiveness, derived from post-marketing studies, observational research, and real-world data sources, complements pre-market clinical trial data and informs regulatory decision-making regarding drug approval, labeling, and post-approval commitments.

Monitoring real-world treatment outcomes is essential for assessing the effectiveness of drugs in routine clinical practice and informing evidence-based decision-making in healthcare. By capturing patient-centered outcomes, clinical endpoints, comparative effectiveness data, longitudinal follow-up, real-time surveillance, quality improvement initiatives, and regulatory evaluation, real-world treatment outcomes enhance our understanding of drug effectiveness in real-world patient populations and support continuous improvement in patient care and healthcare delivery.

10.2.2.2 Comparative Effectiveness Research

Comparative effectiveness research (CER) is a critical approach to evaluating the relative benefits and risks of different treatment options, including drugs, in real-world clinical practice settings. Here's an exploration of how CER contributes to the assessment of drug effectiveness:

1. **Comparison of Treatment Strategies:** CER involves comparing the effectiveness of two or more treatment strategies, which may include different drugs, therapeutic interventions, or healthcare delivery approaches. By evaluating treatments head-to-head in real-world

settings, CER generates evidence to guide clinical decision-making and inform treatment choices based on their relative merits.

2. **Patient-Centered Outcomes:** CER focuses on patient-centered outcomes, such as symptom relief, functional status, quality of life, treatment satisfaction, and adverse events. By assessing outcomes that matter most to patients, CER helps identify treatments that optimize health outcomes and align with patient preferences, values, and goals of care.
3. **Heterogeneous Patient Populations:** CER considers the heterogeneity of patient populations encountered in real-world clinical practice, including individuals with diverse demographic characteristics, clinical presentations, comorbidities, and treatment histories. By studying diverse patient cohorts, CER generates evidence that is more generalizable and applicable to real-world patient care than findings from controlled clinical trials.
4. **Longitudinal Follow-Up:** CER involves longitudinal follow-up of patients over extended periods to assess treatment outcomes, disease progression, and adverse events in routine clinical practice. Longitudinal data capture enables the evaluation of treatment durability, long-term effectiveness, and persistence of treatment benefits beyond the short-term efficacy observed in clinical trials.
5. **Real-World Data Sources:** CER utilizes real-world data sources, such as electronic health records (EHRs), claims databases, disease registries, and patient-reported outcomes databases, to conduct comparative effectiveness studies. These data sources provide comprehensive information on treatment utilization, healthcare utilization, and clinical outcomes across diverse patient populations and healthcare settings.
6. **Methodological Approaches:** CER employs a variety of methodological approaches, including observational studies, pragmatic trials, retrospective analyses, meta-analyses, and decision modeling, to compare treatment effectiveness while accounting for confounding variables, bias, and potential sources of variability. Advanced statistical techniques, such as propensity score matching, instrumental variable analysis, and sensitivity analyses, help address methodological challenges and enhance the validity of CER findings.
7. **Policy and Practice Implications:** CER findings have policy and practice implications for healthcare decision-makers, including clinicians, patients, payers, policymakers, and healthcare organizations. Evidence

from CER studies informs treatment guidelines, formulary decisions, coverage policies, reimbursement decisions, quality improvement initiatives, and healthcare resource allocation strategies aimed at optimizing patient outcomes and healthcare value.

Comparative effectiveness research (CER) plays a vital role in assessing the effectiveness of drugs and other treatment options in real-world clinical practice. By comparing treatment strategies, focusing on patient-centered outcomes, considering heterogeneous patient populations, conducting longitudinal follow-up, utilizing real-world data sources, employing rigorous methodological approaches, and informing policy and practice decisions, CER contributes to evidence-based healthcare delivery, patient-centered care, and continuous improvement in healthcare quality and value.

10.2.3 Regulatory Compliance and Pharmacovigilance

10.2.3.1 Post-Marketing Requirements by Regulatory Agencies

Regulatory agencies impose post-marketing requirements on pharmaceutical companies to ensure ongoing compliance with safety standards and pharmacovigilance practices. These requirements aim to monitor drug safety, detect adverse events, and mitigate potential risks associated with marketed drugs. Here's an exploration of post-marketing requirements by regulatory agencies:

1. **Safety Reporting Obligations:** Regulatory agencies, such as the U.S. Food and Drug Administration (FDA), the European Medicines Agency (EMA), and other global regulatory authorities, mandate pharmaceutical companies to submit periodic safety reports detailing adverse events, medication errors, and other safety-related information for marketed drugs. These reports, often referred to as Periodic Safety Update Reports (PSURs) or Periodic Benefit-Risk Evaluation Reports (PBRERs), provide comprehensive safety assessments based on real-world data and ongoing pharmacovigilance activities.
2. **Risk Evaluation and Mitigation Strategies (REMS):** Some regulatory agencies require pharmaceutical companies to implement Risk Evaluation and Mitigation Strategies (REMS) for certain drugs with known or potential safety risks. REMS programs may include elements such as medication guides, communication plans, restricted distribution systems, and healthcare provider training to minimize the risks associated with drug use while maximizing therapeutic benefits.

Compliance with REMS requirements is monitored closely by regulatory agencies to ensure patient safety.

3. **Post-Marketing Studies:** Regulatory agencies may mandate post-marketing studies, also known as Phase IV or post-approval studies, to further evaluate the safety, effectiveness, or long-term outcomes of marketed drugs in real-world clinical practice. These studies may focus on specific patient populations, treatment indications, or safety concerns identified during pre-market clinical trials or post-marketing surveillance. Pharmaceutical companies are responsible for conducting and reporting the results of post-marketing studies to regulatory agencies in accordance with predefined study protocols and timelines.
4. **Labeling Updates:** Regulatory agencies require pharmaceutical companies to maintain up-to-date drug labeling with accurate information on indications, dosing, safety warnings, precautions, contraindications, adverse reactions, and other relevant information. Companies must promptly update drug labels to reflect new safety findings, emerging risks, or changes in therapeutic recommendations based on post-marketing data, regulatory assessments, or safety advisories issued by regulatory agencies.
5. **Adverse Event Monitoring and Reporting:** Pharmaceutical companies are obligated to establish robust pharmacovigilance systems for the ongoing monitoring, detection, assessment, and reporting of adverse events associated with marketed drugs. Adverse event reports submitted to regulatory agencies are carefully reviewed, analyzed, and evaluated to identify potential safety signals, trends, or patterns that may require further investigation or regulatory action to protect public health.
6. **Compliance Audits and Inspections:** Regulatory agencies conduct compliance audits and inspections of pharmaceutical companies to ensure adherence to post-marketing requirements, pharmacovigilance practices, and regulatory standards for drug safety and quality. Inspections may cover various aspects of pharmacovigilance operations, including adverse event reporting procedures, data management systems, signal detection methodologies, risk management plans, and compliance with regulatory reporting obligations.

Regulatory compliance and pharmacovigilance are essential components of post-marketing surveillance aimed at ensuring the ongoing safety and effectiveness of marketed drugs. Pharmaceutical companies must comply with post-marketing requirements imposed by regulatory agencies, including safety reporting obligations, REMS programs, post-marketing studies, labeling updates, adverse event monitoring, and compliance audits, to maintain regulatory approval and protect patient health. Collaboration between regulatory agencies, pharmaceutical companies, healthcare professionals, and other stakeholders is crucial for effective pharmacovigilance and continuous improvement in drug safety monitoring and risk management practices.

10.2.3.2 Risk Management Plans and REMS Programs

Risk management plans (RMPs) and Risk Evaluation and Mitigation Strategies (REMS) programs are regulatory mechanisms implemented by pharmaceutical companies to proactively identify, assess, and mitigate risks associated with marketed drugs. Here's an overview of RMPs and REMS programs:

1. **Risk Management Plans (RMPs):**

Risk management plans are comprehensive documents developed by pharmaceutical companies in collaboration with regulatory agencies to address potential risks associated with a particular drug. RMPs outline strategies for identifying, characterizing, and managing risks throughout the drug's lifecycle. Key components of RMPs include:

- **Safety Specification:** RMPs specify the known and potential risks associated with the drug, including adverse reactions, safety concerns, and risk factors identified during pre-market clinical trials or post-marketing surveillance.
- **Risk Minimization Measures:** RMPs detail risk minimization measures designed to reduce the likelihood or severity of adverse events associated with the drug. These measures may include healthcare provider education, patient counseling, prescribing restrictions, laboratory monitoring, and medication guides.
- **Pharmacovigilance Plan:** RMPs include a pharmacovigilance plan outlining the procedures for monitoring and reporting adverse events, medication errors, and other safety-related information to regulatory agencies. Pharmacovigilance activities ensure ongoing surveillance of drug safety and facilitate early detection of emerging risks.

- **Post-Authorization Safety Studies (PASS):** RMPs may propose post-authorization safety studies (PASS) to further investigate specific safety concerns or unanswered questions regarding the drug's safety profile. PASS aims to generate additional real-world data to inform risk-benefit assessments and regulatory decision-making.

1. **Risk Evaluation and Mitigation Strategies (REMS) Programs:**

REMS programs are risk management strategies mandated by regulatory agencies for certain drugs with known or potential safety risks that require additional measures to ensure safe use. REMS programs aim to minimize the risks associated with the drug while preserving its benefits for patients who need it. Key components of REMS programs include:

- **Elements to Assure Safe Use (ETASU):** REMS programs may include elements to assure safe use (ETASU) designed to prevent, mitigate, or manage specific risks associated with the drug. ETASU elements may include prescriber certification, patient enrollment, distribution restrictions, medication guides, and laboratory monitoring requirements.
- **Communication and Education:** REMS programs emphasize communication and education initiatives aimed at healthcare providers, patients, caregivers, and pharmacists to raise awareness of the drug's risks, safe use practices, and monitoring requirements. Educational materials, training programs, and outreach efforts help promote informed decision-making and risk mitigation strategies.
- **Implementation and Compliance Monitoring:** Pharmaceutical companies are responsible for implementing REMS programs and monitoring compliance with program requirements. Compliance monitoring may involve tracking prescriber participation, patient enrollment, distribution records, adverse event reporting, and other performance metrics to ensure the effective implementation of risk mitigation measures.
- **Evaluation and Modification:** REMS programs undergo periodic evaluation and modification based on ongoing risk assessments, safety data updates, and feedback from stakeholders. Regulatory agencies review the effectiveness of REMS programs and may require modifications or enhancements to address emerging safety concerns,

optimize risk mitigation strategies, or improve program outcomes.

Risk management plans (RMPs) and Risk Evaluation and Mitigation Strategies (REMS) programs are regulatory mechanisms implemented by pharmaceutical companies to proactively identify, assess, and mitigate risks associated with marketed drugs. RMPs provide a comprehensive framework for managing risks throughout the drug's lifecycle, while REMS programs target specific drugs with known or potential safety risks and require additional measures to ensure safe use. Collaboration between regulatory agencies, pharmaceutical companies, healthcare providers, patients, and other stakeholders is essential for the successful implementation of RMPs and REMS programs to protect patient safety and optimize healthcare outcomes.

CHAPTER ELEVEN

CASE STUDIES AND REAL WORLD APPLICATIONS

11.1 Analysis of Past Clinical Trials

11.1.1 Overview of Clinical Trial Design

11.1.1.1 Phases of Clinical Trials

Clinical trials are organized into distinct phases, each serving specific objectives in drug development and evaluation. Understanding the phases is crucial for designing robust trials and interpreting their outcomes effectively. Here's an overview:

1. **Phase 0:** Phase 0 trials, also known as exploratory investigational new drug (IND) studies, involve administering subtherapeutic doses of the investigational drug to a small number of participants (usually less than 15). The primary goal is to gather initial pharmacokinetic and pharmacodynamic data, such as drug metabolism, distribution, and biological effects, to inform subsequent trial phases. Phase 0 trials help assess drug behavior in humans and refine dosing strategies before proceeding to larger trials.
2. **Phase I:** Phase I trials focus on evaluating the safety, tolerability, pharmacokinetics, and preliminary efficacy of the investigational drug in a small cohort of healthy volunteers or patients with the target disease. These trials typically involve dose escalation studies to identify the maximum tolerated dose (MTD) or recommended phase II dose (RP2D) while monitoring adverse events and pharmacological responses. Phase I trials aim to establish the safety profile and initial efficacy signals necessary for advancing to later phases.

3. **Phase II:** Phase II trials assess the efficacy and safety of the investigational drug in a larger cohort of patients with the target disease. These trials aim to gather preliminary evidence of therapeutic activity, optimal dosing regimens, and potential patient subpopulations that may benefit most from the treatment. Phase II trials often employ randomized controlled designs, biomarker assessments, and surrogate endpoints to evaluate treatment effects compared to standard-of-care or placebo.
4. **Phase III:** Phase III trials are large-scale, randomized, controlled studies designed to confirm the efficacy, safety, and benefits of the investigational drug in a diverse patient population across multiple clinical sites. Phase III trials rigorously evaluate the drug's effectiveness in achieving primary and secondary endpoints, such as disease response rates, progression-free survival, overall survival, and quality of life outcomes. Regulatory approval decisions are often based on the results of well-designed Phase III trials.
5. **Phase IV:** Phase IV trials, also known as post-marketing surveillance studies, occur after regulatory approval and involve monitoring the long-term safety, effectiveness, and real-world outcomes of the marketed drug in a larger patient population. Phase IV trials aim to detect rare or delayed adverse events, assess treatment durability, evaluate comparative effectiveness, and inform clinical practice guidelines. These trials play a critical role in expanding the evidence base for the drug's use in routine clinical practice.

Understanding the sequential nature and objectives of each phase in clinical trial design is essential for ensuring the systematic development, evaluation, and regulatory approval of new drugs. From initial safety assessments in Phase 0 to post-marketing surveillance in Phase IV, each phase contributes valuable data to inform drug development decisions, optimize treatment strategies, and improve patient outcomes in clinical practice.

11.1.1.2 Randomized Controlled Trials (RCTs) vs. Observational Studies

Randomized controlled trials (RCTs) and observational studies are two primary study designs used in clinical research to evaluate the effectiveness, safety, and outcomes of interventions. Understanding their differences and respective strengths is crucial for selecting the appropriate study design based on research objectives and practical considerations. Here's a comparison of RCTs and observational studies:

1. **Randomized Controlled Trials (RCTs):**

- **Study Design:** RCTs are experimental studies where participants are randomly allocated to different treatment groups: intervention (receiving the investigational treatment) and control (receiving standard-of-care or placebo).
- **Randomization:** Randomization minimizes selection bias and ensures that participant characteristics are evenly distributed between treatment groups, allowing for a fair comparison of outcomes.
- **Blinding:** RCTs often incorporate blinding (single-blind or double-blind) to minimize bias related to participants' or investigators' knowledge of treatment assignment.
- **Intervention Control:** RCTs provide a high level of control over the intervention being studied, allowing researchers to standardize treatment protocols and closely monitor adherence.
- **Causality Inference:** RCTs are considered the gold standard for establishing causality between interventions and outcomes due to their strong internal validity and ability to control for confounding factors.
- **Generalizability:** While RCTs offer high internal validity, their strict inclusion criteria and controlled conditions may limit generalizability to real-world clinical settings or specific patient populations.

1. **Observational Studies:**

- **Study Design:** Observational studies observe participants in their natural environment without intervention by the researcher. Common types include cohort studies, case-control studies, cross-sectional studies, and ecological studies.
- **Exposure and Outcome Assessment:** Observational studies rely on existing exposures and outcomes, often collected retrospectively or prospectively from medical records, surveys, registries, or

administrative databases.

- **No Randomization:** Participants are not randomized to different exposure groups in observational studies, leading to potential selection bias and confounding by indication or other unmeasured variables.
- **Real-World Context:** Observational studies reflect real-world clinical practice, allowing researchers to assess treatment effectiveness, safety, and outcomes in diverse patient populations and settings.
- **Causality Inference:** While observational studies can identify associations between exposures and outcomes, establishing causality is challenging due to the potential for confounding and bias. However, well-designed observational studies with appropriate control for confounders can provide valuable insights into real-world treatment effects.
- **Generalizability:** Observational studies offer high external validity, allowing for the generalizability of findings to broader patient populations and clinical practice settings. However, results may be subject to biases related to non-randomized treatment allocation and confounding variables.

Randomized controlled trials (RCTs) and observational studies each have unique strengths and limitations in clinical research. RCTs provide robust evidence for causal inference and treatment efficacy but may lack generalizability. Observational studies offer insights into real-world treatment effects and are often more feasible and ethical in certain scenarios but require careful control for confounding factors. Choosing the appropriate study design depends on research objectives, ethical considerations, feasibility, and the balance between internal validity and external validity requirements.

11.1 Examination of Trial Outcomes

11.1.2 Efficacy Endpoints

Efficacy endpoints in clinical trials serve as crucial measures for evaluating the effectiveness of interventions. These endpoints, selected based on the trial's objectives and the nature of the condition being studied, provide quantifiable outcomes to assess treatment efficacy. Here's an exploration of efficacy endpoints commonly used in clinical trials:

1. **Primary Efficacy Endpoints:**

   - **Definition:** Primary efficacy endpoints represent the key outcomes used to determine the success or failure of the intervention being investigated in the trial.
   - **Selection Criteria:** Primary endpoints are chosen based on their clinical relevance, ability to measure the treatment effect accurately, and sensitivity to changes induced by the intervention.
   - **Examples:** Common primary efficacy endpoints include clinical outcomes such as disease remission, symptom improvement, survival rates, disease progression, or the occurrence of specific clinical events (e.g., myocardial infarction, stroke, relapse).

2. **Secondary Efficacy Endpoints:**

   - **Definition:** Secondary efficacy endpoints provide additional measures of treatment effects beyond the primary endpoint, offering supplementary information on treatment benefits.
   - **Complementarity:** Secondary endpoints may include different aspects of the disease process, alternative clinical outcomes, or exploratory biomarkers to further characterize the intervention's effects.
   - **Examples:** Secondary endpoints encompass a wide range of outcomes, including biomarker levels, quality of life assessments, functional status, adverse event rates, or specific clinical parameters relevant to the disease under investigation.

3. **Composite Endpoints:**

   - **Definition:** Composite endpoints combine multiple individual endpoints into a single composite measure to provide a comprehensive assessment of treatment efficacy.
   - **Advantages:** Composite endpoints enhance statistical power, reduce sample size requirements, and capture the overall treatment effect across multiple dimensions of disease.
   - **Components:** Composite endpoints typically include a combination of clinical events, biomarker changes, or disease progression criteria that collectively reflect the treatment's impact on patient outcomes.

4. **Surrogate Endpoints:**

    - **Definition:** Surrogate endpoints are intermediate markers used as substitutes for clinical outcomes to predict treatment effects more rapidly or conveniently.
    - **Validation:** Surrogate endpoints must undergo rigorous validation to establish their correlation with clinical endpoints and their ability to reliably predict long-term outcomes.
    - **Utility:** Surrogate endpoints are valuable for accelerating drug development, reducing trial duration, and facilitating early decision-making based on interim efficacy assessments.

5. **Patient-Reported Outcomes (PROs):**

    - **Definition:** Patient-reported outcomes capture subjective assessments of treatment benefits directly from patients, reflecting their perceptions of symptom relief, functional improvement, and overall well-being.
    - **Inclusion:** PROs are increasingly included as efficacy endpoints in clinical trials to incorporate patients‘ perspectives, enhance treatment relevance, and inform shared decision-making between patients and healthcare providers.

Selecting appropriate efficacy endpoints is critical for ensuring the validity, reliability, and clinical relevance of trial outcomes. Well-defined endpoints aligned with the trial's objectives facilitate the accurate assessment of treatment effects, support regulatory approval decisions, and inform clinical practice guidelines for optimal patient care.

11.1 Examination of Trial Outcomes

11.1.2 Safety Profiles and Adverse Events

Assessing the safety profile of interventions is paramount in clinical trials to ensure patient well-being and regulatory approval. Monitoring adverse events (AEs) provides crucial insights into the potential risks associated with the intervention. Here's an exploration of safety profiles and adverse events in clinical trials:

1. **Safety Monitoring:**

    - **Continuous Surveillance:** Clinical trials employ systematic methods for monitoring participant safety throughout the study duration. This involves the proactive identification, documentation, and evaluation of adverse events, treatment-related complications, and unexpected reactions.
    - **Reporting Requirements:** Investigators and trial sponsors are responsible for promptly reporting adverse events to regulatory authorities, ethics committees, and institutional review boards in compliance with regulatory guidelines and reporting protocols.

2. **Adverse Event Assessment:**

    - **Definition:** Adverse events encompass any untoward medical occurrences experienced by participants during the course of the trial, regardless of causality or severity.
    - **Classification:** Adverse events are classified based on their severity, causality (relatedness to the intervention), seriousness (resulting in death, hospitalization, disability, or other significant outcomes), and expectedness (listed in the drug's prescribing information).

3. **Common Adverse Events:**

    - **Expected Reactions:** Some adverse events are anticipated based on the known pharmacological properties of the intervention or previous clinical experience. These may include mild-to-moderate side effects such as nausea, headache, fatigue, or transient laboratory abnormalities.
    - **Unanticipated Events:** Unexpected adverse events, particularly serious or life-threatening reactions, require immediate investigation to determine causality, assess patient risk, and implement appropriate management strategies.

4. **Safety Profiles:**

    - **Risk-Benefit Assessment:** Evaluating the safety profile involves assessing the balance between treatment benefits and potential risks.

Trial investigators, regulatory agencies, and independent safety monitoring committees review safety data regularly to make informed risk-benefit decisions.

- **Safety Endpoints:** Safety endpoints in clinical trials include adverse events, laboratory abnormalities, vital sign changes, electrocardiogram findings, and other safety-related parameters used to evaluate treatment tolerability and safety signals.

5. **Risk Management Strategies:**

   - **Risk Minimization:** Trial protocols incorporate risk mitigation strategies to minimize participant exposure to potential harms. This may include dose titration, safety monitoring procedures, participant education, informed consent processes, and treatment discontinuation criteria.
   - **Risk Communication:** Transparent communication of safety information to trial participants, healthcare providers, and regulatory authorities is essential for promoting informed decision-making, ensuring patient autonomy, and maintaining public trust in clinical research.

6. **Post-Marketing Surveillance:**

   - **Long-Term Safety:** Safety monitoring continues beyond the trial's conclusion during post-marketing surveillance to detect rare or delayed adverse events, assess long-term treatment effects, and update safety information in product labeling.
   - **Signal Detection:** Pharmacovigilance activities involve signal detection to identify potential safety concerns, emerging risks, or unexpected patterns of adverse events associated with the marketed intervention.

Effective safety monitoring and adverse event assessment are integral components of clinical trial conduct, contributing to the ethical conduct of research, protection of participant welfare, and evidence-based decision-making in healthcare. A comprehensive understanding of safety profiles and adverse event reporting processes ensures the timely detection, evaluation, and management of treatment-related risks throughout the drug development continuum.

11.1 Examination of Trial Outcomes

11.1.3 Factors Influencing Trial Success

11.1.3.1 Patient Recruitment and Retention

Patient recruitment and retention are critical factors influencing the success and completion of clinical trials. Adequate enrollment of eligible participants and their sustained participation throughout the trial duration are essential for generating reliable data and achieving study objectives. Here's an exploration of patient recruitment and retention strategies:

1. **Recruitment Challenges:**

   - **Limited Eligible Population:** Clinical trial eligibility criteria often restrict participant inclusion to specific demographic, clinical, or disease characteristics, limiting the pool of eligible candidates.
   - **Awareness and Accessibility:** Low awareness of clinical trial opportunities among patients, caregivers, and healthcare providers, coupled with limited access to trial sites or transportation barriers, can hinder recruitment efforts.
   - **Patient Reluctance:** Patient concerns about potential risks, treatment uncertainties, time commitments, inconvenience, or fear of receiving placebo may deter participation in clinical trials.

2. **Recruitment Strategies:**

   - **Targeted Outreach:** Collaborating with healthcare providers, patient advocacy groups, community organizations, and social media platforms to raise awareness about clinical trial opportunities and educate potential participants about the benefits of research participation.
   - **Diverse Recruitment Channels:** Utilizing diverse recruitment channels, including electronic health records, patient registries, online trial databases, advertising campaigns, patient referrals, and community outreach events, to reach a broad and representative patient population.

- **Streamlined Screening Process:** Implementing efficient screening procedures to identify and enroll eligible participants quickly, minimizing administrative burdens, and facilitating timely initiation of study interventions.

3. **Retention Strategies:**

- **Participant Engagement:** Establishing rapport with participants through regular communication, personalized interactions, and ongoing support to foster a sense of trust, engagement, and commitment to the trial.
- **Patient-Centered Care:** Prioritizing patient needs, preferences, and concerns by offering flexible appointment scheduling, reimbursement for travel expenses, caregiver support, and ancillary services to enhance the participant experience and minimize dropout rates.
- **Clear Communication:** Providing clear and concise information about study procedures, expectations, potential risks, and benefits during the informed consent process and throughout the trial to empower participants to make informed decisions and maintain study compliance.
- **Regular Follow-Up:** Implementing proactive follow-up strategies, such as reminder calls, text messages, newsletters, and study newsletters, to maintain ongoing communication with participants, monitor treatment adherence, address concerns, and mitigate barriers to retention.

4. **Data Quality and Integrity:**

- **Retention Impact:** High participant retention rates contribute to data quality and integrity by minimizing missing data, reducing attrition bias, ensuring protocol adherence, and maximizing statistical power to detect treatment effects.
- **Protocol Adherence:** Sustained participant engagement and adherence to study protocols facilitate accurate data collection, protocol compliance, and adherence to regulatory requirements, enhancing the reliability and validity of study findings.

5. **Continuous Monitoring and Adaptation:**

- **Performance Metrics:** Monitoring recruitment and retention metrics, such as enrollment rates, screening-to-enrollment ratios, dropout rates, and protocol deviations, to identify trends, anticipate challenges, and implement timely interventions to optimize trial performance.
- **Adaptive Strategies:** Employing adaptive trial designs, flexible enrollment criteria, protocol amendments, or retention incentives based on real-time data insights and participant feedback to address evolving recruitment and retention challenges and maximize trial success.

Effective patient recruitment and retention strategies are essential for overcoming enrollment barriers, ensuring participant engagement, and maintaining data quality in clinical trials. By employing targeted outreach, patient-centered care, clear communication, proactive follow-up, and continuous monitoring, trial sponsors and investigators can enhance trial efficiency, integrity, and ultimately, the successful completion of clinical research studies.

11.1 Examination of Trial Outcomes

11.1.3 Factors Influencing Trial Success

11.1.3.2 Protocol Design and Implementation Challenges

Protocol design and implementation are pivotal elements in clinical trials, shaping study conduct, data collection, and the interpretation of trial outcomes. However, various challenges may arise during protocol development and execution, impacting trial success. Here, we delve into the key challenges associated with protocol design and implementation:

1. **Complexity and Rigidity:**

- **Balancing Complexity:** Protocols that are overly complex or rigid may pose challenges in recruitment, participant retention, and data collection. Streamlining protocols by focusing on essential endpoints, minimizing procedures, and optimizing visit schedules can enhance trial feasibility and participant adherence.

- **Adaptability:** Incorporating flexibility into protocol design through adaptive trial designs, protocol amendments, or interim analyses allows for adjustments based on emerging data, regulatory feedback, and operational constraints.

2. **Inclusion and Exclusion Criteria:**

- **Striking a Balance:** Defining clear and appropriate inclusion and exclusion criteria is essential for ensuring participant safety, homogeneity, and study validity. However, overly restrictive criteria may limit patient recruitment, delay enrollment, and hinder generalizability.
- **Protocol Amendments:** Protocol amendments may be necessary to modify eligibility criteria based on evolving scientific evidence, patient feedback, or regulatory considerations. Timely implementation of amendments and communication with stakeholders are critical to minimizing disruptions and maintaining trial integrity.

3. **Endpoint Selection and Measurement:**

- **Clinical Relevance:** Selecting clinically meaningful and scientifically sound endpoints is crucial for accurately assessing treatment effects and informing clinical decision-making. Endpoint selection should align with study objectives, patient priorities, regulatory expectations, and the available scientific evidence.
- **Outcome Measurement:** Ensuring consistent and standardized methods for endpoint measurement, data collection, and adjudication across study sites is essential to minimize variability, enhance data quality, and facilitate comparative analyses.

4. **Operational Execution:**

- **Site Training and Support:** Providing comprehensive training, study materials, and ongoing support to site staff ensures protocol adherence, data accuracy, and regulatory compliance. Site readiness assessments, site initiation visits, and regular monitoring visits help identify and address operational challenges promptly.

- **Logistical Considerations:** Anticipating logistical challenges related to drug supply, laboratory testing, imaging procedures, and data management early in protocol development allows for proactive planning and resource allocation to mitigate potential delays or disruptions.

5. **Regulatory Compliance and Ethical Considerations:**

- **Ethical Review:** Obtaining timely approval from institutional review boards (IRBs) or ethics committees and addressing their feedback regarding protocol design, participant safety, and informed consent procedures are critical for ensuring compliance with ethical standards and regulatory requirements.
- **Regulatory Oversight:** Navigating regulatory requirements, protocol deviations, safety reporting obligations, and documentation standards necessitates close collaboration between trial sponsors, investigators, and regulatory authorities to maintain trial integrity and patient safety.

Addressing protocol design and implementation challenges requires a multidisciplinary approach involving input from investigators, trial sponsors, regulatory experts, statisticians, and patient representatives. By prioritizing simplicity, flexibility, scientific rigor, and ethical conduct, stakeholders can optimize protocol development and execution to enhance trial efficiency, validity, and ultimately, the generation of meaningful clinical evidence.

11.2 Discussion of Landmark Case Studies in Pharmaceutical Development

11.2.1 Thalidomide Tragedy

11.2.1.1 Background and Historical Context

The Thalidomide tragedy stands as one of the most significant events in pharmaceutical history, serving as a stark reminder of the critical importance of drug safety and regulatory oversight. Here's an exploration of the background and historical context surrounding the Thalidomide tragedy:

1. **Discovery and Initial Use:**

    - Thalidomide, originally developed by Chemie Grünenthal in the late 1950s, was initially marketed as a sedative and anti-nausea medication for pregnant women experiencing morning sickness.
    - Marketed under various trade names, including Distaval, Contergan, and Softenon, thalidomide gained widespread popularity due to its perceived safety and effectiveness in alleviating pregnancy-related symptoms.

2. **Emergence of Adverse Effects:**

    - In the early 1960s, reports began to surface linking thalidomide use during pregnancy to severe birth defects, particularly limb malformations (phocomelia) in newborns.
    - The alarming increase in the incidence of thalidomide-related birth defects led to widespread public outcry, scientific investigations, and regulatory interventions to address the crisis.

3. **Global Impact:**

    - The Thalidomide tragedy had a profound global impact, affecting thousands of families worldwide and prompting regulatory agencies to reevaluate drug approval processes and safety standards.
    - Countries including Germany, the United Kingdom, Australia, Canada, and Japan witnessed a surge in thalidomide-related birth defects, leading to the withdrawal of the drug from the market and the implementation of stringent regulations governing drug safety and testing.

4. **Investigations and Legal Proceedings:**

    - Intensive investigations and legal proceedings followed the Thalidomide crisis, with affected families seeking compensation for the lifelong disabilities and hardships endured by their children.
    - The Thalidomide scandal highlighted deficiencies in preclinical testing, regulatory oversight, and post-marketing surveillance, prompting reforms aimed at enhancing drug safety, efficacy, and

transparency.

5. **Legacy and Lessons Learned:**

- The Thalidomide tragedy left a lasting legacy in the pharmaceutical industry, catalyzing significant changes in drug development, regulation, and patient safety.
- The establishment of rigorous preclinical testing requirements, enhanced regulatory scrutiny, pharmacovigilance programs, and strengthened informed consent processes reflect some of the enduring lessons learned from the Thalidomide disaster.

The Thalidomide tragedy serves as a sobering reminder of the inherent risks associated with pharmaceutical interventions and the imperative of prioritizing patient safety in drug development and regulatory decision-making. By understanding the historical context and lessons gleaned from the Thalidomide experience, stakeholders can work collaboratively to mitigate risks, uphold ethical standards, and promote public health in the pursuit of innovative therapies.

11.2 Discussion of Landmark Case Studies in Pharmaceutical Development

11.2.2 Sildenafil (Viagra) Discovery

11.2.2.1 Serendipitous Discovery of Sildenafil's Effect on Erectile Dysfunction

The discovery of sildenafil's effect on erectile dysfunction represents a serendipitous breakthrough in pharmaceutical research, leading to the development of Viagra, a groundbreaking therapy for male impotence. Here's an exploration of the serendipitous discovery of sildenafil's therapeutic effect:

1. **Background and Context:**

- Sildenafil, initially synthesized by pharmaceutical company Pfizer as a potential treatment for hypertension and angina, belonged to a class of drugs known as phosphodiesterase type 5 (PDE5) inhibitors.

- Early clinical trials of sildenafil focused on its vasodilatory effects in cardiovascular conditions, with researchers investigating its ability to relax blood vessels and improve blood flow.

2. **Unanticipated Clinical Observation:**

- During Phase I clinical trials in the late 1980s, researchers observed an unexpected side effect of sildenafil: an increase in penile erections among male participants.
- Patients participating in the trial reported sustained and improved erections following sildenafil administration, suggesting a potential therapeutic application for erectile dysfunction.

3. **Exploration of Mechanism of Action:**

- Subsequent investigations revealed that sildenafil's mechanism of action involved the inhibition of phosphodiesterase type 5 (PDE5) enzymes, leading to the accumulation of cyclic guanosine monophosphate (cGMP) in penile tissues.
- Elevated cGMP levels promote smooth muscle relaxation in the corpus cavernosum of the penis, facilitating penile erection by increasing blood flow and engorgement of erectile tissues.

4. **Clinical Development and Regulatory Approval:**

- Building on the serendipitous discovery of sildenafil's effects on erectile function, Pfizer redirected its clinical development program to focus on the treatment of male impotence.
- Subsequent Phase II and Phase III clinical trials demonstrated the safety and efficacy of sildenafil in treating erectile dysfunction, leading to regulatory approval by the U.S. Food and Drug Administration (FDA) in 1998 for the commercialization of Viagra.

5. **Therapeutic Impact and Cultural Significance:**

- The approval of Viagra revolutionized the management of erectile dysfunction, offering millions of men worldwide a safe, effective, and convenient oral therapy for restoring sexual function and enhancing quality of life.

- Viagra's introduction sparked widespread public interest, media attention, and cultural discourse surrounding sexuality, masculinity, aging, and the pharmaceutical industry's role in addressing intimate health concerns.

6. **Legacy and Future Developments:**

- The serendipitous discovery of sildenafil's effects on erectile dysfunction exemplifies the unpredictable nature of drug discovery and underscores the importance of serendipity, curiosity, and scientific exploration in pharmaceutical research.
- Viagra's success paved the way for the development of subsequent PDE5 inhibitors and other pharmacological treatments for erectile dysfunction, highlighting the enduring impact of serendipitous discoveries on therapeutic innovation and patient care.

The serendipitous discovery of sildenafil's therapeutic effect on erectile dysfunction represents a remarkable example of scientific serendipity, transforming a failed cardiovascular medication into a revolutionary treatment for male impotence. By leveraging unexpected observations, researchers can uncover new therapeutic applications, improve patient outcomes, and advance medical science in unforeseen ways.

11.3 Discussion of Landmark Case Studies in Pharmaceutical Development

113.3 Statins for Cardiovascular Disease Prevention

11.3.3.1 Landmark Trials Demonstrating Statins' Efficacy

Statins have emerged as cornerstone therapies for the prevention and management of cardiovascular disease (CVD), with landmark trials providing compelling evidence of their efficacy in reducing cardiovascular events and mortality. Here's an exploration of the key landmark trials demonstrating the efficacy of statins:

1. **Scandinavian Simvastatin Survival Study (4S):**

- Conducted in the early 1990s, the 4S trial was a pivotal study that demonstrated the efficacy of simvastatin, a statin medication, in reducing cardiovascular morbidity and mortality.
- The trial enrolled over 4,000 patients with coronary heart disease (CHD) and elevated cholesterol levels and randomized them to receive either simvastatin or placebo.
- Results showed that simvastatin therapy significantly reduced the risk of major cardiovascular events, including myocardial infarction (MI), stroke, and coronary revascularization, leading to a 30% relative risk reduction in cardiovascular mortality over five years.

2. **Cholesterol Treatment Trialists' (CTT) Collaborators Meta-Analysis:**

- The CTT meta-analysis, published in 1995 and updated subsequently, synthesized data from multiple randomized controlled trials (RCTs) evaluating the efficacy of statins in primary and secondary prevention of CVD.
- By pooling data from over 90,000 participants across various statin trials, the CTT analysis demonstrated the consistent and significant reduction in major vascular events with statin therapy, irrespective of baseline cholesterol levels.
- Statin therapy was associated with a 25% reduction in major vascular events per 1 mmol/L reduction in low-density lipoprotein cholesterol (LDL-C), highlighting the dose-dependent relationship between LDL-C lowering and cardiovascular risk reduction.

3. **Heart Protection Study (HPS):**

- The HPS, conducted in the late 1990s, evaluated the efficacy of simvastatin in a broad population of high-risk individuals, including those with coronary artery disease, peripheral vascular disease, diabetes mellitus, and stroke.
- Over 20,000 participants were randomized to receive either simvastatin or placebo and followed for an average of five years.
- Results demonstrated a significant reduction in major vascular events with simvastatin therapy, including a 24% reduction in major coronary events, a 25% reduction in stroke, and a 13% reduction in all-cause mortality.

4. **Justification for the Use of Statins in Prevention: An Intervention Trial Evaluating Rosuvastatin (JUPITER):**

- The JUPITER trial, conducted in the late 2000s, focused on individuals with low LDL-C levels but elevated high-sensitivity C-reactive protein (hs-CRP) levels, a marker of inflammation associated with increased cardiovascular risk.
- Participants without prior cardiovascular disease were randomized to receive rosuvastatin or placebo and followed for a median of 1.9 years.
- Rosuvastatin therapy led to a significant reduction in major cardiovascular events, including myocardial infarction, stroke, and cardiovascular mortality, despite starting with relatively low LDL-C levels.

These landmark trials have provided robust evidence supporting the efficacy of statin therapy in reducing cardiovascular morbidity and mortality across diverse patient populations. By demonstrating the substantial benefits of statins in both primary and secondary prevention settings, these trials have informed clinical practice guidelines and influenced treatment decisions, contributing to the widespread adoption of statin therapy as a cornerstone of cardiovascular risk management.

www.ingramcontent.com/pod-product-compliance
Ingram Content Group UK Ltd.
Pitfield, Milton Keynes, MK11 3LW, UK
UKHW062310290726
14090UKWH00018B/980